CIRCULAR 92

Copyright Law of the United States

and Related Laws Contained in Title 17 of the United States Code

DECEMBER 2011

The Constitutional Provision Respecting Copyright

The Congress shall have Power . . . To promote the Progress of Science and useful Arts, by securing for limited Times to Authors and Inventors the exclusive Right to their respective Writings and Discoveries.

United States Constitution, Article I, Section 8

For sale by the Superintendent of Documents, U.S. Government Printing Office
Internet: bookstore.gpo.gov Phone: toll free (866) 512-1800; DC area (202) 512-1800
Fax: (202) 512-2104 Mail: Stop IDCC, Washington, DC 20402-0001

ISBN 978-0-16-089891-4

Dedication

This edition is dedicated to Marybeth Peters, the eleventh Register of Copyrights of the United States, who served in that capacity from 1994 until the end of 2010. As the Register of Copyrights for over sixteen years, she was instrumental in the consideration and enactment of most of the forty amendments to Title 17 that were enacted during her tenure, including the most recent amendments incorporated into this edition. Her advice and counsel on copyright law and policy matters were, and continue to be, valued by Members of Congress on both sides of the aisle and by the copyright community at large.

Preface

This volume contains the text of title 17 of the *United States Code*, including all amendments enacted through December 9, 2010, in the second session of the 111th Congress. This publication includes the Copyright Act of 1976 and all subsequent amendments to copyright law; the Semiconductor Chip Protection Act of 1984, as amended; and the Vessel Hull Design Protection Act, as amended. The Copyright Office is responsible for registering intellectual property claims under all three.

The United States copyright law is contained in chapters 1 through 8 and 10 through 12 of title 17 of the *United States Code*. The Copyright Act of 1976, which provides the basic framework for the current copyright law, was enacted on October 19, 1976, as Pub. L. No. 94-553, 90 Stat. 2541. The 1976 Act was a comprehensive revision of the copyright law in title 17. Listed below in chronological order of their enactment are subsequent amendments to title 17.

Chapters 9 and 13 of title 17 contain two types of design protection that are independent of copyright protection. Chapter 9 of title 17 is the Semiconductor Chip Protection Act of 1984 (SCPA), as amended. On November 8, 1984, the SCPA was enacted as title III of Pub. L. No. 98-620, 98 Stat. 3335, 3347. Chapter 13 of title 17 is the Vessel Hull Design Protection Act (VHDPA). It was enacted on October 28, 1998, as title V of the Digital Millennium Copyright Act (DMCA), Pub. L. No. 105-304, 112 Stat. 2860, 2905. Subsequent amendments to the title 17 provisions for SCPA and the VHDPA are also included in the list below, in chronological order of their enactment.

Significant copyright legislation enacted since the last printed edition of this circular in October 2007 includes the Satellite Television Extension and Localism Act of 2010. For more details, this statute appears at the end of the chronological list below of statutory enactments that amend title 17 of the *United States Code*.

For transitional and supplementary provisions that do not amend title 17, see the appendices.

Statutory Enactments Contained in Title 17 of the *United States Code*

- [Copyright Act of 1976], Pub. L. No. 94-553, 90 Stat. 2541 (for the general revision of copyright law, title 17 of the *United States Code*, and for other purposes), October 19, 1976.
- Legislative Branch Appropriation Act, 1978, Pub. L. No. 95-94, 91 Stat. 653, 682 (amending §203 and §708, title 17, *United States Code*, regarding the deposit

of moneys by the Register of Copyrights in the Treasury of the United States), enacted August 5, 1977.

- [Copyright Amendments], Pub. L. No. 95-598, 92 Stat. 2549, 2676 (amending §201(e), title 17, *United States Code*, to permit involuntary transfer under the Bankruptcy Law), enacted November 6, 1978.
- [Copyright Amendments], Pub. L. No. 96-517, 94 Stat. 3015, 3028 (amending §101 and §117, title 17, *United States Code*, regarding computer programs), enacted December 12, 1980.
- Piracy and Counterfeiting Amendments Act of 1982, Pub. L. No. 97-180, 96 Stat. 91, 93 (amending §506(a), title 17, *United States Code* and title 18 of the *United States Code*), enacted May 24, 1982.
- [Copyright Amendments], Pub. L. No. 97-215, 96 Stat. 178 (amending the manufacturing clause in chapter 6, title 17, *United States Code*), enacted July 13, 1982.
- [Copyright Amendments], Pub. L. No. 97-366, 96 Stat. 1759 (amending §110 and §708, title 17, *United States Code*, regarding the redesignation of registration fees as filing fees, and the exemption from copyright liability of certain performances of nondramatic literary or musical works), enacted October 25, 1982.
- Record Rental Amendment of 1984, Pub. L. No. 98-450, 98 Stat. 1727 (amending §109 and §115, title 17, *United States Code*, with respect to rental, lease or lending of sound recordings), enacted October 4, 1984.
- Semiconductor Chip Protection Act of 1984, title III of Pub. L. No. 98-620, 98 Stat. 3335, 3347 (adding chapter 9, title 17, *United States Code*, to provide design protection for semiconductor chips), November 8, 1984.
- [Copyright Amendments], Pub. L. No. 99-397, 100 Stat. 848 (amending §111 and §801, title 17, *United States Code*, to clarify the definition of the local service area of a primary transmitter in the case of a low power television station), enacted on August 27, 1986.
- [Amendments to the Semiconductor Chip Protection Act of 1984], Pub. L. No. 100-159, 101 Stat. 899 (amending chapter 9, title 17, *United States Code*, regarding protection extended to semiconductor chip products of foreign entities), enacted November 9, 1987.
- Berne Convention Implementation Act of 1988, Pub. L. No. 100-568, 102 Stat. 2853, enacted October 31, 1988. (See Appendix J for certain provisions of this Act that do not amend title 17 of the *United States Code*.)

- [Copyright Amendments], Pub. L. No. 100-617, 102 Stat. 3194 (extending for an additional eight-year period certain provisions of title 17, *United States Code*, relating to the rental of sound recordings and for other purposes), enacted November 5, 1988.
- Satellite Home Viewer Act of 1988, title II of Pub. L. No. 100-667, 102 Stat. 3935, 3949, enacted November 16, 1988.
- Judicial Improvements and Access to Justice Act, Pub. L. No. 100-702, 102 Stat. 4642, 4672 (amending §912, title 17, *United States Code*), enacted November 19, 1988.
- Copyright Fees and Technical Amendments Act of 1989, Pub. L. No. 101-318, 104 Stat. 287, enacted on July 3, 1990.
- Copyright Royalty Tribunal Reform and Miscellaneous Pay Act of 1989, Pub. L. No. 101-319, 104 Stat. 290, enacted July 3, 1990.
- Copyright Remedy Clarification Act, Pub. L. No. 101-553, 104 Stat. 2749, enacted November 15, 1990.
- Visual Artists Rights Act of 1990, title VI of the Judicial Improvements Act of 1990, Pub. L. No. 101-650, 104 Stat. 5089, 5128, enacted December 1, 1990.
- Architectural Works Copyright Protection Act, title VII of the Judicial Improvements Act of 1990, Pub. L. No. 101-650, 104 Stat. 5089, 5133, enacted December 1, 1990.
- Computer Software Rental Amendments Act of 1990, title VIII of the Judicial Improvements Act of 1990, Pub. L. No. 101-650, 104 Stat 5089, 5134, enacted December 1, 1990.
- Semiconductor International Protection Extension Act of 1991, Pub. L. No. 102-64, 105 Stat. 320 (amending chapter 9, title 17, *United States Code*, regarding protection extended to semiconductor chip products of foreign entities), enacted June 28, 1991.
- Copyright Amendments Act of 1992, Pub. L. No. 102-307, 106 Stat. 264, 272 (amending chapter 3, title 17, *United States Code*, as described immediately below and by deleting subsection 108(i)), enacted June 26, 1992. (Also, through an independent provision that does not amend title 17 of the *United States Code*, the Act established the National Film Registry under title II, which is the National Film Preservation Act of 1992.)
- Copyright Renewal Act of 1992, title I of the Copyright Amendments Act of 1992, Pub. L. No. 102-307, 106 Stat. 264 (amending chapter 3, title 17 of the *United States Code*, by providing for automatic renewal of copyright for works copyrighted between January 1, 1964, and December 31, 1977), enacted June 26, 1992.

- [Copyright Amendments], Pub. L. No. 102-492, 106 Stat. 3145 (amending §107, title 17, *United States Code*, regarding unpublished works), enacted October 24, 1992.
- [Copyright Amendments], Pub. L. No. 102-561, 106 Stat. 4233 (amending §2319, title 18, *United States Code*, regarding criminal penalties for copyright infringement), enacted October 28, 1992.
- Audio Home Recording Act of 1992, Pub. L. No. 102-563, 106 Stat. 4237 (amending title 17 of the *United States Code* by adding a new chapter 10), enacted October 28, 1992.
- North American Free Trade Agreement Implementation Act, Pub. L. No. 103-182, 107 Stat. 2057, 2114 and 2115 (amending §109, title 17, *United States Code*, and adding a new §104A), enacted December 8, 1993.
- Copyright Royalty Tribunal Reform Act of 1993, Pub. L. No. 103-198, 107 Stat. 2304 (amending, *inter alia*, chapter 8, title 17, *United States Code*), enacted December 17, 1993.
- Satellite Home Viewer Act of 1994, Pub. L. No. 103-369, 108 Stat. 3477 (amending, *inter alia*, §111 and §119, title 17, *United States Code*, relating to the definition of a local service area of a primary transmitter), enacted October 18, 1994.
- Uruguay Round Agreements Act, Pub. L. No. 103-465, 108 Stat. 4809, 4973 (amending, *inter alia*, §104, title 17, *United States Code*, and adding a new chapter 11), enacted December 8, 1994. (See Appendix J for the text of certain provisions of this Act that do not amend title 17 of the *United States Code*.)
- Digital Performance Right in Sound Recordings Act of 1995, Pub. L. No. 104-39, 109 Stat. 336 (amending, *inter alia*, §114 and §115, title 17, *United States Code*), enacted November 1, 1995.
- Anticounterfeiting Consumer Protection Act of 1996, Pub. L. No. 104-153, 110 Stat. 1386, 1388 (amending §603(c), title 17, *United States Code* and §2318, title 18, *United States Code*), enacted July 2, 1996.
- Legislative Branch Appropriations Act, 1997, Pub. L. No. 104-197, 110 Stat. 2394, 2416 (amending, *inter alia*, title 17 of the *United States Code*, by adding a new §121 concerning the limitation on exclusive copyrights for literary works in specialized format for the blind and disabled), enacted September 16, 1996.
- [Copyright Amendments and Amendments to the Semiconductor Chip Protection Act of 1984], Pub. L. No. 105-80, 111 Stat. 1529 (making technical amendments to certain provisions of title 17, *United States Code*), enacted November 13, 1997.

- No Electronic Theft (NET) Act, Pub. L. No. 105-147, 111 Stat. 2678, enacted December 16, 1997.
- Sonny Bono Copyright Term Extension Act, title I of Pub. L. No. 105-298, 112 Stat. 2827 (amending chapter 3, title 17, *United States Code*, to extend the term of copyright protection for most works to life plus 70 years), enacted October 27, 1998.
- Fairness in Music Licensing Act of 1998, title II of Pub. L. No. 105-298, 112 Stat. 2827, 2830 (amending, *inter alia*, §110, title 17, *United States Code*, and adding §513 to provide a music licensing exemption for food service and drinking establishments), enacted October 27, 1998.
- Digital Millennium Copyright Act, Pub. L. No. 105-304, 112 Stat. 2860, 2887 (title IV amending §108, §112, §114, chapter 7 and chapter 8, title 17, *United States Code*), enacted October 28, 1998. (This Act also contains four separate acts within titles I, II, III, and V that amended title 17 of the *United States Code*. These four acts are each separately listed below. See Appendix B for additional provisions of this Act that do not amend title 17 of the *United States Code*.)
- WIPO Copyright and Performances and Phonograms Treaties Implementation Act of 1998, title I of the Digital Millennium Copyright Act, Pub. L. No. 105-304, 112 Stat. 2860, 2861 (amending title 17 of the *United States Code*, *inter alia*, to add a new chapter 12 which prohibits circumvention of copyright protection systems and provides protection for copyright management information), enacted October 28, 1998.
- Online Copyright Infringement Liability Limitation Act, title II of the Digital Millennium Copyright Act, Pub. L. No. 105-304, 112 Stat. 2860, 2877 (amending title 17 of the *United States Code*, to add a new §512), enacted October 28, 1998.
- Computer Maintenance Competition Assurance Act, title III of the Digital Millennium Copyright Act, Pub. L. No. 105-304, 112 Stat. 2860, 2886 (amending §117, title 17, *United States Code*), enacted October 28, 1998.
- Vessel Hull Design Protection Act, title V of the Digital Millennium Copyright Act, Pub. L. No. 105-304, 112 Stat. 2860, 2905 (adding chapter 13, title 17, *United States Code*, to provide design protection for vessel hulls), enacted October 28, 1998.
- [Copyright Amendments and Amendments to the Vessel Hull Design Protection Act], Pub. L. No. 106-44, 113 Stat. 221 (making technical corrections to title 17 of the *United States Code*), enacted August 5, 1999.

- Satellite Home Viewer Improvement Act of 1999, title I of the Intellectual Property and Communications Omnibus Reform Act of 1999, Pub. L. No. 106-113, 113 Stat. 1501, app. I (amending chapters 1 and 5 of title 17 of the *United States Code* to replace the Satellite Home Viewer Act of 1994 and amending chapters 12 and 13 of title 17), enacted November 29, 1999.
- Digital Theft Deterrence and Copyright Damages Improvement Act of 1999, Pub. L. No. 106-160, 113 Stat 1774, (amending chapter 5 of title 17 of the *United States Code* to increase statutory damages for copyright infringement), enacted December 9, 1999.
- Work Made for Hire and Copyright Corrections Act of 2000, Pub. L. No. 106-379, 114 Stat. 1444 (amending the definition of works made for hire in title 17 of the *United States Code*, amending chapter 7 of title 17, including changing the language regarding Copyright Office fees, and making other technical and conforming amendments to title 17), enacted October 27, 2000.
- Intellectual Property and High Technology Technical Amendments Act of 2002, Division C, Title III, Subtitle B of the 21st Century Department of Justice Appropriations Authorization Act, Pub. L. No. 107-273, 116 Stat. 1758, 1901 (making technical corrections both to title 17, *United States Code*, and, as described in footnotes where appropriate, to title I of the Intellectual Property and Communications Omnibus Reform Act of 1999, entitled the Satellite Home Viewer Improvement Act of 1999, Pub. L. No. 106-113, 113 Stat. 1501, app. I), enacted November 2, 2002.
- Technology, Education, and Copyright Harmonization Act of 2002, Division C, Title III, Subtitle C of the 21st Century Department of Justice Appropriations Authorization Act, Pub. L. No. 107-273, 116 Stat. 1758, 1910 (amending chapter 1, title 17, *United States Code*, to incorporate provisions relating to use of copyrighted works for distance education), enacted November 2, 2002.
- Small Webcaster Settlement Act of 2002, Pub. L. No. 107-321, 116 Stat. 2780 (amending chapter 1, title 17, *United States Code*, to incorporate new language into section 114), enacted December 4, 2002.
- Copyright Royalty and Distribution Reform Act of 2004, Pub. L. No. 108-419, 118 Stat. 2341 (revising chapter 8, title 17, *United States Code*, in its entirety), enacted November 30, 2004.
- Individuals with Disabilities Education Improvement Act of 2004, Title III, Pub. L. No. 108-446, 118 Stat. 2647, 2807 (amending section 121, title 17, *United States Code*, to further expand authorized reproduction of copyrighted works for the blind or people with other disabilities), enacted December 3, 2004.
- Satellite Home Viewer Extension and Reauthorization Act of 2004, Title IX, Division J of the Consolidated Appropriations Act, 2005, Pub. L. No. 108-447,

118 Stat. 2809, 3393 (amending section 119, title 17, *United States Code* throughout and by extending for an additional five years the statutory license for satellite carriers retransmitting over-the-air television broadcast stations to their subscribers), enacted December 8, 2004.

- Anti-counterfeiting Amendments Act of 2004, Title I of the Intellectual Property Protection and Courts Amendments Act of 2004, Pub. L. No. 108-482, 118 Stat. 3912 (amending section 2318, title 18, of the *United States Code* concerning trafficking in counterfeit or illicit labels in connection with stolen copyrighted works), enacted December 23, 2004.
- Fraudulent Online Identity Sanctions Act, Title II of the Intellectual Property Protection and Courts Amendments Act of 2004, Pub. L. No. 108-482, 118 Stat. 3912, 3916 (amending section 504(c), title 17, *United States Code*, to add language making it a criminal violation to knowingly provide false contact information for a domain name that is used in connection with copyright infringement when registering the domain name with authorities), enacted December 23, 2004.
- Artists' Rights and Theft Prevention Act of 2005 (also known as the "ART Act"), Title I of the Family Entertainment and Copyright Act of 2005, Pub. L. No. 109-9, 119 Stat. 218 (amending chapter 113, title 18, *United States Code*, to add a new section 2319B authorizing criminal penalties for unauthorized recording of motion pictures; amends section 506(a), title 17, *United States Code*, in its entirety; amending section 2319, title 18, *United States Code*, by adding criminal penalties for section 506(a); amending section 408, title 17, *United States Code*, by adding new language authorizing preregistration of works being prepared for commercial distribution; and directing the United States Sentencing Commission to establish policies and guidelines for intellectual property crimes), enacted April 27, 2005.
- Family Movie Act of 2005, Title II of the Family Entertainment and Copyright Act of 2005, Pub. L. No. 109-9, 119 Stat. 218, 223 (amending section 110, title 17, *United States Code*, to add a new exemption from infringement for imperceptible skipping of audio and video content in motion pictures), enacted April 27, 2005.
- Preservation of Orphan Works Act, Title IV of the Family Entertainment and Copyright Act of 2005, Pub. L. No. 109-9, 119 Stat. 218, 226 (amending section 108(i), title 17, *United States Code*, to add orphan works to the list of works that are exempt from certain limitations on uses by libraries and archives), enacted April 27, 2005.
- Copyright Royalty Judges Program Technical Corrections Act, Pub. L. No. 109-303, 120 Stat. 1478 (to make clarifying and technical corrections to chapter 8, *United States Code*, and related conforming amendments), enacted October 6, 2006.

- Prioritizing Resources and Organization for Intellectual Property Act of 2008, Pub. L. No. 110-403, 122 Stat. 4256 (amending civil and criminal provisions in chapters 4, 5 and 6, title 17, *United States Code*, and related provisions in title 28, *United States Code*), enacted October 13, 2008.
- Vessel Hull Design Protection Amendments of 2008, Pub. L. No. 110-434, 122 Stat. 4972 (amending definitions in section 1301), enacted October 16, 2008.
- Webcaster Settlement Act of 2008, Pub. L. No. 110-435, 122 Stat. 4974 (amending section 114 to implement the webcaster settlement agreement), enacted October 16, 2008.
- Webcaster Settlement Act of 2009, Pub. L. No. 111-36, 123 Stat. 1926 (amending section 114 to authorize 30-day negotiation period for webcasters and copyright holders), enacted June 30, 2009.
- Department of Defense Appropriations Act, 2010, Pub. L. No. 111-118, 123 Stat. 3409 (amending section 119, title 17, *United States Code*, to extend certain time periods to February 28, 2010, and to repeal section 4(a) of the Satellite Home Viewer Act of 1994), enacted December 19, 2009.
- Temporary Extension Act of 2010, Pub. L. No. 111-144, 124 Stat. 42 (amending section 119, title 17, *United States Code*, to extend certain time periods to March 28, 2010) enacted March 2, 2010.
- Satellite Television Extension Act of 2010, Pub. L. No. 111-151, 124 Stat. 1027 (amending section 119, title 17, *United States Code*, to extend certain time periods to April 30, 2010) enacted March 26, 2010.
- Continuing Extension Act of 2010, Pub. L. No. 111-157, 124 Stat. 1116 (amending section 119, title 17, *United States Code*, to extend certain time periods to May 31, 2010) enacted April 15, 2010.
- Satellite Television Extension and Localism Act of 2010, Pub. L. No. 111-175, 124 Stat. 1218 (amending sections 111, 119, 122, 708, and 804 of title 17, *United States Code*) enacted May 27, 2010.
- Copyright Cleanup, Clarification, and Corrections Act of 2010, Pub. L. No. 111-295, 124 Stat. 3180 (making miscellaneous clarifying, conforming, and technical corrections throughout title 17 *United States Code* and section 2318, title 18 *United States Code*, and repealing section 601, title 17 *United States Code*) enacted December 9, 2010.

This 2011 edition would not have been possible without the efforts of Renée Coe, senior attorney in the Office of the General Counsel, who was responsible for updating statutory provisions and drafting text, as well as the Information and Records Division's writer-editor Judith Nierman, who was responsible for proofreading and editorial review, and graphic designer Cecelia Rogers, who was responsible for the document's design and production.

Maria A. Pallante
Register of Copyrights

Contents

Chapter 1[1]

Subject Matter and Scope of Copyright

§101 · Definitions[2]

Except as otherwise provided in this title, as used in this title, the following terms and their variant forms mean the following:

An "anonymous work" is a work on the copies or phonorecords of which no natural person is identified as author.

An "architectural work" is the design of a building as embodied in any tangible medium of expression, including a building, architectural plans, or drawings. The work includes the overall form as well as the arrangement and composition of spaces and elements in the design, but does not include individual standard features.[3]

"Audiovisual works" are works that consist of a series of related images which are intrinsically intended to be shown by the use of machines or devices such as projectors, viewers, or electronic equipment, together with accompanying sounds, if any, regardless of the nature of the material objects, such as films or tapes, in which the works are embodied.

The "Berne Convention" is the Convention for the Protection of Literary and Artistic Works, signed at Berne, Switzerland, on September 9, 1886, and all acts, protocols, and revisions thereto.[4]

The "best edition" of a work is the edition, published in the United States at any time before the date of deposit, that the Library of Congress determines to be most suitable for its purposes.

A person's "children" are that person's immediate offspring, whether legitimate or not, and any children legally adopted by that person.

A "collective work" is a work, such as a periodical issue, anthology, or encyclopedia, in which a number of contributions, constituting separate and independent works in themselves, are assembled into a collective whole.

A "compilation" is a work formed by the collection and assembling of preexisting materials or of data that are selected, coordinated, or arranged in such a way that the resulting work as a whole constitutes an original work of authorship. The term "compilation" includes collective works.

A "computer program" is a set of statements or instructions to be used directly or indirectly in a computer in order to bring about a certain result.[5]

"Copies" are material objects, other than phonorecords, in which a work is fixed by any method now known or later developed, and from which the work can be perceived, reproduced, or otherwise communicated, either directly or with the aid of a machine or device. The term "copies" includes the material object, other than a phonorecord, in which the work is first fixed.

"Copyright owner", with respect to any one of the exclusive rights comprised in a copyright, refers to the owner of that particular right.

A "Copyright Royalty Judge" is a Copyright Royalty Judge appointed under section 802 of this title, and includes any individual serving as an interim Copyright Royalty Judge under such section.[6]

A work is "created" when it is fixed in a copy or phonorecord for the first time; where a work is prepared over a period of time, the portion of it that has been fixed at any particular time constitutes the work as of that time, and where the work has been prepared in different versions, each version constitutes a separate work.

A "derivative work" is a work based upon one or more preexisting works, such as a translation, musical arrangement, dramatization, fictionalization, motion picture version, sound recording, art reproduction, abridgment, condensation, or any other form in which a work may be recast, transformed, or adapted. A work consisting of editorial revisions, annotations, elaborations, or other modifications, which, as a whole, represent an original work of authorship, is a "derivative work".

A "device", "machine", or "process" is one now known or later developed.

A "digital transmission" is a transmission in whole or in part in a digital or other nonanalog format.[7]

To "display" a work means to show a copy of it, either directly or by means of a film, slide, television image, or any other device or process or, in the case of a motion picture or other audiovisual work, to show individual images nonsequentially.

An "establishment" is a store, shop, or any similar place of business open to the general public for the primary purpose of selling goods or services in which the majority of the gross square feet of space that is nonresidential is used for that purpose, and in which nondramatic musical works are performed publicly.[8]

The term "financial gain" includes receipt, or expectation of receipt, of anything of value, including the receipt of other copyrighted works.[9]

A work is "fixed" in a tangible medium of expression when its embodiment in a copy or phonorecord, by or under the authority of the author, is sufficiently permanent or stable to permit it to be perceived, reproduced, or otherwise communicated for a period of more than transitory duration. A work consisting of sounds, images, or both, that are being transmitted, is "fixed" for purposes of this title if a fixation of the work is being made simultaneously with its transmission.

A "food service or drinking establishment" is a restaurant, inn, bar, tavern, or any other similar place of business in which the public or patrons assemble for the primary purpose of being served food or drink, in which the majority of the gross square feet of space that is nonresidential is used for that purpose, and in which nondramatic musical works are performed publicly.[10]

The "Geneva Phonograms Convention" is the Convention for the Protection of Producers of Phonograms Against Unauthorized Duplication of Their Phonograms, concluded at Geneva, Switzerland, on October 29, 1971.[11]

The "gross square feet of space" of an establishment means the entire interior space of that establishment, and any adjoining outdoor space used to serve patrons, whether on a seasonal basis or otherwise.[12]

The terms "including" and "such as" are illustrative and not limitative.

An "international agreement" is—

(1) the Universal Copyright Convention;

(2) the Geneva Phonograms Convention;

(3) the Berne Convention;

(4) the WTO Agreement;

(5) the WIPO Copyright Treaty;[13]

(6) the WIPO Performances and Phonograms Treaty;[14] and

(7) any other copyright treaty to which the United States is a party.[15]

A "joint work" is a work prepared by two or more authors with the intention that their contributions be merged into inseparable or interdependent parts of a unitary whole.

"Literary works" are works, other than audiovisual works, expressed in words, numbers, or other verbal or numerical symbols or indicia, regardless of the nature of the material objects, such as books, periodicals, manuscripts, phonorecords, film, tapes, disks, or cards, in which they are embodied.

The term "motion picture exhibition facility" means a movie theater, screening room, or other venue that is being used primarily for the exhibition of a copyrighted motion picture, if such exhibition is open to the public or is made to an assembled group of viewers outside of a normal circle of a family and its social acquaintances.[16]

"Motion pictures" are audiovisual works consisting of a series of related images which, when shown in succession, impart an impression of motion, together with accompanying sounds, if any.

To "perform" a work means to recite, render, play, dance, or act it, either directly or by means of any device or process or, in the case of a motion picture or other audiovisual work, to show its images in any sequence or to make the sounds accompanying it audible.

A "performing rights society" is an association, corporation, or other entity that licenses the public performance of nondramatic musical works on behalf of copyright owners of such works, such as the American Society of Composers, Authors and Publishers (ASCAP), Broadcast Music, Inc. (BMI), and SESAC, Inc.[17]

"Phonorecords" are material objects in which sounds, other than those accompanying a motion picture or other audiovisual work, are fixed by any method now known or later developed, and from which the sounds can be perceived, reproduced, or otherwise communicated, either directly or with the aid of a machine or device. The term "phonorecords" includes the material object in which the sounds are first fixed.

"Pictorial, graphic, and sculptural works" include two-dimensional and three-dimensional works of fine, graphic, and applied art, photographs, prints and art reproductions, maps, globes, charts, diagrams, models, and technical drawings, including architectural plans. Such works shall include works of artistic craftsmanship insofar as their form but not their mechanical or utilitarian aspects are concerned; the design of a useful article, as defined in this section, shall be considered a pictorial, graphic, or sculptural work only if, and only to the extent that, such design incorporates pictorial, graphic, or sculptural features that can be identified separately from, and are capable of existing independently of, the utilitarian aspects of the article.[18]

For purposes of section 513, a "proprietor" is an individual, corporation, partnership, or other entity, as the case may be, that owns an establishment or a food service or drinking establishment, except that no owner or operator of a radio or television station licensed by the Federal Communications Commission, cable system or satellite carrier, cable or satellite carrier service or programmer, provider of online services or network access or the operator of facilities therefor, telecommunications company, or any other such audio or audiovisual service or programmer now known or as may be developed in the future, commercial subscription music service, or owner or operator of any other transmission service, shall under any circumstances be deemed to be a proprietor.[19]

A "pseudonymous work" is a work on the copies or phonorecords of which the author is identified under a fictitious name.

"Publication" is the distribution of copies or phonorecords of a work to the public by sale or other transfer of ownership, or by rental, lease, or lending. The offering to distribute copies or phonorecords to a group of persons for purposes of further distribution, public performance, or public display, constitutes publication. A public performance or display of a work does not of itself constitute publication.

To perform or display a work "publicly" means—

(1) to perform or display it at a place open to the public or at any place where a substantial number of persons outside of a normal circle of a family and its social acquaintances is gathered; or

(2) to transmit or otherwise communicate a performance or display of the work to a place specified by clause (1) or to the public, by means of any device or process, whether the members of the public capable of receiving the performance or display receive it in the same place or in separate places and at the same time or at different times.

"Registration", for purposes of sections 205(c)(2), 405, 406, 410(d), 411, 412, and 506(e), means a registration of a claim in the original or the renewed and extended term of copyright.[20]

"Sound recordings" are works that result from the fixation of a series of musical, spoken, or other sounds, but not including the sounds accompanying a motion picture or other audiovisual work, regardless of the nature of the material objects, such as disks, tapes, or other phonorecords, in which they are embodied.

"State" includes the District of Columbia and the Commonwealth of Puerto Rico, and any territories to which this title is made applicable by an Act of Congress.

A "transfer of copyright ownership" is an assignment, mortgage, exclusive license, or any other conveyance, alienation, or hypothecation of a copyright or of any of the exclusive rights comprised in a copyright, whether or not it is limited in time or place of effect, but not including a nonexclusive license.

A "transmission program" is a body of material that, as an aggregate, has been produced for the sole purpose of transmission to the public in sequence and as a unit.

To "transmit" a performance or display is to communicate it by any device or process whereby images or sounds are received beyond the place from which they are sent.

A "treaty party" is a country or intergovernmental organization other than the United States that is a party to an international agreement.[21]

The "United States", when used in a geographical sense, comprises the several States, the District of Columbia and the Commonwealth of Puerto Rico, and the organized territories under the jurisdiction of the United States Government.

For purposes of section 411, a work is a "United States work" only if—

(1) in the case of a published work, the work is first published—

(A) in the United States;

(B) simultaneously in the United States and another treaty party or parties, whose law grants a term of copyright protection that is the same as or longer than the term provided in the United States;

(C) simultaneously in the United States and a foreign nation that is not a treaty party; or

(D) in a foreign nation that is not a treaty party, and all of the authors of the work are nationals, domiciliaries, or habitual residents of, or in the case of an audiovisual work legal entities with headquarters in, the United States;

(2) in the case of an unpublished work, all the authors of the work are nationals, domiciliaries, or habitual residents of the United States, or, in the case of an unpublished audiovisual work, all the authors are legal entities with headquarters in the United States; or

(3) in the case of a pictorial, graphic, or sculptural work incorporated in a building or structure, the building or structure is located in the United States.[22]

A "useful article" is an article having an intrinsic utilitarian function that is not merely to portray the appearance of the article or to convey information. An article that is normally a part of a useful article is considered a "useful article".

The author's "widow" or "widower" is the author's surviving spouse under the law of the author's domicile at the time of his or her death, whether or not the spouse has later remarried.

The "WIPO Copyright Treaty" is the WIPO Copyright Treaty concluded at Geneva, Switzerland, on December 20, 1996.[23]

The "WIPO Performances and Phonograms Treaty" is the WIPO Performances and Phonograms Treaty concluded at Geneva, Switzerland, on December 20, 1996.[24]

A "work of visual art" is—

(1) a painting, drawing, print or sculpture, existing in a single copy, in a limited edition of 200 copies or fewer that are signed and consecutively numbered by the author, or, in the case of a sculpture, in multiple cast, carved, or fabricated sculptures of 200 or fewer that are consecutively numbered by the author and bear the signature or other identifying mark of the author; or

(2) a still photographic image produced for exhibition purposes only, existing in a single copy that is signed by the author, or in a limited edition of 200 copies or fewer that are signed and consecutively numbered by the author.

A work of visual art does not include—

(A)(i) any poster, map, globe, chart, technical drawing, diagram, model, applied art, motion picture or other audiovisual work, book, magazine, newspaper, periodical, data base, electronic information service, electronic publication, or similar publication;

(ii) any merchandising item or advertising, promotional, descriptive, covering, or packaging material or container;

(iii) any portion or part of any item described in clause (i) or (ii);

(B) any work made for hire; or

(C) any work not subject to copyright protection under this title.[25]

A "work of the United States Government" is a work prepared by an officer or employee of the United States Government as part of that person's official duties.

A "work made for hire" is—

(1) a work prepared by an employee within the scope of his or her employment; or

(2) a work specially ordered or commissioned for use as a contribution to a collective work, as a part of a motion picture or other audiovisual work, as a translation, as a supplementary work, as a compilation, as an instructional text, as a test, as answer material for a test, or as an atlas, if the parties expressly agree in a written instrument signed by them that the work shall be considered a work made for hire. For the purpose of the foregoing sentence, a "supplementary work" is a work prepared for publication as a secondary adjunct to a work by another author for the purpose of introducing, concluding, illustrating, explaining, revising, commenting upon, or assisting in the use of the other work, such as forewords, afterwords, pictorial illustrations, maps, charts, tables, editorial notes, musical arrangements, answer material for tests, bibliographies, appendixes, and indexes, and an "instructional text" is a literary, pictorial, or graphic work prepared for publication and with the purpose of use in systematic instructional activities.

In determining whether any work is eligible to be considered a work made for hire under paragraph (2), neither the amendment contained in section 1011(d) of the Intellectual Property and Communications Omnibus Reform Act of 1999, as enacted by section 1000(a)(9) of Public Law 106-113, nor the deletion of the words added by that amendment—

(A) shall be considered or otherwise given any legal significance, or

(B) shall be interpreted to indicate congressional approval or disapproval of, or acquiescence in, any judicial determination,

by the courts or the Copyright Office. Paragraph (2) shall be interpreted as if both section 2(a)(1) of the Work Made for Hire and Copyright Corrections Act of 2000 and section 1011(d) of the Intellectual Property and Communications Omnibus Reform Act of 1999, as enacted by section 1000(a)(9) of Public Law 106-113, were never enacted, and without regard to any inaction or awareness by the Congress at any time of any judicial determinations.[26]

The terms "WTO Agreement" and "WTO member country" have the meanings given those terms in paragraphs (9) and (10), respectively, of section 2 of the Uruguay Round Agreements Act.[27]

§102 · Subject matter of copyright: In general[28]

(a) Copyright protection subsists, in accordance with this title, in original works of authorship fixed in any tangible medium of expression, now known or later developed, from which they can be perceived, reproduced, or otherwise communicated, either directly or with the aid of a machine or device. Works of authorship include the following categories:

(1) literary works;

(2) musical works, including any accompanying words;

(3) dramatic works, including any accompanying music;

(4) pantomimes and choreographic works;

(5) pictorial, graphic, and sculptural works;

(6) motion pictures and other audiovisual works;

(7) sound recordings; and

(8) architectural works.

(b) In no case does copyright protection for an original work of authorship extend to any idea, procedure, process, system, method of operation, concept, principle, or discovery, regardless of the form in which it is described, explained, illustrated, or embodied in such work.

§103 · Subject matter of copyright: Compilations and derivative works

(a) The subject matter of copyright as specified by section 102 includes compilations and derivative works, but protection for a work employing preexisting material in which copyright subsists does not extend to any part of the work in which such material has been used unlawfully.

(b) The copyright in a compilation or derivative work extends only to the material contributed by the author of such work, as distinguished from the preexisting material employed in the work, and does not imply any exclusive right in the preexisting material. The copyright in such work is independent of, and does not affect or enlarge the scope, duration, ownership, or subsistence of, any copyright protection in the preexisting material.

§104 · Subject matter of copyright: National origin[29]

(a) Unpublished Works.—The works specified by sections 102 and 103, while unpublished, are subject to protection under this title without regard to the nationality or domicile of the author.

(b) Published Works.—The works specified by sections 102 and 103, when published, are subject to protection under this title if—

(1) on the date of first publication, one or more of the authors is a national or domiciliary of the United States, or is a national, domiciliary, or sovereign authority of a treaty party, or is a stateless person, wherever that person may be domiciled; or

(2) the work is first published in the United States or in a foreign nation that, on the date of first publication, is a treaty party; or

(3) the work is a sound recording that was first fixed in a treaty party; or

(4) the work is a pictorial, graphic, or sculptural work that is incorporated in a building or other structure, or an architectural work that is embodied in a building and the building or structure is located in the United States or a treaty party; or

(5) the work is first published by the United Nations or any of its specialized agencies, or by the Organization of American States; or

(6) the work comes within the scope of a Presidential proclamation. Whenever the President finds that a particular foreign nation extends, to works by authors who are nationals or domiciliaries of the United States or to works that are first published in the United States, copyright protection on substantially the same basis as that on which the foreign nation extends protection to works of its own nationals and domiciliaries and works first published in that nation, the President may by proclamation extend protection under this title to works of which

one or more of the authors is, on the date of first publication, a national, domiciliary, or sovereign authority of that nation, or which was first published in that nation. The President may revise, suspend, or revoke any such proclamation or impose any conditions or limitations on protection under a proclamation.

For purposes of paragraph (2), a work that is published in the United States or a treaty party within 30 days after publication in a foreign nation that is not a treaty party shall be considered to be first published in the United States or such treaty party, as the case may be.

(c) Effect of Berne Convention.—No right or interest in a work eligible for protection under this title may be claimed by virtue of, or in reliance upon, the provisions of the Berne Convention, or the adherence of the United States thereto. Any rights in a work eligible for protection under this title that derive from this title, other Federal or State statutes, or the common law, shall not be expanded or reduced by virtue of, or in reliance upon, the provisions of the Berne Convention, or the adherence of the United States thereto.

(d) Effect of Phonograms Treaties.—Notwithstanding the provisions of subsection (b), no works other than sound recordings shall be eligible for protection under this title solely by virtue of the adherence of the United States to the Geneva Phonograms Convention or the WIPO Performances and Phonograms Treaty.[30]

§104A · Copyright in restored works[31]

(a) Automatic Protection and Term.—

(1) Term.—

(A) Copyright subsists, in accordance with this section, in restored works, and vests automatically on the date of restoration.

(B) Any work in which copyright is restored under this section shall subsist for the remainder of the term of copyright that the work would have otherwise been granted in the United States if the work never entered the public domain in the United States.

(2) Exception.—Any work in which the copyright was ever owned or administered by the Alien Property Custodian and in which the restored copyright would be owned by a government or instrumentality thereof, is not a restored work.

(b) Ownership of Restored Copyright.—A restored work vests initially in the author or initial rightholder of the work as determined by the law of the source country of the work.

(c) Filing of Notice of Intent to Enforce Restored Copyright Against Reliance Parties.—On or after the date of restoration, any person who owns a copyright in a restored work or an exclusive right therein may file with the Copyright Office a notice of intent to enforce that person's copyright or exclusive right or may serve such a notice directly on a reliance party. Acceptance of a notice by the Copyright Office is effective as to any reliance parties but shall not create a presumption of the validity of any of the facts stated therein. Service on a reliance party is effective as to that reliance party and any other reliance parties with actual knowledge of such service and of the contents of that notice.

(d) Remedies for Infringement of Restored Copyrights.—

(1) Enforcement of copyright in restored works in the absence of a reliance party.—As against any party who is not a reliance party, the remedies provided in chapter 5 of this title shall be available on or after the date of restoration of a restored copyright with respect to an act of infringement of the restored copyright that is commenced on or after the date of restoration.

(2) Enforcement of copyright in restored works as against reliance parties.—As against a reliance party, except to the extent provided in paragraphs (3) and (4), the remedies provided in chapter 5 of this title shall be available, with respect to an act of infringement of a restored copyright, on or after the date of restoration of the restored copyright if the requirements of either of the following subparagraphs are met:

(A)(i) The owner of the restored copyright (or such owner's agent) or the owner of an exclusive right therein (or such owner's agent) files with the Copyright Office, during the 24-month period beginning on the date of restoration, a notice of intent to enforce the restored copyright; and

(ii)(I) the act of infringement commenced after the end of the 12-month period beginning on the date of publication of the notice in the Federal Register;

(II) the act of infringement commenced before the end of the 12-month period described in subclause (I) and continued after the end of that 12-month period, in which case remedies shall be available only for infringement occurring after the end of that 12-month period; or

(III) copies or phonorecords of a work in which copyright has been restored under this section are made after publication of the notice of intent in the Federal Register.

(B)(i) The owner of the restored copyright (or such owner's agent) or the owner of an exclusive right therein (or such owner's agent) serves upon a reliance party a notice of intent to enforce a restored copyright; and

(ii)(I) the act of infringement commenced after the end of the 12-month period beginning on the date the notice of intent is received;

(II) the act of infringement commenced before the end of the 12-month period described in subclause (I) and continued after the end of that 12-month period, in which case remedies shall be available only for the infringement occurring after the end of that 12-month period; or

(III) copies or phonorecords of a work in which copyright has been restored under this section are made after receipt of the notice of intent.

In the event that notice is provided under both subparagraphs (A) and (B), the 12-month period referred to in such subparagraphs shall run from the earlier of publication or service of notice.

(3) Existing derivative works.—

(A) In the case of a derivative work that is based upon a restored work and is created—

(i) before the date of the enactment of the Uruguay Round Agreements Act, if the source country of the restored work is an eligible country on such date, or

(ii) before the date on which the source country of the restored work becomes an eligible country, if that country is not an eligible country on such date of enactment,

a reliance party may continue to exploit that derivative work for the duration of the restored copyright if the reliance party pays to the owner of the restored copyright reasonable compensation for conduct which would be subject to a remedy for infringement but for the provisions of this paragraph.

(B) In the absence of an agreement between the parties, the amount of such compensation shall be determined by an action in United States district court, and shall reflect any harm to the actual or potential market for or value of the restored work from the reliance party's continued exploitation of the work, as well as compensation for the relative contributions of expression of the author of the restored work and the reliance party to the derivative work.

(4) Commencement of infringement for reliance parties.—For purposes of section 412, in the case of reliance parties, infringement shall be deemed to have commenced before registration when acts which would have constituted infringement had the restored work been subject to copyright were commenced before the date of restoration.

(e) Notices of Intent to Enforce a Restored Copyright.—

(1) Notices of intent filed with the Copyright Office.—

(A)(i) A notice of intent filed with the Copyright Office to enforce a restored copyright shall be signed by the owner of the restored copyright or the owner of an exclusive right therein, who files the notice under subsection (d)(2)(A)(i) (hereafter in this paragraph referred to as the "owner"), or by the owner's agent, shall identify the title of the restored work, and shall include an English translation of the title and any other alternative titles known to the owner by which the restored work may be identified, and an address and telephone number at which the owner may be contacted. If the notice is signed by an agent, the agency relationship must have been constituted in a writing signed by the owner before the filing of the notice. The Copyright Office may specifically require in regulations other information to be included in the notice, but failure to provide such other information shall not invalidate the notice or be a basis for refusal to list the restored work in the Federal Register.

(ii) If a work in which copyright is restored has no formal title, it shall be described in the notice of intent in detail sufficient to identify it.

(iii) Minor errors or omissions may be corrected by further notice at any time after the notice of intent is filed. Notices of corrections for such minor errors or omissions shall be accepted after the period established in subsection (d)(2)(A)(i). Notices shall be published in the Federal Register pursuant to subparagraph (B).

(B)(i) The Register of Copyrights shall publish in the Federal Register, commencing not later than 4 months after the date of restoration for a particular nation and every 4 months thereafter for a period of 2 years, lists identifying restored works and the ownership thereof if a notice of intent to enforce a restored copyright has been filed.

(ii) Not less than 1 list containing all notices of intent to enforce shall be maintained in the Public Information Office of the Copyright Office and shall be available for public inspection and copying during regular business hours pursuant to sections 705 and 708.

(C) The Register of Copyrights is authorized to fix reasonable fees based on the costs of receipt, processing, recording, and publication of notices of intent to enforce a restored copyright and corrections thereto.

(D)(i) Not later than 90 days before the date the Agreement on Trade-Related Aspects of Intellectual Property referred to in section 101(d)(15) of the Uruguay Round Agreements Act enters into force with respect to the United States, the Copyright Office shall issue and publish in the Federal Register regulations governing the filing under this subsection of notices of intent to enforce a restored copyright.

(ii) Such regulations shall permit owners of restored copyrights to file simultaneously for registration of the restored copyright.

(2) Notices of intent served on a reliance party.—

(A) Notices of intent to enforce a restored copyright may be served on a reliance party at any time after the date of restoration of the restored copyright.

(B) Notices of intent to enforce a restored copyright served on a reliance party shall be signed by the owner or the owner's agent, shall identify the restored work and the work in which the restored work is used, if any, in detail sufficient to identify them, and shall include an English translation of the title, any other alternative titles known to the owner by which the work may be identified, the use or uses to which the owner objects, and an address and telephone number at which the reliance party may contact the owner. If the notice is signed by an agent, the agency relationship must have been constituted in writing and signed by the owner before service of the notice.

(3) EFFECT OF MATERIAL FALSE STATEMENTS.—Any material false statement knowingly made with respect to any restored copyright identified in any notice of intent shall make void all claims and assertions made with respect to such restored copyright.

(f) IMMUNITY FROM WARRANTY AND RELATED LIABILITY.—

(1) IN GENERAL.—Any person who warrants, promises, or guarantees that a work does not violate an exclusive right granted in section 106 shall not be liable for legal, equitable, arbitral, or administrative relief if the warranty, promise, or guarantee is breached by virtue of the restoration of copyright under this section, if such warranty, promise, or guarantee is made before January 1, 1995.

(2) PERFORMANCES.—No person shall be required to perform any act if such performance is made infringing by virtue of the restoration of copyright under the provisions of this section, if the obligation to perform was undertaken before January 1, 1995.

(g) PROCLAMATION OF COPYRIGHT RESTORATION.—Whenever the President finds that a particular foreign nation extends, to works by authors who are nationals or domiciliaries of the United States, restored copyright protection on substantially the same basis as provided under this section, the President may by proclamation extend restored protection provided under this section to any work—

(1) of which one or more of the authors is, on the date of first publication, a national, domiciliary, or sovereign authority of that nation; or

(2) which was first published in that nation.

The President may revise, suspend, or revoke any such proclamation or impose any conditions or limitations on protection under such a proclamation.

(h) DEFINITIONS.—For purposes of this section and section 109(a):

(1) The term "date of adherence or proclamation" means the earlier of the date on which a foreign nation which, as of the date the WTO Agreement enters into force with respect to the United States, is not a nation adhering to the Berne Convention or a WTO member country, becomes—

(A) a nation adhering to the Berne Convention;

(B) a WTO member country;

(C) a nation adhering to the WIPO Copyright Treaty;[32]

(D) a nation adhering to the WIPO Performances and Phonograms Treaty;[33] or

(E) subject to a Presidential proclamation under subsection (g).

(2) The "date of restoration" of a restored copyright is—

(A) January 1, 1996, if the source country of the restored work is a nation adhering to the Berne Convention or a WTO member country on such date, or

(B) the date of adherence or proclamation, in the case of any other source country of the restored work.

(3) The term "eligible country" means a nation, other than the United States, that—

(A) becomes a WTO member country after the date of the enactment of the Uruguay Round Agreements Act;

(B) on such date of enactment is, or after such date of enactment becomes, a nation adhering to the Berne Convention;

(C) adheres to the WIPO Copyright Treaty;[34]

(D) adheres to the WIPO Performances and Phonograms Treaty;[35] or

(E) after such date of enactment becomes subject to a proclamation under subsection (g).

(4) The term "reliance party" means any person who—

(A) with respect to a particular work, engages in acts, before the source country of that work becomes an eligible country, which would have violated section 106 if the restored work had been subject to copyright protection, and who, after the source country becomes an eligible country, continues to engage in such acts;

(B) before the source country of a particular work becomes an eligible country, makes or acquires 1 or more copies or phonorecords of that work; or

(C) as the result of the sale or other disposition of a derivative work covered under subsection (d)(3), or significant assets of a person described in subparagraph (A) or (B), is a successor, assignee, or licensee of that person.

(5) The term "restored copyright" means copyright in a restored work under this section.

(6) The term "restored work" means an original work of authorship that—

(A) is protected under subsection (a);

(B) is not in the public domain in its source country through expiration of term of protection;

(C) is in the public domain in the United States due to—

(i) noncompliance with formalities imposed at any time by United States copyright law, including failure of renewal, lack of proper notice, or failure to comply with any manufacturing requirements;

(ii) lack of subject matter protection in the case of sound recordings fixed before February 15, 1972; or

(iii) lack of national eligibility;

(D) has at least one author or rightholder who was, at the time the work was created, a national or domiciliary of an eligible country, and if published, was first published in an eligible country and not published in the United States during the 30-day period following publication in such eligible country; and

(E) if the source country for the work is an eligible country solely by virtue of its adherence to the WIPO Performances and Phonograms Treaty, is a sound recording.[36]

(7) The term "rightholder" means the person—

(A) who, with respect to a sound recording, first fixes a sound recording with authorization, or

(B) who has acquired rights from the person described in subparagraph (A) by means of any conveyance or by operation of law.

(8) The "source country" of a restored work is—

(A) a nation other than the United States;

(B) in the case of an unpublished work—

(i) the eligible country in which the author or rightholder is a national or domiciliary, or, if a restored work has more than 1 author or rightholder, of which the majority of foreign authors or rightholders are nationals or domiciliaries; or

(ii) if the majority of authors or rightholders are not foreign, the nation other than the United States which has the most significant contacts with the work; and

(C) in the case of a published work—

(i) the eligible country in which the work is first published, or

(ii) if the restored work is published on the same day in 2 or more eligible countries, the eligible country which has the most significant contacts with the work.

§105 · Subject matter of copyright: United States Government works[37]

Copyright protection under this title is not available for any work of the United States Government, but the United States Government is not precluded from receiving and holding copyrights transferred to it by assignment, bequest, or otherwise.

§106 · Exclusive rights in copyrighted works[38]

Subject to sections 107 through 122, the owner of copyright under this title has the exclusive rights to do and to authorize any of the following:

(1) to reproduce the copyrighted work in copies or phonorecords;

(2) to prepare derivative works based upon the copyrighted work;

(3) to distribute copies or phonorecords of the copyrighted work to the public by sale or other transfer of ownership, or by rental, lease, or lending;

(4) in the case of literary, musical, dramatic, and choreographic works, pantomimes, and motion pictures and other audiovisual works, to perform the copyrighted work publicly;

(5) in the case of literary, musical, dramatic, and choreographic works, pantomimes, and pictorial, graphic, or sculptural works, including the individual images of a motion picture or other audiovisual work, to display the copyrighted work publicly; and

(6) in the case of sound recordings, to perform the copyrighted work publicly by means of a digital audio transmission.

§106A · Rights of certain authors to attribution and integrity[39]

(a) Rights of Attribution and Integrity.—Subject to section 107 and independent of the exclusive rights provided in section 106, the author of a work of visual art—

(1) shall have the right—

(A) to claim authorship of that work, and

(B) to prevent the use of his or her name as the author of any work of visual art which he or she did not create;

(2) shall have the right to prevent the use of his or her name as the author of the work of visual art in the event of a distortion, mutilation, or other modification of the work which would be prejudicial to his or her honor or reputation; and

(3) subject to the limitations set forth in section 113(d), shall have the right—

(A) to prevent any intentional distortion, mutilation, or other modification of that work which would be prejudicial to his or her honor or reputation, and any intentional distortion, mutilation, or modification of that work is a violation of that right, and

(B) to prevent any destruction of a work of recognized stature, and any intentional or grossly negligent destruction of that work is a violation of that right.

(b) Scope and Exercise of Rights.—Only the author of a work of visual art has the rights conferred by subsection (a) in that work, whether or not the author is the copyright owner. The authors of a joint work of visual art are coowners of the rights conferred by subsection (a) in that work.

(c) Exceptions.—(1) The modification of a work of visual art which is the result of the passage of time or the inherent nature of the materials is not a distortion, mutilation, or other modification described in subsection (a)(3)(A).

(2) The modification of a work of visual art which is the result of conservation, or of the public presentation, including lighting and placement, of the work is not a destruction, distortion, mutilation, or other modification described in subsection (a)(3) unless the modification is caused by gross negligence.

(3) The rights described in paragraphs (1) and (2) of subsection (a) shall not apply to any reproduction, depiction, portrayal, or other use of a work in, upon, or in any connection with any item described in subparagraph (A) or (B) of the definition of "work of visual art" in section 101, and any such reproduction, depiction, portrayal, or other use of a work is not a destruction, distortion, mutilation, or other modification described in paragraph (3) of subsection (a).

(d) Duration of Rights.—(1) With respect to works of visual art created on or after the effective date set forth in section 610(a) of the Visual Artists Rights Act of 1990, the rights conferred by subsection (a) shall endure for a term consisting of the life of the author.

(2) With respect to works of visual art created before the effective date set forth in section 610(a) of the Visual Artists Rights Act of 1990, but title to which has not, as of such effective date, been transferred from the author, the rights conferred by subsection (a) shall be coextensive with, and shall expire at the same time as, the rights conferred by section 106.

(3) In the case of a joint work prepared by two or more authors, the rights conferred by subsection (a) shall endure for a term consisting of the life of the last surviving author.

(4) All terms of the rights conferred by subsection (a) run to the end of the calendar year in which they would otherwise expire.

(e) Transfer and Waiver.—(1) The rights conferred by subsection (a) may not be transferred, but those rights may be waived if the author expressly agrees to such waiver in a written instrument signed by the author. Such instrument shall specifically identify the work, and uses of that work, to which the waiver applies, and the waiver shall apply only to the work and uses so identified. In the case of a joint work prepared by two or more authors, a waiver of rights under this paragraph made by one such author waives such rights for all such authors.

(2) Ownership of the rights conferred by subsection (a) with respect to a work of visual art is distinct from ownership of any copy of that work, or of a copyright or any exclusive right under a copyright in that work. Transfer of ownership of any copy of a work of visual art, or of a copyright or any exclusive right under a copyright, shall not constitute a waiver of the rights conferred by subsection (a). Except as may otherwise be agreed by the author in a written instrument signed by the author, a waiver of the rights conferred

by subsection (a) with respect to a work of visual art shall not constitute a transfer of ownership of any copy of that work, or of ownership of a copyright or of any exclusive right under a copyright in that work.

§107 · Limitations on exclusive rights: Fair use[40]

Notwithstanding the provisions of sections 106 and 106A, the fair use of a copyrighted work, including such use by reproduction in copies or phonorecords or by any other means specified by that section, for purposes such as criticism, comment, news reporting, teaching (including multiple copies for classroom use), scholarship, or research, is not an infringement of copyright. In determining whether the use made of a work in any particular case is a fair use the factors to be considered shall include—

(1) the purpose and character of the use, including whether such use is of a commercial nature or is for nonprofit educational purposes;

(2) the nature of the copyrighted work;

(3) the amount and substantiality of the portion used in relation to the copyrighted work as a whole; and

(4) the effect of the use upon the potential market for or value of the copyrighted work.

The fact that a work is unpublished shall not itself bar a finding of fair use if such finding is made upon consideration of all the above factors.

§108 · Limitations on exclusive rights: Reproduction by libraries and archives[41]

(a) Except as otherwise provided in this title and notwithstanding the provisions of section 106, it is not an infringement of copyright for a library or archives, or any of its employees acting within the scope of their employment, to reproduce no more than one copy or phonorecord of a work, except as provided in subsections (b) and (c), or to distribute such copy or phonorecord, under the conditions specified by this section, if—

(1) the reproduction or distribution is made without any purpose of direct or indirect commercial advantage;

(2) the collections of the library or archives are (i) open to the public, or (ii) available not only to researchers affiliated with the library or archives or with the institution of which it is a part, but also to other persons doing research in a specialized field; and

(3) the reproduction or distribution of the work includes a notice of copyright that appears on the copy or phonorecord that is reproduced under the

provisions of this section, or includes a legend stating that the work may be protected by copyright if no such notice can be found on the copy or phonorecord that is reproduced under the provisions of this section.

(b) The rights of reproduction and distribution under this section apply to three copies or phonorecords of an unpublished work duplicated solely for purposes of preservation and security or for deposit for research use in another library or archives of the type described by clause (2) of subsection (a), if—

(1) the copy or phonorecord reproduced is currently in the collections of the library or archives; and

(2) any such copy or phonorecord that is reproduced in digital format is not otherwise distributed in that format and is not made available to the public in that format outside the premises of the library or archives.

(c) The right of reproduction under this section applies to three copies or phonorecords of a published work duplicated solely for the purpose of replacement of a copy or phonorecord that is damaged, deteriorating, lost, or stolen, or if the existing format in which the work is stored has become obsolete, if—

(1) the library or archives has, after a reasonable effort, determined that an unused replacement cannot be obtained at a fair price; and

(2) any such copy or phonorecord that is reproduced in digital format is not made available to the public in that format outside the premises of the library or archives in lawful possession of such copy.

For purposes of this subsection, a format shall be considered obsolete if the machine or device necessary to render perceptible a work stored in that format is no longer manufactured or is no longer reasonably available in the commercial marketplace.

(d) The rights of reproduction and distribution under this section apply to a copy, made from the collection of a library or archives where the user makes his or her request or from that of another library or archives, of no more than one article or other contribution to a copyrighted collection or periodical issue, or to a copy or phonorecord of a small part of any other copyrighted work, if—

(1) the copy or phonorecord becomes the property of the user, and the library or archives has had no notice that the copy or phonorecord would be used for any purpose other than private study, scholarship, or research; and

(2) the library or archives displays prominently, at the place where orders are accepted, and includes on its order form, a warning of copyright in accordance with requirements that the Register of Copyrights shall prescribe by regulation.

(e) The rights of reproduction and distribution under this section apply to the entire work, or to a substantial part of it, made from the collection of a library or archives where the user makes his or her request or from that of another library or archives, if the library or archives has first determined, on the basis of a reasonable investigation, that a copy or phonorecord of the copyrighted work cannot be obtained at a fair price, if—

(1) the copy or phonorecord becomes the property of the user, and the library or archives has had no notice that the copy or phonorecord would be used for any purpose other than private study, scholarship, or research; and

(2) the library or archives displays prominently, at the place where orders are accepted, and includes on its order form, a warning of copyright in accordance with requirements that the Register of Copyrights shall prescribe by regulation.

(f) Nothing in this section—

(1) shall be construed to impose liability for copyright infringement upon a library or archives or its employees for the unsupervised use of reproducing equipment located on its premises: *Provided,* That such equipment displays a notice that the making of a copy may be subject to the copyright law;

(2) excuses a person who uses such reproducing equipment or who requests a copy or phonorecord under subsection (d) from liability for copyright infringement for any such act, or for any later use of such copy or phonorecord, if it exceeds fair use as provided by section 107;

(3) shall be construed to limit the reproduction and distribution by lending of a limited number of copies and excerpts by a library or archives of an audiovisual news program, subject to clauses (1), (2), and (3) of subsection (a); or

(4) in any way affects the right of fair use as provided by section 107, or any contractual obligations assumed at any time by the library or archives when it obtained a copy or phonorecord of a work in its collections.

(g) The rights of reproduction and distribution under this section extend to the isolated and unrelated reproduction or distribution of a single copy or phonorecord of the same material on separate occasions, but do not extend to cases where the library or archives, or its employee—

(1) is aware or has substantial reason to believe that it is engaging in the related or concerted reproduction or distribution of multiple copies or phonorecords of the same material, whether made on one occasion or over a period of time, and whether intended for aggregate use by one or more individuals or for separate use by the individual members of a group; or

(2) engages in the systematic reproduction or distribution of single or multiple copies or phonorecords of material described in subsection (d): *Provided,* That nothing in this clause prevents a library or archives from participating in interlibrary arrangements that do not have, as their purpose or effect, that the library or archives receiving such copies or phonorecords for distribution does so in such aggregate quantities as to substitute for a subscription to or purchase of such work.

(h)(1) For purposes of this section, during the last 20 years of any term of copyright of a published work, a library or archives, including a nonprofit educational institution that functions as such, may reproduce, distribute, display, or perform in facsimile or digital form a copy or phonorecord of such work, or portions thereof, for purposes of preservation, scholarship, or research, if such library or archives has first determined, on the basis of a reasonable investigation, that none of the conditions set forth in subparagraphs (A), (B), and (C) of paragraph (2) apply.

(2) No reproduction, distribution, display, or performance is authorized under this subsection if—

(A) the work is subject to normal commercial exploitation;

(B) a copy or phonorecord of the work can be obtained at a reasonable price; or

(C) the copyright owner or its agent provides notice pursuant to regulations promulgated by the Register of Copyrights that either of the conditions set forth in subparagraphs (A) and (B) applies.

(3) The exemption provided in this subsection does not apply to any subsequent uses by users other than such library or archives.

(i) The rights of reproduction and distribution under this section do not apply to a musical work, a pictorial, graphic or sculptural work, or a motion picture or other audiovisual work other than an audiovisual work dealing with news, except that no such limitation shall apply with respect to rights granted by subsections (b), (c), and (h), or with respect to pictorial or graphic works published as illustrations, diagrams, or similar adjuncts to works of which copies are reproduced or distributed in accordance with subsections (d) and (e).

§109 · Limitations on exclusive rights: Effect of transfer of particular copy or phonorecord[42]

(a) Notwithstanding the provisions of section 106(3), the owner of a particular copy or phonorecord lawfully made under this title, or any person authorized by such owner, is entitled, without the authority of the copyright owner, to sell or otherwise dispose of the possession of that copy or phonorecord. Notwithstanding the preceding sentence, copies or phonorecords of works subject to restored copyright under section 104A that are manufactured before the date of restoration of copyright or, with respect to reliance parties, before publication or service of notice under section 104A(e), may be sold or otherwise disposed of without the authorization of the owner of the restored copyright for purposes of direct or indirect commercial advantage only during the 12-month period beginning on—

(1) the date of the publication in the Federal Register of the notice of intent filed with the Copyright Office under section 104A(d)(2)(A), or

(2) the date of the receipt of actual notice served under section 104A(d)(2)(B), whichever occurs first.

(b)(1)(A) Notwithstanding the provisions of subsection (a), unless authorized by the owners of copyright in the sound recording or the owner of copyright in a computer program (including any tape, disk, or other medium embodying such program), and in the case of a sound recording in the musical works embodied therein, neither the owner of a particular phonorecord nor any person in possession of a particular copy of a computer program (including any tape, disk, or other medium embodying such program), may, for the purposes of direct or indirect commercial advantage, dispose of, or authorize the disposal of, the possession of that phonorecord or computer program (including any tape, disk, or other medium embodying such program) by rental, lease, or lending, or by any other act or practice in the nature of rental, lease, or lending. Nothing in the preceding sentence shall apply to the rental, lease, or lending of a phonorecord for nonprofit purposes by a nonprofit library or nonprofit educational institution. The transfer of possession of a lawfully made copy of a computer program by a nonprofit educational institution to another nonprofit educational institution or to faculty, staff, and students does not constitute rental, lease, or lending for direct or indirect commercial purposes under this subsection.

(B) This subsection does not apply to—

(i) a computer program which is embodied in a machine or product and which cannot be copied during the ordinary operation or use of the machine or product; or

(ii) a computer program embodied in or used in conjunction with a limited purpose computer that is designed for playing video games and may be designed for other purposes.

(C) Nothing in this subsection affects any provision of chapter 9 of this title.

(2)(A) Nothing in this subsection shall apply to the lending of a computer program for nonprofit purposes by a nonprofit library, if each copy of a computer program which is lent by such library has affixed to the packaging containing the program a warning of copyright in accordance with requirements that the Register of Copyrights shall prescribe by regulation.

(B) Not later than three years after the date of the enactment of the Computer Software Rental Amendments Act of 1990, and at such times thereafter as the Register of Copyrights considers appropriate, the Register of Copyrights, after consultation with representatives of copyright owners and librarians, shall submit to the Congress a report stating whether this paragraph has achieved its intended purpose of maintaining the integrity of the copyright system while providing nonprofit libraries the capability to fulfill their function. Such report shall advise the Congress as to any information or recommendations that the Register of Copyrights considers necessary to carry out the purposes of this subsection.

(3) Nothing in this subsection shall affect any provision of the antitrust laws. For purposes of the preceding sentence, "antitrust laws" has the meaning given that term in the first section of the Clayton Act and includes section 5 of

the Federal Trade Commission Act to the extent that section relates to unfair methods of competition.

(4) Any person who distributes a phonorecord or a copy of a computer program (including any tape, disk, or other medium embodying such program) in violation of paragraph (1) is an infringer of copyright under section 501 of this title and is subject to the remedies set forth in sections 502, 503, 504, and 505. Such violation shall not be a criminal offense under section 506 or cause such person to be subject to the criminal penalties set forth in section 2319 of title 18.

(c) Notwithstanding the provisions of section 106(5), the owner of a particular copy lawfully made under this title, or any person authorized by such owner, is entitled, without the authority of the copyright owner, to display that copy publicly, either directly or by the projection of no more than one image at a time, to viewers present at the place where the copy is located.

(d) The privileges prescribed by subsections (a) and (c) do not, unless authorized by the copyright owner, extend to any person who has acquired possession of the copy or phonorecord from the copyright owner, by rental, lease, loan, or otherwise, without acquiring ownership of it.

(e) Notwithstanding the provisions of sections 106(4) and 106(5), in the case of an electronic audiovisual game intended for use in coin-operated equipment, the owner of a particular copy of such a game lawfully made under this title, is entitled, without the authority of the copyright owner of the game, to publicly perform or display that game in coin-operated equipment, except that this subsection shall not apply to any work of authorship embodied in the audiovisual game if the copyright owner of the electronic audiovisual game is not also the copyright owner of the work of authorship.

§110 · Limitations on exclusive rights: Exemption of certain performances and displays[43]

Notwithstanding the provisions of section 106, the following are not infringements of copyright:

(1) performance or display of a work by instructors or pupils in the course of face-to-face teaching activities of a nonprofit educational institution, in a classroom or similar place devoted to instruction, unless, in the case of a motion picture or other audiovisual work, the performance, or the display of individual images, is given by means of a copy that was not lawfully made under this title, and that the person responsible for the performance knew or had reason to believe was not lawfully made;

(2) except with respect to a work produced or marketed primarily for performance or display as part of mediated instructional activities transmitted via

digital networks, or a performance or display that is given by means of a copy or phonorecord that is not lawfully made and acquired under this title, and the transmitting government body or accredited nonprofit educational institution knew or had reason to believe was not lawfully made and acquired, the performance of a nondramatic literary or musical work or reasonable and limited portions of any other work, or display of a work in an amount comparable to that which is typically displayed in the course of a live classroom session, by or in the course of a transmission, if—

(A) the performance or display is made by, at the direction of, or under the actual supervision of an instructor as an integral part of a class session offered as a regular part of the systematic mediated instructional activities of a governmental body or an accredited nonprofit educational institution;

(B) the performance or display is directly related and of material assistance to the teaching content of the transmission;

(C) the transmission is made solely for, and, to the extent technologically feasible, the reception of such transmission is limited to—

(i) students officially enrolled in the course for which the transmission is made; or

(ii) officers or employees of governmental bodies as a part of their official duties or employment; and

(D) the transmitting body or institution—

(i) institutes policies regarding copyright, provides informational materials to faculty, students, and relevant staff members that accurately describe, and promote compliance with, the laws of the United States relating to copyright, and provides notice to students that materials used in connection with the course may be subject to copyright protection; and

(ii) in the case of digital transmissions—

(I) applies technological measures that reasonably prevent—

(aa) retention of the work in accessible form by recipients of the transmission from the transmitting body or institution for longer than the class session; and

(bb) unauthorized further dissemination of the work in accessible form by such recipients to others; and

(II) does not engage in conduct that could reasonably be expected to interfere with technological measures used by copyright owners to prevent such retention or unauthorized further dissemination;

(3) performance of a nondramatic literary or musical work or of a dramatico-musical work of a religious nature, or display of a work, in the course of services at a place of worship or other religious assembly;

(4) performance of a nondramatic literary or musical work otherwise than in a transmission to the public, without any purpose of direct or indirect

commercial advantage and without payment of any fee or other compensation for the performance to any of its performers, promoters, or organizers, if—

(A) there is no direct or indirect admission charge; or

(B) the proceeds, after deducting the reasonable costs of producing the performance, are used exclusively for educational, religious, or charitable purposes and not for private financial gain, except where the copyright owner has served notice of objection to the performance under the following conditions:

(i) the notice shall be in writing and signed by the copyright owner or such owner's duly authorized agent; and

(ii) the notice shall be served on the person responsible for the performance at least seven days before the date of the performance, and shall state the reasons for the objection; and

(iii) the notice shall comply, in form, content, and manner of service, with requirements that the Register of Copyrights shall prescribe by regulation;

(5)(A) except as provided in subparagraph (B), communication of a transmission embodying a performance or display of a work by the public reception of the transmission on a single receiving apparatus of a kind commonly used in private homes, unless—

(i) a direct charge is made to see or hear the transmission; or

(ii) the transmission thus received is further transmitted to the public;

(B) communication by an establishment of a transmission or retransmission embodying a performance or display of a nondramatic musical work intended to be received by the general public, originated by a radio or television broadcast station licensed as such by the Federal Communications Commission, or, if an audiovisual transmission, by a cable system or satellite carrier, if—

(i) in the case of an establishment other than a food service or drinking establishment, either the establishment in which the communication occurs has less than 2,000 gross square feet of space (excluding space used for customer parking and for no other purpose), or the establishment in which the communication occurs has 2,000 or more gross square feet of space (excluding space used for customer parking and for no other purpose) and—

(I) if the performance is by audio means only, the performance is communicated by means of a total of not more than 6 loudspeakers, of which not more than 4 loudspeakers are located in any 1 room or adjoining outdoor space; or

(II) if the performance or display is by audiovisual means, any visual portion of the performance or display is communicated by means of a total of not more than 4 audiovisual devices, of which not more than 1 audiovisual device is located in any 1 room, and no such audiovisual device has a diagonal screen size greater than 55 inches, and any audio portion of the performance or display is communicated by means of a total of not more than 6 loudspeakers, of which not more than 4 loudspeakers are located in any 1 room or adjoining outdoor space;

(ii) in the case of a food service or drinking establishment, either the establishment in which the communication occurs has less than 3,750 gross square feet of space (excluding space used for customer parking and for no other purpose), or the establishment in which the communication occurs has 3,750 gross square feet of space or more (excluding space used for customer parking and for no other purpose) and—

(I) if the performance is by audio means only, the performance is communicated by means of a total of not more than 6 loudspeakers, of which not more than 4 loudspeakers are located in any 1 room or adjoining outdoor space; or

(II) if the performance or display is by audiovisual means, any visual portion of the performance or display is communicated by means of a total of not more than 4 audiovisual devices, of which not more than 1 audiovisual device is located in any 1 room, and no such audiovisual device has a diagonal screen size greater than 55 inches, and any audio portion of the performance or display is communicated by means of a total of not more than 6 loudspeakers, of which not more than 4 loudspeakers are located in any 1 room or adjoining outdoor space;

(iii) no direct charge is made to see or hear the transmission or retransmission;

(iv) the transmission or retransmission is not further transmitted beyond the establishment where it is received; and

(v) the transmission or retransmission is licensed by the copyright owner of the work so publicly performed or displayed;

(6) performance of a nondramatic musical work by a governmental body or a nonprofit agricultural or horticultural organization, in the course of an annual agricultural or horticultural fair or exhibition conducted by such body or organization; the exemption provided by this clause shall extend to any liability for copyright infringement that would otherwise be imposed on such body or organization, under doctrines of vicarious liability or related infringement, for a performance by a concessionaire, business establishment, or other person at such fair or exhibition, but shall not excuse any such person from liability for the performance;

(7) performance of a nondramatic musical work by a vending establishment open to the public at large without any direct or indirect admission charge, where the sole purpose of the performance is to promote the retail sale of

copies or phonorecords of the work, or of the audiovisual or other devices utilized in such performance, and the performance is not transmitted beyond the place where the establishment is located and is within the immediate area where the sale is occurring;

(8) performance of a nondramatic literary work, by or in the course of a transmission specifically designed for and primarily directed to blind or other handicapped persons who are unable to read normal printed material as a result of their handicap, or deaf or other handicapped persons who are unable to hear the aural signals accompanying a transmission of visual signals, if the performance is made without any purpose of direct or indirect commercial advantage and its transmission is made through the facilities of: (i) a governmental body; or (ii) a noncommercial educational broadcast station (as defined in section 397 of title 47); or (iii) a radio subcarrier authorization (as defined in 47 CFR 73.293–73.295 and 73.593–73.595); or (iv) a cable system (as defined in section 111 (f));

(9) performance on a single occasion of a dramatic literary work published at least ten years before the date of the performance, by or in the course of a transmission specifically designed for and primarily directed to blind or other handicapped persons who are unable to read normal printed material as a result of their handicap, if the performance is made without any purpose of direct or indirect commercial advantage and its transmission is made through the facilities of a radio subcarrier authorization referred to in clause (8) (iii), *Provided,* That the provisions of this clause shall not be applicable to more than one performance of the same work by the same performers or under the auspices of the same organization;

(10) notwithstanding paragraph (4), the following is not an infringement of copyright: performance of a nondramatic literary or musical work in the course of a social function which is organized and promoted by a nonprofit veterans' organization or a nonprofit fraternal organization to which the general public is not invited, but not including the invitees of the organizations, if the proceeds from the performance, after deducting the reasonable costs of producing the performance, are used exclusively for charitable purposes and not for financial gain. For purposes of this section the social functions of any college or university fraternity or sorority shall not be included unless the social function is held solely to raise funds for a specific charitable purpose; and

(11) the making imperceptible, by or at the direction of a member of a private household, of limited portions of audio or video content of a motion picture, during a performance in or transmitted to that household for private home viewing, from an authorized copy of the motion picture, or the creation or provision of a computer program or other technology that enables such making imperceptible and that is designed and marketed to be used, at the direction of a member of a private household, for such making imperceptible,

if no fixed copy of the altered version of the motion picture is created by such computer program or other technology.

The exemptions provided under paragraph (5) shall not be taken into account in any administrative, judicial, or other governmental proceeding to set or adjust the royalties payable to copyright owners for the public performance or display of their works. Royalties payable to copyright owners for any public performance or display of their works other than such performances or displays as are exempted under paragraph (5) shall not be diminished in any respect as a result of such exemption.

In paragraph (2), the term "mediated instructional activities" with respect to the performance or display of a work by digital transmission under this section refers to activities that use such work as an integral part of the class experience, controlled by or under the actual supervision of the instructor and analogous to the type of performance or display that would take place in a live classroom setting. The term does not refer to activities that use, in 1 or more class sessions of a single course, such works as textbooks, course packs, or other material in any media, copies or phonorecords of which are typically purchased or acquired by the students in higher education for their independent use and retention or are typically purchased or acquired for elementary and secondary students for their possession and independent use.

For purposes of paragraph (2), accreditation—

(A) with respect to an institution providing post-secondary education, shall be as determined by a regional or national accrediting agency recognized by the Council on Higher Education Accreditation or the United States Department of Education; and

(B) with respect to an institution providing elementary or secondary education, shall be as recognized by the applicable state certification or licensing procedures.

For purposes of paragraph (2), no governmental body or accredited nonprofit educational institution shall be liable for infringement by reason of the transient or temporary storage of material carried out through the automatic technical process of a digital transmission of the performance or display of that material as authorized under paragraph (2). No such material stored on the system or network controlled or operated by the transmitting body or institution under this paragraph shall be maintained on such system or network in a manner ordinarily accessible to anyone other than anticipated recipients. No such copy shall be maintained on the system or network in a manner ordinarily accessible to such anticipated recipients for a longer period than is reasonably necessary to facilitate the transmissions for which it was made.

For purposes of paragraph (11), the term "making imperceptible" does not include the addition of audio or video content that is performed or displayed over or in place of existing content in a motion picture.

Nothing in paragraph (11) shall be construed to imply further rights under section 106 of this title, or to have any effect on defenses or limitations on rights granted under any other section of this title or under any other paragraph of this section.

§111 · Limitations on exclusive rights: Secondary transmissions of broadcast programming by cable[44]

(a) Certain Secondary Transmissions Exempted.—The secondary transmission of a performance or display of a work embodied in a primary transmission is not an infringement of copyright if—

(1) the secondary transmission is not made by a cable system, and consists entirely of the relaying, by the management of a hotel, apartment house, or similar establishment, of signals transmitted by a broadcast station licensed by the Federal Communications Commission, within the local service area of such station, to the private lodgings of guests or residents of such establishment, and no direct charge is made to see or hear the secondary transmission; or

(2) the secondary transmission is made solely for the purpose and under the conditions specified by paragraph (2) of section 110; or

(3) the secondary transmission is made by any carrier who has no direct or indirect control over the content or selection of the primary transmission or over the particular recipients of the secondary transmission, and whose activities with respect to the secondary transmission consist solely of providing wires, cables, or other communications channels for the use of others: *Provided,* That the provisions of this paragraph extend only to the activities of said carrier with respect to secondary transmissions and do not exempt from liability the activities of others with respect to their own primary or secondary transmissions;

(4) the secondary transmission is made by a satellite carrier pursuant to a statutory license under section 119 or section 122;

(5) the secondary transmission is not made by a cable system but is made by a governmental body, or other nonprofit organization, without any purpose of direct or indirect commercial advantage, and without charge to the recipients of the secondary transmission other than assessments necessary to defray the actual and reasonable costs of maintaining and operating the secondary transmission service.

(b) Secondary Transmission of Primary Transmission to Controlled Group.—Notwithstanding the provisions of subsections (a) and (c), the secondary transmission to the public of a performance or display of a work embodied in a primary transmission is actionable as an act of infringement under section 501, and is fully subject to the remedies provided by sections 502 through 506, if the primary transmission is not made for reception by the public at large but is controlled and limited to reception by particular members of the public: *Provided*, however, That such secondary transmission is not actionable as an act of infringement if—

(1) the primary transmission is made by a broadcast station licensed by the Federal Communications Commission; and

(2) the carriage of the signals comprising the secondary transmission is required under the rules, regulations, or authorizations of the Federal Communications Commission; and

(3) the signal of the primary transmitter is not altered or changed in any way by the secondary transmitter.

(c) Secondary Transmissions by Cable Systems.—

(1) Subject to the provisions of paragraphs (2), (3), and (4) of this subsection and section 114(d), secondary transmissions to the public by a cable system of a performance or display of a work embodied in a primary transmission made by a broadcast station licensed by the Federal Communications Commission or by an appropriate governmental authority of Canada or Mexico shall be subject to statutory licensing upon compliance with the requirements of subsection (d) where the carriage of the signals comprising the secondary transmission is permissible under the rules, regulations, or authorizations of the Federal Communications Commission.

(2) Notwithstanding the provisions of paragraph (1) of this subsection, the willful or repeated secondary transmission to the public by a cable system of a primary transmission made by a broadcast station licensed by the Federal Communications Commission or by an appropriate governmental authority of Canada or Mexico and embodying a performance or display of a work is actionable as an act of infringement under section 501, and is fully subject to the remedies provided by sections 502 through 506, in the following cases:

(A) where the carriage of the signals comprising the secondary transmission is not permissible under the rules, regulations, or authorizations of the Federal Communications Commission; or

(B) where the cable system has not deposited the statement of account and royalty fee required by subsection (d).

(3) Notwithstanding the provisions of paragraph (1) of this subsection and subject to the provisions of subsection (e) of this section, the secondary transmission to the public by a cable system of a performance or display of a work embodied in a primary transmission made by a broadcast station licensed by the Federal Communications Commission or by an appropriate governmental authority of Canada or Mexico is actionable as an act of infringement under section 501, and is fully subject to the remedies provided by sections 502 through 506 and section 510, if the content of the particular program in which the performance or display is embodied, or any commercial advertising or station announcements transmitted by the primary transmitter during,

or immediately before or after, the transmission of such program, is in any way willfully altered by the cable system through changes, deletions, or additions, except for the alteration, deletion, or substitution of commercial advertisements performed by those engaged in television commercial advertising market research: *Provided,* That the research company has obtained the prior consent of the advertiser who has purchased the original commercial advertisement, the television station broadcasting that commercial advertisement, and the cable system performing the secondary transmission: *And provided further,* That such commercial alteration, deletion, or substitution is not performed for the purpose of deriving income from the sale of that commercial time.

(4) Notwithstanding the provisions of paragraph (1) of this subsection, the secondary transmission to the public by a cable system of a performance or display of a work embodied in a primary transmission made by a broadcast station licensed by an appropriate governmental authority of Canada or Mexico is actionable as an act of infringement under section 501, and is fully subject to the remedies provided by sections 502 through 506, if (A) with respect to Canadian signals, the community of the cable system is located more than 150 miles from the United States–Canadian border and is also located south of the forty-second parallel of latitude, or (B) with respect to Mexican signals, the secondary transmission is made by a cable system which received the primary transmission by means other than direct interception of a free space radio wave emitted by such broadcast television station, unless prior to April 15, 1976, such cable system was actually carrying, or was specifically authorized to carry, the signal of such foreign station on the system pursuant to the rules, regulations, or authorizations of the Federal Communications Commission.

(d) STATUTORY LICENSE FOR SECONDARY TRANSMISSIONS BY CABLE SYSTEMS.[45]—

(1) STATEMENT OF ACCOUNT AND ROYALTY FEES.— Subject to paragraph (5), a cable system whose secondary transmissions have been subject to statutory licensing under subsection (c) shall, on a semiannual basis, deposit with the Register of Copyrights, in accordance with requirements that the Register shall prescribe by regulation the following—

(A) A statement of account, covering the six months next preceding, specifying the number of channels on which the cable system made secondary transmissions to its subscribers, the names and locations of all primary transmitters whose transmissions were further transmitted by the cable system, the total number of subscribers, the gross amounts paid to the cable system for the basic service of providing secondary transmissions of primary broadcast transmitters, and such other data as the Register of Copyrights may from time to time prescribe by regulation. In determining the total number of subscribers and the gross amounts paid to the cable system for the basic service of providing secondary transmissions of primary broadcast transmitters, the cable system shall not include subscribers and amounts collected from subscribers receiving secondary transmissions pursuant to section 119. Such statement shall also include a special statement of account covering any non-network television programming that was carried by the cable system in whole or in part beyond the local service area of the primary transmitter, under rules, regulations, or authorizations of the Federal Communications Commission permitting the substitution or addition of signals under certain circumstances, together with logs showing the times, dates, stations, and programs involved in such substituted or added carriage.

(B) Except in the case of a cable system whose royalty fee is specified in subparagraph (E) or (F), a total royalty fee payable to copyright owners pursuant to paragraph (3) for the period covered by the statement, computed on the basis of specified percentages of the gross receipts from subscribers to the cable service during such period for the basic service of providing secondary transmissions of primary broadcast transmitters, as follows:

(i) 1.064 percent of such gross receipts for the privilege of further transmitting, beyond the local service area of such primary transmitter, any non-network programming of a primary transmitter in whole or in part, such amount to be applied against the fee, if any, payable pursuant to clauses (ii) through (iv);

(ii) 1.064 percent of such gross receipts for the first distant signal equivalent;

(iii) 0.701 percent of such gross receipts for each of the second, third, and fourth distant signal equivalents; and

(iv) 0.330 percent of such gross receipts for the fifth distant signal equivalent and each distant signal equivalent thereafter.

(C) In computing amounts under clauses (ii) through (iv) of subparagraph (B)—

(i) any fraction of a distant signal equivalent shall be computed at its fractional value;

(ii) in the case of any cable system located partly within and partly outside of the local service area of a primary transmitter, gross receipts shall be limited to those gross receipts derived from subscribers located outside of the local service area of such primary transmitter; and

(iii) if a cable system provides a secondary transmission of a primary transmitter to some but not all communities served by that cable system—

(I) the gross receipts and the distant signal equivalent values for such secondary transmission shall be derived solely on the basis of the subscribers in those communities where the cable system provides such secondary transmission; and

(II) the total royalty fee for the period paid by such system shall not be less than the royalty fee calculated under subparagraph (B)(i) multiplied by the gross receipts from all subscribers to the system.

(D) A cable system that, on a statement submitted before the date of the enactment of the Satellite Television Extension and Localism Act of 2010, computed its royalty fee consistent with the methodology under subparagraph (C)(iii), or that amends a statement filed before such date of enactment to compute the royalty fee due using such methodology, shall not be subject to an action for infringement, or eligible for any royalty refund or offset, arising out of its use of such methodology on such statement.

(E) If the actual gross receipts paid by subscribers to a cable system for the period covered by the statement for the basic service of providing secondary transmissions of primary broadcast transmitters are $263,800 or less—

(i) gross receipts of the cable system for the purpose of this paragraph shall be computed by subtracting from such actual gross receipts the amount by which $263,800 exceeds such actual gross receipts, except that in no case shall a cable system's gross receipts be reduced to less than $10,400; and

(ii) the royalty fee payable under this paragraph to copyright owners pursuant to paragraph (3) shall be 0.5 percent, regardless of the number of distant signal equivalents, if any.

(F) If the actual gross receipts paid by subscribers to a cable system for the period covered by the statement for the basic service of providing secondary transmissions of primary broadcast transmitters are more than $263,800 but less than $527,600, the royalty fee payable under this paragraph to copyright owners pursuant to paragraph (3) shall be—

(i) 0.5 percent of any gross receipts up to $263,800, regardless of the number of distant signal equivalents, if any; and

(ii) 1 percent of any gross receipts in excess of $263,800, but less than $527,600, regardless of the number of distant signal equivalents, if any.

(G) A filing fee, as determined by the Register of Copyrights pursuant to section 708(a).

(2) Handling of fees.— The Register of Copyrights shall receive all fees (including the filing fee specified in paragraph (1)(G)) deposited under this section and, after deducting the reasonable costs incurred by the Copyright Office under this section, shall deposit the balance in the Treasury of the United States, in such manner as the Secretary of the Treasury directs. All funds held by the Secretary of the Treasury shall be invested in interest-bearing United States securities for later distribution with interest by the Librarian of Congress upon authorization by the Copyright Royalty Judges.

(3) Distribution of royalty fees to copyright owners.— The royalty fees thus deposited shall, in accordance with the procedures provided by clause (4), be distributed to those among the following copyright owners who claim that their works were the subject of secondary transmissions by cable systems during the relevant semiannual period:

(A) Any such owner whose work was included in a secondary transmission made by a cable system of a non-network television program in whole or in part beyond the local service area of the primary transmitter.

(B) Any such owner whose work was included in a secondary transmission identified in a special statement of account deposited under clause (1)(A).

(C) Any such owner whose work was included in non-network programming consisting exclusively of aural signals carried by a cable system in whole or in part beyond the local service area of the primary transmitter of such programs.

(4) Procedures for royalty fee distribution.— The royalty fees thus deposited shall be distributed in accordance with the following procedures:

(A) During the month of July in each year, every person claiming to be entitled to statutory license fees for secondary transmissions shall file a claim with the Copyright Royalty Judges, in accordance with requirements that the Copyright Royalty Judges shall prescribe by regulation. Notwithstanding any provisions of the antitrust laws, for purposes of this clause any claimants may agree among themselves as to the proportionate division of statutory licensing fees among them, may lump their claims together and file them jointly or as a single claim, or may designate a common agent to receive payment on their behalf.

(B) After the first day of August of each year, the Copyright Royalty Judges shall determine whether there exists a controversy concerning the distribution of royalty fees. If the Copyright Royalty Judges determine that no such controversy exists, the Copyright Royalty Judges shall authorize the Librarian of Congress to proceed to distribute such fees to the copyright owners entitled to receive them, or to their designated agents, subject to the deduction of reasonable administrative costs under this section. If the Copyright Royalty Judges find the existence of a controversy, the Copyright Royalty Judges shall, pursuant to chapter 8 of this title, conduct a proceeding to determine the distribution of royalty fees.

(C) During the pendency of any proceeding under this subsection, the Copyright Royalty Judges shall have the discretion to authorize the Librarian of Congress to proceed to distribute any amounts that are not in controversy.

(5) 3.75 Percent rate and syndicated exclusivity surcharge not applicable to multicast streams.— The royalty rates specified in sections 256.2(c) and 256.2(d) of title 37, Code of Federal Regulations (commonly

referred to as the "3.75 percent rate" and the "syndicated exclusivity surcharge", respectively), as in effect on the date of the enactment of the Satellite Television Extension and Localism Act of 2010, as such rates may be adjusted, or such sections redesignated, thereafter by the Copyright Royalty Judges, shall not apply to the secondary transmission of a multicast stream.

(6) VERIFICATION OF ACCOUNTS AND FEE PAYMENTS.— The Register of Copyrights shall issue regulations to provide for the confidential verification by copyright owners whose works were embodied in the secondary transmissions of primary transmissions pursuant to this section of the information reported on the semiannual statements of account filed under this subsection for accounting periods beginning on or after January 1, 2010, in order that the auditor designated under subparagraph (A) is able to confirm the correctness of the calculations and royalty payments reported therein. The regulations shall—

(A) establish procedures for the designation of a qualified independent auditor—

(i) with exclusive authority to request verification of such a statement of account on behalf of all copyright owners whose works were the subject of secondary transmissions of primary transmissions by the cable system (that deposited the statement) during the accounting period covered by the statement; and

(ii) who is not an officer, employee, or agent of any such copyright owner for any purpose other than such audit;

(B) establish procedures for safeguarding all nonpublic financial and business information provided under this paragraph;

(C)(i) require a consultation period for the independent auditor to review its conclusions with a designee of the cable system;

(ii) establish a mechanism for the cable system to remedy any errors identified in the auditor's report and to cure any underpayment identified; and

(iii) provide an opportunity to remedy any disputed facts or conclusions;

(D) limit the frequency of requests for verification for a particular cable system and the number of audits that a multiple system operator can be required to undergo in a single year; and

(E) permit requests for verification of a statement of account to be made only within 3 years after the last day of the year in which the statement of account is filed.

(7) ACCEPTANCE OF ADDITIONAL DEPOSITS.—Any royalty fee payments received by the Copyright Office from cable systems for the secondary transmission of primary transmissions that are in addition to the payments calculated and deposited in accordance with this subsection shall be deemed to

have been deposited for the particular accounting period for which they are received and shall be distributed as specified under this subsection.

(e) Nonsimultaneous Secondary Transmissions by Cable Systems.—

(1) Notwithstanding those provisions of the subsection (f)(2) relating to nonsimultaneous secondary transmissions by a cable system, any such transmissions are actionable as an act of infringement under section 501, and are fully subject to the remedies provided by sections 502 through 506 and section 510, unless—

(A) the program on the videotape is transmitted no more than one time to the cable system's subscribers;

(B) the copyrighted program, episode, or motion picture videotape, including the commercials contained within such program, episode, or picture, is transmitted without deletion or editing;

(C) an owner or officer of the cable system

(i) prevents the duplication of the videotape while in the possession of the system,

(ii) prevents unauthorized duplication while in the possession of the facility making the videotape for the system if the system owns or controls the facility, or takes reasonable precautions to prevent such duplication if it does not own or control the facility,

(iii) takes adequate precautions to prevent duplication while the tape is being transported, and

(iv) subject to paragraph (2), erases or destroys, or causes the erasure or destruction of, the videotape;

(D) within forty-five days after the end of each calendar quarter, an owner or officer of the cable system executes an affidavit attesting

(i) to the steps and precautions taken to prevent duplication of the videotape, and

(ii) subject to paragraph (2), to the erasure or destruction of all videotapes made or used during such quarter;

(E) such owner or officer places or causes each such affidavit, and affidavits received pursuant to paragraph (2)(C), to be placed in a file, open to public inspection, at such system's main office in the community where the transmission is made or in the nearest community where such system maintains an office; and

(F) the nonsimultaneous transmission is one that the cable system would be authorized to transmit under the rules, regulations, and authorizations of the Federal Communications Commission in effect at the time of the nonsimultaneous transmission if the transmission had been made simultaneously, except that this subparagraph shall not apply to inadvertent or accidental transmissions.

(2) If a cable system transfers to any person a videotape of a program nonsimultaneously transmitted by it, such transfer is actionable as an act of infringement under section 501, and is fully subject to the remedies provided by sections 502 through 506, except that, pursuant to a written, nonprofit contract providing for the equitable sharing of the costs of such videotape and its transfer, a videotape nonsimultaneously transmitted by it, in accordance with paragraph (1), may be transferred by one cable system in Alaska to another system in Alaska, by one cable system in Hawaii permitted to make such nonsimultaneous transmissions to another such cable system in Hawaii, or by one cable system in Guam, the Northern Mariana Islands, or the Trust Territory of the Pacific Islands, to another cable system in any of those five entities, if—

(A) each such contract is available for public inspection in the offices of the cable systems involved, and a copy of such contract is filed, within thirty days after such contract is entered into, with the Copyright Office (which Office shall make each such contract available for public inspection); and

(B) the cable system to which the videotape is transferred complies with paragraph (1)(A), (B), (C) (i), (iii), and (iv), and (D) through (F);

(C) such system provides a copy of the affidavit required to be made in accordance with paragraph (1)(D) to each cable system making a previous nonsimultaneous transmission of the same videotape.

(3) This subsection shall not be construed to supersede the exclusivity protection provisions of any existing agreement, or any such agreement hereafter entered into, between a cable system and a television broadcast station in the area in which the cable system is located, or a network with which such station is affiliated.

(4) As used in this subsection, the term "videotape" means the reproduction of the images and sounds of a program or programs broadcast by a television broadcast station licensed by the Federal Communications Commission, regardless of the nature of the material objects, such as tapes or films, in which the reproduction is embodied.

(f) Definitions.—As used in this section, the following terms mean the following:

(1) Primary transmission.— A "primary transmission" is a transmission made to the public by a transmitting facility whose signals are being received and further transmitted by a secondary transmission service, regardless of where or when the performance or display was first transmitted. In the case of a television broadcast station, the primary stream and any multicast streams transmitted by the station constitute primary transmissions.

(2) Secondary transmission.— A "secondary transmission" is the further transmitting of a primary transmission simultaneously with the primary transmission, or nonsimultaneously with the primary transmission if by a

cable system not located in whole or in part within the boundary of the forty-eight contiguous States, Hawaii, or Puerto Rico: *Provided, however*, That a nonsimultaneous further transmission by a cable system located in Hawaii of a primary transmission shall be deemed to be a secondary transmission if the carriage of the television broadcast signal comprising such further transmission is permissible under the rules, regulations, or authorizations of the Federal Communications Commission.

(3) Cable system.— A "cable system" is a facility, located in any State, territory, trust territory, or possession of the United States, that in whole or in part receives signals transmitted or programs broadcast by one or more television broadcast stations licensed by the Federal Communications Commission, and makes secondary transmissions of such signals or programs by wires, cables, microwave, or other communications channels to subscribing members of the public who pay for such service. For purposes of determining the royalty fee under subsection (d)(1), two or more cable systems in contiguous communities under common ownership or control or operating from one headend shall be considered as one system.

(4) Local service area of a primary transmitter.— The "local service area of a primary transmitter", in the case of both the primary stream and any multicast streams transmitted by a primary transmitter that is a television broadcast station, comprises the area where such primary transmitter could have insisted upon its signal being retransmitted by a cable system pursuant to the rules, regulations, and authorizations of the Federal Communications Commission in effect on April 15, 1976, or such station's television market as defined in section 76.55(e) of title 47, Code of Federal Regulations (as in effect on September 18, 1993), or any modifications to such television market made, on or after September 18, 1993, pursuant to section 76.55(e) or 76.59 of title 47, Code of Federal Regulations or within the noise-limited contour as defined in 73.622(e)(1) of title 47, Code of Federal Regulations, or in the case of a television broadcast station licensed by an appropriate governmental authority of Canada or Mexico, the area in which it would be entitled to insist upon its signal being retransmitted if it were a television broadcast station subject to such rules, regulations, and authorizations. In the case of a low power television station, the "local service area of a primary transmitter" comprises the area within 35 miles of the transmitter site, except that in the case of such a station located in a standard metropolitan statistical area which has one of the 50 largest populations of all standard metropolitan statistical areas (based on the 1980 decennial census of population taken by the Secretary of Commerce), the number of miles shall be 20 miles. The "local service area of a primary transmitter", in the case of a radio broadcast station, comprises the primary service area of such station, pursuant to the rules and regulations of the Federal Communications Commission.

(5) Distant signal equivalent.—

(A) In general.— Except as provided under subparagraph (B), a "distant signal equivalent"—

(i) is the value assigned to the secondary transmission of any nonnetwork television programming carried by a cable system in whole or in part beyond the local service area of the primary transmitter of such programming; and

(ii) is computed by assigning a value of one to each primary stream and to each multicast stream (other than a simulcast) that is an independent station, and by assigning a value of one-quarter to each primary stream and to each multicast stream (other than a simulcast) that is a network station or a noncommercial educational station.

(B) Exceptions.— The values for independent, network, and noncommercial educational stations specified in subparagraph (A) are subject to the following:

(i) Where the rules and regulations of the Federal Communications Commission require a cable system to omit the further transmission of a particular program and such rules and regulations also permit the substitution of another program embodying a performance or display of a work in place of the omitted transmission, or where such rules and regulations in effect on the date of the enactment of the Copyright Act of 1976 permit a cable system, at its election, to effect such omission and substitution of a nonlive program or to carry additional programs not transmitted by primary transmitters within whose local service area the cable system is located, no value shall be assigned for the substituted or additional program.

(ii) Where the rules, regulations, or authorizations of the Federal Communications Commission in effect on the date of the enactment of the Copyright Act of 1976 permit a cable system, at its election, to omit the further transmission of a particular program and such rules, regulations, or authorizations also permit the substitution of another program embodying a performance or display of a work in place of the omitted transmission, the value assigned for the substituted or additional program shall be, in the case of a live program, the value of one full distant signal equivalent multiplied by a fraction that has as its numerator the number of days in the year in which such substitution occurs and as its denominator the number of days in the year.

(iii) In the case of the secondary transmission of a primary transmitter that is a television broadcast station pursuant to the late-night or specialty programming rules of the Federal Communications Commission, or the secondary transmission of a primary transmitter that is a television broadcast station on a part-time basis where full-time carriage is not possible because the cable system lacks the activated channel capacity to retransmit on a full-time basis all signals that it is authorized to carry, the values for independent, network, and noncommercial educational stations set forth in subparagraph (A), as the case may be, shall be multiplied by a fraction that is equal to the ratio of the broadcast hours of such primary transmitter retransmitted by the cable system to the total broadcast hours of the primary transmitter.

(iv) No value shall be assigned for the secondary transmission of the primary stream or any multicast streams of a primary transmitter that is a television broadcast station in any community that is within the local service area of the primary transmitter.

(6) NETWORK STATION.—

(A) TREATMENT OF PRIMARY STREAM.— The term "network station" shall be applied to a primary stream of a television broadcast station that is owned or operated by, or affiliated with, one or more of the television networks in the United States providing nationwide transmissions, and that transmits a substantial part of the programming supplied by such networks for a substantial part of the primary stream's typical broadcast day.

(B) TREATMENT OF MULTICAST STREAMS.— The term "network station" shall be applied to a multicast stream on which a television broadcast station transmits all or substantially all of the programming of an interconnected program service that—

(i) is owned or operated by, or affiliated with, one or more of the television networks described in subparagraph (A); and

(ii) offers programming on a regular basis for 15 or more hours per week to at least 25 of the affiliated television licensees of the interconnected program service in 10 or more States.

(7) INDEPENDENT STATION.— The term "independent station" shall be applied to the primary stream or a multicast stream of a television broadcast station that is not a network station or a noncommercial educational station.

(8) NONCOMMERCIAL EDUCATIONAL STATION.— The term "noncommercial educational station" shall be applied to the primary stream or a multicast stream of a television broadcast station that is a noncommercial educational broadcast station as defined in section 397 of the Communications Act of 1934, as in effect on the date of the enactment of the Satellite Television Extension and Localism Act of 2010.

(9) PRIMARY STREAM.— A "primary stream" is—

(A) the single digital stream of programming that, before June 12, 2009, was substantially duplicating the programming transmitted by the television broadcast station as an analog signal; or

(B) if there is no stream described in subparagraph (A), then the single digital stream of programming transmitted by the television broadcast station for the longest period of time.

(10) Primary transmitter.— A "primary transmitter" is a television or radio broadcast station licensed by the Federal Communications Commission, or by an appropriate governmental authority of Canada or Mexico, that makes primary transmissions to the public.

(11) Multicast stream.— A "multicast stream" is a digital stream of programming that is transmitted by a television broadcast station and is not the station's primary stream.

(12) Simulcast.— A "simulcast" is a multicast stream of a television broadcast station that duplicates the programming transmitted by the primary stream or another multicast stream of such station.

(13) Subscriber; subscribe.—

(A) Subscriber.— The term "subscriber" means a person or entity that receives a secondary transmission service from a cable system and pays a fee for the service, directly or indirectly, to the cable system.

(B) Subscribe.— The term "subscribe" means to elect to become a subscriber.

§ 112 · Limitations on exclusive rights: Ephemeral recordings[46]

(a)(1) Notwithstanding the provisions of section 106, and except in the case of a motion picture or other audiovisual work, it is not an infringement of copyright for a transmitting organization entitled to transmit to the public a performance or display of a work, under a license, including a statutory license under section 114(f), or transfer of the copyright or under the limitations on exclusive rights in sound recordings specified by section 114 (a) or for a transmitting organization that is a broadcast radio or television station licensed as such by the Federal Communications Commission and that makes a broadcast transmission of a performance of a sound recording in a digital format on a nonsubscription basis, to make no more than one copy or phonorecord of a particular transmission program embodying the performance or display, if—

(A) the copy or phonorecord is retained and used solely by the transmitting organization that made it, and no further copies or phonorecords are reproduced from it; and

(B) the copy or phonorecord is used solely for the transmitting organization's own transmissions within its local service area, or for purposes of archival preservation or security; and

(C) unless preserved exclusively for archival purposes, the copy or phonorecord is destroyed within six months from the date the transmission program was first transmitted to the public.

(2) In a case in which a transmitting organization entitled to make a copy or phonorecord under paragraph (1) in connection with the transmission to the public of a performance or display of a work is prevented from making such copy or phonorecord by reason of the application by the copyright owner of technical measures that prevent the reproduction of the work, the copyright owner shall make available to the transmitting organization the necessary means for permitting the making of such copy or phonorecord as permitted under that paragraph, if it is technologically feasible and economically reasonable for the copyright owner to do so. If the copyright owner fails to do so in a timely manner in light of the transmitting organization's reasonable business requirements, the transmitting organization shall not be liable for a violation of section 1201(a)(1) of this title for engaging in such activities as are necessary to make such copies or phonorecords as permitted under paragraph (1) of this subsection.

(b) Notwithstanding the provisions of section 106, it is not an infringement of copyright for a governmental body or other nonprofit organization entitled to transmit a performance or display of a work, under section 110(2) or under the limitations on exclusive rights in sound recordings specified by section 114(a), to make no more than thirty copies or phonorecords of a particular transmission program embodying the performance or display, if—

(1) no further copies or phonorecords are reproduced from the copies or phonorecords made under this clause; and

(2) except for one copy or phonorecord that may be preserved exclusively for archival purposes, the copies or phonorecords are destroyed within seven years from the date the transmission program was first transmitted to the public.

(c) Notwithstanding the provisions of section 106, it is not an infringement of copyright for a governmental body or other nonprofit organization to make for distribution no more than one copy or phonorecord, for each transmitting organization specified in clause (2) of this subsection, of a particular transmission program embodying a performance of a nondramatic musical work of a religious nature, or of a sound recording of such a musical work, if—

(1) there is no direct or indirect charge for making or distributing any such copies or phonorecords; and

(2) none of such copies or phonorecords is used for any performance other than a single transmission to the public by a transmitting organization entitled to transmit to the public a performance of the work under a license or transfer of the copyright; and

(3) except for one copy or phonorecord that may be preserved exclusively for archival purposes, the copies or phonorecords are all destroyed within one year from the date the transmission program was first transmitted to the public.

(d) Notwithstanding the provisions of section 106, it is not an infringement of copyright for a governmental body or other nonprofit organization entitled to transmit a performance of a work under section 110(8) to make no more than ten copies or phonorecords embodying the performance, or to permit the use of any such copy or phonorecord by any governmental body or nonprofit organization entitled to transmit a performance of a work under section 110(8), if—

(1) any such copy or phonorecord is retained and used solely by the organization that made it, or by a governmental body or nonprofit organization entitled to transmit a performance of a work under section 110(8), and no further copies or phonorecords are reproduced from it; and

(2) any such copy or phonorecord is used solely for transmissions authorized under section 110(8), or for purposes of archival preservation or security; and

(3) the governmental body or nonprofit organization permitting any use of any such copy or phonorecord by any governmental body or nonprofit organization under this subsection does not make any charge for such use.

(e) Statutory License.—(1) A transmitting organization entitled to transmit to the public a performance of a sound recording under the limitation on exclusive rights specified by section 114(d)(1)(C)(iv) or under a statutory license in accordance with section 114(f) is entitled to a statutory license, under the conditions specified by this subsection, to make no more than 1 phonorecord of the sound recording (unless the terms and conditions of the statutory license allow for more), if the following conditions are satisfied:

(A) The phonorecord is retained and used solely by the transmitting organization that made it, and no further phonorecords are reproduced from it.

(B) The phonorecord is used solely for the transmitting organization's own transmissions originating in the United States under a statutory license in accordance with section 114(f) or the limitation on exclusive rights specified by section 114(d)(1)(C)(iv).

(C) Unless preserved exclusively for purposes of archival preservation, the phonorecord is destroyed within 6 months from the date the sound recording was first transmitted to the public using the phonorecord.

(D) Phonorecords of the sound recording have been distributed to the public under the authority of the copyright owner or the copyright owner authorizes the transmitting entity to transmit the sound recording, and the transmitting entity makes the phonorecord under this subsection from a phonorecord lawfully made and acquired under the authority of the copyright owner.

(2) Notwithstanding any provision of the antitrust laws, any copyright owners of sound recordings and any transmitting organizations entitled to a statu-

tory license under this subsection may negotiate and agree upon royalty rates and license terms and conditions for making phonorecords of such sound recordings under this section and the proportionate division of fees paid among copyright owners, and may designate common agents to negotiate, agree to, pay, or receive such royalty payments.

(3) Proceedings under chapter 8 shall determine reasonable rates and terms of royalty payments for the activities specified by paragraph (1) during the 5-year period beginning on January 1 of the second year following the year in which the proceedings are to be commenced, or such other period as the parties may agree. Such rates shall include a minimum fee for each type of service offered by transmitting organizations. Any copyright owners of sound recordings or any transmitting organizations entitled to a statutory license under this subsection may submit to the Copyright Royalty Judges licenses covering such activities with respect to such sound recordings. The parties to each proceeding shall bear their own costs.

(4) The schedule of reasonable rates and terms determined by the Copyright Royalty Judges shall, subject to paragraph (5), be binding on all copyright owners of sound recordings and transmitting organizations entitled to a statutory license under this subsection during the 5-year period specified in paragraph (3), or such other period as the parties may agree. Such rates shall include a minimum fee for each type of service offered by transmitting organizations. The Copyright Royalty Judges shall establish rates that most clearly represent the fees that would have been negotiated in the marketplace between a willing buyer and a willing seller. In determining such rates and terms, the Copyright Royalty Judges shall base their decision on economic, competitive, and programming information presented by the parties, including—

(A) whether use of the service may substitute for or may promote the sales of phonorecords or otherwise interferes with or enhances the copyright owner's traditional streams of revenue; and

(B) the relative roles of the copyright owner and the transmitting organization in the copyrighted work and the service made available to the public with respect to relative creative contribution, technological contribution, capital investment, cost, and risk.

In establishing such rates and terms, the Copyright Royalty Judges may consider the rates and terms under voluntary license agreements described in paragraphs (2) and (3). The Copyright Royalty Judges shall also establish requirements by which copyright owners may receive reasonable notice of the use of their sound recordings under this section, and under which records of such use shall be kept and made available by transmitting organizations entitled to obtain a statutory license under this subsection.

(5) License agreements voluntarily negotiated at any time between 1 or more copyright owners of sound recordings and 1 or more transmitting organizations entitled to obtain a statutory license under this subsection shall be given effect in lieu of any decision by the Librarian of Congress or determination by the Copyright Royalty Judges.

(6)(A) Any person who wishes to make a phonorecord of a sound recording under a statutory license in accordance with this subsection may do so without infringing the exclusive right of the copyright owner of the sound recording under section 106(1)—

(i) by complying with such notice requirements as the Copyright Royalty Judges shall prescribe by regulation and by paying royalty fees in accordance with this subsection; or

(ii) if such royalty fees have not been set, by agreeing to pay such royalty fees as shall be determined in accordance with this subsection.

(B) Any royalty payments in arrears shall be made on or before the 20th day of the month next succeeding the month in which the royalty fees are set.

(7) If a transmitting organization entitled to make a phonorecord under this subsection is prevented from making such phonorecord by reason of the application by the copyright owner of technical measures that prevent the reproduction of the sound recording, the copyright owner shall make available to the transmitting organization the necessary means for permitting the making of such phonorecord as permitted under this subsection, if it is technologically feasible and economically reasonable for the copyright owner to do so. If the copyright owner fails to do so in a timely manner in light of the transmitting organization's reasonable business requirements, the transmitting organization shall not be liable for a violation of section 1201(a)(1) of this title for engaging in such activities as are necessary to make such phonorecords as permitted under this subsection.

(8) Nothing in this subsection annuls, limits, impairs, or otherwise affects in any way the existence or value of any of the exclusive rights of the copyright owners in a sound recording, except as otherwise provided in this subsection, or in a musical work, including the exclusive rights to reproduce and distribute a sound recording or musical work, including by means of a digital phonorecord delivery, under section 106(1), 106(3), and 115, and the right to perform publicly a sound recording or musical work, including by means of a digital audio transmission, under sections 106(4) and 106(6).

(f)(1) Notwithstanding the provisions of section 106, and without limiting the application of subsection (b), it is not an infringement of copyright for a governmental body or other nonprofit educational institution entitled under section 110(2) to transmit a performance or display to make copies or phonorecords of a work that is in digital form and, solely to the extent permitted in paragraph (2), of a work that is in analog form, embodying the performance or display to be used for making transmissions authorized under section 110(2), if—

(A) such copies or phonorecords are retained and used solely by the body or institution that made them, and no further copies or phonorecords are reproduced from them, except as authorized under section 110(2); and

(B) such copies or phonorecords are used solely for transmissions authorized under section 110(2).

(2) This subsection does not authorize the conversion of print or other analog versions of works into digital formats, except that such conversion is permitted hereunder, only with respect to the amount of such works authorized to be performed or displayed under section 110(2), if—

(A) no digital version of the work is available to the institution; or

(B) the digital version of the work that is available to the institution is subject to technological protection measures that prevent its use for section 110(2).

(g) The transmission program embodied in a copy or phonorecord made under this section is not subject to protection as a derivative work under this title except with the express consent of the owners of copyright in the preexisting works employed in the program.

§113 · Scope of exclusive rights in pictorial, graphic, and sculptural works[47]

(a) Subject to the provisions of subsections (b) and (c) of this section, the exclusive right to reproduce a copyrighted pictorial, graphic, or sculptural work in copies under section 106 includes the right to reproduce the work in or on any kind of article, whether useful or otherwise.

(b) This title does not afford, to the owner of copyright in a work that portrays a useful article as such, any greater or lesser rights with respect to the making, distribution, or display of the useful article so portrayed than those afforded to such works under the law, whether title 17 or the common law or statutes of a State, in effect on December 31, 1977, as held applicable and construed by a court in an action brought under this title.

(c) In the case of a work lawfully reproduced in useful articles that have been offered for sale or other distribution to the public, copyright does not include any right to prevent the making, distribution, or display of pictures or photographs of such articles in connection with advertisements or commentaries related to the distribution or display of such articles, or in connection with news reports.

(d)(1) In a case in which—

(A) a work of visual art has been incorporated in or made part of a building in such a way that removing the work from the building will cause the destruction, distortion, mutilation, or other modification of the work as described in section 106A(a)(3), and

(B) the author consented to the installation of the work in the building either before the effective date set forth in section 610(a) of the Visual Artists Rights Act of 1990, or in a written instrument executed on or after such effective date that is signed by the owner of the building and the author and that specifies that installation of the work may subject the work to destruction, distortion, mutilation, or other modification, by reason of its removal, then the rights conferred by paragraphs (2) and (3) of section 106A(a) shall not apply.

(2) If the owner of a building wishes to remove a work of visual art which is a part of such building and which can be removed from the building without the destruction, distortion, mutilation, or other modification of the work as described in section 106A(a)(3), the author's rights under paragraphs (2) and (3) of section 106A(a) shall apply unless—

(A) the owner has made a diligent, good faith attempt without success to notify the author of the owner's intended action affecting the work of visual art, or

(B) the owner did provide such notice in writing and the person so notified failed, within 90 days after receiving such notice, either to remove the work or to pay for its removal.

For purposes of subparagraph (A), an owner shall be presumed to have made a diligent, good faith attempt to send notice if the owner sent such notice by registered mail to the author at the most recent address of the author that was recorded with the Register of Copyrights pursuant to paragraph (3). If the work is removed at the expense of the author, title to that copy of the work shall be deemed to be in the author.

(3) The Register of Copyrights shall establish a system of records whereby any author of a work of visual art that has been incorporated in or made part of a building, may record his or her identity and address with the Copyright Office. The Register shall also establish procedures under which any such author may update the information so recorded, and procedures under which owners of buildings may record with the Copyright Office evidence of their efforts to comply with this subsection.

§ 114 · Scope of exclusive rights in sound recordings[48]

(a) The exclusive rights of the owner of copyright in a sound recording are limited to the rights specified by clauses (1), (2), (3) and (6) of section 106, and do not include any right of performance under section 106(4).

(b) The exclusive right of the owner of copyright in a sound recording under clause (1) of section 106 is limited to the right to duplicate the sound recording in the form of phonorecords or copies that directly or indirectly recapture the actual sounds fixed in the recording. The exclusive right of the owner of copyright in a sound recording under clause (2) of section 106 is limited to the right to prepare a derivative work in which the actual sounds fixed in the sound recording are rearranged, remixed, or otherwise altered in sequence or quality. The exclusive rights of the owner of copyright in a sound recording under clauses (1) and (2) of section 106 do not extend to the making or duplication of another sound recording that consists entirely of an independent fixation of other sounds, even though such sounds imitate or simulate those in the copyrighted sound recording. The exclusive rights of the owner of copyright in a sound recording under clauses (1), (2), and (3) of section 106 do not apply to sound recordings included in educational television and radio programs (as defined in section 397 of title 47) distributed or transmitted by or through public broadcasting entities (as defined by section 118(f)): *Provided*, That copies or phonorecords of said programs are not commercially distributed by or through public broadcasting entities to the general public.

(c) This section does not limit or impair the exclusive right to perform publicly, by means of a phonorecord, any of the works specified by section 106(4).

(d) Limitations on Exclusive Right.—Notwithstanding the provisions of section 106(6)—

(1) Exempt transmissions and retransmissions.—The performance of a sound recording publicly by means of a digital audio transmission, other than as a part of an interactive service, is not an infringement of section 106(6) if the performance is part of—

(A) a nonsubscription broadcast transmission;

(B) a retransmission of a nonsubscription broadcast transmission: *Provided*, That, in the case of a retransmission of a radio station's broadcast transmission—

(i) the radio station's broadcast transmission is not willfully or repeatedly retransmitted more than a radius of 150 miles from the site of the radio broadcast transmitter, however—

(I) the 150 mile limitation under this clause shall not apply when a nonsubscription broadcast transmission by a radio station licensed by the Federal Communications Commission is retransmitted on a nonsubscription basis by a terrestrial broadcast station, terrestrial translator, or terrestrial repeater licensed by the Federal Communications Commission; and

(II) in the case of a subscription retransmission of a nonsubscription broadcast retransmission covered by subclause (I), the 150 mile radius shall be measured from the transmitter site of such broadcast retransmitter;

(ii) the retransmission is of radio station broadcast transmissions that are—

(I) obtained by the retransmitter over the air;

(II) not electronically processed by the retransmitter to deliver separate and discrete signals; and

(III) retransmitted only within the local communities served by the retransmitter;

(iii) the radio station's broadcast transmission was being retransmitted to cable systems (as defined in section 111(f)) by a satellite carrier on January 1, 1995, and that retransmission was being retransmitted by cable systems as a separate and discrete signal, and the satellite carrier obtains the radio station's broadcast transmission in an analog format: *Provided*, That the broadcast transmission being retransmitted may embody the programming of no more than one radio station; or

(iv) the radio station's broadcast transmission is made by a noncommercial educational broadcast station funded on or after January 1, 1995, under section 396(k) of the Communications Act of 1934 (47 U.S.C. 396(k)), consists solely of noncommercial educational and cultural radio programs, and the retransmission, whether or not simultaneous, is a nonsubscription terrestrial broadcast retransmission; or

(C) a transmission that comes within any of the following categories—

(i) a prior or simultaneous transmission incidental to an exempt transmission, such as a feed received by and then retransmitted by an exempt transmitter: *Provided*, That such incidental transmissions do not include any subscription transmission directly for reception by members of the public;

(ii) a transmission within a business establishment, confined to its premises or the immediately surrounding vicinity;

(iii) a retransmission by any retransmitter, including a multichannel video programming distributor as defined in section 602(12) of the Communications Act of 1934 (47 U.S.C. 522 (12)), of a transmission by a transmitter licensed to publicly perform the sound recording as a part of that transmission, if the retransmission is simultaneous with the licensed transmission and authorized by the transmitter; or

(iv) a transmission to a business establishment for use in the ordinary course of its business: *Provided*, That the business recipient does not retransmit the transmission outside of its premises or the immediately surrounding vicinity, and that the transmission does not exceed the sound recording performance complement. Nothing in this clause shall limit the scope of the exemption in clause (ii).

(2) STATUTORY LICENSING OF CERTAIN TRANSMISSIONS.—

The performance of a sound recording publicly by means of a subscription digital audio transmission not exempt under paragraph (1), an eligible nonsubscription transmission, or a transmission not exempt under paragraph (1) that is made by a preexisting satellite digital audio radio service shall be subject to statutory licensing, in accordance with subsection (f) if—

(A)(i) the transmission is not part of an interactive service;

(ii) except in the case of a transmission to a business establishment, the transmitting entity does not automatically and intentionally cause any device receiving the transmission to switch from one program channel to another; and

(iii) except as provided in section 1002(e), the transmission of the sound recording is accompanied, if technically feasible, by the information encoded in that sound recording, if any, by or under the authority of the copyright owner of that sound recording, that identifies the title of the sound recording, the featured recording artist who performs on the sound recording, and related information, including information concerning the underlying musical work and its writer;

(B) in the case of a subscription transmission not exempt under paragraph (1) that is made by a preexisting subscription service in the same transmission medium used by such service on July 31, 1998, or in the case of a transmission not exempt under paragraph (1) that is made by a preexisting satellite digital audio radio service—

(i) the transmission does not exceed the sound recording performance complement; and

(ii) the transmitting entity does not cause to be published by means of an advance program schedule or prior announcement the titles of the specific sound recordings or phonorecords embodying such sound recordings to be transmitted; and

(C) in the case of an eligible nonsubscription transmission or a subscription transmission not exempt under paragraph (1) that is made by a new subscription service or by a preexisting subscription service other than in the same transmission medium used by such service on July 31, 1998—

(i) the transmission does not exceed the sound recording performance complement, except that this requirement shall not apply in the case of a retransmission of a broadcast transmission if the retransmission is made by a transmitting entity that does not have the right or ability to control the programming of the broadcast station making the broadcast transmission, unless—

(I) the broadcast station makes broadcast transmissions—

(aa) in digital format that regularly exceed the sound recording performance complement; or (bb) in analog format, a substantial portion of which, on a weekly basis, exceed the sound recording performance complement; and

(II) the sound recording copyright owner or its representative has notified the transmitting entity in writing that broadcast transmissions of the copyright owner's sound recordings exceed the sound recording performance complement as provided in this clause;

(ii) the transmitting entity does not cause to be published, or induce or facilitate the publication, by means of an advance program schedule or prior announcement, the titles of the specific sound recordings to be transmitted, the phonorecords embodying such sound recordings, or, other than for illustrative purposes, the names of the featured recording artists, except that this clause does not disqualify a transmitting entity that makes a prior announcement that a particular artist will be featured within an unspecified future time period, and in the case of a retransmission of a broadcast transmission by a transmitting entity that does not have the right or ability to control the programming of the broadcast transmission, the requirement of this clause shall not apply to a prior oral announcement by the broadcast station, or to an advance program schedule published, induced, or facilitated by the broadcast station, if the transmitting entity does not have actual knowledge and has not received written notice from the copyright owner or its representative that the broadcast station publishes or induces or facilitates the publication of such advance program schedule, or if such advance program schedule is a schedule of classical music programming published by the broadcast station in the same manner as published by that broadcast station on or before September 30, 1998;

(iii) the transmission—

(I) is not part of an archived program of less than 5 hours duration;

(II) is not part of an archived program of 5 hours or greater in duration that is made available for a period exceeding 2 weeks;

(III) is not part of a continuous program which is of less than 3 hours duration; or

(IV) is not part of an identifiable program in which performances of sound recordings are rendered in a predetermined order, other than an archived or continuous program, that is transmitted at—

(aa) more than 3 times in any 2-week period that have been publicly announced in advance, in the case of a program of less than 1 hour in duration, or

(bb) more than 4 times in any 2-week period that have been publicly announced in advance, in the case of a program of 1 hour or more in duration, except that the requirement of this subclause shall not apply in the case of a retransmission of a broadcast transmission by a transmitting entity that does not have the right or ability to control the programming of the broadcast transmission, unless the transmitting entity is given notice in writing by the copyright owner of the sound recording that the broadcast station makes broadcast transmissions that regularly violate such requirement;

(iv) the transmitting entity does not knowingly perform the sound recording, as part of a service that offers transmissions of visual images contemporaneously with transmissions of sound recordings, in a manner that is likely to cause confusion, to cause mistake, or to deceive, as to the affiliation, connection, or association of the copyright owner or featured recording artist with the transmitting entity or a particular product or service advertised by the transmitting entity, or as to the origin, sponsorship, or approval by the copyright owner or featured recording artist of the activities of the transmitting entity other than the performance of the sound recording itself;

(v) the transmitting entity cooperates to prevent, to the extent feasible without imposing substantial costs or burdens, a transmission recipient or any other person or entity from automatically scanning the transmitting entity's transmissions alone or together with transmissions by other transmitting entities in order to select a particular sound recording to be transmitted to the transmission recipient, except that the requirement of this clause shall not apply to a satellite digital audio service that is in operation, or that is licensed by the Federal Communications Commission, on or before July 31, 1998;

(vi) the transmitting entity takes no affirmative steps to cause or induce the making of a phonorecord by the transmission recipient, and if the technology used by the transmitting entity enables the transmitting entity to limit the making by the transmission recipient of phonorecords of the transmission directly in a digital format, the transmitting entity sets such technology to limit such making of phonorecords to the extent permitted by such technology;

(vii) phonorecords of the sound recording have been distributed to the public under the authority of the copyright owner or the copyright owner authorizes the transmitting entity to transmit the sound recording, and the transmitting entity makes the transmission from a phonorecord lawfully made under the authority of the copyright owner, except that the requirement of this clause shall not apply to a retransmission of a broadcast transmission by a transmitting entity that does not have the right or ability to control the programming of the broadcast transmission, unless the transmitting entity is given notice in writing by the copyright owner of the sound recording that the broadcast station makes broadcast transmissions that regularly violate such requirement;

(viii) the transmitting entity accommodates and does not interfere with the transmission of technical measures that are widely used by sound recording copyright owners to identify or protect copyrighted works, and that are technically feasible of being transmitted by the transmitting entity without imposing substantial costs on the transmitting entity or resulting in perceptible aural or visual degradation of the digital signal, except that the requirement of this clause shall not apply to a satellite digital audio service that is in operation, or that is licensed under the authority of the Federal Communications Commission, on or before July 31, 1998, to the extent that such service has designed, developed, or made commitments to procure equipment or technology that is not compatible with such technical measures before such technical measures are widely adopted by sound recording copyright owners; and

(ix) the transmitting entity identifies in textual data the sound recording during, but not before, the time it is performed, including the title of the sound recording, the title of the phonorecord embodying such sound recording, if any, and the featured recording artist, in a manner to permit it to be displayed to the transmission recipient by the device or technology intended for receiving the service provided by the transmitting entity, except that the obligation in this clause shall not take effect until 1 year after the date of the enactment of the Digital Millennium Copyright Act and shall not apply in the case of a retransmission of a broadcast transmission by a transmitting entity that does not have the right or ability to control the programming of the broadcast transmission, or in the case in which devices or technology intended for receiving the service provided by the transmitting entity that have the capability to display such textual data are not common in the marketplace.

(3) Licenses for transmissions by interactive services.—

(A) No interactive service shall be granted an exclusive license under section 106(6) for the performance of a sound recording publicly by means of digital audio transmission for a period in excess of 12 months, except that with respect to an exclusive license granted to an interactive service by a licensor that holds the copyright to 1,000 or fewer sound recordings, the period of such license shall not exceed 24 months: Provided, however, That the grantee of such exclusive license shall be ineligible to receive another exclusive license for the performance of that sound recording for a period of 13 months from the expiration of the prior exclusive license.

(B) The limitation set forth in subparagraph (A) of this paragraph shall not apply if—

(i) the licensor has granted and there remain in effect licenses under section 106(6) for the public performance of sound recordings by means of digital audio transmission by at least 5 different interactive services; Provided, however, That each such license must be for a minimum of 10 percent of the copyrighted sound recordings owned by the licensor that have been licensed to interactive services, but in no event less than 50 sound recordings; or

(ii) the exclusive license is granted to perform publicly up to 45 seconds of a sound recording and the sole purpose of the performance is to promote the distribution or performance of that sound recording.

(C) Notwithstanding the grant of an exclusive or nonexclusive license of the right of public performance under section 106(6), an interactive service may not publicly perform a sound recording unless a license has been granted for the public performance of any copyrighted musical work contained in the sound recording: Provided, That such license to publicly perform the copyrighted musical work may be granted either by a performing rights society representing the copyright owner or by the copyright owner.

(D) The performance of a sound recording by means of a retransmission of a digital audio transmission is not an infringement of section 106(6) if—

(i) the retransmission is of a transmission by an interactive service licensed to publicly perform the sound recording to a particular member of the public as part of that transmission; and

(ii) the retransmission is simultaneous with the licensed transmission, authorized by the transmitter, and limited to that particular member of the public intended by the interactive service to be the recipient of the transmission.

(E) For the purposes of this paragraph—

(i) a "licensor" shall include the licensing entity and any other entity under any material degree of common ownership, management, or control that owns copyrights in sound recordings; and

(ii) a "performing rights society" is an association or corporation that licenses the public performance of nondramatic musical works on behalf of the copyright owner, such as the American Society of Composers, Authors and Publishers, Broadcast Music, Inc., and SESAC, Inc.

(4) Rights not otherwise limited.—

(A) Except as expressly provided in this section, this section does not limit or impair the exclusive right to perform a sound recording publicly by means of a digital audio transmission under section 106(6).

(B) Nothing in this section annuls or limits in any way—

(i) the exclusive right to publicly perform a musical work, including by means of a digital audio transmission, under section 106(4);

(ii) the exclusive rights in a sound recording or the musical work embodied therein under sections 106(1), 106(2) and 106(3); or

(iii) any other rights under any other clause of section 106, or remedies available under this title as such rights or remedies exist either before or after the date of enactment of the Digital Performance Right in Sound Recordings Act of 1995.

(C) Any limitations in this section on the exclusive right under section 106(6) apply only to the exclusive right under section 106(6) and not to any other exclusive rights under section 106. Nothing in this section shall be construed to annul, limit, impair or otherwise affect in any way the ability of the owner of a copyright in a sound recording to exercise the rights under sections 106(1), 106(2) and 106(3), or to obtain the remedies available under this title pursuant to such rights, as such rights and remedies exist either before or after the date of enactment of the Digital Performance Right in Sound Recordings Act of 1995.

(e) AUTHORITY FOR NEGOTIATIONS.—

(1) Notwithstanding any provision of the antitrust laws, in negotiating statutory licenses in accordance with subsection (f), any copyright owners of sound recordings and any entities performing sound recordings affected by this section may negotiate and agree upon the royalty rates and license terms and conditions for the performance of such sound recordings and the proportionate division of fees paid among copyright owners, and may designate common agents on a nonexclusive basis to negotiate, agree to, pay, or receive payments.

(2) For licenses granted under section 106(6), other than statutory licenses, such as for performances by interactive services or performances that exceed the sound recording performance complement—

(A) copyright owners of sound recordings affected by this section may designate common agents to act on their behalf to grant licenses and receive and remit royalty payments: *Provided*, That each copyright owner shall establish the royalty rates and material license terms and conditions unilaterally, that is, not in agreement, combination, or concert with other copyright owners of sound recordings; and

(B) entities performing sound recordings affected by this section may designate common agents to act on their behalf to obtain licenses and collect and pay royalty fees: *Provided*, That each entity performing sound recordings shall determine the royalty rates and material license terms and conditions unilaterally, that is, not in agreement, combination, or concert with other entities performing sound recordings.

(f) LICENSES FOR CERTAIN NONEXEMPT TRANSMISSIONS.

(1)(A) Proceedings under chapter 8 shall determine reasonable rates and terms of royalty payments for subscription transmissions by preexisting subscription services and transmissions by preexisting satellite digital audio radio services specified by subsection (d)(2) during the 5-year period beginning on January 1 of the second year following the year in which the proceedings are to be commenced, except in the case of a different transitional period provided under section 6(b)(3) of the Copyright Royalty and Distribution Reform Act of 2004, or such other period as the parties may agree. Such terms and rates shall distinguish among the different types of digital audio transmission services then in operation. Any copyright owners of sound recordings, preexisting subscription services, or preexisting satellite digital audio radio services may submit to the Copyright Royalty Judges licenses covering such subscription transmissions with respect to such sound recordings. The parties to each proceeding shall bear their own costs.

(B) The schedule of reasonable rates and terms determined by the Copyright Royalty Judges shall, subject to paragraph (3), be binding on all copyright owners of sound recordings and entities performing sound recordings affected by this paragraph during the 5-year period specified in subparagraph (A), a transitional period provided under section 6(b)(3) of the Copyright Royalty and Distribution Reform Act of 2004, or such other period as the parties may agree. In establishing rates and terms for preexisting subscription services and preexisting satellite digital audio radio services, in addition to the objectives set forth in section 801(b)(1), the Copyright Royalty Judges may consider the rates and terms for comparable types of subscription digital audio transmission services and comparable circumstances under voluntary license agreements described in subparagraph (A).

(C) The procedures under subparagraphs (A) and (B) also shall be initiated pursuant to a petition filed by any copyright owners of sound recordings, any preexisting subscription services, or any preexisting satellite digital audio radio services indicating that a new type of subscription digital audio transmission service on which sound recordings are performed is or is about to become operational, for the purpose of determining reasonable terms and rates of royalty payments with respect to such new type of transmission service for the period beginning with the inception of such new type of service and ending on the date on which the royalty rates and terms for subscription digital audio transmission services most recently determined under subparagraph (A) or (B) and chapter 8 expire, or such other period as the parties may agree.

(2)(A) Proceedings under chapter 8 shall determine reasonable rates and terms of royalty payments for public performances of sound recordings by means of eligible nonsubscription transmission services and new subscription services specified by subsection (d)(2) during the 5-year period beginning on

January 1 of the second year following the year in which the proceedings are to be commenced, except in the case of a different transitional period provided under section 6(b)(3) of the Copyright Royalty and Distribution Reform Act of 2004, or such other period as the parties may agree. Such rates and terms shall distinguish among the different types of eligible nonsubscription transmission services and new subscription services then in operation and shall include a minimum fee for each such type of service. Any copyright owners of sound recordings or any entities performing sound recordings affected by this paragraph may submit to the Copyright Royalty Judges licenses covering such eligible nonsubscription transmissions and new subscription services with respect to such sound recordings. The parties to each proceeding shall bear their own costs.

(B) The schedule of reasonable rates and terms determined by the Copyright Royalty Judges shall, subject to paragraph (3), be binding on all copyright owners of sound recordings and entities performing sound recordings affected by this paragraph during the 5-year period specified in subparagraph (A), a transitional period provided under section 6(b)(3) of the Copyright Royalty and Distribution Act of 2004, or such other period as the parties may agree. Such rates and terms shall distinguish among the different types of eligible nonsubscription transmission services then in operation and shall include a minimum fee for each such type of service, such differences to be based on criteria including, but not limited to, the quantity and nature of the use of sound recordings and the degree to which use of the service may substitute for or may promote the purchase of phonorecords by consumers. In establishing rates and terms for transmissions by eligible nonsubscription services and new subscription services, the Copyright Royalty Judges shall establish rates and terms that most clearly represent the rates and terms that would have been negotiated in the marketplace between a willing buyer and a willing seller. In determining such rates and terms, the Copyright Royalty Judges shall base their[49] decision on economic, competitive and programming information presented by the parties, including—

(i) whether use of the service may substitute for or may promote the sales of phonorecords or otherwise may interfere with or may enhance the sound recording copyright owner's other streams of revenue from its sound recordings; and

(ii) the relative roles of the copyright owner and the transmitting entity in the copyrighted work and the service made available to the public with respect to relative creative contribution, technological contribution, capital investment, cost, and risk.

In establishing such rates and terms, the Copyright Royalty Judges may consider the rates and terms for comparable types of digital audio transmission services and comparable circumstances under voluntary license agreements described in subparagraph (A).

(C) The procedures under subparagraphs (A) and (B) shall also be initiated pursuant to a petition filed by any copyright owners of sound recordings or any eligible nonsubscription service or new subscription service indicating that a new type of eligible nonsubscription service or new subscription service on which sound recordings are performed is or is about to become operational, for the purpose of determining reasonable terms and rates of royalty payments with respect to such new type of service for the period beginning with the inception of such new type of service and ending on the date on which the royalty rates and terms for eligible nonsubscription services and new subscription services, as the case may be, most recently determined under subparagraph (A) or (B) and chapter 8 expire, or such other period as the parties may agree.

(3) License agreements voluntarily negotiated at any time between 1 or more copyright owners of sound recordings and 1 or more entities performing sound recordings shall be given effect in lieu of any decision by the Librarian of Congress or determination by the Copyright Royalty Judges.

(4)(A) The Copyright Royalty Judges shall also establish requirements by which copyright owners may receive reasonable notice of the use of their sound recordings under this section, and under which records of such use shall be kept and made available by entities performing sound recordings. The notice and recordkeeping rules in effect on the day before the effective date of the Copyright Royalty and Distribution Reform Act of 2004 shall remain in effect unless and until new regulations are promulgated by the Copyright Royalty Judges. If new regulations are promulgated under this subparagraph, the Copyright Royalty Judges shall take into account the substance and effect of the rules in effect on the day before the effective date of the Copyright Royalty and Distribution Reform Act of 2004 and shall, to the extent practicable, avoid significant disruption of the functions of any designated agent authorized to collect and distribute royalty fees.

(B) Any person who wishes to perform a sound recording publicly by means of a transmission eligible for statutory licensing under this subsection may do so without infringing the exclusive right of the copyright owner of the sound recording—

(i) by complying with such notice requirements as the Copyright Royalty Judges shall prescribe by regulation and by paying royalty fees in accordance with this subsection; or

(ii) if such royalty fees have not been set, by agreeing to pay such royalty fees as shall be determined in accordance with this subsection.

(C) Any royalty payments in arrears shall be made on or before the twentieth day of the month next succeeding the month in which the royalty fees are set.

(5)(A) Notwithstanding section 112(e) and the other provisions of this subsection, the receiving agent may enter into agreements for the reproduction and performance of sound recordings under section 112(e) and this section by any 1 or more commercial webcasters or noncommercial webcasters for a period of not more than 11 years beginning on January 1, 2005, that, once published in the Federal Register pursuant to subparagraph (B), shall be binding on all copyright owners of sound recordings and other persons entitled to payment under this section, in lieu of any determination by the Copyright Royalty Judges. Any such agreement for commercial webcasters may include provisions for payment of royalties on the basis of a percentage of revenue or expenses, or both, and include a minimum fee. Any such agreement may include other terms and conditions, including requirements by which copyright owners may receive notice of the use of their sound recordings and under which records of such use shall be kept and made available by commercial webcasters or noncommercial webcasters. The receiving agent shall be under no obligation to negotiate any such agreement. The receiving agent shall have no obligation to any copyright owner of sound recordings or any other person entitled to payment under this section in negotiating any such agreement, and no liability to any copyright owner of sound recordings or any other person entitled to payment under this section for having entered into such agreement.

(B) The Copyright Office shall cause to be published in the Federal Register any agreement entered into pursuant to subparagraph (A). Such publication shall include a statement containing the substance of subparagraph (C). Such agreements shall not be included in the Code of Federal Regulations. Thereafter, the terms of such agreement shall be available, as an option, to any commercial webcaster or noncommercial webcaster meeting the eligibility conditions of such agreement.

(C) Neither subparagraph (A) nor any provisions of any agreement entered into pursuant to subparagraph (A), including any rate structure, fees, terms, conditions, or notice and recordkeeping requirements set forth therein, shall be admissible as evidence or otherwise taken into account in any administrative, judicial, or other government proceeding involving the setting or adjustment of the royalties payable for the public performance or reproduction in ephemeral phonorecords or copies of sound recordings, the determination of terms or conditions related thereto, or the establishment of notice or recordkeeping requirements by the Copyright Royalty Judges under paragraph (4) or section 112(e)(4). It is the intent of Congress that any royalty rates, rate structure, definitions, terms, conditions, or notice and recordkeeping requirements, included in such agreements shall be considered as a compromise motivated by the unique business, economic and political circumstances of webcasters, copyright owners, and performers rather than as matters that would have been negotiated in the marketplace between a willing buyer and a willing seller, or otherwise meet the objectives set forth in section 801(b). This subparagraph shall not apply to the extent that the receiving agent and a webcaster that is party to an agreement entered into pursuant to subparagraph (A) expressly authorize the submission of the agreement in a proceeding under this subsection.

(D) Nothing in the Webcaster Settlement Act of 2008, the Webcaster Settlement Act of 2009, or any agreement entered into pursuant to subparagraph (A) shall be taken into account by the United States Court of Appeals for the District of Columbia Circuit in its review of the determination by the Copyright Royalty Judges of May 1, 2007, of rates and terms for the digital performance of sound recordings and ephemeral recordings, pursuant to sections 112 and 114.

(E) As used in this paragraph—

(i) the term "noncommercial webcaster" means a webcaster that—

(I) is exempt from taxation under section 501 of the Internal Revenue Code of 1986 (26 U.S.C. 501);

(II) has applied in good faith to the Internal Revenue Service for exemption from taxation under section 501 of the Internal Revenue Code and has a commercially reasonable expectation that such exemption shall be granted; or

(III) is operated by a State or possession or any governmental entity or subordinate thereof, or by the United States or District of Columbia, for exclusively public purposes;

(ii) the term "receiving agent" shall have the meaning given that term in section 261.2 of title 37, Code of Federal Regulations, as published in the Federal Register on July 8, 2002; and

(iii) the term "webcaster" means a person or entity that has obtained a compulsory license under section 112 or 114 and the implementing regulations therefor.

(F) The authority to make settlements pursuant to subparagraph (A) shall expire at 11:59 p.m. Eastern time on the 30th day after the date of the enactment of the Webcaster Settlement Act of 2009.

(g) Proceeds from Licensing of Transmissions.—

(1) Except in the case of a transmission licensed under a statutory license in accordance with subsection (f) of this section—

(A) a featured recording artist who performs on a sound recording that has been licensed for a transmission shall be entitled to receive payments from the copyright owner of the sound recording in accordance with the terms of the artist's contract; and

(B) a nonfeatured recording artist who performs on a sound recording that has been licensed for a transmission shall be entitled to receive payments from the copyright owner of the sound recording in accordance with the terms of the nonfeatured recording artist's applicable contract or other applicable agreement.

(2) An agent designated to distribute receipts from the licensing of transmissions in accordance with subsection (f) shall distribute such receipts as follows:

(A) 50 percent of the receipts shall be paid to the copyright owner of the exclusive right under section 106(6) of this title to publicly perform a sound recording by means of a digital audio transmission.

(B) 2½ percent of the receipts shall be deposited in an escrow account managed by an independent administrator jointly appointed by copyright owners of sound recordings and the American Federation of Musicians (or any successor entity) to be distributed to nonfeatured musicians (whether or not members of the American Federation of Musicians) who have performed on sound recordings.

(C) 2½ percent of the receipts shall be deposited in an escrow account managed by an independent administrator jointly appointed by copyright owners of sound recordings and the American Federation of Television and Radio Artists (or any successor entity) to be distributed to nonfeatured vocalists (whether or not members of the American Federation of Television and Radio Artists) who have performed on sound recordings.

(D) 45 percent of the receipts shall be paid, on a per sound recording basis, to the recording artist or artists featured on such sound recording (or the persons conveying rights in the artists' performance in the sound recordings).

(3) A nonprofit agent designated to distribute receipts from the licensing of transmissions in accordance with subsection (f) may deduct from any of its receipts, prior to the distribution of such receipts to any person or entity entitled thereto other than copyright owners and performers who have elected to receive royalties from another designated agent and have notified such nonprofit agent in writing of such election, the reasonable costs of such agent incurred after November 1, 1995, in—

(A) the administration of the collection, distribution, and calculation of the royalties;

(B) the settlement of disputes relating to the collection and calculation of the royalties; and

(C) the licensing and enforcement of rights with respect to the making of ephemeral recordings and performances subject to licensing under section 112 and this section, including those incurred in participating in negotiations or arbitration proceedings under section 112 and this section, except that all costs incurred relating to the section 112 ephemeral recordings right may only be deducted from the royalties received pursuant to section 112.

(4) Notwithstanding paragraph (3), any designated agent designated to distribute receipts from the licensing of transmissions in accordance with subsection (f) may deduct from any of its receipts, prior to the distribution of such receipts, the reasonable costs identified in paragraph (3) of such agent incurred after November 1, 1995, with respect to such copyright owners and performers who have entered with such agent a contractual relationship that specifies that such costs may be deducted from such royalty receipts.

(h) Licensing to Affiliates.—

(1) If the copyright owner of a sound recording licenses an affiliated entity the right to publicly perform a sound recording by means of a digital audio transmission under section 106(6), the copyright owner shall make the licensed sound recording available under section 106(6) on no less favorable terms and conditions to all bona fide entities that offer similar services, except that, if there are material differences in the scope of the requested license with respect to the type of service, the particular sound recordings licensed, the frequency of use, the number of subscribers served, or the duration, then the copyright owner may establish different terms and conditions for such other services.

(2) The limitation set forth in paragraph (1) of this subsection shall not apply in the case where the copyright owner of a sound recording licenses—

(A) an interactive service; or

(B) an entity to perform publicly up to 45 seconds of the sound recording and the sole purpose of the performance is to promote the distribution or performance of that sound recording.

(i) No Effect on Royalties for Underlying Works.—License fees payable for the public performance of sound recordings under section 106(6) shall not be taken into account in any administrative, judicial, or other governmental proceeding to set or adjust the royalties payable to copyright owners of musical works for the public performance of their works. It is the intent of Congress that royalties payable to copyright owners of musical works for the public performance of their works shall not be diminished in any respect as a result of the rights granted by section 106(6).

(j) Definitions.—As used in this section, the following terms have the following meanings:

(1) An "affiliated entity" is an entity engaging in digital audio transmissions covered by section 106(6), other than an interactive service, in which the licensor has any direct or indirect partnership or any ownership interest amounting to 5 percent or more of the outstanding voting or nonvoting stock.

(2) An "archived program" is a predetermined program that is available repeatedly on the demand of the transmission recipient and that is performed in the same order from the beginning, except that an archived program shall not include a recorded event or broadcast transmission that makes no more than an incidental use of sound recordings, as long as such recorded event or broadcast transmission does not contain an entire sound recording or feature a particular sound recording.

(3) A "broadcast" transmission is a transmission made by a terrestrial broadcast station licensed as such by the Federal Communications Commission.

(4) A "continuous program" is a predetermined program that is continuously performed in the same order and that is accessed at a point in the program that is beyond the control of the transmission recipient.

(5) A "digital audio transmission" is a digital transmission as defined in section 101, that embodies the transmission of a sound recording. This term does not include the transmission of any audiovisual work.

(6) An "eligible nonsubscription transmission" is a noninteractive nonsubscription digital audio transmission not exempt under subsection (d)(1) that is made as part of a service that provides audio programming consisting, in whole or in part, of performances of sound recordings, including retransmissions of broadcast transmissions, if the primary purpose of the service is to provide to the public such audio or other entertainment programming, and the primary purpose of the service is not to sell, advertise, or promote particular products or services other than sound recordings, live concerts, or other music-related events.

(7) An "interactive service" is one that enables a member of the public to receive a transmission of a program specially created for the recipient, or on request, a transmission of a particular sound recording, whether or not as part of a program, which is selected by or on behalf of the recipient. The ability of individuals to request that particular sound recordings be performed for reception by the public at large, or in the case of a subscription service, by all subscribers of the service, does not make a service interactive, if the programming on each channel of the service does not substantially consist of sound recordings that are performed within 1 hour of the request or at a time designated by either the transmitting entity or the individual making such request. If an entity offers both interactive and noninteractive services (either concurrently or at different times), the noninteractive component shall not be treated as part of an interactive service.

(8) A "new subscription service" is a service that performs sound recordings by means of noninteractive subscription digital audio transmissions and that is not a preexisting subscription service or a preexisting satellite digital audio radio service.

(9) A "nonsubscription" transmission is any transmission that is not a subscription transmission.

(10) A "preexisting satellite digital audio radio service" is a subscription satellite digital audio radio service provided pursuant to a satellite digital audio radio service license issued by the Federal Communications Commission on or before July 31, 1998, and any renewal of such license to the extent of the scope of the original license, and may include a limited number of sample channels representative of the subscription service that are made available on a nonsubscription basis in order to promote the subscription service.

(11) A "preexisting subscription service" is a service that performs sound recordings by means of noninteractive audio-only subscription digital audio transmissions, which was in existence and was making such transmissions to the public for a fee on or before July 31, 1998, and may include a limited number of sample channels representative of the subscription service that are made available on a nonsubscription basis in order to promote the subscription service.

(12) A "retransmission" is a further transmission of an initial transmission, and includes any further retransmission of the same transmission. Except as provided in this section, a transmission qualifies as a "retransmission" only if it is simultaneous with the initial transmission. Nothing in this definition shall be construed to exempt a transmission that fails to satisfy a separate element required to qualify for an exemption under section 114(d)(1).

(13) The "sound recording performance complement" is the transmission during any 3-hour period, on a particular channel used by a transmitting entity, of no more than—

(A) 3 different selections of sound recordings from any one phonorecord lawfully distributed for public performance or sale in the United States, if no more than 2 such selections are transmitted consecutively; or

(B) 4 different selections of sound recordings—

(i) by the same featured recording artist; or

(ii) from any set or compilation of phonorecords lawfully distributed together as a unit for public performance or sale in the United States,

if no more than three such selections are transmitted consecutively:

Provided, That the transmission of selections in excess of the numerical limits provided for in clauses (A) and (B) from multiple phonorecords shall nonetheless qualify as a sound recording performance complement if the programming of the multiple phonorecords was not willfully intended to avoid the numerical limitations prescribed in such clauses.

(14) A "subscription" transmission is a transmission that is controlled and limited to particular recipients, and for which consideration is required to be paid or otherwise given by or on behalf of the recipient to receive the transmission or a package of transmissions including the transmission.

(15) A "transmission" is either an initial transmission or a retransmission.

§115 · Scope of exclusive rights in nondramatic musical works: Compulsory license for making and distributing phonorecords[50]

In the case of nondramatic musical works, the exclusive rights provided by clauses (1) and (3) of section 106, to make and to distribute phonorecords of such works, are subject to compulsory licensing under the conditions specified by this section.

(a) Availability and Scope of Compulsory License.—

(1) When phonorecords of a nondramatic musical work have been distributed to the public in the United States under the authority of the copyright owner, any other person, including those who make phonorecords or digital phonorecord deliveries, may, by complying with the provisions of this section, obtain a compulsory license to make and distribute phonorecords of the work. A person may obtain a compulsory license only if his or her primary purpose in making phonorecords is to distribute them to the public for private use, including by means of a digital phonorecord delivery. A person may not obtain a compulsory license for use of the work in the making of phonorecords duplicating a sound recording fixed by another, unless:

(i) such sound recording was fixed lawfully; and

(ii) the making of the phonorecords was authorized by the owner of copyright in the sound recording or, if the sound recording was fixed before February 15, 1972, by any person who fixed the sound recording pursuant to an express license from the owner of the copyright in the musical work or pursuant to a valid compulsory license for use of such work in a sound recording.

(2) A compulsory license includes the privilege of making a musical arrangement of the work to the extent necessary to conform it to the style or manner of interpretation of the performance involved, but the arrangement shall not change the basic melody or fundamental character of the work, and shall not be subject to protection as a derivative work under this title, except with the express consent of the copyright owner.

(b) Notice of Intention to Obtain Compulsory License.—

(1) Any person who wishes to obtain a compulsory license under this section shall, before or within thirty days after making, and before distributing any phonorecords of the work, serve notice of intention to do so on the copyright owner. If the registration or other public records of the Copyright Office do not identify the copyright owner and include an address at which notice can be served, it shall be sufficient to file the notice of intention in the

Copyright Office. The notice shall comply, in form, content, and manner of service, with requirements that the Register of Copyrights shall prescribe by regulation.

(2) Failure to serve or file the notice required by clause (1) forecloses the possibility of a compulsory license and, in the absence of a negotiated license, renders the making and distribution of phonorecords actionable as acts of infringement under section 501 and fully subject to the remedies provided by sections 502 through 506 and 509.

(c) Royalty Payable under Compulsory License.[51] —

(1) To be entitled to receive royalties under a compulsory license, the copyright owner must be identified in the registration or other public records of the Copyright Office. The owner is entitled to royalties for phonorecords made and distributed after being so identified, but is not entitled to recover for any phonorecords previously made and distributed.

(2) Except as provided by clause (1), the royalty under a compulsory license shall be payable for every phonorecord made and distributed in accordance with the license. For this purpose, and other than as provided in paragraph (3), a phonorecord is considered "distributed" if the person exercising the compulsory license has voluntarily and permanently parted with its possession. With respect to each work embodied in the phonorecord, the royalty shall be either two and three-fourths cents, or one-half of one cent per minute of playing time or fraction thereof, whichever amount is larger.

(3)(A) A compulsory license under this section includes the right of the compulsory licensee to distribute or authorize the distribution of a phonorecord of a nondramatic musical work by means of a digital transmission which constitutes a digital phonorecord delivery, regardless of whether the digital transmission is also a public performance of the sound recording under section 106(6) of this title or of any nondramatic musical work embodied therein under section 106(4) of this title. For every digital phonorecord delivery by or under the authority of the compulsory licensee—

(i) on or before December 31, 1997, the royalty payable by the compulsory licensee shall be the royalty prescribed under paragraph (2) and chapter 8 of this title; and

(ii) on or after January 1, 1998, the royalty payable by the compulsory licensee shall be the royalty prescribed under subparagraphs (B) through (E) and chapter 8 of this title.

(B) Notwithstanding any provision of the antitrust laws, any copyright owners of nondramatic musical works and any persons entitled to obtain a compulsory license under subsection (a)(1) may negotiate and agree upon the terms and rates of royalty payments under this section and the proportionate division of fees paid among copyright owners, and may designate common agents on a nonexclusive basis to negotiate, agree to, pay or receive such royalty payments. Such authority to negotiate the terms and rates of royalty payments includes, but is not limited to, the authority to negotiate the year during which the royalty rates prescribed under this subparagraph and subparagraphs (C) through (E) and chapter 8 of this title shall next be determined.

(C) Proceedings under chapter 8 shall determine reasonable rates and terms of royalty payments for the activities specified by this section during the period beginning with the effective date of such rates and terms, but not earlier than January 1 of the second year following the year in which the petition requesting the proceeding is filed, and ending on the effective date of successor rates and terms, or such other period as the parties may agree. Such terms and rates shall distinguish between (i) digital phonorecord deliveries where the reproduction or distribution of a phonorecord is incidental to the transmission which constitutes the digital phonorecord delivery, and (ii) digital phonorecord deliveries in general. Any copyright owners of nondramatic musical works and any persons entitled to obtain a compulsory license under subsection (a)(1) may submit to the Copyright Royalty Judges licenses covering such activities. The parties to each proceeding shall bear their own costs.

(D) The schedule of reasonable rates and terms determined by the Copyright Royalty Judges shall, subject to subparagraph (E), be binding on all copyright owners of nondramatic musical works and persons entitled to obtain a compulsory license under subsection (a)(1) during the period specified in subparagraph (C), such other period as may be determined pursuant to subparagraphs (B) and (C), or such other period as the parties may agree. Such terms and rates shall distinguish between (i) digital phonorecord deliveries where the reproduction or distribution of a phonorecord is incidental to the transmission which constitutes the digital phonorecord delivery, and (ii) digital phonorecord deliveries in general. In addition to the objectives set forth in section 801(b)(1), in establishing such rates and terms, the Copyright Royalty Judges may consider rates and terms under voluntary license agreements described in subparagraphs (B) and (C). The royalty rates payable for a compulsory license for a digital phonorecord delivery under this section shall be established de novo and no precedential effect shall be given to the amount of the royalty payable by a compulsory licensee for digital phonorecord deliveries on or before December 31, 1997. The Copyright Royalty Judges shall also establish requirements by which copyright owners may receive reasonable notice of the use of their works under this section, and under which records of such use shall be kept and made available by persons making digital phonorecord deliveries.

(E)(i) License agreements voluntarily negotiated at any time between one or more copyright owners of nondramatic musical works and one or more persons entitled to obtain a compulsory license under subsection (a)(1) shall be given effect in lieu of any determination by the Librarian of Congress and Copyright Royalty Judges. Subject to clause (ii), the royalty rates determined pursuant to subparagraph (C) and (D) shall be given effect as to digital phonorecord deliveries in lieu of any contrary royalty rates specified in a contract pursuant to which a recording artist who is the author of a nondramatic musical work grants a license under that person's exclusive rights in the musical work under paragraphs (1) and (3) of section 106 or commits another person to grant a license in that musical work under paragraphs (1) and (3) of section 106, to a person desiring to fix in a tangible medium of expression a sound recording embodying the musical work.

(ii) The second sentence of clause (i) shall not apply to—

(I) a contract entered into on or before June 22, 1995 and not modified thereafter for the purpose of reducing the royalty rates determined pursuant to subparagraph (C) and (D) or of increasing the number of musical works within the scope of the contract covered by the reduced rates, except if a contract entered into on or before June 22, 1995, is modified thereafter for the purpose of increasing the number of musical works within the scope of the contract, any contrary royalty rates specified in the contract shall be given effect in lieu of royalty rates determined pursuant to subparagraph (C) and (D) for the number of musical works within the scope of the contract as of June 22, 1995; and

(II) a contract entered into after the date that the sound recording is fixed in a tangible medium of expression substantially in a form intended for commercial release, if at the time the contract is entered into, the recording artist retains the right to grant licenses as to the musical work under paragraphs (1) and (3) of section 106.

(F) Except as provided in section 1002(e) of this title, a digital phonorecord delivery licensed under this paragraph shall be accompanied by the information encoded in the sound recording, if any, by or under the authority of the copyright owner of that sound recording, that identifies the title of the sound recording, the featured recording artist who performs on the sound recording, and related information, including information concerning the underlying musical work and its writer.

(G)(i) A digital phonorecord delivery of a sound recording is actionable as an act of infringement under section 501, and is fully subject to the remedies provided by sections 502 through 506,[52] unless—

(I) the digital phonorecord delivery has been authorized by the copyright owner of the sound recording; and

(II) the owner of the copyright in the sound recording or the entity making the digital phonorecord delivery has obtained a compulsory license under this section or has otherwise been authorized by the copyright owner of the musical work to distribute or authorize the distribution, by means of a digital phonorecord delivery, of each musical work embodied in the sound recording.

(ii) Any cause of action under this subparagraph shall be in addition to those available to the owner of the copyright in the nondramatic musical work under subsection (c)(6) and section 106(4) and the owner of the copyright in the sound recording under section 106(6).

(H) The liability of the copyright owner of a sound recording for infringement of the copyright in a nondramatic musical work embodied in the sound recording shall be determined in accordance with applicable law, except that the owner of a copyright in a sound recording shall not be liable for a digital phonorecord delivery by a third party if the owner of the copyright in the sound recording does not license the distribution of a phonorecord of the nondramatic musical work.

(I) Nothing in section 1008 shall be construed to prevent the exercise of the rights and remedies allowed by this paragraph, paragraph (6), and chapter 5 in the event of a digital phonorecord delivery, except that no action alleging infringement of copyright may be brought under this title against a manufacturer, importer or distributor of a digital audio recording device, a digital audio recording medium, an analog recording device, or an analog recording medium, or against a consumer, based on the actions described in such section.

(J) Nothing in this section annuls or limits

(i) the exclusive right to publicly perform a sound recording or the musical work embodied therein, including by means of a digital transmission, under sections 106(4) and 106(6), (ii) except for compulsory licensing under the conditions specified by this section, the exclusive rights to reproduce and distribute the sound recording and the musical work embodied therein under sections 106(1) and 106(3), including by means of a digital phonorecord delivery, or (iii) any other rights under any other provision of section 106, or remedies available under this title, as such rights or remedies exist either before or after the date of enactment of the Digital Performance Right in Sound Recordings Act of 1995.

(K) The provisions of this section concerning digital phonorecord deliveries shall not apply to any exempt transmissions or retransmissions under section 114(d)(1). The exemptions created in section 114(d)(1) do not expand or reduce the rights of copyright owners under section 106(1) through (5) with respect to such transmissions and retransmissions.

(4) A compulsory license under this section includes the right of the maker of a phonorecord of a nondramatic musical work under subsection (a)(1) to distribute or authorize distribution of such phonorecord by rental, lease, or lending (or by acts or practices in the nature of rental, lease, or lending). In addition to any royalty payable under clause (2) and chapter 8 of this title, a royalty shall be payable by the compulsory licensee for every act of distribution of a phonorecord by or in the nature of rental, lease, or lending, by or under the authority of the compulsory licensee. With respect to each nondramatic musical work embodied in the phonorecord, the royalty shall be a proportion of the revenue received by the compulsory licensee from every such act of distribution of the phonorecord under this clause equal to the proportion of the revenue received by the compulsory licensee from distribution of the phonorecord under clause (2) that is payable by a compulsory licensee under that clause and under chapter 8. The Register of Copyrights shall issue regulations to carry out the purpose of this clause.

(5) Royalty payments shall be made on or before the twentieth day of each month and shall include all royalties for the month next preceding. Each monthly payment shall be made under oath and shall comply with requirements that the Register of Copyrights shall prescribe by regulation. The Register shall also prescribe regulations under which detailed cumulative annual statements of account, certified by a certified public accountant, shall be filed for every compulsory license under this section. The regulations covering both the monthly and the annual statements of account shall prescribe the form, content, and manner of certification with respect to the number of records made and the number of records distributed.

(6) If the copyright owner does not receive the monthly payment and the monthly and annual statements of account when due, the owner may give written notice to the licensee that, unless the default is remedied within thirty days from the date of the notice, the compulsory license will be automatically terminated. Such termination renders either the making or the distribution, or both, of all phonorecords for which the royalty has not been paid, actionable as acts of infringement under section 501 and fully subject to the remedies provided by sections 502 through 506.

(d) Definition.—As used in this section, the following term has the following meaning: A "digital phonorecord delivery" is each individual delivery of a phonorecord by digital transmission of a sound recording which results in a specifically identifiable reproduction by or for any transmission recipient of a phonorecord of that sound recording, regardless of whether the digital transmission is also a public performance of the sound recording or any nondramatic musical work embodied therein. A digital phonorecord delivery does not result from a real-time, non-interactive subscription transmission of a sound recording where no reproduction of the sound recording or the musical work embodied therein is made from the inception of the transmission through to its receipt by the transmission recipient in order to make the sound recording audible.

§116 · Negotiated licenses for public performances by means of coin-operated phonorecord players[53]

(a) Applicability of Section.—This section applies to any nondramatic musical work embodied in a phonorecord.

(b) Negotiated Licenses.—

(1) Authority for negotiations.—Any owners of copyright in works to which this section applies and any operators of coin-operated phonorecord players may negotiate and agree upon the terms and rates of royalty payments for the performance of such works and the proportionate division of fees paid among copyright owners, and may designate common agents to negotiate, agree to, pay, or receive such royalty payments.

(2) Chapter 8 proceeding.—Parties not subject to such a negotiation may have the terms and rates and the division of fees described in paragraph (1) determined in a proceeding in accordance with the provisions of chapter 8.

(c) License Agreements Superior to Determinations by Copyright Royalty Judges.—License agreements between one or more copyright owners and one or more operators of coin-operated phonorecord players, which are negotiated in accordance with subsection (b), shall be given effect in lieu of any otherwise applicable determination by the Copyright Royalty Judges.

(d) Definitions.—As used in this section, the following terms mean the following:

(1) A "coin-operated phonorecord player" is a machine or device that—

(A) is employed solely for the performance of nondramatic musical works by means of phonorecords upon being activated by the insertion of coins, currency, tokens, or other monetary units or their equivalent;

(B) is located in an establishment making no direct or indirect charge for admission;

(C) is accompanied by a list which is comprised of the titles of all the musical works available for performance on it, and is affixed to the phonorecord player or posted in the establishment in a prominent position where it can be readily examined by the public; and

(D) affords a choice of works available for performance and permits the choice to be made by the patrons of the establishment in which it is located.

(2) An "operator" is any person who, alone or jointly with others—
(A) owns a coin-operated phonorecord player;
(B) has the power to make a coin-operated phonorecord player available for placement in an establishment for purposes of public performance; or
(C) has the power to exercise primary control over the selection of the musical works made available for public performance on a coin-operated phonorecord player.

§117 · Limitations on exclusive rights: Computer programs[54]

(a) Making of Additional Copy or Adaptation by Owner of Copy.—Notwithstanding the provisions of section 106, it is not an infringement for the owner of a copy of a computer program to make or authorize the making of another copy or adaptation of that computer program provided:

(1) that such a new copy or adaptation is created as an essential step in the utilization of the computer program in conjunction with a machine and that it is used in no other manner, or

(2) that such new copy or adaptation is for archival purposes only and that all archival copies are destroyed in the event that continued possession of the computer program should cease to be rightful.

(b) Lease, Sale, or Other Transfer of Additional Copy or Adaptation.—Any exact copies prepared in accordance with the provisions of this section may be leased, sold, or otherwise transferred, along with the copy from which such copies were prepared, only as part of the lease, sale, or other transfer of all rights in the program. Adaptations so prepared may be transferred only with the authorization of the copyright owner.

(c) Machine Maintenance or Repair.—Notwithstanding the provisions of section 106, it is not an infringement for the owner or lessee of a machine to make or authorize the making of a copy of a computer program if such copy is made solely by virtue of the activation of a machine that lawfully contains an authorized copy of the computer program, for purposes only of maintenance or repair of that machine, if—

(1) such new copy is used in no other manner and is destroyed immediately after the maintenance or repair is completed; and

(2) with respect to any computer program or part thereof that is not necessary for that machine to be activated, such program or part thereof is not accessed or used other than to make such new copy by virtue of the activation of the machine.

(d) Definitions.—For purposes of this section—

(1) the "maintenance" of a machine is the servicing of the machine in order to make it work in accordance with its original specifications and any changes to those specifications authorized for that machine; and

(2) the "repair" of a machine is the restoring of the machine to the state of working in accordance with its original specifications and any changes to those specifications authorized for that machine.

§ 118 · Scope of exclusive rights: Use of certain works in connection with noncommercial broadcasting[55]

(a) The exclusive rights provided by section 106 shall, with respect to the works specified by subsection (b) and the activities specified by subsection (d), be subject to the conditions and limitations prescribed by this section.

(b) Notwithstanding any provision of the antitrust laws, any owners of copyright in published nondramatic musical works and published pictorial, graphic, and sculptural works and any public broadcasting entities, respectively, may negotiate and agree upon the terms and rates of royalty payments and the proportionate division of fees paid among various copyright owners, and may designate common agents to negotiate, agree to, pay, or receive payments.

(1) Any owner of copyright in a work specified in this subsection or any public broadcasting entity may submit to the Copyright Royalty Judges proposed licenses covering such activities with respect to such works.

(2) License agreements voluntarily negotiated at any time between one or more copyright owners and one or more public broadcasting entities shall be given effect in lieu of any determination by the Librarian of Congress or the Copyright Royalty Judges, if copies of such agreements are filed with the Copyright Royalty Judges within 30 days of execution in accordance with regulations that the Copyright Royalty Judges shall issue.

(3) Voluntary negotiation proceedings initiated pursuant to a petition filed under section 804(a) for the purpose of determining a schedule of terms and rates of royalty payments by public broadcasting entities to owners of copyright in works specified by this subsection and the proportionate division of fees paid among various copyright owners shall cover the 5-year period beginning on January 1 of the second year following the year in which the petition is filed. The parties to each negotiation proceeding shall bear their own costs.

(4) In the absence of license agreements negotiated under paragraph (2) or (3), the Copyright Royalty Judges shall, pursuant to chapter 8, conduct a proceeding to determine and publish in the Federal Register a schedule of rates and terms which, subject to paragraph (2), shall be binding on all owners of copyright in works specified by this subsection and public broad-

casting entities, regardless of whether such copyright owners have submitted proposals to the Copyright Royalty Judges. In establishing such rates and terms the Copyright Royalty Judges may consider the rates for comparable circumstances under voluntary license agreements negotiated as provided in paragraph (2) or (3). The Copyright Royalty Judges shall also establish requirements by which copyright owners may receive reasonable notice of the use of their works under this section, and under which records of such use shall be kept by public broadcasting entities.

(c) Subject to the terms of any voluntary license agreements that have been negotiated as provided by subsection (b) (2) or (3), a public broadcasting entity may, upon compliance with the provisions of this section, including the rates and terms established by the Copyright Royalty Judges under subsection (b)(4), engage in the following activities with respect to published nondramatic musical works and published pictorial, graphic, and sculptural works:

(1) performance or display of a work by or in the course of a transmission made by a noncommercial educational broadcast station referred to in subsection (f); and

(2) production of a transmission program, reproduction of copies or phonorecords of such a transmission program, and distribution of such copies or phonorecords, where such production, reproduction, or distribution is made by a nonprofit institution or organization solely for the purpose of transmissions specified in paragraph (1); and

(3) the making of reproductions by a governmental body or a nonprofit institution of a transmission program simultaneously with its transmission as specified in paragraph (1), and the performance or display of the contents of such program under the conditions specified by paragraph (1) of section 110, but only if the reproductions are used for performances or displays for a period of no more than seven days from the date of the transmission specified in paragraph (1), and are destroyed before or at the end of such period. No person supplying, in accordance with paragraph (2), a reproduction of a transmission program to governmental bodies or nonprofit institutions under this paragraph shall have any liability as a result of failure of such body or institution to destroy such reproduction: *Provided*, That it shall have notified such body or institution of the requirement for such destruction pursuant to this paragraph: *And provided further*, That if such body or institution itself fails to destroy such reproduction it shall be deemed to have infringed.

(d) Except as expressly provided in this subsection, this section shall have no applicability to works other than those specified in subsection (b). Owners of copyright in nondramatic literary works and public broadcasting entities may, during the course of voluntary negotiations, agree among themselves, respectively, as to the terms and rates of royalty payments without liability under the antitrust laws. Any such terms and rates of royalty payments shall be effective upon filing with the Copyright Royalty Judges, in accordance with regulations that the Copyright Royalty Judges shall prescribe as provided in section 803(b)(6).

(e) Nothing in this section shall be construed to permit, beyond the limits of fair use as provided by section 107, the unauthorized dramatization of a nondramatic musical work, the production of a transmission program drawn to any substantial extent from a published compilation of pictorial, graphic, or sculptural works, or the unauthorized use of any portion of an audiovisual work.

(f) As used in this section, the term "public broadcasting entity" means a noncommercial educational broadcast station as defined in section 397 of title 47 and any nonprofit institution or organization engaged in the activities described in paragraph (2) of subsection (c).

§119 · Limitations on exclusive rights: Secondary transmissions of distant television programming by satellite[56]

(a) Secondary Transmissions by Satellite Carriers.—

(1) Non-network Stations.—Subject to the provisions of paragraphs (4), (5), and (7) of this subsection and section 114(d), secondary transmissions of a performance or display of a work embodied in a primary transmission made by a non-network station shall be subject to statutory licensing under this section if the secondary transmission is made by a satellite carrier to the public for private home viewing or for viewing in a commercial establishment, with regard to secondary transmissions the satellite carrier is in compliance with the rules, regulations, or authorizations of the Federal Communications Commission governing the carriage of television broadcast station signals, and the carrier makes a direct or indirect charge for each retransmission service to each subscriber receiving the secondary transmission or to a distributor that has contracted with the carrier for direct or indirect delivery of the secondary transmission to the public for private home viewing or for viewing in a commercial establishment.[57]

(2) Network stations.—

(A) In general.—Subject to the provisions of subparagraph (B) of this paragraph and paragraphs (4), (5), (6), and (7) of this subsection and section 114(d), secondary transmissions of a performance or display of a work embodied in a primary transmission made by a network station shall be subject to statutory licensing under this section if the secondary transmission is made by a satellite carrier to the public for private home viewing, with regard to secondary transmissions the satellite carrier is in compliance with the rules, regulations, or authorizations of the Federal Communications

Commission governing the carriage of television broadcast station signals, and the carrier makes a direct or indirect charge for such retransmission service to each subscriber receiving the secondary transmission.

(B) SECONDARY TRANSMISSIONS TO UNSERVED HOUSEHOLDS.—

(i) IN GENERAL.—The statutory license provided for in subparagraph (A) shall be limited to secondary transmissions of the signals of no more than two network stations in a single day for each television network to persons who reside in unserved households.

(ii) ACCURATE DETERMINATIONS OF ELIGIBILITY.—

(I) ACCURATE PREDICTIVE MODEL.—In determining presumptively whether a person resides in an unserved household under subsection (d)(10)(A), a court shall rely on the Individual Location Longley-Rice model set forth by the Federal Communications Commission in Docket No. 98-201, as that model may be amended by the Commission over time under section 339(c)(3) of the Communications Act of 1934 to increase the accuracy of that model.

(II) ACCURATE MEASUREMENTS.—For purposes of site measurements to determine whether a person resides in an unserved household under subsection (d)(10)(A), a court shall rely on section 339(c)(4) of the Communications Act of 1934.

(iii) C-BAND EXEMPTION TO UNSERVED HOUSEHOLDS.—

(I) IN GENERAL.—The limitations of clause (i) shall not apply to any secondary transmissions by C-band services of network stations that a subscriber to C-band service received before any termination of such secondary transmissions before October 31, 1999.

(II) DEFINITION.—In this clause, the term "C-band service" means a service that is licensed by the Federal Communications Commission and operates in the Fixed Satellite Service under part 25 of title 47, Code of Federal Regulations.

(III) ACCURATE PREDICTIVE MODEL WITH RESPECT TO DIGITAL SIGNALS.— Notwithstanding subclause (I), in determining presumptively whether a person resides in an unserved household under subsection (d)(10)(A) with respect to digital signals, a court shall rely on a predictive model set forth by the Federal Communications Commission pursuant to a rulemaking as provided in section 339(c)(3) of the Communications Act of 1934 (47 U.S.C. 339(c)(3)), as that model may be amended by the Commission over time under such section to increase the accuracy of that model. Until such time as the Commission sets forth such model, a court shall rely on the predictive model as recommended by the Commission with respect to digital signals in its Report to Congress in ET Docket No. 05–182, FCC 05–199 (released December 9, 2005).

(C) Submission of subscriber lists to networks.—

(i) Initial lists.— A satellite carrier that makes secondary transmissions of a primary transmission made by a network station pursuant to subparagraph (A) shall, not later than 90 days after commencing such secondary transmissions, submit to the network that owns or is affiliated with the network station a list identifying (by name and address, including street or rural route number, city, State, and 9-digit zip code) all subscribers to which the satellite carrier makes secondary transmissions of that primary transmission to subscribers in unserved households.

(ii) Monthly lists.— After the submission of the initial lists under clause (i), the satellite carrier shall, not later than the 15th of each month, submit to the network a list, aggregated by designated market area, identifying (by name and address, including street or rural route number, city, State, and 9-digit zip code) any persons who have been added or dropped as subscribers under clause (i) since the last submission under this subparagraph.

(iii) Use of subscriber information.—Subscriber information submitted by a satellite carrier under this subparagraph may be used only for purposes of monitoring compliance by the satellite carrier with this subsection.

(iv) Applicability.—The submission requirements of this subparagraph shall apply to a satellite carrier only if the network to which the submissions are to be made places on file with the Register of Copyrights a document identifying the name and address of the person to whom such submissions are to be made. The Register shall maintain for public inspection a file of all such documents.

(3) Statutory license where retransmissions into local market available.—

(A) Rules for subscribers to signals under subsection (e).—

(i) For those receiving distant signals.—In the case of a subscriber of a satellite carrier who is eligible to receive the secondary transmission of the primary transmission of a network station solely by reason of subsection (e) (in this subparagraph referred to as a "distant signal"), and who, as of October 1, 2004, is receiving the distant signal of that network station, the following shall apply:

(I) In a case in which the satellite carrier makes available to the subscriber the secondary transmission of the primary transmission of a local network station affiliated with the same television network pursuant to the statutory license under section 122, the statutory license under paragraph (2) shall apply only to secondary transmissions by that satellite carrier to that subscriber of the distant signal of a station affiliated with the same television network—

(aa) if, within 60 days after receiving the notice of the satellite carrier under section 338(h)(1) of the Communications Act of 1934, the subscriber elects to retain the distant signal; but

(bb) only until such time as the subscriber elects to receive such local signal.

(II) Notwithstanding subclause (I), the statutory license under paragraph (2) shall not apply with respect to any subscriber who is eligible to receive the distant signal of a television network station solely by reason of subsection (e), unless the satellite carrier, within 60 days after the date of the enactment of the Satellite Home Viewer Extension and Reauthorization Act of 2004, submits to that television network a list, aggregated by designated market area (as defined in section 122(j)(2)(C)), that—

(aa) identifies that subscriber by name and address (street or rural route number, city, State, and zip code) and specifies the distant signals received by the subscriber; and

(bb) states, to the best of the satellite carrier's knowledge and belief, after having made diligent and good faith inquiries, that the subscriber is eligible under subsection (e) to receive the distant signals.

(ii) For those not receiving distant signals.—In the case of any subscriber of a satellite carrier who is eligible to receive the distant signal of a network station solely by reason of subsection (e) and who did not receive a distant signal of a station affiliated with the same network on October 1, 2004, the statutory license under paragraph (2) shall not apply to secondary transmissions by that satellite carrier to that subscriber of the distant signal of a station affiliated with the same network.

(B) Rules for lawful subscribers as of date of enactment of 2010 act.— In the case of a subscriber of a satellite carrier who, on the day before the date of the enactment of the Satellite Television Extension and Localism Act of 2010, was lawfully receiving the secondary transmission of the primary transmission of a network station under the statutory license under paragraph (2) (in this subparagraph referred to as the distant signal), other than subscribers to whom subparagraph (A) applies, the statutory license under paragraph (2) shall apply to secondary transmissions by that satellite carrier to that subscriber of the distant signal of a station affiliated with the same television network, and the subscriber's household shall continue to be considered to be an unserved household with respect to such network, until such time as the subscriber elects to terminate such secondary transmissions, whether or not the subscriber elects to subscribe to receive the secondary transmission of the primary transmission of a local network station affiliated with the same network pursuant to the statutory license under section 122.

(C) Future applicability.—

(i) When local signal available at time of subscription.— The statutory license under paragraph (2) shall not apply to the secondary transmission by a satellite carrier of the primary transmission of a network station to a person who is not a subscriber lawfully receiving such secondary transmission as of the date of the enactment of the Satellite Television Extension and Localism Act of 2010 and, at the time such person seeks to subscribe to receive such secondary transmission, resides in a local market where the satellite carrier makes available to that person the secondary transmission of the primary transmission of a local network station affiliated with the same network pursuant to the statutory license under section 122.

(ii) When local signal available after subscription.— In the case of a subscriber who lawfully subscribes to and receives the secondary transmission by a satellite carrier of the primary transmission of a network station under the statutory license under paragraph (2) (in this clause referred to as the "distant signal") on or after the date of the enactment of the Satellite Television Extension and Localism Act of 2010, the statutory license under paragraph (2) shall apply to secondary transmissions by that satellite carrier to that subscriber of the distant signal of a station affiliated with the same television network, and the subscriber's household shall continue to be considered to be an unserved household with respect to such network, until such time as the subscriber elects to terminate such secondary transmissions, but only if such subscriber subscribes to the secondary transmission of the primary transmission of a local network station affiliated with the same network within 60 days after the satellite carrier makes available to the subscriber such secondary transmission of the primary transmission of such local network station.

(D) Other provisions not affected.—This paragraph shall not affect the applicability of the statutory license to secondary transmissions to unserved households included under paragraph (11).

(E) Waiver.—A subscriber who is denied the secondary transmission of a network station under subparagraph (B) or (C) may request a waiver from such denial by submitting a request, through the subscriber's satellite carrier, to the network station in the local market affiliated with the same network where the subscriber is located. The network station shall accept or reject the subscriber's request for a waiver within 30 days after receipt of the request. If the network station fails to accept or reject the subscriber's request for a waiver within that 30-day period, that network station shall be deemed to agree to the waiver request. Unless specifically stated by the network station, a waiver that was granted before the date of the enactment of the Satellite Home Viewer Extension and Reauthorization Act of 2004 under section 339(c)(2) of the Communications Act of 1934 shall not constitute a waiver for purposes of this subparagraph.

(F) Available defined.—For purposes of this paragraph, a satellite carrier makes available a secondary transmission of the primary transmission of a local station to a subscriber or person if the satellite carrier offers that secondary transmission to other subscribers who reside in the same 9-digit zip code as that subscriber or person.

(4) Noncompliance with reporting and payment requirements.—Notwithstanding the provisions of paragraphs (1) and (2), the willful or repeated secondary transmission to the public by a satellite carrier of a primary transmission made by a non-network station or a network station and embodying a performance or display of a work is actionable as an act of infringement under section 501, and is fully subject to the remedies provided by sections 502 through 506, where the satellite carrier has not deposited the statement of account and royalty fee required by subsection (b), or has failed to make the submissions to networks required by paragraph (2)(C).

(5) Willful alterations.—Notwithstanding the provisions of paragraphs (1) and (2), the secondary transmission to the public by a satellite carrier of a performance or display of a work embodied in a primary transmission made by a non-network station or a network station is actionable as an act of infringement under section 501, and is fully subject to the remedies provided by sections 502 through 506 and section 510, if the content of the particular program in which the performance or display is embodied, or any commercial advertising or station announcement transmitted by the primary transmitter during, or immediately before or after, the transmission of such program, is in any way willfully altered by the satellite carrier through changes, deletions, or additions, or is combined with programming from any other broadcast signal.

(6) Violation of territorial restrictions on statutory license for network stations.—

(A) Individual violations.—The willful or repeated secondary transmission by a satellite carrier of a primary transmission made by a network station and embodying a performance or display of a work to a subscriber who is not eligible to receive the transmission under this section is actionable as an act of infringement under section 501 and is fully subject to the remedies provided by sections 502 through 506, except that—

(i) no damages shall be awarded for such act of infringement if the satellite carrier took corrective action by promptly withdrawing service from the ineligible subscriber, and

(ii) any statutory damages shall not exceed $250 for such subscriber for each month during which the violation occurred.

(B) Pattern of violations.—If a satellite carrier engages in a willful or repeated pattern or practice of delivering a primary transmission made by a network station and embodying a performance or display of a work to subscribers who are not eligible to receive the transmission under this section, then in addition to the remedies set forth in subparagraph (A)—

(i) if the pattern or practice has been carried out on a substantially nationwide basis, the court shall order a permanent injunction barring the secondary transmission by the satellite carrier, for private home viewing, of the primary transmissions of any primary network station affiliated with the same network, and the court may order statutory damages of not to exceed $2,500,000 for each 3-month period during which the pattern or practice was carried out; and

(ii) if the pattern or practice has been carried out on a local or regional basis, the court shall order a permanent injunction barring the secondary transmission, for private home viewing in that locality or region, by the satellite carrier of the primary transmissions of any primary network station affiliated with the same network, and the court may order statutory damages of not to exceed $2,500,000 for each 6-month period during which the pattern or practice was carried out.

The court shall direct one half of any statutory damages ordered under clause (i) to be deposited with the Register of Copyrights for distribution to copyright owners pursuant to subsection (b). The Copyright Royalty Judges shall issue regulations establishing procedures for distributing such funds, on a proportional basis, to copyright owners whose works were included in the secondary transmissions that were the subject of the statutory damages.

(C) Previous subscribers excluded.—Subparagraphs (A) and (B) do not apply to secondary transmissions by a satellite carrier to persons who subscribed to receive such secondary transmissions from the satellite carrier or a distributor before November 16, 1988.

(D) Burden of proof.[58]—In any action brought under this paragraph, the satellite carrier shall have the burden of proving that its secondary transmission of a primary transmission by a network station is to a subscriber who is eligible to receive the secondary transmission under this section.

(E) Exception.—The secondary transmission by a satellite carrier of a performance or display of a work embodied in a primary transmission made by a network station to subscribers who do not reside in unserved households shall not be an act of infringement if—

(i) the station on May 1, 1991, was retransmitted by a satellite carrier and was not on that date owned or operated by or affiliated with a television network that offered interconnected program service on a regular basis for 15 or more hours per week to at least 25 affiliated television licensees in 10 or more States;

(ii) as of July 1, 1998, such station was retransmitted by a satellite carrier under the statutory license of this section; and

(iii) the station is not owned or operated by or affiliated with a television network that, as of January 1, 1995, offered interconnected program service on a regular basis for 15 or more hours per week to at least 25 affiliated television licensees in 10 or more States.

(7) Discrimination by a satellite carrier.—Notwithstanding the provisions of paragraph (1), the willful or repeated secondary transmission to the public by a satellite carrier of a performance or display of a work embodied in a primary transmission made by a non-network station or a network station is actionable as an act of infringement under section 501, and is fully subject to the remedies provided by sections 502 through 506, if the satellite carrier unlawfully discriminates against a distributor.[59]

(8) Geographic limitation on secondary transmissions.—The statutory license created by this section shall apply only to secondary transmissions to households located in the United States.

(9) Loser pays for signal intensity measurement; recovery of measurement costs in a civil action.—In any civil action filed relating to the eligibility of subscribing households as unserved households—

(A) a network station challenging such eligibility shall, within 60 days after receipt of the measurement results and a statement of such costs, reimburse the satellite carrier for any signal intensity measurement that is conducted by that carrier in response to a challenge by the network station and that establishes the household is an unserved household; and

(B) a satellite carrier shall, within 60 days after receipt of the measurement results and a statement of such costs, reimburse the network station challenging such eligibility for any signal intensity measurement that is conducted by that station and that establishes the household is not an unserved household.

(10) Inability to conduct measurement.—If a network station makes a reasonable attempt to conduct a site measurement of its signal at a subscriber's household and is denied access for the purpose of conducting the measurement, and is otherwise unable to conduct a measurement, the satellite carrier shall within 60 days notice thereof, terminate service of the station's network to that household.

(11) Service to recreational vehicles and commercial trucks.—

(A) Exemption.—

(i) In general.—For purposes of this subsection, and subject to clauses (ii) and (iii), the term "unserved household" shall include—

(I) recreational vehicles as defined in regulations of the Secretary of Housing and Urban Development under section 3282.8 of title 24, Code of Federal Regulations; and

(II) commercial trucks that qualify as commercial motor vehicles under regulations of the Secretary of Transportation under section 383.5 of title 49, Code of Federal Regulations.

(ii) LIMITATION.—Clause (i) shall apply only to a recreational vehicle or commercial truck if any satellite carrier that proposes to make a secondary transmission of a network station to the operator of such a recreational vehicle or commercial truck complies with the documentation requirements under subparagraphs (B) and (C).

(iii) EXCLUSION.—For purposes of this subparagraph, the terms "recreational vehicle" and "commercial truck" shall not include any fixed dwelling, whether a mobile home or otherwise.

(B) DOCUMENTATION REQUIREMENTS.—A recreational vehicle or commercial truck shall be deemed to be an unserved household beginning 10 days after the relevant satellite carrier provides to the network that owns or is affiliated with the network station that will be secondarily transmitted to the recreational vehicle or commercial truck the following documents:

(i) DECLARATION.—A signed declaration by the operator of the recreational vehicle or commercial truck that the satellite dish is permanently attached to the recreational vehicle or commercial truck, and will not be used to receive satellite programming at any fixed dwelling.

(ii) REGISTRATION.—In the case of a recreational vehicle, a copy of the current State vehicle registration for the recreational vehicle.

(iii) REGISTRATION AND LICENSE.—In the case of a commercial truck, a copy of—

(I) the current State vehicle registration for the truck; and

(II) a copy of a valid, current commercial driver's license, as defined in regulations of the Secretary of Transportation under section 383 of title 49, Code of Federal Regulations, issued to the operator.

(C) UPDATED DOCUMENTATION REQUIREMENTS.—If a satellite carrier wishes to continue to make secondary transmissions to a recreational vehicle or commercial truck for more than a 2-year period, that carrier shall provide each network, upon request, with updated documentation in the form described under subparagraph (B) during the 90 days before expiration of that 2-year period.

(12) STATUTORY LICENSE CONTINGENT ON COMPLIANCE WITH FCC RULES AND REMEDIAL STEPS.—Notwithstanding any other provision of this section, the willful or repeated secondary transmission to the public by a satellite carrier of a primary transmission embodying a performance or display of a work made by a broadcast station licensed by the Federal Communications Com-

mission is actionable as an act of infringement under section 501, and is fully subject to the remedies provided by sections 502 through 506, if, at the time of such transmission, the satellite carrier is not in compliance with the rules, regulations, and authorizations of the Federal Communications Commission concerning the carriage of television broadcast station signals.[60]

(13) WAIVERS.—A subscriber who is denied the secondary transmission of a signal of a network station under subsection (a)(2)(B) may request a waiver from such denial by submitting a request, through the subscriber's satellite carrier, to the network station asserting that the secondary transmission is prohibited. The network station shall accept or reject a subscriber's request for a waiver within 30 days after receipt of the request. If a television network station fails to accept or reject a subscriber's request for a waiver within the 30-day period after receipt of the request, that station shall be deemed to agree to the waiver request and have filed such written waiver. Unless specifically stated by the network station, a waiver that was granted before the date of the enactment of the Satellite Home Viewer Extension and Reauthorization Act of 2004 under section 339(c)(2) of the Communications Act of 1934, and that was in effect on such date of enactment, shall constitute a waiver for purposes of this paragraph.

(14) RESTRICTED TRANSMISSION OF OUT-OF-STATE DISTANT NETWORK SIGNALS INTO CERTAIN MARKETS.—

(A) OUT-OF-STATE NETWORK AFFILIATES.—Notwithstanding any other provision of this title, the statutory license in this subsection and subsection (b) shall not apply to any secondary transmission of the primary transmission of a network station located outside of the State of Alaska to any subscriber in that State to whom the secondary transmission of the primary transmission of a television station located in that State is made available by the satellite carrier pursuant to section 122.

(B) EXCEPTION.—The limitation in subparagraph (A) shall not apply to the secondary transmission of the primary transmission of a digital signal of a network station located outside of the State of Alaska if at the time that the secondary transmission is made, no television station licensed to a community in the State and affiliated with the same network makes primary transmissions of a digital signal.

(b) DEPOSIT OF STATEMENTS AND FEES; VERIFICATION PROCEDURES.—

(1) DEPOSITS WITH THE REGISTER OF COPYRIGHTS.—A satellite carrier whose secondary transmissions are subject to statutory licensing under subsection (a) shall, on a semiannual basis, deposit with the Register of Copyrights, in accordance with requirements that the Register shall prescribe by regulation—

(A) a statement of account, covering the preceding 6-month period, specifying the names and locations of all non-network and network stations whose signals were retransmitted, at any time during that period, to subscribers as described in subsections (a)(1) and (a)(2), the total number of subscribers that received such retransmissions, and such other data as the Register of Copyrights may from time to time prescribe by regulation;

(B) a royalty fee payable to copyright owners pursuant to paragraph (4) for that 6-month period, computed by multiplying the total number of subscribers receiving each secondary transmission of a primary stream or multicast stream of each non-network station or network station during each calendar year month by the appropriate rate in effect under this subsection; and

(C) a filing fee, as determined by the Register of Copyrights pursuant to section 708(a).

(2) Verification of accounts and fee payments.— The Register of Copyrights shall issue regulations to permit interested parties to verify and audit the statements of account and royalty fees submitted by satellite carriers under this subsection.

(3) Investment of fees.—The Register of Copyrights shall receive all fees (including the filing fee specified in paragraph (1)(c)) deposited under this section and, after deducting the reasonable costs incurred by the Copyright Office under this section (other than the costs deducted under paragraph (5)), shall deposit the balance in the Treasury of the United States, in such manner as the Secretary of the Treasury directs. All funds held by the Secretary of the Treasury shall be invested in interest-bearing securities of the United States for later distribution with interest by the Librarian of Congress as provided by this title.

(4) Persons to whom fees are distributed.—The royalty fees deposited under paragraph (3) shall, in accordance with the procedures provided by paragraph (5), be distributed to those copyright owners whose works were included in a secondary transmission made by a satellite carrier during the applicable 6-month accounting period and who file a claim with the Copyright Royalty Judges under paragraph (5).

(5) Procedures for distribution.—The royalty fees deposited under paragraph (3) shall be distributed in accordance with the following procedures:

(A) Filing of claims for fees.—During the month of July in each year, each person claiming to be entitled to statutory license fees for secondary transmissions shall file a claim with the Copyright Royalty Judges, in accordance with requirements that the Copyright Royalty Judges shall prescribe by regulation. For purposes of this paragraph, any claimants may agree among themselves as to the proportionate division of statutory license fees among them, may lump their claims together and file them jointly or as a single claim, or may designate a common agent to receive payment on their behalf.

(B) Determination of controversy; distributions.—After the first day of August of each year, the Copyright Royalty Judges shall determine whether there exists a controversy concerning the distribution of royalty fees. If the Copyright Royalty Judges determine that no such controversy exists, the Copyright Royalty Judges shall authorize the Librarian of Congress to proceed to distribute such fees to the copyright owners entitled to receive them, or to their designated agents, subject to the deduction of reasonable administrative costs under this section. If the Copyright Royalty Judges find the existence of a controversy, the Copyright Royalty Judges shall, pursuant to chapter 8 of this title, conduct a proceeding to determine the distribution of royalty fees.

(C) WITHHOLDING OF FEES DURING CONTROVERSY.—During the pendency of any proceeding under this subsection, the Copyright Royalty Judges shall have the discretion to authorize the Librarian of Congress to proceed to distribute any amounts that are not in controversy.

(c) ADJUSTMENT OF ROYALTY FEES.—

(1) APPLICABILITY AND DETERMINATION OF ROYALTY FEES FOR SIGNALS.—

(A) INITIAL FEE.—The appropriate fee for purposes of determining the royalty fee under subsection (b)(1)(B) for the secondary transmission of the primary transmissions of network stations and non-network stations shall be the appropriate fee set forth in part 258 of title 37, Code of Federal Regulations, as in effect on July 1, 2009, as modified under this paragraph.

(B) FEE SET BY VOLUNTARY NEGOTIATION.—On or before June 1, 2010, the Copyright Royalty Judges shall cause to be published in the Federal Register of the initiation of voluntary negotiation proceedings for the purpose of determining the royalty fee to be paid by satellite carriers for the secondary transmission of the primary transmission of network stations and non-network stations under subsection (b)(1)(B).

(C) NEGOTIATIONS.—Satellite carriers, distributors, and copyright owners entitled to royalty fees under this section shall negotiate in good faith in an effort to reach a voluntary agreement or agreements for the payment of royalty fees. Any such satellite carriers, distributors and copyright owners may at any time negotiate and agree to the royalty fee, and may designate common agents to negotiate, agree to, or pay such fees. If the parties fail to identify common agents, the Copyright Royalty Judges shall do so, after requesting recommendations from the parties to the negotiation proceeding. The parties to each negotiation proceeding shall bear the cost thereof.

(D) AGREEMENTS BINDING ON PARTIES; FILING OF AGREEMENTS; PUBLIC NOTICE.—(i) VOLUNTARY AGREEMENTS; FILING.—Voluntary agreements negotiated at any time in accordance with this paragraph shall be binding upon all satellite carriers, distributors, and copyright owners that are parties thereto. Copies of such agreements shall be filed with the Copyright Office within 30 days after execution in accordance with regulations that the Register of Copyrights shall prescribe.

(ii) Procedure for adoption of fees.—

(I) Publication of notice.—Within 10 days after publication in the Federal Register of a notice of the initiation of voluntary negotiation proceedings, parties who have reached a voluntary agreement may request that the royalty fees in that agreement be applied to all satellite carriers, distributors, and copyright owners without convening a proceeding under subparagraph (F).

(II) Public notice of fees.— Upon receiving a request under subclause (I), the Copyright Royalty Judges shall immediately provide public notice of the royalty fees from the voluntary agreement and afford parties an opportunity to state that they object to those fees.

(III) Adoption of fees.— The Copyright Royalty Judges shall adopt the royalty fees from the voluntary agreement for all satellite carriers, distributors, and copyright owners without convening the proceeding under subparagraph (F) unless a party with an intent to participate in that proceeding and a significant interest in the outcome of that proceeding objects under subclause (II).

(E) Period agreement is in effect.—The obligation to pay the royalty fees established under a voluntary agreement which has been filed with the Copyright Royalty Judges in accordance with this paragraph shall become effective on the date specified in the agreement, and shall remain in effect until December 31, 2014[61], in accordance with the terms of the agreement, whichever is later.

(F) Fee set by copyright royalty judges proceeding.—

(i) Notice of initiation of the proceeding.—On or before September 1, 2010, the Copyright Royalty Judges shall cause notice to be published in the Federal Register of the initiation of a proceeding for the purpose of determining the royalty fees to be paid for the secondary transmission of the primary transmissions of network stations and non-network stations under subsection (b)(1)(B) by satellite carriers and distributors—

(I) in the absence of a voluntary agreement filed in accordance with subparagraph (D) that establishes royalty fees to be paid by all satellite carriers and distributors; or

(II) if an objection to the fees from a voluntary agreement submitted for adoption by the Copyright Royalty Judges to apply to all satellite carriers, distributors, and copyright owners is received under subparagraph (D) from a party with an intent to participate in the proceeding and a significant interest in the outcome of that proceeding.

Such proceeding shall be conducted under chapter 8.

(ii) Establishment of royalty fees.— In determining royalty fees under this subparagraph, the Copyright Royalty Judges shall establish fees for the secondary transmissions of the primary transmissions of network stations and non-network stations that most clearly represent the fair market value of secondary transmissions, except that the Copyright Royalty Judges shall adjust royalty fees to account for the obligations of the parties under any applicable voluntary agreement filed with the Copyright Royalty Judges in accordance with subparagraph (D). In determining the fair market value, the Judges shall base their decision on economic, competitive, and programming information presented by the parties, including—

(I) the competitive environment in which such programming is distributed, the cost of similar signals in similar private and compulsory license marketplaces, and any special features and conditions of the retransmission marketplace;

(II) the economic impact of such fees on copyright owners and satellite carriers; and

(III) the impact on the continued availability of secondary transmissions to the public.

(iii) Effective date for decision of copyright royalty judges.— The obligation to pay the royalty fees established under a determination that is made by the Copyright Royalty Judges in a proceeding under this paragraph shall be effective as of January 1, 2010.

(iv) Persons subject to royalty fees.—The royalty fees referred to in clause (iii) shall be binding on all satellite carriers, distributors and copyright owners, who are not party to a voluntary agreement filed with the Copyright Office under subparagraph (D).

(2) Annual royalty fee adjustment.—Effective January 1 of each year, the royalty fee payable under subsection (b)(1)(B) for the secondary transmission of the primary transmissions of network stations and non-network stations shall be adjusted by the Copyright Royalty Judges to reflect any changes occurring in the cost of living as determined by the most recent Consumer Price Index (for all consumers and for all items) published by the Secretary of Labor before December 1 of the preceding year. Notification of the adjusted fees shall be published in the Federal Register at least 25 days before January 1.

(d) Definitions.—As used in this section—

(1) Distributor.—The term "distributor" means an entity that contracts to distribute secondary transmissions from a satellite carrier and, either as a single channel or in a package with other programming, provides the secondary transmission either directly to individual subscribers or indirectly through other program distribution entities in accordance with the provisions of this section.

(2) Network station.—The term "network station" means—

(A) a television station licensed by the Federal Communications Commission, including any translator station or terrestrial satellite station that rebroadcasts all or substantially all of the programming broadcast by a network station, that is owned or operated by, or affiliated with, one or more of the television networks in the United States that offer an interconnected program service on a regular basis for 15 or more hours per week to at least 25 of its affiliated television licensees in 10 or more States; or

(B) a noncommercial educational broadcast station (as defined in section 397 of the Communications Act of 1934).

(3) Primary network station.—The term "primary network station" means a network station that broadcasts or rebroadcasts the basic programming service of a particular national network.

(4) Primary transmission.—The term "primary transmission" has the meaning given that term in section 111(f) of this title.

(5) Private home viewing.—The term "private home viewing" means the viewing, for private use in a household by means of satellite reception equipment that is operated by an individual in that household and that serves only such household, of a secondary transmission delivered by a satellite carrier of a primary transmission of a television station licensed by the Federal Communications Commission.

(6) Satellite carrier.—The term "satellite carrier" means an entity that uses the facilities of a satellite or satellite service licensed by the Federal Communications Commission and operates in the Fixed-Satellite Service under part 25 of title 47, Code of Federal Regulations, or the Direct Broadcast Satellite Service under part 100 of title 47, Code of Federal Regulations to establish and operate a channel of communications for point-to-multipoint distribution of television station signals, and that owns or leases a capacity or service on a satellite in order to provide such point-to-multipoint distribution, except to the extent that such entity provides such distribution pursuant to tariff under the Communications Act of 1934, other than for private home viewing pursuant to this section.

(7) Secondary transmission.—The term "secondary transmission" has the meaning given that term in section 111(f) of this title.

(8) Subscriber; subscribe.—

(A) Subscriber.—The term "subscriber" means a person or entity that receives a secondary transmission service from a satellite carrier and pays a fee for the service, directly or indirectly, to the satellite carrier or to a distributor.

(B) Subscribe.—The term "subscribe" means to elect to become a subscriber.

(9) Non-network station.—The term "non-network station" means a television station, other than a network station, licensed by the Federal Communications Commission, that is secondarily transmitted by a satellite carrier.

(10) Unserved household.—The term "unserved household", with respect to a particular television network, means a household that—

(A) cannot receive, through the use of an antenna, an over-the-air signal containing the primary stream, or, on or after the qualifying date, the multicast stream, originating in that household's local market and affiliated with that network of—

(i) if the signal originates as an analog signal, Grade B intensity as defined by the Federal Communications Commission in section 73.683(a) of title 47, Code of Federal Regulations, as in effect on January 1, 1999; or

(ii) if the signal originates as a digital signal, intensity defined in the values for the digital television noise-limited service contour, as defined in regulations issued by the Federal Communications Commission (section 73.622(e) of title 47, Code of Federal Regulations), as such regulations may be amended from time to time;

(B) is subject to a waiver that meets the standards of subsection (a)(13) whether or not the waiver was granted before the date of the enactment of the Satellite Television Extension and Localism Act of 2010;

(C) is a subscriber to whom subsection (e) applies;

(D) is a subscriber to whom subsection (a)(11) applies; or

(E) is a subscriber to whom the exemption under subsection (a)(2)(B)(iii) applies.

(11) Local market.—The term "local market" has the meaning given such term under section 122(j).

(12) Commercial establishment.—The term "commercial establishment"—

(A) means an establishment used for commercial purposes, such as a bar, restaurant, private office, fitness club, oil rig, retail store, bank or other financial institution, supermarket, automobile or boat dealership, or any other establishment with a common business area; and

(B) does not include a multi-unit permanent or temporary dwelling where private home viewing occurs, such as a hotel, dormitory, hospital, apartment, condominium, or prison.

(13) Qualifying date.—The term "qualifying date", for purposes of paragraph (10)(A), means—

(A) October 1, 2010, for multicast streams that exist on March 31, 2010; and

(B) January 1, 2011, for all other multicast streams.

(14) Multicast stream.—The term "multicast stream" means a digital stream containing programming and program-related material affiliated with a television network, other than the primary stream.

(15) Primary stream.—The term "primary stream" means—

(A) the single digital stream of programming as to which a television broadcast station has the right to mandatory carriage with a satellite carrier under the rules of the Federal Communications Commission in effect on July 1, 2009; or

(B) if there is no stream described in subparagraph (A), then either—

(i) the single digital stream of programming associated with the network last transmitted by the station as an analog signal; or

(ii) if there is no stream described in clause (i), then the single digital stream of programming affiliated with the network that, as of July 1, 2009, had been offered by the television broadcast station for the longest period of time.

(e) Moratorium on Copyright Liability.—Until December 31, 2014[62], a subscriber who does not receive a signal of Grade A intensity (as defined in the regulations of the Federal Communications Commission under section 73.683(a) of title 47, Code of Federal Regulations, as in effect on January 1, 1999, or predicted by the Federal Communications Commission using the Individual Location Longley-Rice methodology described by the Federal Communications Commission in Docket No. 98-201) of a local network television broadcast station shall remain eligible to receive signals of network stations affiliated with the same network, if that subscriber had satellite service of such network signal terminated after July 11, 1998, and before October 31, 1999, as required by this section, or received such service on October 31, 1999.

(f) Expedited Consideration by Justice Department of Voluntary Agreements to Provide Satellite Secondary Transmissions to Local Markets.—

(1) In general.—In a case in which no satellite carrier makes available, to subscribers located in a local market, as defined in section 122(j)(2), the secondary transmission into that market of a primary transmission of one or more television broadcast stations licensed by the Federal Communications Commission, and two or more satellite carriers request a business review letter in accordance with section 50.6 of title 28, Code of Federal Regulations (as in effect on July 7, 2004), in order to assess the legality under the antitrust laws of proposed business conduct to make or carry out an agreement to provide such secondary transmission into such local market, the appropriate official of the Department of Justice shall respond to the request no later than 90 days after the date on which the request is received.

(2) Definition.—For purposes of this subsection, the term "antitrust laws"—

(A) has the meaning given that term in subsection (a) of the first section of the Clayton Act (15 U.S.C. 12(a)), except that such term includes section 5 of the Federal Trade Commission Act (15 U.S.C. 45) to the extent such section 5 applies to unfair methods of competition; and

(B) includes any State law similar to the laws referred to in paragraph (1).

(g) Certain Waivers Granted to Providers of Local-into-Local Service to All DMAs.—

(1) Injunction waiver.—A court that issued an injunction pursuant to subsection (a)(7)(B) before the date of the enactment of this subsection shall waive such injunction if the court recognizes the entity against which the injunction was issued as a qualified carrier.

(2) Limited temporary waiver.—

(A) In general.—Upon a request made by a satellite carrier, a court that issued an injunction against such carrier under subsection (a)(7)(B) before the date of the enactment of this subsection shall waive such injunction with respect to the statutory license provided under subsection (a)(2) to the extent necessary to allow such carrier to make secondary transmissions of primary transmissions made by a network station to unserved households located in short markets in which such carrier was not providing local service pursuant to the license under section 122 as of December 31, 2009.

(B) Expiration of temporary waiver.—A temporary waiver of an injunction under subparagraph (A) shall expire after the end of the 120-day period beginning on the date such temporary waiver is issued unless extended for good cause by the court making the temporary waiver.

(C) Failure to provide local-into-local service to all dmas.—

(i) Failure to act reasonably in good faith.—If the court issuing a temporary waiver under subparagraph (A) determines that the satellite carrier that made the request for such waiver has failed to act reasonably or has failed to make a good faith effort to provide local-into-local service to all DMAs, such failure—

(I) is actionable as an act of infringement under section 501 and the court may in its discretion impose the remedies provided for in sections 502 through 506 and subsection (a)(6)(B) of this section; and

(II) shall result in the termination of the waiver issued under subparagraph (A).

(ii) Failure to provide local-into-local service.—If the court issuing a temporary waiver under subparagraph (A) determines that the satellite carrier that made the request for such waiver has failed to provide local-into-local service to all DMAs, but determines that the carrier acted reasonably and in good faith, the court may in its discretion impose financial penalties that reflect—

(I) the degree of control the carrier had over the circumstances that resulted in the failure;

(II) the quality of the carrier's efforts to remedy the failure; and

(III) the severity and duration of any service interruption.

(D) Single temporary waiver available.—An entity may only receive one temporary waiver under this paragraph.

(E) Short market defined.—For purposes of this paragraph, the term "short market" means a local market in which programming of one or more of the four most widely viewed television networks nationwide as measured on the date of the enactment of this subsection is not offered on the primary stream transmitted by any local television broadcast station.

(3) Establishment of qualified carrier recognition.—

(A) Statement of eligibility.—An entity seeking to be recognized as a qualified carrier under this subsection shall file a statement of eligibility with the court that imposed the injunction. A statement of eligibility must include—

(i) an affidavit that the entity is providing local-into-local service to all DMAs;

(ii) a motion for a waiver of the injunction;

(iii) a motion that the court appoint a special master under Rule 53 of the Federal Rules of Civil Procedure;

(iv) an agreement by the carrier to pay all expenses incurred by the special master under paragraph (4)(B)(ii); and

(v) a certification issued pursuant to section 342(a) of Communications Act of 1934.

(B) Grant of recognition as a qualified carrier.—Upon receipt of a statement of eligibility, the court shall recognize the entity as a qualified carrier and issue the waiver under paragraph (1). Upon motion pursuant to subparagraph (A)(iii), the court shall appoint a special master to conduct the examination and provide a report to the court as provided in paragraph (4)(B).

(C) Voluntary termination.—At any time, an entity recognized as a qualified carrier may file a statement of voluntary termination with the court certifying that it no longer wishes to be recognized as a qualified carrier. Upon receipt of such statement, the court shall reinstate the injunction waived under paragraph (1).

(D) Loss of recognition prevents future recognition.—No entity may be recognized as a qualified carrier if such entity had previously been recognized as a qualified carrier and subsequently lost such recognition or voluntarily terminated such recognition under subparagraph (C).

(4) Qualified carrier obligations and compliance.—

(A) Continuing obligations.—

(i) In general.—An entity recognized as a qualified carrier shall continue to provide local-into-local service to all DMAs.

(ii) Cooperation with compliance examination.—An entity recognized as a qualified carrier shall fully cooperate with the special master appointed by the court under paragraph (3)(B) in an examination set forth in subparagraph (B).

(B) Qualified carrier compliance examination.—

(i) Examination and report.—A special master appointed by the court under paragraph (3)(B) shall conduct an examination of, and file a report on, the qualified carrier's compliance with the royalty payment and household eligibility requirements of the license under this section. The report shall address the qualified carrier's conduct during the period beginning on the date on which the qualified carrier is recognized as such under paragraph (3)(B) and ending on April 30, 2012.

(ii) Records of qualified carrier.—Beginning on the date that is one year after the date on which the qualified carrier is recognized as such under paragraph (3)(B), but not later than December 1, 2011, the qualified carrier shall provide the special master with all records that the special master considers to be directly pertinent to the following requirements under this section:

(I) Proper calculation and payment of royalties under the statutory license under this section.

(II) Provision of service under this license to eligible subscribers only.

(iii) Submission of report.—The special master shall file the report required by clause (i) not later than July 24, 2012, with the court referred to in paragraph (1) that issued the injunction, and the court shall transmit a copy of the report to the Register of Copyrights, the Committees on the Judiciary and on Energy and Commerce of the House of Representatives, and the Committees on the Judiciary and on Commerce, Science, and Transportation of the Senate.

(iv) Evidence of infringement.—The special master shall include in the report a statement of whether the examination by the special master indicated that there is substantial evidence that a copyright holder could bring a successful action under this section against the qualified carrier for infringement.

(v) Subsequent examination.—If the special master's report includes a statement that its examination indicated the existence of substantial evidence that a copyright holder could bring a successful action under this section against the qualified carrier for infringement, the special master shall, not later than 6 months after the report under clause (i) is filed, initiate another examination of the qualified carrier's compliance with the royalty payment and household eligibility requirements of the license under this section since the last report was filed under clause (iii). The special master shall file a report on the results of the examination conducted under this clause with the court referred to in paragraph (1) that issued the injunction, and the court shall transmit a copy to the Register of Copyrights, the Committees on the Judiciary and on Energy and Commerce of the House of Representatives, and the Committees on the Judiciary and on Commerce, Science, and Transportation of the Senate. The report shall include a statement described in clause (iv).

(vi) Compliance.—Upon motion filed by an aggrieved copyright owner, the court recognizing an entity as a qualified carrier shall terminate such designation upon finding that the entity has failed to cooperate with an examination required by this subparagraph.

(vii) Oversight.—During the period of time that the special master is conducting an examination under this subparagraph, the Comptroller General shall monitor the degree to which the entity seeking to be recognized or recognized as a qualified carrier under paragraph (3) is complying with the special master's examination. The qualified carrier shall make available to the Comptroller General all records and individuals that the Comptroller General considers necessary to meet the Comptroller General's obligations under this clause. The Comptroller General shall report the results of the monitoring required by this clause to the Committees on the Judiciary and on Energy and Commerce of the House of Representatives and the Committees on the Judiciary and on Commerce, Science, and Transportation of the Senate at intervals of not less than six months during such period.

(C) Affirmation.—A qualified carrier shall file an affidavit with the district court and the Register of Copyrights 30 months after such status was granted stating that, to the best of the affiant's knowledge, it is in compliance with the requirements for a qualified carrier. The qualified carrier shall attach to its affidavit copies of all reports or orders issued by the court, the special master, and the Comptroller General.

(D) Compliance determination.—Upon the motion of an aggrieved television broadcast station, the court recognizing an entity as a qualified carrier may make a determination of whether the entity is providing local-into-local service to all DMAs.

(E) Pleading requirement.—In any motion brought under subparagraph (D), the party making such motion shall specify one or more designated market areas (as such term is defined in section 122(j)(2)(C)) for which the failure to provide service is being alleged, and, for each such designated market area, shall plead with particularity the circumstances of the alleged failure.

(F) Burden of proof.—In any proceeding to make a determination under subparagraph (D), and with respect to a designated market area for which failure to provide service is alleged, the entity recognized as a qualified carrier shall have the burden of proving that the entity provided local-into-local service with a good quality satellite signal to at least 90 percent of the households in such designated market area (based on the most recent census data released by the United States Census Bureau) at the time and place alleged.

(5) Failure to provide service.—

(A) Penalties.—If the court recognizing an entity as a qualified carrier finds that such entity has willfully failed to provide local-into-local service to all DMAs, such finding shall result in the loss of recognition of the entity as a qualified carrier and the termination of the waiver provided under paragraph (1), and the court may, in its discretion—

(i) treat such failure as an act of infringement under section 501, and subject such infringement to the remedies provided for in sections 502 through 506 and subsection (a)(6)(B) of this section; and

(ii) impose a fine of not less than $250,000 and not more than $5,000,000.

(B) Exception for nonwillful violation.—If the court determines that the failure to provide local-into-local service to all DMAs is nonwillful, the court may in its discretion impose financial penalties for noncompliance that reflect—

(i) the degree of control the entity had over the circumstances that resulted in the failure;

(ii) the quality of the entity's efforts to remedy the failure and restore service; and

(iii) the severity and duration of any service interruption.

(6) Penalties for violation of license.—A court that finds, under subsection (a)(6)(A), that an entity recognized as a qualified carrier has willfully made a secondary transmission of a primary transmission made by a network station and embodying a performance or display of a work to a subscriber who is not eligible to receive the transmission under this section shall reinstate the injunction waived under paragraph (1), and the court may order statutory damages of not more than $2,500,000.

(7) Local-into-local service to all DMAs defined.—For purposes of this subsection:

(A) In general.—An entity provides "local-into-local service to all DMAs" if the entity provides local service in all designated market areas (as such term is defined in section 122(j)(2)(C)) pursuant to the license under section 122.

(B) Household coverage.—For purposes of subparagraph (A), an entity that makes available local-into-local service with a good quality satellite signal to at least 90 percent of the households in a designated market area based on the most recent census data released by the United States Census Bureau shall be considered to be providing local service to such designated market area.

(C) Good quality satellite signal defined.—The term "good quality satellite signal" has the meaning given such term under section 342(e)(2) of Communications Act of 1934.

§120 · Scope of exclusive rights in architectural works[63]

(a) Pictorial Representations Permitted.—The copyright in an architectural work that has been constructed does not include the right to prevent the making, distributing, or public display of pictures, paintings, photographs, or other pictorial representations of the work, if the building in which the work is embodied is located in or ordinarily visible from a public place.

(b) Alterations to and Destruction of Buildings.—Notwithstanding the provisions of section 106(2), the owners of a building embodying an architectural work may, without the consent of the author or copyright owner of the architectural work, make or authorize the making of alterations to such building, and destroy or authorize the destruction of such building.

§121 · Limitations on exclusive rights: Reproduction for blind or other people with disabilities[64]

(a) Notwithstanding the provisions of section 106, it is not an infringement of copyright for an authorized entity to reproduce or to distribute copies or phonorecords of a previously published, nondramatic literary work if such copies or phonorecords are reproduced or distributed in specialized formats exclusively for use by blind or other persons with disabilities.

(b)(1) Copies or phonorecords to which this section applies shall—

(A) not be reproduced or distributed in a format other than a specialized format exclusively for use by blind or other persons with disabilities;

(B) bear a notice that any further reproduction or distribution in a format other than a specialized format is an infringement; and

(C) include a copyright notice identifying the copyright owner and the date of the original publication.

(2) The provisions of this subsection shall not apply to standardized, secure, or norm-referenced tests and related testing material, or to computer programs, except the portions thereof that are in conventional human language (including descriptions of pictorial works) and displayed to users in the ordinary course of using the computer programs.

(c) Notwithstanding the provisions of section 106, it is not an infringement of copyright for a publisher of print instructional materials for use in elementary or secondary schools to create and distribute to the National Instructional Materials Access Center copies of the electronic files described in sections 612(a)(23)(C), 613(a)(6), and section 674(e) of the Individuals with Disabilities Education Act that contain the contents of print instructional materials using the National Instructional Material Accessibility Standard (as defined in section 674(e)(3) of that Act), if—

(1) the inclusion of the contents of such print instructional materials is required by any State educational agency or local educational agency;

(2) the publisher had the right to publish such print instructional materials in print formats; and

(3) such copies are used solely for reproduction or distribution of the contents of such print instructional materials in specialized formats.

(d) For purposes of this section, the term—

(1) "authorized entity" means a nonprofit organization or a governmental agency that has a primary mission to provide specialized services relating to training, education, or adaptive reading or information access needs of blind or other persons with disabilities;

(2) "blind or other persons with disabilities" means individuals who are eligible or who may qualify in accordance with the Act entitled "An Act to provide books for the adult blind", approved March 3, 1931 (2 U.S.C. 135a; 46 Stat. 1487) to receive books and other publications produced in specialized formats;

(3) "print instructional materials" has the meaning given under section 674(e)(3)(C) of the Individuals with Disabilities Education Act; and

(4) "specialized formats" means—

(A) braille, audio, or digital text which is exclusively for use by blind or other persons with disabilities; and

(B) with respect to print instructional materials, includes large print formats when such materials are distributed exclusively for use by blind or other persons with disabilities.

§122 · Limitations on exclusive rights: Secondary transmissions of local television programming by satellite[65]

(a) Secondary Transmissions into Local Markets.—

(1) Secondary transmissions of television broadcast stations within a local market.—A secondary transmission of a performance or display of a work embodied in a primary transmission of a television broadcast station into the station's local market shall be subject to statutory licensing under this section if—

(A) the secondary transmission is made by a satellite carrier to the public;

(B) with regard to secondary transmissions, the satellite carrier is in compliance with the rules, regulations, or authorizations of the Federal Communications Commission governing the carriage of television broadcast station signals; and

(C) the satellite carrier makes a direct or indirect charge for the secondary transmission to—

(i) each subscriber receiving the secondary transmission; or

(ii) a distributor that has contracted with the satellite carrier for direct or indirect delivery of the secondary transmission to the public.

(2) Significantly viewed stations.—

(A) In general.—A secondary transmission of a performance or display of a work embodied in a primary transmission of a television broadcast station to subscribers who receive secondary transmissions of primary transmissions under paragraph (1) shall be subject to statutory licensing under this paragraph if the secondary transmission is of the primary transmission of a network station or a nonnetwork station to a subscriber who resides outside the station's local market but within a community in which the signal has been determined by the Federal Communications Commission to be significantly viewed in such community, pursuant to the rules, regulations, and authorizations of the Federal Communications Commission in effect on April 15, 1976, applicable to determining with respect to a cable system whether signals are significantly viewed in a community.

(B) Waiver.—A subscriber who is denied the secondary transmission of the primary transmission of a network station or a non-network station under subparagraph (A) may request a waiver from such denial by submitting a request, through the subscriber's satellite carrier, to the network station or non-network station in the local market affiliated with the same network or non-network where the subscriber is located. The network station or non-network station shall accept or reject the subscriber's request for a waiver within 30 days after receipt of the request. If the network station or non-network station fails to accept or reject the subscriber's request for a waiver within that 30-day period, that network station or non-network station shall be deemed to agree to the waiver request.

(3) Secondary transmission of low power programming.—

(A) In general.—Subject to subparagraphs (B) and (C), a secondary transmission of a performance or display of a work embodied in a primary transmission of a television broadcast station to subscribers who receive secondary transmissions of primary transmissions under paragraph (1) shall be subject to statutory licensing under this paragraph if the secondary transmission is of the primary transmission of a television broadcast station that is licensed as a low power television station, to a subscriber who resides within the same designated market area as the station that originates the transmission.

(B) NO APPLICABILITY TO REPEATERS AND TRANSLATORS.—Secondary transmissions provided for in subparagraph (A) shall not apply to any low power television station that retransmits the programs and signals of another television station for more than 2 hours each day.

(C) NO IMPACT ON OTHER SECONDARY TRANSMISSIONS OBLIGATIONS.—A satellite carrier that makes secondary transmissions of a primary transmission of a low power television station under a statutory license provided under this section is not required, by reason of such secondary transmissions, to make any other secondary transmissions.

(4) SPECIAL EXCEPTIONS.—A secondary transmission of a performance or display of a work embodied in a primary transmission of a television broadcast station to subscribers who receive secondary transmissions of primary transmissions under paragraph (1) shall, if the secondary transmission is made by a satellite carrier that complies with the requirements of paragraph (1), be subject to statutory licensing under this paragraph as follows:

(A) STATES WITH SINGLE FULL-POWER NETWORK STATION.—In a State in which there is licensed by the Federal Communications Commission a single full-power station that was a network station on January 1, 1995, the statutory license provided for in this paragraph shall apply to the secondary transmission by a satellite carrier of the primary transmission of that station to any subscriber in a community that is located within that State and that is not within the first 50 television markets as listed in the regulations of the Commission as in effect on such date (47 C.F.R. 76.51).

(B) STATES WITH ALL NETWORK STATIONS AND NON-NETWORK STATIONS IN SAME LOCAL MARKET.—In a State in which all network stations and non-network stations licensed by the Federal Communications Commission within that State as of January 1, 1995, are assigned to the same local market and that local market does not encompass all counties of that State, the statutory license provided under this paragraph shall apply to the secondary transmission by a satellite carrier of the primary transmissions of such station to all subscribers in the State who reside in a local market that is within the first 50 major television markets as listed in the regulations of the Commission as in effect on such date (section 76.51 of title 47, Code of Federal Regulations).

(C) ADDITIONAL STATIONS.—In the case of that State in which are located 4 counties that—

(i) on January 1, 2004, were in local markets principally comprised of counties in another State, and

(ii) had a combined total of 41,340 television households, according to the U.S. Television Household Estimates by Nielsen Media Research for 2004,

the statutory license provided under this paragraph shall apply to secondary transmissions by a satellite carrier to subscribers in any such county of the primary transmissions of any network station located in that State, if the satellite carrier was making such secondary transmissions to any subscribers in that county on January 1, 2004.

(D) Certain additional stations.—If 2 adjacent counties in a single State are in a local market comprised principally of counties located in another State, the statutory license provided for in this paragraph shall apply to the secondary transmission by a satellite carrier to subscribers in those 2 counties of the primary transmissions of any network station located in the capital of the State in which such 2 counties are located, if—

(i) the 2 counties are located in a local market that is in the top 100 markets for the year 2003 according to Nielsen Media Research; and

(ii) the total number of television households in the 2 counties combined did not exceed 10,000 for the year 2003 according to Nielsen Media Research.

(E) Networks of noncommercial educational broadcast stations.—In the case of a system of three or more noncommercial educational broadcast stations licensed to a single State, public agency, or political, educational, or special purpose subdivision of a State, the statutory license provided for in this paragraph shall apply to the secondary transmission of the primary transmission of such system to any subscriber in any county or county equivalent within such State, if such subscriber is located in a designated market area that is not otherwise eligible to receive the secondary transmission of the primary transmission of a noncommercial educational broadcast station located within the State pursuant to paragraph (1).

(5) Applicability of royalty rates and procedures.—The royalty rates and procedures under section 119(b) shall apply to the secondary transmissions to which the statutory license under paragraph (4) applies.

(b) Reporting Requirements.—

(1) Initial lists.—A satellite carrier that makes secondary transmissions of a primary transmission made by a network station under subsection (a) shall, within 90 days after commencing such secondary transmissions, submit to the network that owns or is affiliated with the network station—

(A) a list identifying (by name in alphabetical order and street address, including county and 9-digit zip code) all subscribers to which the satellite carrier makes secondary transmissions of that primary transmission under subsection (a);

(B) a separate list, aggregated by designated market area (by name and address, including street or rural route number, city, State, and 9-digit zip code), which shall indicate those subscribers being served pursuant to paragraph (2) of subsection (a).

(2) SUBSEQUENT LISTS.—After the list is submitted under paragraph (1), the satellite carrier shall, on the 15th of each month, submit to the network—

(A) a list identifying (by name in alphabetical order and street address, including county and 9-digit zip code) any subscribers who have been added or dropped as subscribers since the last submission under this subsection; and

(B) a separate list, aggregated by designated market area (by name and street address, including street or rural route number, city, State, and 9-digit zip code), identifying those subscribers whose service pursuant to paragraph (2) of subsection (a) has been added or dropped since the last submission under this subsection.

(3) USE OF SUBSCRIBER INFORMATION.—Subscriber information submitted by a satellite carrier under this subsection may be used only for the purposes of monitoring compliance by the satellite carrier with this section.

(4) REQUIREMENTS OF NETWORKS.—The submission requirements of this subsection shall apply to a satellite carrier only if the network to which the submissions are to be made places on file with the Register of Copyrights a document identifying the name and address of the person to whom such submissions are to be made. The Register of Copyrights shall maintain for public inspection a file of all such documents.

(c) NO ROYALTY FEE REQUIRED FOR CERTAIN SECONDARY TRANSMISSIONS.—A satellite carrier whose secondary transmissions are subject to statutory licensing under paragraphs (1), (2), and (3) of subsection (a) shall have no royalty obligation for such secondary transmissions.

(d) NONCOMPLIANCE WITH REPORTING AND REGULATORY REQUIREMENTS.—Notwithstanding subsection (a), the willful or repeated secondary transmission to the public by a satellite carrier into the local market of a television broadcast station of a primary transmission embodying a performance or display of a work made by that television broadcast station is actionable as an act of infringement under section 501, and is fully subject to the remedies provided under sections 502 through 506, if the satellite carrier has not complied with the reporting requirements of subsection (b) or with the rules, regulations, and authorizations of the Federal Communications Commission concerning the carriage of television broadcast signals.

(e) WILLFUL ALTERATIONS.—Notwithstanding subsection (a), the secondary transmission to the public by a satellite carrier into the local market of a television broadcast station of a performance or display of a work embodied in a primary transmission made by that television broadcast station is actionable as an act of infringement under section 501, and is fully subject to the remedies provided by sections 502 through 506 and section 510, if the content of the particular program in which the performance or display is embodied, or any commercial advertising or station announcement transmitted by the primary transmitter during, or immediately before or after, the transmission of such program, is in any way willfully altered by the satellite carrier through changes, deletions, or additions, or is combined with programming from any other broadcast signal.

(f) Violation of Territorial Restrictions on Statutory License for Television Broadcast Stations.—

(1) Individual violations.—The willful or repeated secondary transmission to the public by a satellite carrier of a primary transmission embodying a performance or display of a work made by a television broadcast station to a subscriber who does not reside in that station's local market, and is not subject to statutory licensing under section 119, subject to statutory licensing by reason of paragraph (2)(A), (3), or (4) of subsection (a), or subject to a private licensing agreement, is actionable as an act of infringement under section 501 and is fully subject to the remedies provided by sections 502 through 506 and 509, except that—

(A) no damages shall be awarded for such act of infringement if the satellite carrier took corrective action by promptly withdrawing service from the ineligible subscriber; and

(B) any statutory damages shall not exceed $250 for such subscriber for each month during which the violation occurred.

(2) Pattern of violations.—If a satellite carrier engages in a willful or repeated pattern or practice of secondarily transmitting to the public a primary transmission embodying a performance or display of a work made by a television broadcast station to subscribers who do not reside in that station's local market, and are not subject to statutory licensing under section 119, subject to statutory licensing by reason of paragraph (2)(A), (3), or (4) of subsection (a), or subject to a private licensing agreement, then in addition to the remedies under paragraph (1)—

(A) if the pattern or practice has been carried out on a substantially nationwide basis, the court—

(i) shall order a permanent injunction barring the secondary transmission by the satellite carrier of the primary transmissions of that television broadcast station (and if such television broadcast station is a network station, all other television broadcast stations affiliated with such network); and

(ii) may order statutory damages not exceeding $2,500,000 for each 6-month period during which the pattern or practice was carried out; and

(B) if the pattern or practice has been carried out on a local or regional basis with respect to more than one television broadcast station, the court—

(i) shall order a permanent injunction barring the secondary transmission in that locality or region by the satellite carrier of the primary transmissions of any television broadcast station; and

(ii) may order statutory damages not exceeding $2,500,000 for each 6-month period during which the pattern or practice was carried out.

(g) Burden of Proof.—In any action brought under subsection (f), the satellite carrier shall have the burden of proving that its secondary transmission of a primary transmission by a television broadcast station is made only to subscribers located within that station's local market or subscribers being served in compliance with section 119, paragraph (2)(A), (3), or (4) of subsection (a), or a private licensing agreement.

(h) Geographic Limitations on Secondary Transmissions.—The statutory license created by this section shall apply to secondary transmissions to locations in the United States.

(i) Exclusivity with Respect to Secondary Transmissions of Broadcast Stations by Satellite to Members of the Public.—No provision of section 111 or any other law (other than this section and section 119) shall be construed to contain any authorization, exemption, or license through which secondary transmissions by satellite carriers of programming contained in a primary transmission made by a television broadcast station may be made without obtaining the consent of the copyright owner.

(j) Definitions.—In this section—

(1) Distributor.—The term "distributor" means an entity that contracts to distribute secondary transmissions from a satellite carrier and, either as a single channel or in a package with other programming, provides the secondary transmission either directly to individual subscribers or indirectly through other program distribution entities.

(2) Local market.—

(A) In general.—The term "local market", in the case of both commercial and noncommercial television broadcast stations, means the designated market area in which a station is located, and—

(i) in the case of a commercial television broadcast station, all commercial television broadcast stations licensed to a community within the same designated market area are within the same local market; and

(ii) in the case of a noncommercial educational television broadcast station, the market includes any station that is licensed to a community within the same designated market area as the noncommercial educational television broadcast station.

(B) County of license.—In addition to the area described in subparagraph (A), a station's local market includes the county in which the station's community of license is located.

(C) Designated market area.—For purposes of subparagraph (A), the term "designated market area" means a designated market area, as determined by Nielsen Media Research and published in the 1999–2000 Nielsen Station Index Directory and Nielsen Station Index United States Television Household Estimates or any successor publication.

(D) Certain areas outside of any designated market area.—Any census area, borough, or other area in the State of Alaska that is outside of a designated market area, as determined by Nielsen Media Research, shall be deemed to be part of one of the local markets in the State of Alaska. A satellite carrier may determine which local market in the State of Alaska will be deemed to be the relevant local market in connection with each subscriber in such census area, borough, or other area.

(3) Low power television station.—The term "low power television station" means a low power TV station as defined in section 74.701(f) of title 47, Code of Federal Regulations, as in effect on June 1, 2004. For purposes of this paragraph, the term "low power television station" includes a low power television station that has been accorded primary status as a Class A television licensee under section 73.6001(a) of title 47, Code of Federal Regulations.

(4) Network station; non-network station; satellite carrier; secondary transmission.—The terms "network station", "non-network station", "satellite carrier", and "secondary transmission" have the meanings given such terms under section 119(d).

(5) Noncommercial educational broadcast station.—The term "noncommercial educational broadcast station" means a television broadcast station that is a noncommercial educational broadcast station as defined in section 397 of the Communications Act of 1934, as in effect on the date of the enactment of the Satellite Television Extension and Localism Act of 2010.

(6) Subscriber.—The term "subscriber" means a person or entity that receives a secondary transmission service from a satellite carrier and pays a fee for the service, directly or indirectly, to the satellite carrier or to a distributor.

(7) Television broadcast station.—The term "television broadcast station"—

(A) means an over-the-air, commercial or noncommercial television broadcast station licensed by the Federal Communications Commission under subpart E of part 73 of title 47, Code of Federal Regulations, except that such term does not include a low-power or translator television station; and

(B) includes a television broadcast station licensed by an appropriate governmental authority of Canada or Mexico if the station broadcasts primarily in the English language and is a network station as defined in section 119(d)(2)(A).

Chapter 1 · Notes

1. In 1980, section 117 was amended in its entirety and given a new title. However, the table of sections was not changed to reflect the new title. Pub. L. No. 96-517, 94 Stat. 3015, 3028. In 1997, a technical amendment made that change. Pub. L. No. 105-80, 111 Stat. 1529, 1534.

The Satellite Television Extension and Localism Act of 2010 Act amended the title for section 111 by adding "of broadcast programming by cable." Pub. L. No. 111-175, 124 Stat. 1218, 1231. It amended the title for section 119 by substituting "distant television programming by satellite" for "superstations and network stations for private home viewing." *Id.*, 124 Stat. 1219. The Act also amended the title for section 122 by deleting "by satellite carriers within local markets" from the title and inserting "of local television programming by satellite." *Id.*, 124 Stat. 1227.

2. The Audio Home Recording Act of 1992 amended section 101 by inserting "Except as otherwise provided in this title," at the beginning of the first sentence. Pub. L. No. 102-563, 106 Stat. 4237, 4248.

The Berne Convention Implementation Act of 1988 amended section 101 by adding a definition for "Berne Convention work." Pub. L. No. 100-568, 102 Stat. 2853, 2854. In 1990, the Architectural Works Copyright Protection Act amended the definition of "Berne Convention work" by adding paragraph (5). Pub. L. No. 101-650, 104 Stat. 5089, 5133. The WIPO Copyright and Performances and Phonograms Treaties Implementation Act of 1998 deleted the definition of "Berne Convention work" from section 101. Pub. L. No. 105-304, 112 Stat. 2860, 2861. The definition of "Berne Convention work," as deleted, is contained in Appendix N.

3. In 1990, the Architectural Works Copyright Protection Act amended section 101 by adding the definition for "architectural work." Pub. L. No. 101-650, 104 Stat. 5089, 5133. That Act states that the definition is applicable to "any architectural work that, on the date of the enactment of this Act, is unconstructed and embodied in unpublished plans or drawings, except that protection for such architectural work under title 17, *United States Code*, by virtue of the amendments made by this title, shall terminate on December 31, 2002, unless the work is constructed by that date."

4. The Berne Convention Implementation Act of 1988 amended section 101 by adding the definition of "Berne Convention." Pub. L. No. 100-568, 102 Stat. 2853, 2854.

5. In 1980, the definition of "computer program" was added to section 101 and placed at the end. Pub. L. No. 96-517, 94 Stat. 3015, 3028. The Intellectual Property and High Technology Technical Amendments Act of 2002 amended section 101 by moving the definition for computer program from the end of section 101 to be in alphabetical order, after "compilation." Pub. L. No. 107-273, 116 Stat. 1758, 1909.

6. The Copyright Royalty and Distribution Reform Act of 2004 amended section 101 by adding the definition for "Copyright Royalty Judge." That Act inserted the definition in the wrong alphabetical order, placing it after "copies," instead of "copyright owner." Pub. L. No. 108-419, 118 Stat. 2341, 2361. A technical correction in the Copyright Cleanup, Clarification, and Corrections Act of 2010 put it after the definition for copyright owner. Pub. L. No. 111-295, 124 Stat. 3180, 3181.

7. The Digital Performance Right in Sound Recordings Act of 1995 amended section 101 by adding the definition of "digital transmission." Pub. L. No.104-39, 109 Stat. 336, 348.

8. The Fairness in Music Licensing Act of 1998 amended section 101 by adding the definition of "establishment." Pub. L. No. 105-298, 112 Stat. 2827, 2833.

9. In 1997, the No Electronic Theft (NET) Act amended section 101 by adding the definition for "financial gain." Pub. L. No. 105-147, 111 Stat. 2678.

10. The Fairness in Music Licensing Act of 1998 amended section 101 by adding the definition for "food service or drinking establishment." It inserted the definition in the wrong alphabetical order, placing it after "establishment" instead of "fixed." Pub. L. No. 105-298, 112 Stat. 2827, 2833. A technical correction in the Copyright Cleanup, Clarification, and Corrections Act of 2010 placed it after the definition for fixed. Pub. L. No. 111-295, 124 Stat. 3180, 3181.

11. The WIPO Copyright and Performances and Phonograms Treaties Implementation Act of 1998 amended section 101 by adding the definition of "Geneva Phonograms Convention." Pub. L. No. 105-304, 112 Stat. 2860, 2861.

12. The Fairness in Music Licensing Act of 1998 amended section 101 by adding the definition of "gross square feet of space." Pub. L. No. 105-298, 112 Stat. 2827, 2833.

13. The WIPO Copyright and Performances and Phonograms Treaties Implementation Act of 1998 requires that paragraph (5) of the definition of "international agreement" take effect upon entry into force of the WIPO Copyright Treaty with respect to the United States, which occurred March 6, 2002. Pub. L. No. 105-304, 112 Stat. 2860, 2877.

14. The WIPO Copyright and Performances and Phonograms Treaties Implementation Act of 1998 requires that paragraph (6) of the definition of "international agreement" take effect upon entry into force of the WIPO Performances and Phonograms Treaty with respect to the United States, which occurred May 20, 2002. Pub. L. No. 105-304, 112 Stat. 2860, 2877.

15. The WIPO Copyright and Performances and Phonograms Treaties Implementation Act of 1998 amended section 101 by adding the definition of "international agreement." Pub. L. No. 105-304, 112 Stat. 2860, 2861.

16. The Artists' Rights and Theft Prevention Act of 2005 amended section 101 by adding the definition for "motion picture exhibition facility." That Act inserted the definition in the wrong alphabetical order, placing it after "motion pictures," instead of before. Pub. L. No. 109-9, 119 Stat. 218, 220. A technical correction in the Copyright Cleanup, Clarification, and Corrections Act of 2010 put it after the definition for literary works. Pub. L. No. 111-295, 124 Stat. 3180, 3181.

17. The Fairness in Music Licensing Act of 1998 amended section 101 by adding the definition of "performing rights society." Pub. L. No. 105-298, 112 Stat. 2827, 2833.

18. The Berne Convention Implementation Act of 1988 amended the definition of "Pictorial, graphic, and sculptural works" by inserting "diagrams, models, and technical drawings, including architectural plans" in the first sentence, in lieu of "technical drawings, diagrams, and models." Pub. L. No. 100-568, 102 Stat. 2853, 2854.

19. The Fairness in Music Licensing Act of 1998 amended section 101 by adding the definition of "proprietor." Pub. L. No. 105-298, 112 Stat. 2827, 2833. In 1999, a technical amendment added the phrase "For purposes of section 513,", to the beginning of the definition of "proprietor." Pub. L. No. 106-44, 113 Stat. 221, 222.

20. The Copyright Renewal Act of 1992 amended section 101 by adding the definition of "registration." Pub. L. No. 102-307, 106 Stat. 264, 266.

21. The WIPO Copyright and Performances and Phonograms Treaties Implementation Act of 1998 amended section 101 by adding the definition of "treaty party." Pub. L. No. 105-304, 112 Stat. 2860, 2861.

22. The Berne Convention Implementation Act of 1988 amended section 101 by adding the definition of "country of origin" of a Berne Convention work, for purposes of section 411. Pub. L. No. 100-568, 102 Stat. 2853, 2854. The WIPO Copyright and Performances and Phonograms Treaties Implementation Act of 1998 amended that definition by changing it to a definition for "United States work," for purposes of section 411. Pub. L. No. 105-304, 112 Stat. 2860, 2861. In 1999, a technical amendment moved the definition of "United States work" to place it in alphabetical order, after the definition for "United States." Pub. L. No. 106-44, 113 Stat. 221, 222.

23. The WIPO Copyright and Performances and Phonograms Treaties Implementation Act of 1998 amended section 101 by adding the definition of "WIPO Copyright Treaty." Pub. L. No. 105-304, 112 Stat. 2860, 2861. That definition is required to take effect upon entry into force of the WIPO Copyright Treaty with respect to the United States, which occurred March 6, 2002. Pub. L. No. 105-304, 112 Stat. 2860, 2877.

24. The WIPO Copyright and Performances and Phonograms Treaties Implementation Act of 1998 amended section 101 by adding the definition of "WIPO Performances and Phonograms Treaty." Pub. L. No. 105-304, 112 Stat. 2860, 2862. That definition is required to take effect upon entry into force of the WIPO Performances and Phonograms Treaty with respect to the United States, which occurred May 20, 2002. Pub. L. No. 105-304, 112 Stat. 2860, 2877.

25. The Visual Artists Rights Act of 1990 amended section 101 by adding the definition of "work of visual art." Pub. L. No. 101-650, 104 Stat. 5089, 5128.

26. The Satellite Home Viewer Improvement Act of 1999 amended the definition of "a work made for hire" by inserting "as a sound recording" after "audiovisual work." Pub. L. No. 106-113, 113 Stat. 1501, app. I at 1501A-544. The Work Made for Hire and Copyright Corrections Act of 2000 amended the definition of "work made for hire" by deleting "as a sound recording" after "audiovisual work." Pub. L. No. 106-379, 114 Stat. 1444. The Act also added a second paragraph to part (2) of that definition. *Id.* These changes are effective retroactively, as of November 29, 1999.

27. The WIPO Copyright and Performances and Phonograms Treaties Implementation Act of 1998 amended section 101 by adding the definitions of "WTO Agreement" and "WTO member country," thereby transferring those definitions to section 101 from section 104A. Pub. L. No. 105-304, 112 Stat. 2860, 2862. See also note 31, *infra*.

28. In 1990, the Architectural Works Copyright Protection Act amended subsection 102(a) by adding at the end thereof paragraph (8). Pub. L. No. 101-650, 104 Stat. 5089, 5133.

29. The Berne Convention Implementation Act of 1988 amended section 104(b) by redesignating paragraph (4) as paragraph (5), by inserting after paragraph (3) a new paragraph (4), and by adding subsection (c) at the end. Pub. L. No. 100-568, 102 Stat. 2853, 2855. The WIPO Copyright and Performances and Phonograms Treaties Implementation Act of 1998 amended section 104 as follows: 1) by amending subsection (b) to redesignate paragraphs (3) and (5) as (5) and (6), respectively, and by adding a new paragraph (3); 2) by amending section 104(b), throughout; and 3) by adding section 104(d). Pub. L. No. 105-304, 112 Stat. 2860, 2862.

30. The WIPO Copyright and Performances and Phonograms Treaties Implementation Act of 1998 requires that subsection (d), regarding the effect of phonograms treaties, take effect upon entry into force of the WIPO Performances and Phonograms Treaty with respect to the United States, which occurred May 20, 2002. Pub. L. No. 105-304, 112 Stat. 2860, 2877.

31. In 1993, the North American Free Trade Agreement Implementation Act added section 104A. Pub. L. No. 103-182, 107 Stat. 2057, 2115. In 1994, the Uruguay Round Agreements Act amended section 104A in its entirety with an amendment in the nature of a substitute. Pub. L. No. 103-465, 108 Stat. 4809, 4976. On November 13, 1997, section 104A was amended by replacing subsection (d)(3)(A), by striking the last sentence of subsection (e)(1)(B)(ii), and by rewriting paragraphs (2) and (3) of subsection (h). Pub. L. No. 105-80, 111 Stat. 1529, 1530. The WIPO Copyright and Performances and Phonograms Treaties Implementation Act of 1998 amended section 104A by rewriting paragraphs (1) and (3) of subsection (h); by adding subparagraph (E) to subsection (h)(6); and by amending subsection (h)(8)(B)(i). Pub. L. No. 105-304, 112 Stat. 2860, 2862. That Act also deleted paragraph (9), thereby transferring the definitions for "WTO Agreement" and "WTO member country" from section 104A to section 101. Pub. L. No. 105-304, 112 Stat. 2860, 2863. See also note 27, *supra*.

32. The WIPO Copyright and Performances and Phonograms Treaties Implementation Act of 1998 requires that subparagraph (C) of the definition of "date of adherence or proclamation" take effect upon entry into force of the WIPO Copyright Treaty with respect to the United States, which occurred March 6, 2002. Pub. L. No. 105-304, 112 Stat. 2860, 2877.

33. The WIPO Copyright and Performances and Phonograms Treaties Implementation Act of 1998 requires that subparagraph (D) of the definition of "date of adherence or proclamation" take effect upon entry into force of the WIPO Performances and Phonograms Treaty with respect to the United States, which occurred May 20, 2002. Pub. L. No. 105-304, 112 Stat. 2860, 2877.

34. The WIPO Copyright and Performances and Phonograms Treaties Implementation Act of 1998 requires that subparagraph (C) of the definition of "eligible country" take effect upon entry into force of the WIPO Copyright Treaty with respect to the United States, which occurred March 6, 2002. Pub. L. No. 105-304, 112 Stat. 2860, 2877.

35. The WIPO Copyright and Performances and Phonograms Treaties Implementation Act of 1998 requires that subparagraph (D) of the definition of "eligible country" take effect upon entry into force of the WIPO Performance and Phonograms Treaty with respect to the United States, which occurred May 20, 2002. Pub. L. No. 105-304, 112 Stat. 2860, 2877.

36. The WIPO Copyright and Performances and Phonograms Treaties Implementation Act of 1998 requires that subparagraph (E) of the definition of "restored work" take effect upon entry into force of the WIPO Performances and Phonograms Treaty with respect to the United States, which occurred May 20, 2002. Pub. L. No. 105-304, 112 Stat. 2860, 2877.

37. In 1968, the Standard Reference Data Act provided an exception to section 105, Pub. L. No. 90-396, 82 Stat. 339. Section 6 of that act amended title 15 of the *United States Code* by authorizing the Secretary of Commerce, at 15 *U.S.C.* 290e, to secure copyright and renewal thereof on behalf of the United States as author or proprietor "in all or any part of any standard reference data which he prepares or makes available under this chapter," and to "authorize the reproduction and publication thereof by others." See also section 105(f) of the Transitional and Supplementary Provisions of the Copyright Act of 1976, in Appendix A. Pub. L. No. 94-553, 90 Stat. 2541.

Concerning the liability of the United States Government for copyright infringement, also see 28 *U.S.C.* 1498. Title 28 of the *United States Code* is entitled "Judiciary and Judicial Procedure," included in the appendices to this volume.

38. The Digital Performance Right in Sound Recordings Act of 1995 amended section 106 by adding paragraph (6). Pub. L. No. 104-39, 109 Stat. 336. In 1999, a technical amendment substituted "121" for "120." Pub. L. No. 106-44, 113 Stat. 221, 222. The Intellectual Property and High Technology Technical Amendments Act of 2002 amended section 106 by substituting sections "107 through 122" for "107 through 121." Pub. L. No. 107-273, 116 Stat. 1758, 1909.

39. The Visual Artists Rights Act of 1990 added section 106A. Pub. L. No. 101-650, 104 Stat. 5089, 5128. The Act states that, generally, section 106A is to take effect 6 months after its date of enactment, December 1, 1990, and that the rights created by section 106A shall apply to (1) works created before such effective date but title to which has not, as of such effective date, been transferred from the author and (2) works created on or after such effective date, but shall not apply to any destruction, distortion, mutilation, or other modification (as described in section 106A(a)(3)) of any work which occurred before such effective date. See also, note 3, chapter 3.

40. The Visual Artists Rights Act of 1990 amended section 107 by adding the reference to section 106A. Pub. L. No. 101-650, 104 Stat. 5089, 5132. In 1992, section 107 was also amended to add the last sentence. Pub. L. No. 102-492, 106 Stat. 3145.

41. The Copyright Amendments Act of 1992 amended section 108 by repealing subsection (i) in its entirety. Pub. L. No. 102-307, 106 Stat. 264, 272. In 1998, the Sonny Bono Copyright Term Extension Act amended section 108 by redesignating subsection (h) as (i) and adding a new subsection (h). Pub. L. No. 105-298, 112 Stat. 2827, 2829. Also in 1998, the Digital Millennium Copyright Act amended section 108 by making changes in subsections (a), (b), and (c). Pub. L. No. 105-304, 112 Stat. 2860, 2889.

In 2005, the Preservation of Orphan Works Act amended subsection 108(i) by adding a reference to subsection (h). It substituted "(b), (c), and (h)" for "(b) and (c)." Pub. L. No. 109-9, 119 Stat. 218, 226, 227.

42. The Record Rental Amendment of 1984 amended section 109 by redesignating subsections (b) and (c) as subsections (c) and (d), respectively, and by inserting a new subsection (b) after subsection (a). Pub. L. No. 98-450, 98 Stat. 1727. Section 4(b) of the Act states that the provisions of section 109(b), as added by section 2 of the Act, "shall not affect the right of an owner of a particular phonorecord of a sound recording, who acquired such ownership before [October 4, 1984], to dispose of the possession of that particular phonorecord on or after such date of enactment in any manner permitted by section 109 of title 17, *United States Code*, as in effect on the day before the date of the enactment of this Act." Pub. L. No. 98-450, 98 Stat. 1727, 1728. Section 4(c) of the Act also states that the amendments "shall not apply to rentals, leasings, lendings (or acts or practices in the nature of rentals, leasings, or lendings) occurring after the date which is 13 years after [October 4, 1984]." In 1988, the Record Rental Amendment Act of 1984 was amended to extend the time period in section 4(c) from 5 years to 13 years. Pub. L. No. 100-617, 102 Stat. 3194. In 1993, the North American Free Trade Agreement Implementation Act repealed section 4(c) of the Record Rental Amendment of 1984. Pub. L. No. 103-182, 107 Stat. 2057, 2114. Also in 1988, technical amendments to section 109(d) inserted "(c)" in lieu of "(b)" and substituted "copyright" in lieu of "coyright." Pub. L. No. 100-617, 102 Stat. 3194.

The Computer Software Rental Amendments Act of 1990 amended section 109(b) as follows: 1) paragraphs (2) and (3) were redesignated as paragraphs (3) and (4), respectively; 2) paragraph (1) was struck out and new paragraphs (1) and (2) were inserted in lieu thereof; and 3) paragraph (4), as redesignated, was amended in its entirety with a new paragraph (4) inserted in lieu thereof. Pub. L. No. 101-650, 104 Stat. 5089, 5134. The Act states that section 109(b), as amended, "shall not affect the right of a person in possession of a particular copy of a computer program, who acquired such copy before the date of the enactment of this Act, to dispose of the possession of that copy on or after such date of enactment in any manner permitted by section 109 of title 17, *United States Code*, as in effect on the day before such date of enactment." The Act also states that the amendments made to section 109(b) "shall not apply to rentals, leasings, or lendings (or acts or practices in the nature of rentals, leasings, or lendings) occurring on or after October 1, 1997." However, this limitation, which is set forth in the first sentence of section 804 (c) of the Computer Software Rental Amendments Act of 1990, at 104 Stat. 5136, was subsequently deleted in 1994 by the Uruguay Round Agreements Act. Pub. L. No. 103-465, 108 Stat. 4809, 4974.

The Computer Software Rental Amendments Act of 1990 also amended section 109 by adding at the end thereof subsection (e). Pub. L. No. 101-650, 104 Stat. 5089, 5135. That Act states that the provisions contained in the new subsection (e) shall take effect 1 year after its date of enactment. It was enacted on December 1, 1990. The Act also states that such amendments so made "shall not apply to public performances or displays that occur on or after October 1, 1995."

In 1994, the Uruguay Round Agreements Act amended section 109(a) by adding the second sentence, which begins with "Notwithstanding the preceding sentence." Pub. L. No. 103-465, 108 Stat. 4809, 4981.

The Prioritizing Resources and Organization for Intellectual Property Act of 2008 amended part (4) of subsection 109(b) by removing the reference to section 509 (which was repealed). Pub. L. No. 110-403, 122 Stat. 4256, 4264.

43. In 1988, the Extension of Record Rental Amendment amended section 110 by adding paragraph (10). Pub. L. No. 97-366, 96 Stat. 1759. In 1997, the Technical Corrections to the Satellite Home Viewer Act amended section 110 by inserting a semicolon in lieu of the period at the end of paragraph (8); by inserting "; and" in lieu of the period at the end of paragraph (9); and by inserting "(4)" in lieu of "4 above" in paragraph (10). Pub. L. No. 105-80, 111 Stat. 1529, 1534. The Fairness in Music Licensing Act of 1998 amended section 110, in paragraph 5, by adding subparagraph (B) and by making conforming amendments to subparagraph (A); by adding the phrase "or of the audiovisual or other devices utilized in such performance" to paragraph 7; and by adding the last paragraph to section 110 that begins "The exemptions provided under paragraph (5)." Pub. L. No. 105-298, 112 Stat. 2827, 2830. In 1999, a technical amendment made corrections to conform paragraph designations that were affected by amendments previously made by the Fairness in Music Licensing Act of 1998. Pub. L. No. 106-44, 113 Stat. 221. The Technology, Education, and Copyright Harmonization Act of 2002 amended section 110 by substituting new language for paragraph 110(2) and by adding all the language at the end of section 110 that concerns paragraph 110(2). Pub. L. No. 107-273, 116 Stat. 1758, 1910.

The Family Movie Act of 2005 amended section 110 by adding paragraph (11) and by adding a new paragraph at the end of that section. Pub. L. No. 109-9, 119 Stat. 218, 223.

44. Throughout section 111 the date of enactment of the Satellite Television and Localism Act of 2010 (STELA) is incorporated by reference. STELA was enacted on May 27, 2010. Pub. L. No. 111-175, 124 Stat. 1218. There are also references to the date of enactment for the Copyright Act of 1976, which is October 19, 1976. Pub. L. No. 94-553, 90 Stat. 2541.

In 1986, section 111(d) was amended by striking out paragraph (1) and by redesignating paragraphs (2), (3), (4), and (5) as paragraphs (1), (2), (3), and (4), respectively. Pub. L. 99-397, 100 Stat. 848. Also, in 1986, section 111(f) was amended by substituting "subsection (d)(1)" for "subsection (d)(2)" in the last sentence of the definition of "secondary transmission" and by adding a new sentence after the first sentence in the definition of "local service area of a primary transmitter." Pub. L. No. 99-397, 100 Stat. 848.

The Satellite Home Viewer Act of 1988 amended subsection 111(a) by striking "or" at the end of paragraph (3), by redesignating paragraph (4) as paragraph (5), and by inserting a new paragraph (4). Pub. L. No. 100-667, 102 Stat. 3935, 3949. That Act also amended section (d)(1)(A) by adding the second sentence, which begins with "In determining the total number." *Id.*

The Copyright Royalty Tribunal Reform Act of 1993 amended section 111(d) by substituting "Librarian of Congress" for "Copyright Royalty Tribunal" where appropriate, by inserting a new sentence in lieu of the second and third sentences of paragraph (2), and, in paragraph (4), by amending subparagraph (B) in its entirety. Pub. L. No. 103-198, 107 Stat. 2304, 2311.

The Satellite Home Viewer Act of 1994 amended section 111(f) by inserting "microwave" after "wires, cables," in the paragraph relating to the definition of "cable system" and by inserting new matter after "April 15, 1976," in the paragraph relating to the definition of "local service area of a primary transmitter." Pub. L. No. 103-369, 108 Stat. 3477, 3480. That Act provides that the amendment "relating to the definition of the local service area of a primary transmitter, shall take effect on July 1, 1994." *Id.*

In 1995, the Digital Performance in Sound Recordings Act amended section 111(c)(1) by inserting "and section 114(d)" in the first sentence, after "of this subsection." Pub. L. No. 104-39, 109 Stat. 336, 348.

The Satellite Home Viewer Improvement Act of 1999 amended section 111 by substituting "statutory" for "compulsory" and "programming" for "programing," wherever they appeared. Pub. L. No. 106-113, 113 Stat. 1501, app. I at 1501A-543. The Act also amended sections 111(a) and (b) by inserting "performance or display of a work embodied in a primary transmission" in lieu of "primary transmission embodying a performance or display of a work." It amended paragraph (1) of section 111(c) by inserting "a performance or display of a work embodied in" after "by a cable system of" and by striking "and embodying a performance or display of a work." It amended subparagraphs (3) and (4) of section 111(a) by inserting "a performance or display of a work embodied in a primary transmission" in lieu of "a primary transmission" and by striking "and embodying a performance or display of a work." *Id.*

The Copyright Royalty and Distribution Reform Act of 2004 made amendments to subsection 111(d) to conform it to revised chapter 8, substituting "Copyright Royalty Judges" for "Librarian of Congress" where appropriate, along with making other conforming amendments. Pub. L. No. 108-419, 118 Stat. 2341, 2361. The Satellite Home Viewer Extension and Reauthorization Act of 2004 amended section 111 by deleting "for private home viewing" in subsections (a)(4) and (d)(1)(A). Pub. L. No. 108-447, 118 Stat. 2809, 3393, 3406.

In 2006, the Copyright Royalty Judges Program Technical Corrections Act amended section 111(d)(2) by substituting "upon authorization by the Copyright Royalty Judges for everything in the second sentence after "Librarian of Congress"; by substituting new text for the second sentence of (4)(B); by making a technical correction in the last sentence of (4)(B) to change "finds" to "find"; and by revising (4)(C) in its entirety. Pub. L. No. 109-303, 120 Stat. 1478, 1481.

The Prioritizing Resources and Organization for Intellectual Property Act of 2008 amended section 111 by deleting all references to section 509 (which was repealed). Pub. L. No. 110-403, 122 Stat. 4256, 4264.

The Satellite Television Extension and Localism Act of 2010 amended subsection 111(d)(1) by deleting subparagraphs (B) through (D) and replacing them with new subparagraphs (B) through (G); by amending paragraph 111(d)(2) to insert the parenthetical language in the first sentence; and by adding new paragraphs (5) through (7). Pub. L. No. 111-175, 124 Stat. 1218, 1232-35. It amended subsection 111(f) by numbering the previously undesignated paragraphs and adding subtitles to them; by substituting new language for the definition for primary transmissions; by amending the definition for local service area of a primary transmitter; by substituting new provisions to define distant signal equivalent, network station, independent station, and noncommercial educational station; and by adding definitions for primary stream, primary transmitter, multicast stream, simulcast, subscriber, and subscribe. *Id.*, at 124 Stat. 1235-38. The Act also added "of broadcast programming by cable" to the section title and made perfecting, technical, and clarifying amendments throughout section 111. *Id.*

45. Royalty rates specified by the compulsory licensing provisions of this section are subject to adjustment by copyright royalty judges appointed by the Librarian of Congress in accordance with the provisions of chapter 8 of title 17 of the *United States Code*, as amended by the Copyright Royalty and Distribution Reform Act of 2004, Pub. L. No. 108-419, 118 Stat. 2341. See chapter 8, *infra*. Regulations for adjusting royalty rates may be found in subchapter B of chapter 11, title 37, *Code of Federal Regulations*.

46. In 1998, the Digital Millennium Copyright Act amended section 112 by redesignating subsection (a) as subsection (a)(1); by redesignating former sections (a)(1), (a)(2), and (a)(3) as subsections (a)(1)(A), (a)(1)(B), and (a)(1)(C), respectively; by adding subsection (a)(2); and by amending the language in new subsection (a)(1). Pub. L. No. 105-304, 112 Stat. 2860, 2888. The Digital Millennium Copyright Act also amended section 112 by redesignating subsection (e) as subsection (f) and adding a new subsection (e). Pub. L. No. 105-304, 112 Stat. 2860, 2899. In 1999, a technical amendment to section 112(e) redesignated paragraphs (3) through (10) as (2) through (9) and corrected the paragraph references throughout that section to conform to those redesignations. Pub. L. No. 106-44, 113 Stat. 221. The Technology, Education, and Copyright Harmonization Act of 2002 amended section 112 by redesignating subsection 112(f) as 112(g) and adding a new paragraph (f). Pub. L. No. 107-273, 116 Stat. 1758, 1912.

The Copyright Royalty and Distribution Reform Act of 2004 amended subsection 112(e) to conform it to revised chapter 8, by substituting new language for the first sentences of paragraphs (3) and (4); by deleting paragraph (6) and renumbering paragraphs (7) through (9) as (6) through (8); by changing references to the "Librarian of Congress" to "Copyright Royalty Judges," with corresponding grammatical changes, throughout; and by striking references to negotiations in paragraphs (3) and (4) along with making other conforming amendments. Pub. L. No. 108-419, 118 Stat. 2341, 2361.

47. The Visual Artists Rights Act of 1990 amended section 113 by adding subsection (d) at the end thereof. Pub. L. No. 101-650, 104 Stat. 5089, 5130.

48. The Digital Performance Right in Sound Recordings Act of 1995 amended section 114 as follows: 1) in subsection (a), by striking "and (3)" and inserting in lieu thereof "(3) and (6)"; 2) in subsection (b) in the first sentence, by striking "phonorecords, or of copies of motion pictures and other audiovisual works," and inserting "phonorecords or copies"; and 3) by striking subsection (d) and inserting in lieu thereof new subsections (d), (e), (f), (g), (h), (i), and (j). Pub. L. No. 104-39, 109 Stat. 336. In 1997, subsection 114(f) was amended in paragraph (1) by inserting all the text that appears after "December 31, 2000" and in paragraph (2) by striking "and publish in the Federal Register." Pub. L. No. 105-80, 111 Stat. 1529, 1531.

In 1998, the Digital Millennium Copyright Act amended section 114(d) by replacing paragraphs (1)(A) and (2) with amendments in the nature of substitutes. Pub. L. No. 105-304, 112 Stat. 2860, 2890. That Act also amended section 114(f) by revising the title; by redesignating paragraph (1) as paragraph (1)(A); by adding paragraph (1)(B) in lieu of paragraphs (2), (3), (4), and (5); and by amending the language in newly designated paragraph (1)(A), including revising the effective date from December 31, 2000, to December 31, 2001. Pub. L. No. 105-304, 112 Stat. 2860, 2894. The Digital Millennium Copyright Act also amended subsection 114(g) by substituting "transmission" in lieu of "subscription transmission," wherever it appears and, in the first sentence in paragraph (g)(1), by substituting "transmission licensed under a statutory license" in lieu of "subscription transmission licensed." Pub. L. No. 105-304, 112 Stat. 2860, 2897. That Act also amended subsection 114(j) by redesignating paragraphs (2), (3), (5), (6), (7), and (8) as (3), (5), (9), (12), (13), and (14), respectively; by amending paragraphs (4) and (9) in their entirety and redesignating them as paragraphs (7) and (15), respectively; and by adding new definitions, including, paragraph (2) defining "archived program," paragraph (4) defining "continuous program," paragraph (6) defining "eligible nonsubscription transmission," paragraph (8) defining "new subscription service," paragraph (10) defining "preexisting satellite digital audio radio service," and paragraph (11) defining "preexisting subscription service." Pub. L. No. 105-304, 112 Stat. 2860, 2897.

The Small Webcaster Settlement Act of 2002 amended section 114 by adding paragraph (5) to subsection 114(f), by amending paragraph 114(g)(2), and by adding paragraph 114(g)(3). Pub. L. No. 107-321, 116 Stat. 2780, 2781 and 2784.

The Copyright Royalty and Distribution Reform Act of 2004 amended subsection 114(f) to conform it to revised chapter 8, by substituting new language for the first sentences of subparagraphs (1)(A), (1)(B), (2)(A), and (2)(B); by substituting new language for subparagraphs (1)(C) and (2)(C); by changing references to the "Librarian of Congress" in paragraphs (1), (2), (3), and (4) to "Copyright Royalty Judges," and making corresponding grammatical changes; by striking references to negotiations in paragraphs (1), (2), (3), and (4) and replacing with corresponding grammatical changes and conforming language; and by adding new language at the end of subparagraph (4)(A). Pub. L. No. 108-419, 118 Stat. 2341, 2362-2364.

In 2006, the Copyright Royalty Judges Program Technical Corrections Act amended section 114 by substituting new text after "proceedings are to be commenced" in the first sentence in (f)(1)(A); by amending (2)(A) in its entirety; and by inserting "described in" in the last sentence of (2)(B) which repeats an amendment already made by the Copyright Royalty and Distribution Reform Act of 2004, Pub. L. No. 108 419, 118 Stat. 2341, 2364. Pub. L. No. 109-303, 120 Stat. 1478, 1481-82.

The Webcaster Settlement Act of 2008 amended part (5) of subsection 114(f) by deleting "small" wherever it appears before "commercial webcasters." Pub. L. No. 110-435, 122 Stat. 4974. The Webcaster Settlement Act of 2008 also amended subpart (5)(A) by substituting "for a period of not more than 11 years beginning on January 1, 2005" for "during the period beginning on October 28, 1998, and ending on December 31, 2004," by substituting "the Copyright Royalty Judges" in place of references to the copyright arbitration royalty panel and the Librarian of Congress and by changing "shall" to "may" at the beginning of the second sentence. *Id.* It amended subpart (5)(C) by adding a sentence at the end that states, "This subparagraph shall not apply to the extent that the receiving agent and a webcaster that is party to an agreement entered into pursuant to subparagraph (A) expressly authorize the submission of the agreement in a proceeding under this subsection." *Id.* It amended subpart (5)(D) by changing the reference in the first sentence from "the Small Webcaster Settlement Act of 2002" to "the Webcaster Settlement Act of 2008" and by substituting "Copyright Royalty Judges of May 1, 2007" for "Librarian of Congress of July 8, 2002." *Id.* It also amended subpart (5)(F) by substituting "February 15, 2009" for "December 15, 2002, except with respect to noncommercial webcasters for whom the authority shall expire May 31, 2003." *Id.*

The Webcaster Settlement Act of 2009 amended section 114 by adding a reference to itself in the first sentence of subpart (f)(5)(D); by deleting this text: "to make eligible nonsubscription transmissions and ephemeral recordings" at the end of subpart (f)(5)(E)(iii); and, in subpart (f)(5)(F), by changing the expiration to 11:59 p.m. on July 30, 2009, which is 30 days after the Webcaster Settlement Act of 2009 was enacted on June 30, 2009. Pub. L. No. 111-36, 123 Stat. 1926.

A technical correction in the Copyright Cleanup, Clarification, and Corrections Act of 2010 amended section 114(b) to change the reference from "section 118(g)" to "section 118(f)." Pub. L. No. 111-295, 124 Stat. 3180, 3181. It also amended subparagraph 114(f)(2)(C) by substituting "eligible nonsubscription services and new subscription services" for "preexisting subscription digital audio transmission services or preexisting satellite digital radio audio services." *Id.*

49. The Copyright Royalty and Distribution Reform Act of 2004 did not conform the pronoun "its" to "their" when it substituted "Copyright Royalty Judges" for "copyright arbitration royalty panel." Pub. L. No. 108-419, 118 Stat. 2341, 2362. A technical amendment in the Copyright Cleanup, Clarification, and Corrections Act of 2010 corrected this error. Pub. L. No. 111-295, 124 Stat. 3180, 3181.

50. The Record Rental Amendment of 1984 amended section 115 by redesignating paragraphs (3) and (4) of subsection (c) as paragraphs (4) and (5), respectively, and by adding a new paragraph (3). Pub. L. No. 98-450, 98 Stat. 1727.

The Digital Performance Right in Sound Recordings Act of 1995 amended section 115 as follows: 1) in the first sentence of subsection (a)(1), by striking "any other person" and inserting in lieu thereof "any other person, including those who make phonorecords or digital phonorecord deliveries,"; 2) in the second sentence of the same subsection, by inserting before the period "including by means of a digital phonorecord delivery"; 3) in the second sentence of subsection (c)(2), by inserting "and other than as provided in paragraph (3)," after "For this purpose,"; 4) by redesignating paragraphs (3), (4), and (5) of subsection

(c) as paragraphs (4), (5), and (6), respectively, and by inserting after paragraph (2) a new paragraph (3); and (5) by adding after subsection (c) a new subsection (d). Pub. L. No. 104-39, 109 Stat. 336, 344.

In 1997, section 115 was amended by striking "and publish in the Federal Register" in subparagraph 115(c)(3)(D). Pub. L. No. 105-80, 111 Stat. 1529, 1531. The same legislation also amended section 115(c)(3)(E) by replacing the phrases "sections 106(1) and (3)" and "sections 106(1) and 106(3)" with "paragraphs (1) and (3) of section 106." Pub. L. No. 105-80, 111 Stat. 1529, 1534.

The Copyright Royalty and Distribution Reform Act of 2004 amended paragraph 115(c)(3) to conform it to revised chapter 8, by substituting new language for the first sentences of subparagraphs (3)(C) and (3)(D); by changing references to the "Librarian of Congress" in subparagraphs (3)(C), (3)(D), and (3)(E) to "Copyright Royalty Judges," with corresponding grammatical changes; by striking references to negotiations in subparagraphs (3)(C) and (D) and making corresponding grammatical changes and conforming language; by deleting subparagraph (F); and by redesignating paragraphs (G) through (L) as paragraphs (F) through (K) with corresponding technical changes in subparagraphs (A), (B), and (E) to conform references to the subparagraphs subject to that redesignation. Pub. L. No. 108-419, 118 Stat. 2341, 2364–2365. The Copyright Royalty and Distribution Act of 2004 also amended the first sentence of subparagraph 115(c)(3)(B) by substituting "section" for "paragraph" and by inserting "on a nonexclusive basis" after "common agents." *Id.* at 2364. It also amended subparagraph 115(c)(3)(E) by inserting "as to digital phonorecord deliveries" after "shall be given effect." *Id.* at 2365.

In 2006, the Copyright Royalty Judges Program Technical Corrections Act amended 115(c)(3)(B) by inserting "this subparagraph and subparagraphs (C) through (E)" in lieu of "subparagraphs (B) through (F)." The Act also amended the third sentence of 115(c)(3)(D) by inserting "in subparagraphs (B) and (C)" after "described"; and 115(c)(3)(E)(i) and (ii)(I) by substituting "(C) and (D)" for "(C) or (D)" wherever it appears. Pub. L. No. 109-303, 120 Stat. 1478, 1482.

The Prioritizing Resources and Organization for Intellectual Property Act of 2008 amended subparts (3)(G)(i) and (6) of subsection 115(c) by removing the reference to section 509 (which was repealed). Pub. L. No. 110-403, 122 Stat. 4256, 4264.

51. See note 45, *supra.*

52. There was a minor drafting error for this text in the Prioritizing Resources and Organization for Intellectual Property Act of 2008. Pub. L. No. 110-403, 122 Stat. 4256, 5264. To delete the reference to "and section 509," it deleted "and 509," thereby, technically, not including the word "section" in the amendment. A technical amendment in the Copyright Cleanup, Clarification, and Corrections Act of 2010 corrected this error. Pub. L. No. 111-295, 124 Stat. 3180, 3181.

53. The Berne Convention Implementation Act of 1988 added section 116A. Pub. L. No. 100-568, 102 Stat. 2853, 2855. The Copyright Royalty Tribunal Reform Act of 1993 redesignated section 116A as section 116; repealed the preexisting section 116; in the redesignated section 116, struck subsections (b), (e), (f), and (g), and redesignated subsections (c) and (d) as subsections (b) and (c), respectively; and substituted, where appropriate, "Librarian of Congress" or "copyright arbitration royalty panel" for "Copyright Royalty Tribunal." Pub. L.

No. 103-198, 107 Stat. 2304, 2309. In 1997, section 116 was amended by rewriting subsection (b)(2) and by adding a new subsection (d). Pub. L. No. 105-80, 111 Stat. 1529, 1531.

The Copyright Royalty and Distribution Reform Act of 2004 amended section 116 to conform it to revised chapter 8, by substituting new language for subsection (b)(2); by changing the title of subsection (c) to "License Agreements Superior to Determinations by Copyright Royalty Judges" from "License Agreements Superior to Copyright Arbitration Royalty Panel Determinations"; and, in subsection (c), by striking "copyright arbitration royalty panel" and replacing it with "Copyright Royalty Judges." Pub. L. No. 108-419, 118 Stat. 2341, 2365.

54. In 1980, section 117 was amended in its entirety. Pub. L. No. 96-517, 94 Stat. 3015, 3028. In 1998, the Computer Maintenance Competition Assurance Act amended section 117 by inserting headings for subsections (a) and (b) and by adding subsections (c) and (d). Pub. L. No. 105-304, 112 Stat. 2860, 2887.

55. The Copyright Royalty Tribunal Reform Act of 1993 amended section 118 by striking the first two sentences of subsection (b), by substituting a new first sentence in paragraph (3), and by making general conforming amendments throughout. Pub. L. 103-198, 107 Stat. 2304, 2309. In 1999, a technical amendment deleted paragraph (2) from section 118(e). Pub. L. No. 106-44, 113 Stat. 221, 222. The Intellectual Property and High Technology Technical Amendments Act of 2002 amended section 118 by deleting "to it" in the second sentence in subsection (b)(1). Pub. L. No. 107-273, 116 Stat. 1758, 1909.

The Copyright Royalty and Distribution Reform Act of 2004 amended section 118 to conform it to revised chapter 8, by deleting the last sentence in paragraph (b)(1); by revising paragraph (b)(2) by rewriting the end of sentence after "determination by the"; by substituting new language for the first sentence of paragraph (3), thereby, creating new paragraphs (3) and (4); by deleting subsection (c) and redesignating sections (d) through (g) as (c) through (f) with a corresponding technical change in section (f) to refer to "subsection (c)" instead of "subsection (d)"; and by changing references to the "Librarian of Congress" in subsections (b) and (d), as redesignated, to "Copyright Royalty Judges," with corresponding grammatical or procedural changes. Pub. L. No. 108-419, 118 Stat. 2341, 2365–2366. The Copyright Royalty and Distribution Act of 2004 also amended section 116 in text that became the second sentence of new subparagraph (4), see *supra*, by inserting "or (3)" after "paragraph 2". *Id.* at 2366. It further amended subsection 116(c) by inserting "or (3)" after "provided by subsection (b)(2)" and by inserting "to the extent that they were accepted by the Librarian of Congress" after "under subsection (b)(3)" and before the comma. *Id.*

In 2006, the Copyright Royalty Judges Program Technical Corrections Act amended subsection 118(b)(3) by inserting "owners of copyright in works" in lieu of "copyright owners in works"; by amending the first sentence of (c); and by substituting "(f)" for "(g)" in (c)(1). Pub. L. No. 109-303, 120 Stat. 1478, 1482.

The Prioritizing Resources and Organization for Intellectual Property Act of 2008 amended subparts (6), (7)(A), (8) and (13) of subsection 119(a) by removing the reference to section 509 (which was repealed). Pub. L. No. 110-403, 122 Stat. 4256, 4264.

56. Throughout section 119 the date of enactment of the Satellite Television and Localism Act of 2010 (STELA) is incorporated by reference. STELA was enacted on May 27, 2010. Pub. L. No. 111-175, 124 Stat. 1218.

The Satellite Home Viewer Act of 1988 added section 119. Pub. L. No. 100-667, 102 Stat. 3935, 3949. The Copyright Royalty Tribunal Reform Act of 1993 amended subsections (b) and (c) of section 119 by substituting "Librarian of Congress" in lieu of "Copyright Royalty Tribunal" wherever it appeared and by making related conforming amendments. Pub. L. No. 103-198, 107 Stat. 2304, 2310. The Copyright Royalty Tribunal Reform Act of 1993 also amended paragraph (c)(3) by deleting subparagraphs (B), (C), (E), and (F) and by redesignating subparagraph (D) as (B), (G) as (C), and (H) as (D). The redesignated subparagraph (C) was amended in its entirety and paragraph (c)(4) was deleted. *Id.*

The Satellite Home Viewer Act of 1994 further amended section 119. Pub. L. No. 103-369, 108 Stat. 3477. In 1997, technical corrections and clarifications were made to the Satellite Home Viewer Act of 1994. Pub. L. No. 105-80, 111 Stat. 1529. Those two acts amended section 119 as follows: 1) by deleting or replacing obsolete effective dates; 2) in subsection (a)(5), by adding subparagraph (D); 3) in subsection (a), by adding paragraphs (8), (9), and (10); 4) in subsection (b)(1)(B), by adjusting the royalty rate for retransmitted superstations; 5) in subsection (c)(3), by replacing subparagraph (B) with an amendment in the nature of a substitute; 6) in subsections (d)(2) and (d)(6), by modifying the definition of "network station" and "satellite carrier"; and 7) in subsection (d), by adding paragraph 11 to define "local market."

Pursuant to section 4 of the Satellite Home Viewer Act of 1994, the changes made by that Act to section 119 of the *United States Code* ceased to be effective on December 31, 1999. Pub. L. No. 103-369, 108 Stat. 3477, 3481. However, section 1003 of the Satellite Home Viewer Improvement Act of 1999 extended that date to December 31, 2004. Pub. L. No. 106-113, 113 Stat. 1501, app. I at 1501A-527.

The Digital Performance Right in Sound Recordings Act of 1995 amended section 119 in the first sentence of subsections (a)(1) and (a)(2)(A), respectively, by inserting the words "and section 114(d)" after "of this subsection." Pub. L. No. 104-39, 109 Stat. 336, 348. In 1999, a technical amendment substituted "network station's" for "network's stations" in section 119(a)(8)(C)(ii). Pub. L. No. 106-44, 113 Stat. 221, 222.

The Satellite Home Viewer Improvement Act of 1999 amended section 119(a)(1) as follows: 1) by inserting "and PBS satellite feed" after "Superstations" in the paragraph heading; 2) by inserting "performance or display of a work embodied in a primary transmission made by a superstation or by the Public Broadcasting Service satellite feed" in lieu of "primary transmission made by a superstation and embodying a performance or display of a work," (see this note, *infra*); and 3) by adding the last sentence, which begins "In the case of the Public Broadcasting Service." Pub. L. No. 106-113, 113 Stat. 1501, app. I at 1501A-530 and 543. The Act states that these amendments shall be effective as of July 1, 1999, except for a portion of the second item, starting with "performance or display" through "superstation." Pub. L. No. 106-113, 113 Stat. 1501, app. I at 1501A-544. The Act also amended section 119(a) by inserting the phrase "with regard to secondary transmissions the satellite carrier is in compliance with the rules, regulations, or authorization of the Federal Communications Commission governing the carriage of television broadcast stations signals" in paragraphs (1) and (2) and by inserting into paragraph (2), "a performance or display of a work embodied in a primary transmission made by a network station" in lieu of "programming contained in a primary transmission made by a network station and embodying a performance or display of a work." *Id.* at 1501A-531 and 544. The Act amended section 119(a)(2) by substituting new language for paragraph (B) and, in paragraph (C), by deleting "currently" after "the satellite carrier" near the end of the first sentence. *Id.* at 1501A-528 and 544. It also amended section 119(a)(4) by inserting "a performance or display of a work embodied in" after "by a satellite carrier of" and by deleting "and embodying a performance or display of a work." *Id.* at 1501A-544. The Satellite Home Viewer Improvement Act of 1999 further amended section 119(a) by adding subparagraph (E) to paragraph (5). *Id.* at 1501A-528. It amended section 19(a)(6) by inserting "performance or display of a work embodied in" after "by a satellite carrier of" and by deleting "and embodying a performance or display of a work." *Id.* The Act also amended section 119(a) by adding paragraphs (11) and (12). *Id.* at 1501A-529 and 531.

The Satellite Home Viewer Improvement Act of 1999 amended section 119(b)(1) by inserting "or the Public Broadcasting Service satellite feed" into subparagraph (B). *Id.* at 1501A-530. The Act amended section 119(c) by adding a new paragraph (4). *Id.* at 1501A-527. The Act amended section 119(d) by substituting new language for paragraphs (9) through (11) and by adding paragraph (12). *Id.* at 1501A-527, 530, and 531. The Act substituted new language for section 119(e). *Id.* at 1501A-529.

The Intellectual Property and High Technology Technical Amendments Act of 2002 amended section 119(a)(6) by substituting "of a performance" for "of performance." Pub. L. No. 107-273, 116 Stat. 1758, 1909. The Act also amended section 119(b)(1)(A) by substituting "retransmitted" and "retransmissions" for "transmitted" and "transmitted," respectively, in paragraph (1)(A). *Id.*

The Copyright Royalty and Distribution Reform Act of 2004 amended section 119 to conform it to revised chapter 8 by changing references to the "Librarian of Congress" in subsections (b) and (c) to "Copyright Royalty Judges," with corresponding grammatical adjustments and procedural references; by substituting new language for subparagraphs (b)(4)(B) and (C); by deleting the term "arbitration" wherever it appears with "proceedings," along with corresponding grammatical adjustments; by amending the title of subparagraph 119(c)(3)(C) to insert "Determination under Chapter 8" in lieu of "Decision of Arbitration Panel or Order of Librarian"; and, also, in subparagraph (c)(3)(C), by substituting new language for clauses (i) and (ii). Pub. L. No. 108-419, 118 Stat. 2341, 2364–2365.

The Satellite Home Viewer Extension and Reauthorization Act of 2004 amended paragraph 119(a)(1) by deleting "and PBS satellite feed" from the title; by deleting "or by the Public Broadcasting Service satellite feed" from the first sentence; by deleting the last sentence, which concerned Public Broadcasting Service satellite feed; by inserting "or for viewing in a commercial establishment" after "for private home viewing"; and by substituting "subscriber" for "household." Pub. L. No. 108-447, 118 Stat. 2809, 3393, 3394 and 3406. It amended subparagraph 119(a)(2)(B) by inserting at the end of clause (i) "The limitation in this clause shall not apply to secondary transmissions under paragraph (3)." *Id.* at 3397. It amended subsection (C) in its entirety by substituting new language. *Id.* at 3394. It amended paragraph 119(a)(5), which is now renumbered as 119(a)(7), in the first sentence of subparagraph (A), by inserting "who is not eligible to receive the transmission under this section" in lieu of "who does not reside in an unserved household" and, in the first sentence of subparagraph (B), by making the same change but using "are" instead of "is"; and, in subparagraph (D), by substituting "is to a subscriber who is eligible to receive the secondary transmission under this section" in lieu of "is for private home viewing to an unserved household." *Id.* at 3404. The Act further amended subsection 119(a) by adding new paragraphs, redesignated as paragraphs (3) and (4); by deleting paragraph eight; by renumbering the paragraphs affected by those changes; and by revising the references to old paragraph numbers, accordingly, in paragraphs (1) and (2), to be the new numbers as redesignated. *Id.* at 3394, 3396, and 3397. The Act further amended subsection 119(a) by adding at the end three new paragraphs, designated as new paragraphs (14), (15) and (16). *Id.* at 3400, 3404 and 3408.

The Satellite Home Viewer Extension and Reauthorization Act of 2004 amended the title of subsection 119(b) by deleting "for Private Home Viewing." *Id.* at 3406. It also amended subparagraph 119(b)(A) and paragraph 119(b)(3) by deleting "for private home viewing." *Id.* The Act amended subparagraph (119)(b)(1)(B) in its entirety by substituting new language. *Id.* at 3400. It added a new paragraph at the end of paragraph 119(b)(1). *Id.* at 3401.

The Satellite Home Viewer Extension and Reauthorization Act of 2004 amended subsection 119(c) in its entirety. *Id.* The Satellite Home Viewer Extension and Reauthorization Act of 2004 amended paragraph 119(d)(1) by deleting "for private home viewing" after "individual subscribers" and by adding at the end "in accordance with the provisions of this section." *Id.* at 3406. It amended paragraph 119(d)(2)(A) by substituting, at the beginning of the first sentence, "a television station licensed by the Federal Communications Commission" in lieu of "a television broadcast station." *Id.* The Act amended paragraph 119(d)(8) by substituting "or entity that" in lieu of "who"; by deleting "for private home viewing"; and by inserting at the end "in accordance with the provisions of this section." *Id.* It amended subparagraph 119(d)(10)(D) by changing "(a)(11)" to "(a)(12)". *Id.* at 3405. It amended in their entireties paragraph 119(d)(9), subparagraph (119)(d)(10)(B) and paragraphs 119(d)(11) and (12). *Id.* at 3405 and 3406.

The Satellite Home Viewer Extension and Reauthorization Act of 2004 amended subsection 119(e) by changing the date at the beginning of the sentence from "December 31, 2004" to "December 31, 2009". *Id.* at 3394. The Satellite Home Viewer Extension and Reauthorization Act of 2004 amended section 119 by adding a new subsection (f). *Id.* at 3394.

In 2006, the Copyright Royalty Judges Program Technical Corrections Act amended section 119 by revising the second sentence of (b)(4)(B); by amending (b)(4)(C) in its entirety; and by making a technical correction to substitute "arbitration" for "arbitrary" in (c)(1)(F)(i). Pub. L. No. 109-303, 120 Stat. 1478, 1482–83. The Prioritizing Resources and Organization for Intellectual Property Act of 2008 amended subparts (6), (7)(A), (8) and (13) of subsection 119(a) by removing the reference to section 509 (which was repealed). Pub. L. No. 110-403, 122 Stat. 4256, 4264.

Besides the changes described below, the Satellite Television Extension and Localism Act of 2010 made perfecting, technical, and clarifying amendments throughout section 119. Pub. L. No. 111-175, 124 Stat. 1218. It also substituted "non-network station" for "superstation" throughout section 119, revised the title to substitute "distant television programming by satellite" for "superstations and network stations for private home viewing" and added a new subsection (g) at the end. *Id.*, at 124 Stat. 1219, 1233, 1239-44.

In addition, the Satellite Television Extension and Localism Act of 2010 amended subsection 119(a) by deleting the last sentence in subparagraph (a)(2)(B)(i); by deleting paragraph (a)(2)(C); by revising subparagraphs (a)(2)(C)(i) and (ii) in the newly designated paragraph (C); by deleting subsection (a)(3); in the newly designated paragraph (3), by revising subparagraphs (a)(3)(B) and (C) and deleting "analog" wherever it appeared; in newly designated subsection (a)(6), by increasing the statutory damages in (6)(A)(ii) and (6)(B)(ii) from $5 and $250,000 to $250 and $2,500,000, respectively, and, in (6)(B)(i), by substituting "$2,500,000 for each 3-month period" for "$250,000 for each 6 month period;" by adding the last paragraph of subsection (a)(6) and by deleting subsection (a)(15). Pub. L. No. 111-175, 124 Stat. 1218, 1219, 1223-28.

Furthermore, the Satellite Television Extension and Localism Act of 2010 amended the title of subsection 119(b) by deleting "Statutory License for Secondary Transmissions" and inserting "Deposit of Statements and Fees; Verification Procedures. *Id.*, 124 Stat. 1220. It amended subsection 119(b) by revising subparagraph (b)(1)(B), adding new subparagraph (b)(1)(C), and deleting the last sentence of (b)(1); by adding a new subsection (b)(2); and by inserting "(including the filing fee specified in paragraph (1)(C))" into the first sentence of subsection (b)(3). *Id.*, at 124 Stat. 1220, 1223-24.

Public Law No. 111-175 amended subsection 119(c) throughout by deleting the references to "analog" and to "arbitration" and by substituting "Copyright Royalty Judges" for "Librarian of Congress." *Id.*, at 124 Stat. 1220, 21. It also amended subsection 119(c) by changing the reference in paragraph (c)(1)(A) from July 1, 2004, to July 1, 2009, to designate the regulation that establishes royalty fees and by changing the deadline in paragraph (c)(1)(A) from January 2, 2004, to January 2, 2010, for publishing notice in the *Federal Register* of initiation of voluntary negotiations. *Id.*, at 124 Stat. 1220. The Act further amended subsection 119(c) by adding subtitles for the subparagraphs in paragraph (c)(1)(D); by substituting "Copyright Royalty Judges" for "Copyright Office" in paragraph (c)(1)(E); by amending the subtitle for paragraph (c)(1)(F) to substitute "Copyright Royalty Judges Proceeding" for "Compulsory Arbitration;" and by revising subparagraphs (c)(1)(F)(ii) and (iii). *Id.*, at 124 Stat. 1221. The Act revised subsection 119(c)(2). *Id.*, at 124 Stat. 1222.

Public Law No. 111-175 amended subsection 119(d) by revising the definitions for subscriber and subscribe at (d)(8), for unserved household at (d)(10) and for local market at (d)(11). *Id.*, at 124 Stat. 1219, 1222-23. It deleted the definition for low power television station at (d)(12) and added definitions for qualifying date in newly designated paragraph (d)(13), multicast stream at (d)(14), and primary stream at (d)(15). *Id.*, at 124 Stat. 1219-20, 1223. The Act amended subsection 119(e) to extend the moratorium on copyright liability for satellite subscribers from December 31, 2009, to December 31, 2014. See note 62.

A technical correction in the Copyright Cleanup, Clarification, and Corrections Act of 2010 amended subparagraph 119(g)(4)(B)(vi) to substitute "an examination" for "the examinations." Pub. L. No. 111-295, 124 Stat. 3180, 3181.

57. The Satellite Home Viewer Improvement Act of 1999 amended section 119(a)(1) by deleting "primary transmission made by a superstation and embodying a performance or display of a work" and inserting in its place "performance or display of a work embodied in a primary transmission made by a superstation." Pub. L. No. 106-113, 113 Stat. 1501, app. I at 1501A-543. This amendatory language did not take into account a prior amendment that had inserted "or by the Public Broadcasting Service satellite feed" after "superstation" into the phrase quoted above that was deleted. Pub. L. No. 106-113, 113 Stat. 1501, app. I at 1501A-530. There was no mention of the phrase "or by the Public Broadcasting Service satellite feed" in that second amendment. The Intellectual Property and High Technology Technical Amendments Act of 2002 clarified these provisions. Pub. L. No. 107-273, 116 Stat. 1758, 1908. The Act deleted the first change and amended the second to clarify that the amended language should read, "performance or display of a work embodied in a primary transmission made by a superstation or by the Public Broadcasting Service satellite feed." *Id.* The Prioritizing

Resources and Organization for Intellectual Property Act of 2008 amended subparts (6), (7) (A), (8) and (13) of subsection 119(a) by removing the reference to section 509 (which was repealed). Pub. L. No. 110-403, 122 Stat. 4256, 4264.

58. The Satellite Home Viewer Act of 1994 states that "The provisions of section 119 (a) (5)(D) … relating to the burden of proof of satellite carriers, shall take effect on January 1, 1997, with respect to civil actions relating to the eligibility of subscribers who subscribed to service as an unserved household before the date of the enactment of this Act [, October 18, 1994]." Pub. L. No. 103-369, 108 Stat. 3477, 3481.

59. The Intellectual Property and High Technology Technical Amendments Act of 2002 made a technical correction to insert the word "a" before "performance." Pub. L. No. 107-273, 116 Stat. 1758, 1909.

60. The Satellite Home Viewer Improvement Act of 1999 stated that section 119(a), "as amended by section 1005(e)" of the same Act, was amended to add a new paragraph (12). Pub. L. No. 106-113, 113 Stat. 1501, app. I at 1501A-531. The Intellectual Property and High Technology Technical Amendments Act of 2002 made a technical correction to clarify that the amendment was to section 119(a) as amended by "section 1005(d)" of the Satellite Home Viewer Improvement Act of 1999 rather than "section 1005(e)." Pub. L. No. 107-273, 116 Stat. 1758, 1908.

61. Section 119(c)(1)(E) establishes the time period during which the obligation to pay royalty fees established under a voluntary agreement that is filed with the Copyright Royalty Judges is in effect. The December 31, 2009, expiration date was extended several times. The 2010 Department of Defense Appropriations Act extended the date to February 28, 2010. Pub. L. No. 111-118, 123 Stat. 3409, 3469. The Temporary Extension Act of 2010 extended it to March 28, 2010. Pub. L. No. 111-144, 124 Stat. 42, 47. The Satellite Television Extension Act of 2010 extended it to April 30, 2010. Pub. L. No. 111-151, 124 Stat. 1027. The Continuing Extension Act of 2010 extended the date to May 31, 2010. Pub. L. No. 111-157, 124 Stat. 1116, 1119. Finally, the Satellite Television Extension and Localism Act of 2010 extended it to December 31, 2014. Pub. L. No. 111-175, 124 Stat. 1218, 1221.

62. Subsection 119(e) establishes a moratorium on copyright liability for satellite subscribers that was due to expire on December 31, 2009, but was extended several times. The 2010 Department of Defense Appropriations Act extended the date to February 28, 2010. Pub. L. No. 111-118, 123 Stat. 3409, 3469. The Temporary Extension Act of 2010 extended it to March 28, 2010. Pub. L. No. 111-144, 124 Stat. 42, 47. The Satellite Television Extension Act of 2010 extended it to April 30, 2010. Pub. L. No. 111-151, 124 Stat. 1027. The Continuing Extension Act of 2010 extended the date to May 31, 2010. Pub. L. No. 111-157, 124 Stat. 1116, 1119. Finally, the Satellite Television Extension and Localism Act of 2010 extended it to December 31, 2014. Pub. L. No. 111-175, 124 Stat. 1218, 1221.

63. In 1990, the Architectural Works Copyright Protection Act added section 120. Pub. L. No. 101-650, 104 Stat. 5089, 5133. The effective date provision of the Act states that its amendments apply to any work created on or after the date it was enacted, which was December 1, 1990. It also states that the amendments apply to "any architectural work that, on [December 1, 1990], is unconstructed and embodied in unpublished plans or drawings, except that protection for such architectural work under title 17, *United States Code*, by virtue of the amendments made by [the Act], shall terminate on December 31, 2002, unless the work is constructed by that date." *Id.*, 104 Stat. 5089, 5134.

64. The Legislative Branch Appropriations Act, 1997, added section 121. Pub. L. No. 104-197, 110 Stat. 2394, 2416. The Work Made for Hire and Copyright Corrections Act of 2000 amended section 121 by substituting "section 106" for "sections 106 and 710." Pub. L. No. 106-379, 114 Stat. 1444, 1445.

The Individuals with Disabilities Education Improvement Act of 2004 amended section 121 by amending paragraph (c)(3) in its entirety; by adding a new paragraph (c)(4); by redesignating subsection (c) as (d); and by adding a new subsection (c). Pub. L. No. 108-446, 118 Stat. 2647, 2807.

65. Throughout section 122 the date of enactment of the Satellite Television and Localism Act of 2010 (STELA) is incorporated by reference. STELA was enacted on May 27, 2010. Pub. L. No. 111-175, 124 Stat. 1218.

The Satellite Home Viewer Improvement Act of 1999 added section 122. Pub. L. No. 106-113, 113 Stat. 1501, app. I at 1501A-523. The Act states that section 122 shall be effective as of November 29, 1999. Pub. L. No. 106-113, 113 Stat. 1501, app. I at 1501A-544.

The Satellite Home Viewer Extension and Reauthorization Act of 2004 amended section 122 by adding a subparagraph (D) to paragraph (j)(2). Pub. L. No. 108-447, 118 Stat. 2809, 3393, 3409.

The Prioritizing Resources and Organization for Intellectual Property Act of 2008 amended subsections 122(a) and (b) by removing the reference to section 509 (which was repealed). Pub. L. No. 110-403, 122 Stat. 4256, 4264.

The Satellite Television Extension and Localism Act of 2010 amended section 122 by deleting "by satellite carriers within local markets" from the title and replacing that text with "of local television programming by satellite;" by revising subsection (a); by deleting the second half of the first sentence in paragraph (b)(1) and adding subparagraphs (A) and (B); by revising subparagraph (b)(2) to add paragraphs (A) and (B); and by inserting, "For Certain Secondary Transmissions" at the end of the title for subsection (c) and adding "paragraphs (1), (2), and (3) of" to the text. Pub. L. No. 111-175, 124 Stat. 1218, 1227-30. The Act amended subsection 122(f) by inserting "subject to statutory licensing by reason of paragraph (2)(A), (3), or (4) of subsection (a), or subject to" into paragraphs (1) and (2); by increasing the statutory damages in subparagraph (1)(B) from $5 to $250; by increasing the statutory damages in subparts (2)(A)(ii) and (B)(ii) from $250,000 to $2,500,000; and by inserting "paragraph (2)(A), (3), or (4) of subsection (a)" into subsection (g). *Id.*, at 124 Stat. 1230. It also amended subsection (j) by inserting new paragraphs (3) and (5); by revising newly designated paragraph (6); and by inserting "non-network station" into the title of newly designated paragraph (4) and its text. *Id.*, at 124 Stat. 1231.

Chapter 2

Copyright Ownership and Transfer

§ 201 · Ownership of copyright[1]

(a) Initial Ownership.—Copyright in a work protected under this title vests initially in the author or authors of the work. The authors of a joint work are coowners of copyright in the work.

(b) Works Made for Hire.—In the case of a work made for hire, the employer or other person for whom the work was prepared is considered the author for purposes of this title, and, unless the parties have expressly agreed otherwise in a written instrument signed by them, owns all of the rights comprised in the copyright.

(c) Contributions to Collective Works.—Copyright in each separate contribution to a collective work is distinct from copyright in the collective work as a whole, and vests initially in the author of the contribution. In the absence of an express transfer of the copyright or of any rights under it, the owner of copyright in the collective work is presumed to have acquired only the privilege of reproducing and distributing the contribution as part of that particular collective work, any revision of that collective work, and any later collective work in the same series.

(d) Transfer of Ownership.—

(1) The ownership of a copyright may be transferred in whole or in part by any means of conveyance or by operation of law, and may be bequeathed by will or pass as personal property by the applicable laws of intestate succession.

(2) Any of the exclusive rights comprised in a copyright, including any subdivision of any of the rights specified by section 106, may be transferred as provided by clause (1) and owned separately. The owner of any particular exclusive right is entitled, to the extent of that right, to all of the protection and remedies accorded to the copyright owner by this title.

(e) Involuntary Transfer.—When an individual author's ownership of a copyright, or of any of the exclusive rights under a copyright, has not previously been transferred voluntarily by that individual author, no action by any governmental body or other official or organization purporting to seize, expropriate, transfer, or exercise rights of ownership with respect to the copyright, or any of the exclusive rights under a copyright, shall be given effect under this title, except as provided under title 11.[2]

§ 202 · Ownership of copyright as distinct from ownership of material object

Ownership of a copyright, or of any of the exclusive rights under a copyright, is distinct from ownership of any material object in which the work is embodied. Transfer of ownership of any material object, including the copy or phonorecord in which the work is first fixed, does not of itself convey any rights in the copyrighted work embodied in the object; nor, in the absence of an agreement, does transfer of ownership of a copyright or of any exclusive rights under a copyright convey property rights in any material object.

§203 · Termination of transfers and licenses granted by the author[3]

(a) Conditions for Termination.—In the case of any work other than a work made for hire, the exclusive or nonexclusive grant of a transfer or license of copyright or of any right under a copyright, executed by the author on or after January 1, 1978, otherwise than by will, is subject to termination under the following conditions:

(1) In the case of a grant executed by one author, termination of the grant may be effected by that author or, if the author is dead, by the person or persons who, under clause (2) of this subsection, own and are entitled to exercise a total of more than one-half of that author's termination interest. In the case of a grant executed by two or more authors of a joint work, termination of the grant may be effected by a majority of the authors who executed it; if any of such authors is dead, the termination interest of any such author may be exercised as a unit by the person or persons who, under clause (2) of this subsection, own and are entitled to exercise a total of more than one-half of that author's interest.

(2) Where an author is dead, his or her termination interest is owned, and may be exercised, as follows:

(A) The widow or widower owns the author's entire termination interest unless there are any surviving children or grandchildren of the author, in which case the widow or widower owns one-half of the author's interest.

(B) The author's surviving children, and the surviving children of any dead child of the author, own the author's entire termination interest unless there is a widow or widower, in which case the ownership of one-half of the author's interest is divided among them.

(C) The rights of the author's children and grandchildren are in all cases divided among them and exercised on a per stirpes basis according to the number of such author's children represented; the share of the children of a dead child in a termination interest can be exercised only by the action of a majority of them.

(D) In the event that the author's widow or widower, children, and grandchildren are not living, the author's executor, administrator, personal representative, or trustee shall own the author's entire termination interest.

(3) Termination of the grant may be effected at any time during a period of five years beginning at the end of thirty-five years from the date of execution

of the grant; or, if the grant covers the right of publication of the work, the period begins at the end of thirty-five years from the date of publication of the work under the grant or at the end of forty years from the date of execution of the grant, whichever term ends earlier.

(4) The termination shall be effected by serving an advance notice in writing, signed by the number and proportion of owners of termination interests required under clauses (1) and (2) of this subsection, or by their duly authorized agents, upon the grantee or the grantee's successor in title.

(A) The notice shall state the effective date of the termination, which shall fall within the five-year period specified by clause (3) of this subsection, and the notice shall be served not less than two or more than ten years before that date. A copy of the notice shall be recorded in the Copyright Office before the effective date of termination, as a condition to its taking effect.

(B) The notice shall comply, in form, content, and manner of service, with requirements that the Register of Copyrights shall prescribe by regulation.

(5) Termination of the grant may be effected notwithstanding any agreement to the contrary, including an agreement to make a will or to make any future grant.

(b) Effect of Termination.—Upon the effective date of termination, all rights under this title that were covered by the terminated grants revert to the author, authors, and other persons owning termination interests under clauses (1) and (2) of subsection (a), including those owners who did not join in signing the notice of termination under clause (4) of subsection (a), but with the following limitations:

(1) A derivative work prepared under authority of the grant before its termination may continue to be utilized under the terms of the grant after its termination, but this privilege does not extend to the preparation after the termination of other derivative works based upon the copyrighted work covered by the terminated grant.

(2) The future rights that will revert upon termination of the grant become vested on the date the notice of termination has been served as provided by clause (4) of subsection (a). The rights vest in the author, authors, and other persons named in, and in the proportionate shares provided by, clauses (1) and (2) of subsection (a).

(3) Subject to the provisions of clause (4) of this subsection, a further grant, or agreement to make a further grant, of any right covered by a terminated grant is valid only if it is signed by the same number and proportion of the owners, in whom the right has vested under clause (2) of this subsection, as are required to terminate the grant under clauses (1) and (2) of subsection (a). Such further grant or agreement is effective with respect to all of the persons in whom the right it covers has vested under clause (2) of this subsection, including those who did not join in signing it. If any person dies after rights under a

terminated grant have vested in him or her, that person's legal representatives, legatees, or heirs at law represent him or her for purposes of this clause.

(4) A further grant, or agreement to make a further grant, of any right covered by a terminated grant is valid only if it is made after the effective date of the termination. As an exception, however, an agreement for such a further grant may be made between the persons provided by clause (3) of this subsection and the original grantee or such grantee's successor in title, after the notice of termination has been served as provided by clause (4) of subsection (a).

(5) Termination of a grant under this section affects only those rights covered by the grants that arise under this title, and in no way affects rights arising under any other Federal, State, or foreign laws.

(6) Unless and until termination is effected under this section, the grant, if it does not provide otherwise, continues in effect for the term of copyright provided by this title.

§204 · Execution of transfers of copyright ownership

(a) A transfer of copyright ownership, other than by operation of law, is not valid unless an instrument of conveyance, or a note or memorandum of the transfer, is in writing and signed by the owner of the rights conveyed or such owner's duly authorized agent.

(b) A certificate of acknowledgment is not required for the validity of a transfer, but is prima facie evidence of the execution of the transfer if—

(1) in the case of a transfer executed in the United States, the certificate is issued by a person authorized to administer oaths within the United States; or

(2) in the case of a transfer executed in a foreign country, the certificate is issued by a diplomatic or consular officer of the United States, or by a person authorized to administer oaths whose authority is proved by a certificate of such an officer.

§205 · Recordation of transfers and other documents[4]

(a) Conditions for Recordation.—Any transfer of copyright ownership or other document pertaining to a copyright may be recorded in the Copyright Office if the document filed for recordation bears the actual signature of the person who executed it, or if it is accompanied by a sworn or official certification that it is a true copy of the original, signed document. A sworn or official certification may be submitted to the Copyright Office electronically, pursuant to regulations established by the Register of Copyrights.

(b) Certificate of Recordation.—The Register of Copyrights shall, upon receipt of a document as provided by subsection (a) and of the fee provided by section 708, record the document and return it with a certificate of recordation.

(c) Recordation as Constructive Notice.—Recordation of a document in the Copyright Office gives all persons constructive notice of the facts stated in the recorded document, but only if—

(1) the document, or material attached to it, specifically identifies the work to which it pertains so that, after the document is indexed by the Register of Copyrights, it would be revealed by a reasonable search under the title or registration number of the work; and

(2) registration has been made for the work.

(d) Priority between Conflicting Transfers.—As between two conflicting transfers, the one executed first prevails if it is recorded, in the manner required to give constructive notice under subsection (c), within one month after its execution in the United States or within two months after its execution outside the United States, or at any time before recordation in such manner of the later transfer. Otherwise the later transfer prevails if recorded first in such manner, and if taken in good faith, for valuable consideration or on the basis of a binding promise to pay royalties, and without notice of the earlier transfer.

(e) Priority between Conflicting Transfer of Ownership and Nonexclusive License.—A nonexclusive license, whether recorded or not, prevails over a conflicting transfer of copyright ownership if the license is evidenced by a written instrument signed by the owner of the rights licensed or such owner's duly authorized agent, and if

(1) the license was taken before execution of the transfer; or

(2) the license was taken in good faith before recordation of the transfer and without notice of it.

Chapter 2 · Notes

1. In 1978, section 201(e) was amended by deleting the period at the end and adding ", except as provided under title 11." See note 2, *infra*.

2. Title 11 of the *United States Code* is entitled "Bankruptcy."

3. In 1998, the Sonny Bono Copyright Term Extension Act amended section 203 by deleting "by his widow or her widower and his or her grandchildren" from the first sentence in paragraph (2) of subsection (a) and by adding subparagraph (D) to paragraph (2). Pub. L. No. 105-298, 112 Stat. 2827, 2829.

4. The Berne Convention Implementation Act of 1988 amended section 205 by deleting subsection (d) and redesignating subsections (e) and (f) as subsections (d) and (e), respectively. Pub. L. No. 100-568, 102 Stat. 2853, 2857. The Copyright Cleanup, Clarification, and Corrections Act of 2010 amended section 205(a) to add the last sentence. Pub. L. No. 111-295, 124 Stat. 3180.

Chapter 3[1]

Duration of Copyright

§301 · Preemption with respect to other laws[2]

(a) On and after January 1, 1978, all legal or equitable rights that are equivalent to any of the exclusive rights within the general scope of copyright as specified by section 106 in works of authorship that are fixed in a tangible medium of expression and come within the subject matter of copyright as specified by sections 102 and 103, whether created before or after that date and whether published or unpublished, are governed exclusively by this title. Thereafter, no person is entitled to any such right or equivalent right in any such work under the common law or statutes of any State.

(b) Nothing in this title annuls or limits any rights or remedies under the common law or statutes of any State with respect to—

(1) subject matter that does not come within the subject matter of copyright as specified by sections 102 and 103, including works of authorship not fixed in any tangible medium of expression; or

(2) any cause of action arising from undertakings commenced before January 1, 1978;

(3) activities violating legal or equitable rights that are not equivalent to any of the exclusive rights within the general scope of copyright as specified by section 106; or

(4) State and local landmarks, historic preservation, zoning, or building codes, relating to architectural works protected under section 102(a)(8).

(c) With respect to sound recordings fixed before February 15, 1972, any rights or remedies under the common law or statutes of any State shall not be annulled or limited by this title until February 15, 2067. The preemptive provisions of subsection (a) shall apply to any such rights and remedies pertaining to any cause of action arising from undertakings commenced on and after February 15, 2067. Notwithstanding the provisions of section 303, no sound recording fixed before February 15, 1972, shall be subject to copyright under this title before, on, or after February 15, 2067.

(d) Nothing in this title annuls or limits any rights or remedies under any other Federal statute.

(e) The scope of Federal preemption under this section is not affected by the adherence of the United States to the Berne Convention or the satisfaction of obligations of the United States thereunder.

(f)(1) On or after the effective date set forth in section 610(a) of the Visual Artists Rights Act of 1990, all legal or equitable rights that are equivalent to any of the rights conferred by section 106A with respect to works of visual art to which the rights conferred by section 106A apply are governed exclusively by section 106A and section 113(d) and the provisions of this title relating to such sections. Thereafter, no person is entitled to any such right or equivalent right in any work of visual art under the common law or statutes of any State.[3]

(2) Nothing in paragraph (1) annuls or limits any rights or remedies under the common law or statutes of any State with respect to—

(A) any cause of action from undertakings commenced before the effective date set forth in section 610(a) of the Visual Artists Rights Act of 1990;

(B) activities violating legal or equitable rights that are not equivalent to any of the rights conferred by section 106A with respect to works of visual art; or

(C) activities violating legal or equitable rights which extend beyond the life of the author.

§302 · Duration of copyright: Works created on or after January 1, 1978[4]

(a) In General.—Copyright in a work created on or after January 1, 1978, subsists from its creation and, except as provided by the following subsections, endures for a term consisting of the life of the author and 70 years after the author's death.

(b) Joint Works.—In the case of a joint work prepared by two or more authors who did not work for hire, the copyright endures for a term consisting of the life of the last surviving author and 70 years after such last surviving author's death.

(c) Anonymous Works, Pseudonymous Works, and Works Made for Hire.—In the case of an anonymous work, a pseudonymous work, or a work made for hire, the copyright endures for a term of 95 years from the year of its first publication, or a term of 120 years from the year of its creation, whichever expires first. If, before the end of such term, the identity of one or more of the authors of an anonymous or pseudonymous work is revealed in the records of a registration made for that work under subsections (a) or (d) of section 408, or in the records provided by this subsection, the copyright in the work endures for the term specified by subsection (a) or (b), based on the life of the author or authors whose identity has been revealed. Any person having an interest in the copyright in an anonymous or pseudonymous work may at any time record, in records to be maintained by the Copyright Office for that purpose, a statement identifying one or more authors of the work; the statement shall also identify the person filing it, the nature of that person's interest, the source of the information recorded, and the particular work affected, and shall comply in form and content with requirements that the Register of Copyrights shall prescribe by regulation.

(d) Records Relating to Death of Authors.—Any person having an interest in a copyright may at any time record in the Copyright Office a statement of the date of death of the author of the copyrighted work, or a statement that the author is still living on a particular date. The statement shall identify the person filing it, the nature of that person's interest, and the source of the information recorded, and shall comply in form and content with requirements that the Register of Copyrights shall prescribe by regulation. The Register shall maintain current records of information relating to the death of authors of copyrighted works, based on such recorded statements and, to the extent the Register considers practicable, on data contained in any of the records of the Copyright Office or in other reference sources.

(e) Presumption as to Author's Death.—After a period of 95 years from the year of first publication of a work, or a period of 120 years from the year of its creation, whichever expires first, any person who obtains from the Copyright Office a certified report that the records provided by subsection (d) disclose nothing to indicate that the author of the work is living, or died less than 70 years before, is entitled to the benefit of a presumption that the author has been dead for at least 70 years. Reliance in good faith upon this presumption shall be a complete defense to any action for infringement under this title.

§303 · Duration of copyright: Works created but not published or copyrighted before January 1, 1978[5]

(a) Copyright in a work created before January 1, 1978, but not theretofore in the public domain or copyrighted, subsists from January 1, 1978, and endures for the term provided by section 302. In no case, however, shall the term of copyright in such a work expire before December 31, 2002; and, if the work is published on or before December 31, 2002, the term of copyright shall not expire before December 31, 2047.

(b) The distribution before January 1, 1978, of a phonorecord shall not for any purpose constitute a publication of any musical work, dramatic work, or literary work embodied therein.

§304 · Duration of copyright: Subsisting copyrights[6]

(a) Copyrights in Their First Term on January 1, 1978.—

(1)(A) Any copyright, in the first term of which is subsisting on January 1, 1978, shall endure for 28 years from the date it was originally secured.

(B) In the case of—

(i) any posthumous work or of any periodical, cyclopedic, or other composite work upon which the copyright was originally secured by the proprietor thereof, or

(ii) any work copyrighted by a corporate body (otherwise than as assignee or licensee of the individual author) or by an employer for whom such work is made for hire, the proprietor of such copyright shall be entitled to a renewal and extension of the copyright in such work for the further term of 67 years.

(C) In the case of any other copyrighted work, including a contribution by an individual author to a periodical or to a cyclopedic or other composite work—

(i) the author of such work, if the author is still living,

(ii) the widow, widower, or children of the author, if the author is not living,

(iii) the author's executors, if such author, widow, widower, or children are not living, or

(iv) the author's next of kin, in the absence of a will of the author,

shall be entitled to a renewal and extension of the copyright in such work for a further term of 67 years.

(2)(A) At the expiration of the original term of copyright in a work specified in paragraph (1)(B) of this subsection, the copyright shall endure for a renewed and extended further term of 67 years, which—

(i) if an application to register a claim to such further term has been made to the Copyright Office within 1 year before the expiration of the original term of copyright, and the claim is registered, shall vest, upon the beginning of such further term, in the proprietor of the copyright who is entitled to claim the renewal of copyright at the time the application is made; or

(ii) if no such application is made or the claim pursuant to such application is not registered, shall vest, upon the beginning of such further term, in the person or entity that was the proprietor of the copyright as of the last day of the original term of copyright.

(B) At the expiration of the original term of copyright in a work specified in paragraph (1)(C) of this subsection, the copyright shall endure for a renewed and extended further term of 67 years, which—

(i) if an application to register a claim to such further term has been made to the Copyright Office within 1 year before the expiration of the original term of copyright, and the claim is registered, shall vest, upon the beginning of such further term, in any person who is entitled under paragraph (1)(C) to the renewal and extension of the copyright at the time the application is made; or

(ii) if no such application is made or the claim pursuant to such application is not registered, shall vest, upon the beginning of such further term, in any person entitled under paragraph (1)(C), as of the last day of the original term of copyright, to the renewal and extension of the copyright.

(3)(A) An application to register a claim to the renewed and extended term of copyright in a work may be made to the Copyright Office—

(i) within 1 year before the expiration of the original term of copyright by any person entitled under paragraph (1)(B) or (C) to such further term of 67 years; and

(ii) at any time during the renewed and extended term by any person in whom such further term vested, under paragraph (2)(A) or (B), or by any successor or assign of such person, if the application is made in the name of such person.

(B) Such an application is not a condition of the renewal and extension of the copyright in a work for a further term of 67 years.

(4)(A) If an application to register a claim to the renewed and extended term of copyright in a work is not made within 1 year before the expiration of the original term of copyright in a work, or if the claim pursuant to such application is not registered, then a derivative work prepared under authority of a grant of a transfer or license of the copyright that is made before the expiration of the original term of copyright may continue to be used under the terms of the grant during the renewed and extended term of copyright without infringing the copyright, except that such use does not extend to the preparation during such renewed and extended term of other derivative works based upon the copyrighted work covered by such grant.

(B) If an application to register a claim to the renewed and extended term of copyright in a work is made within 1 year before its expiration, and the claim is registered, the certificate of such registration shall constitute prima facie evidence as to the validity of the copyright during its renewed and extended term and of the facts stated in the certificate. The evidentiary weight to be accorded the certificates of a registration of a renewed and extended term of copyright made after the end of that 1-year period shall be within the discretion of the court.

(b) Copyrights in Their Renewal Term at the Time of the Effective Date of the Sonny Bono Copyright Term Extension Act[7]—Any copyright still in its renewal term at the time that the Sonny Bono Copyright Term Extension Act becomes effective shall have a copyright term of 95 years from the date copyright was originally secured.[8]

(c) Termination of Transfers and Licenses Covering Extended Renewal Term.—In the case of any copyright subsisting in either its first or renewal term on January 1, 1978, other than a copyright in a work made for hire, the exclusive or nonexclusive grant of a transfer or license of the renewal copyright or any right under it, executed before January 1, 1978, by any of the persons designated by subsection (a)(1)(C) of this section, otherwise than by will, is subject to termination under the following conditions:

(1) In the case of a grant executed by a person or persons other than the author, termination of the grant may be effected by the surviving person or persons who executed it. In the case of a grant executed by one or more of the

authors of the work, termination of the grant may be effected, to the extent of a particular author's share in the ownership of the renewal copyright, by the author who executed it or, if such author is dead, by the person or persons who, under clause (2) of this subsection, own and are entitled to exercise a total of more than one-half of that author's termination interest.

(2) Where an author is dead, his or her termination interest is owned, and may be exercised, as follows:

(A) The widow or widower owns the author's entire termination interest unless there are any surviving children or grandchildren of the author, in which case the widow or widower owns one-half of the author's interest.

(B) The author's surviving children, and the surviving children of any dead child of the author, own the author's entire termination interest unless there is a widow or widower, in which case the ownership of one-half of the author's interest is divided among them.

(C) The rights of the author's children and grandchildren are in all cases divided among them and exercised on a per stirpes basis according to the number of such author's children represented; the share of the children of a dead child in a termination interest can be exercised only by the action of a majority of them.

(D) In the event that the author's widow or widower, children, and grandchildren are not living, the author's executor, administrator, personal representative, or trustee shall own the author's entire termination interest.

(3) Termination of the grant may be effected at any time during a period of five years beginning at the end of fifty-six years from the date copyright was originally secured, or beginning on January 1, 1978, whichever is later.

(4) The termination shall be effected by serving an advance notice in writing upon the grantee or the grantee's successor in title. In the case of a grant executed by a person or persons other than the author, the notice shall be signed by all of those entitled to terminate the grant under clause (1) of this subsection, or by their duly authorized agents. In the case of a grant executed by one or more of the authors of the work, the notice as to any one author's share shall be signed by that author or his or her duly authorized agent or, if that author is dead, by the number and proportion of the owners of his or her termination interest required under clauses (1) and (2) of this subsection, or by their duly authorized agents.

(A) The notice shall state the effective date of the termination, which shall fall within the five-year period specified by clause (3) of this subsection, or, in the case of a termination under subsection (d), within the five-year period specified by subsection (d)(2), and the notice shall be served not less than two or more than ten years before that date. A copy of the notice shall be recorded in the Copyright Office before the effective date of termination, as a condition to its taking effect.

(B) The notice shall comply, in form, content, and manner of service, with requirements that the Register of Copyrights shall prescribe by regulation.

(5) Termination of the grant may be effected notwithstanding any agreement to the contrary, including an agreement to make a will or to make any future grant.

(6) In the case of a grant executed by a person or persons other than the author, all rights under this title that were covered by the terminated grant revert, upon the effective date of termination, to all of those entitled to terminate the grant under clause (1) of this subsection. In the case of a grant executed by one or more of the authors of the work, all of a particular author's rights under this title that were covered by the terminated grant revert, upon the effective date of termination, to that author or, if that author is dead, to the persons owning his or her termination interest under clause (2) of this subsection, including those owners who did not join in signing the notice of termination under clause (4) of this subsection. In all cases the reversion of rights is subject to the following limitations:

(A) A derivative work prepared under authority of the grant before its termination may continue to be utilized under the terms of the grant after its termination, but this privilege does not extend to the preparation after the termination of other derivative works based upon the copyrighted work covered by the terminated grant.

(B) The future rights that will revert upon termination of the grant become vested on the date the notice of termination has been served as provided by clause (4) of this subsection.

(C) Where the author's rights revert to two or more persons under clause (2) of this subsection, they shall vest in those persons in the proportionate shares provided by that clause. In such a case, and subject to the provisions of subclause (D) of this clause, a further grant, or agreement to make a further grant, of a particular author's share with respect to any right covered by a terminated grant is valid only if it is signed by the same number and proportion of the owners, in whom the right has vested under this clause, as are required to terminate the grant under clause (2) of this subsection. Such further grant or agreement is effective with respect to all of the persons in whom the right it covers has vested under this subclause, including those who did not join in signing it. If any person dies after rights under a terminated grant have vested in him or her, that person's legal representatives, legatees, or heirs at law represent him or her for purposes of this subclause.

(D) A further grant, or agreement to make a further grant, of any right covered by a terminated grant is valid only if it is made after the effective date of the termination. As an exception, however, an agreement for such a further grant may be made between the author or any of the persons provided by the first sentence of clause (6) of this subsection, or between the persons provided by subclause (C) of this clause, and the original grantee or such grantee's successor in title, after the notice of termination has been served as provided by clause (4) of this subsection.

(E) Termination of a grant under this subsection affects only those rights covered by the grant that arise under this title, and in no way affects rights arising under any other Federal, State, or foreign laws.

(F) Unless and until termination is effected under this subsection, the grant, if it does not provide otherwise, continues in effect for the remainder of the extended renewal term.

(d) Termination Rights Provided in Subsection (c) Which Have Expired on or before the Effective Date of the Sonny Bono Copyright Term Extension Act.—In the case of any copyright other than a work made for hire, subsisting in its renewal term on the effective date of the Sonny Bono Copyright Term Extension Act[9] for which the termination right provided in subsection (c) has expired by such date, where the author or owner of the termination right has not previously exercised such termination right, the exclusive or nonexclusive grant of a transfer or license of the renewal copyright or any right under it, executed before January 1, 1978, by any of the persons designated in subsection (a)(1)(C) of this section, other than by will, is subject to termination under the following conditions:

(1) The conditions specified in subsections (c) (1), (2), (4), (5), and (6) of this section apply to terminations of the last 20 years of copyright term as provided by the amendments made by the Sonny Bono Copyright Term Extension Act.

(2) Termination of the grant may be effected at any time during a period of 5 years beginning at the end of 75 years from the date copyright was originally secured.

§305 · Duration of copyright: Terminal date

All terms of copyright provided by sections 302 through 304 run to the end of the calendar year in which they would otherwise expire.

Chapter 3 · Notes

1. Private Law 92-60, 85 Stat. 857, effective December 15, 1971, states that:

[A]ny provision of law to the contrary notwithstanding, copyright is hereby granted to the trustees under the will of Mary Baker Eddy, their successors, and assigns, in the work "Science and Health with Key to the Scriptures" (entitled also in some editions "Science and Health" or "Science and Health; with a Key to the Scriptures"), by Mary Baker Eddy, including all editions thereof in English and translation heretofore published, or hereafter published by or on behalf of said trustees, their successors or assigns, for a term of seventy-five years from the effective date of this Act or from the date of first publication, whichever is later.

But *cf. United Christian Scientists* v. *Christian Science Board of Directors, First Church of Christ, Scientist*, 829 F.2d 1152, 4 USPQ2d 1177 (D.C. Cir. 1987) (holding Priv. L. 92-60, 85 Stat. 857, to be unconstitutional because it violates the Establishment Clause).

2. The Berne Convention Implementation Act of 1988 amended section 301 by adding at the end thereof subsection (e). Pub. L. No. 100-568, 102 Stat. 2853, 2857. In 1990, the Architectural Works Copyright Protection Act amended section 301(b) by adding at the end thereof paragraph (4). Pub. L. No. 101-650, 104 Stat. 5133, 5134. The Visual Artists Rights Act of 1990 amended section 301 by adding at the end thereof subsection (f). Pub. L. No. 101-650, 104 Stat. 5089, 5131. In 1998, the Sonny Bono Copyright Term Extension Act amended section 301 by changing "February 15, 2047" to "February 15, 2067" each place it appeared in subsection (c). Pub. L. No. 105-298, 112 Stat. 2827.

3. The Visual Artists Rights Act of 1990, which added subsection (f), states, "Subject to subsection (b) and except as provided in subsection (c), this title and the amendments made by this title take effect 6 months after the date of the enactment of this Act," that is, 6 months after December 1, 1990. Pub. L. No. 101-650, 104 Stat. 5089, 5132. See also note 39, chapter 1.

4. In 1998, the Sonny Bono Copyright Term Extension Act amended section 302 by substituting "70" for "fifty," "95" for "seventy-five," and "120" for "one hundred" each place they appeared. Pub. L. No. 105-298, 112 Stat. 2827. This change was effective October 27, 1998. *Id.*

5. In 1997, section 303 was amended by adding subsection (b). Pub. L. No. 105-80, 111 Stat. 1529, 1534. In 1998, the Sonny Bono Copyright Term Extension Act amended section 303 by substituting "December 31, 2047" for "December 31, 2027." Pub. L. No. 105-298, 112 Stat. 2827. The Copyright Cleanup, Clarification, and Corrections Act of 2010 amended section 303(b) to substitute "any musical work, dramatic work, or literary work" for "the musical work." Pub. L. No. 111-295, 124 Stat. 3180, 3181.

6. The Copyright Renewal Act of 1992 amended section 304 by substituting a new subsection (a) and by making a conforming amendment in the matter preceding paragraph (1) of subsection (c). Pub. L. No. 102-307, 106 Stat. 264. The Act, as amended by the Sonny Bono Copyright Term Extension Act, states that the renewal and extension of a copyright for a further term of 67 years "shall have the same effect with respect to any grant, before the effective date of the Sonny Bono Copyright Term Extension Act [October 27, 1998], of a transfer or license of the further term as did the renewal of a copyright before the effective date of the Sonny Bono Copyright Term Extension Act [October 27, 1998] under the law in effect at the time of such grant." The Act also states that the 1992 amendments "shall apply only to those copyrights secured between January 1, 1964, and December 31, 1977. Copyrights secured before January 1, 1964, shall be governed by the provisions of section 304(a) of title 17, United States Code, as in effect on the day before … [enactment on June 26, 1992], except each reference to forty-seven years in such provisions shall be deemed to be 67 years." Pub. L. No. 102-307, 106 Stat. 264, 266, as amended by the Sonny Bono Copyright Term Extension Act, Pub. L. No. 105-298, 112 Stat. 2827, 2828.

In 1998, the Sonny Bono Copyright Term Extension Act amended section 304 by substituting "67" for "47" wherever it appeared in subsection (a), by substituting a new subsection (b), and by adding subsection (d) at the end thereof. Pub. L. No. 105-298, 112 Stat. 2827. That Act also amended subsection 304(c) by deleting "by his widow or her widower and his or her children or grandchildren" from the first sentence of paragraph (2), by adding subparagraph (D) at the end of paragraph (2) and by inserting "or, in the case of a termination under subsection (d), within the five-year period specified by subsection (d)(2)," into the first sentence of subparagraph (4)(A). *Id.*

7. In 1998, the Sonny Bono Copyright Term Extension Act amendment to subsection 304(b) completely deleted the previous language that was originally part of the 1976 Copyright Act. Pub. L. No. 105-298, 112 Stat. 2827. That earlier statutory language continues to be relevant for calculating the term of protection for copyrights commencing between September 19, 1906, and December 31, 1949. The 1976 Copyright Act extended the terms for those copyrights by 20 years, provided they were in their renewal term between December 31, 1976, and December 31, 1977. The deleted language states:

The duration of any copyright, the renewal term of which is subsisting at any time between December 31, 1976, and December 31, 1977, inclusive, or for which renewal registration is made between December 31, 1976, and December 31, 1977, inclusive, is extended to endure for a term of seventy-five years from the date copyright was originally secured.

The effective date of this provision was October 19, 1976. That effective date provision is contained in Appendix A, herein, as section 102 of the Transitional and Supplementary Provisions of the Copyright Act of 1976. Copyright Act of 1976, Pub. L. No. 94-553, 90 Stat. 2541, 2598.

In addition, prior to the 1976 Copyright Act, Congress enacted a series of nine interim extensions for works whose copyright protection began between September 19, 1906, and December 31, 1918, if they were in their renewal terms. Without these interim extensions, copyrights commencing during that time period would have otherwise expired after 56 years, at the end of their renewal terms, between September 19, 1962, and December 31, 1976. The nine Acts authorizing the interim extensions are as follows, in chronological order:

Pub. L. No. 87-668, 76 Stat. 555 (extending copyrights from September 19, 1962, to December 31, 1965)
Pub. L. No. 89-142, 79 Stat. 581 (extending copyrights to December 31, 1967)
Pub. L. No. 90-141, 81 Stat. 464 (extending copyrights to December 31, 1968)
Pub. L. No. 90-416, 82 Stat. 397 (extending copyrights to December 31, 1969)
Pub. L. No. 91-147, 83 Stat. 360 (extending copyrights to December 31, 1970)
Pub. L. No. 91-555, 84 Stat. 1441 (extending copyrights to December 31, 1971)
Pub. L. No. 92-170, 85 Stat. 490 (extending copyrights to December 31, 1972)
Pub. L. No. 92-566, 86 Stat. 1181 (extending copyrights to December 31, 1974)
Pub. L. No. 93-573, 88 Stat. 1873 (extending copyrights to December 31, 1976)

8. The effective date of the Sonny Bono Copyright Term Extension Act is October 27, 1998.
9. See note 8, *supra*.

Chapter 4

Copyright Notice, Deposit, and Registration

§401 · Notice of copyright: Visually perceptible copies[2]

(a) General Provisions.—Whenever a work protected under this title is published in the United States or elsewhere by authority of the copyright owner, a notice of copyright as provided by this section may be placed on publicly distributed copies from which the work can be visually perceived, either directly or with the aid of a machine or device.

(b) Form of Notice.—If a notice appears on the copies, it shall consist of the following three elements:

(1) the symbol © (the letter C in a circle), or the word "Copyright", or the abbreviation "Copr."; and

(2) the year of first publication of the work; in the case of compilations or derivative works incorporating previously published material, the year date of first publication of the compilation or derivative work is sufficient. The year date may be omitted where a pictorial, graphic, or sculptural work, with accompanying text matter, if any, is reproduced in or on greeting cards, postcards, stationery, jewelry, dolls, toys, or any useful articles; and

(3) the name of the owner of copyright in the work, or an abbreviation by which the name can be recognized, or a generally known alternative designation of the owner.

(c) Position of Notice.—The notice shall be affixed to the copies in such manner and location as to give reasonable notice of the claim of copyright. The Register of Copyrights shall prescribe by regulation, as examples, specific methods of affixation and positions of the notice on various types of works that will satisfy this requirement, but these specifications shall not be considered exhaustive.

(d) Evidentiary Weight of Notice.—If a notice of copyright in the form and position specified by this section appears on the published copy or copies to which a defendant in a copyright infringement suit had access, then no weight shall be given to such a defendant's interposition of a defense based on innocent infringement in mitigation of actual or statutory damages, except as provided in the last sentence of section 504(c)(2).

§402 · Notice of copyright: Phonorecords of sound recordings[3]

(a) General Provisions.—Whenever a sound recording protected under this title is published in the United States or elsewhere by authority of the copyright owner, a notice of copyright as provided by this section may be placed on publicly distributed phonorecords of the sound recording.

(b) Form of Notice.—If a notice appears on the phonorecords, it shall consist of the following three elements:

(1) the symbol ℗ (the letter P in a circle); and

(2) the year of first publication of the sound recording; and

(3) the name of the owner of copyright in the sound recording, or an abbreviation by which the name can be recognized, or a generally known alternative designation of the owner; if the producer of the sound recording is named on the phonorecord labels or containers, and if no other name appears in conjunction with the notice, the producer's name shall be considered a part of the notice.

(c) Position of Notice.—The notice shall be placed on the surface of the phonorecord, or on the phonorecord label or container, in such manner and location as to give reasonable notice of the claim of copyright.

(d) Evidentiary Weight of Notice.—If a notice of copyright in the form and position specified by this section appears on the published phonorecord or phonorecords to which a defendant in a copyright infringement suit had access, then no weight shall be given to such a defendant's interposition of a defense based on innocent infringement in mitigation of actual or statutory damages, except as provided in the last sentence of section 504(c)(2).

§403 · Notice of copyright: Publications incorporating United States Government works[4]

Sections 401(d) and 402(d) shall not apply to a work published in copies or phonorecords consisting predominantly of one or more works of the United States Government unless the notice of copyright appearing on the published copies or phonorecords to which a defendant in the copyright infringement suit had access includes a statement identifying, either affirmatively or negatively, those portions of the copies or phonorecords embodying any work or works protected under this title.

§404 · Notice of copyright: Contributions to collective works[5]

(a) A separate contribution to a collective work may bear its own notice of copyright, as provided by sections 401 through 403. However, a single notice applicable to the collective work as a whole is sufficient to invoke the provisions of section 401(d) or 402(d), as applicable with respect to the separate contributions it contains (not including advertisements inserted on behalf of persons other than the owner of copyright in the collective work), regardless of the ownership of copyright in the contributions and whether or not they have been previously published.

(b) With respect to copies and phonorecords publicly distributed by authority of the copyright owner before the effective date of the Berne Convention

Implementation Act of 1988, where the person named in a single notice applicable to a collective work as a whole is not the owner of copyright in a separate contribution that does not bear its own notice, the case is governed by the provisions of section 406(a).

§405 · Notice of copyright: Omission of notice on certain copies and phonorecords[6]

(a) Effect of Omission on Copyright.—With respect to copies and phonorecords publicly distributed by authority of the copyright owner before the effective date of the Berne Convention Implementation Act of 1988, the omission of the copyright notice described in sections 401 through 403 from copies or phonorecords publicly distributed by authority of the copyright owner does not invalidate the copyright in a work if—

(1) the notice has been omitted from no more than a relatively small number of copies or phonorecords distributed to the public; or

(2) registration for the work has been made before or is made within five years after the publication without notice, and a reasonable effort is made to add notice to all copies or phonorecords that are distributed to the public in the United States after the omission has been discovered; or

(3) the notice has been omitted in violation of an express requirement in writing that, as a condition of the copyright owner's authorization of the public distribution of copies or phonorecords, they bear the prescribed notice.

(b) Effect of Omission on Innocent Infringers.—Any person who innocently infringes a copyright, in reliance upon an authorized copy or phonorecord from which the copyright notice has been omitted and which was publicly distributed by authority of the copyright owner before the effective date of the Berne Convention Implementation Act of 1988, incurs no liability for actual or statutory damages under section 504 for any infringing acts committed before receiving actual notice that registration for the work has been made under section 408, if such person proves that he or she was misled by the omission of notice. In a suit for infringement in such a case the court may allow or disallow recovery of any of the infringer's profits attributable to the infringement, and may enjoin the continuation of the infringing undertaking or may require, as a condition for permitting the continuation of the infringing undertaking, that the infringer pay the copyright owner a reasonable license fee in an amount and on terms fixed by the court.

(c) Removal of Notice.—Protection under this title is not affected by the removal, destruction, or obliteration of the notice, without the authorization of the copyright owner, from any publicly distributed copies or phonorecords.

§406 · Notice of copyright: Error in name or date on certain copies and phonorecords[7]

(a) Error in Name.—With respect to copies and phonorecords publicly distributed by authority of the copyright owner before the effective date of the Berne Convention Implementation Act of 1988, where the person named in the copyright notice on copies or phonorecords publicly distributed by authority of the copyright owner is not the owner of copyright, the validity and ownership of the copyright are not affected. In such a case, however, any person who innocently begins an undertaking that infringes the copyright has a complete defense to any action for such infringement if such person proves that he or she was misled by the notice and began the undertaking in good faith under a purported transfer or license from the person named therein, unless before the undertaking was begun—

(1) registration for the work had been made in the name of the owner of copyright; or

(2) a document executed by the person named in the notice and showing the ownership of the copyright had been recorded.

The person named in the notice is liable to account to the copyright owner for all receipts from transfers or licenses purportedly made under the copyright by the person named in the notice.

(b) Error in Date.—When the year date in the notice on copies or phonorecords distributed before the effective date of the Berne Convention Implementation Act of 1988 by authority of the copyright owner is earlier than the year in which publication first occurred, any period computed from the year of first publication under section 302 is to be computed from the year in the notice. Where the year date is more than one year later than the year in which publication first occurred, the work is considered to have been published without any notice and is governed by the provisions of section 405.

(c) Omission of Name or Date.—Where copies or phonorecords publicly distributed before the effective date of the Berne Convention Implementation Act of 1988 by authority of the copyright owner contain no name or no date that could reasonably be considered a part of the notice, the work is considered to have been published without any notice and is governed by the provisions of section 405 as in effect on the day before the effective date of the Berne Convention Implementation Act of 1988.

§407 · Deposit of copies or phonorecords for Library of Congress[8]

(a) Except as provided by subsection (c), and subject to the provisions of subsection (e), the owner of copyright or of the exclusive right of publication in a work published in the United States shall deposit, within three months after the date of such publication—

(1) two complete copies of the best edition; or

(2) if the work is a sound recording, two complete phonorecords of the best edition, together with any printed or other visually perceptible material published with such phonorecords.

Neither the deposit requirements of this subsection nor the acquisition provisions of subsection (e) are conditions of copyright protection.

(b) The required copies or phonorecords shall be deposited in the Copyright Office for the use or disposition of the Library of Congress. The Register of Copyrights shall, when requested by the depositor and upon payment of the fee prescribed by section 708, issue a receipt for the deposit.

(c) The Register of Copyrights may by regulation exempt any categories of material from the deposit requirements of this section, or require deposit of only one copy or phonorecord with respect to any categories. Such regulations shall provide either for complete exemption from the deposit requirements of this section, or for alternative forms of deposit aimed at providing a satisfactory archival record of a work without imposing practical or financial hardships on the depositor, where the individual author is the owner of copyright in a pictorial, graphic, or sculptural work and (i) less than five copies of the work have been published, or (ii) the work has been published in a limited edition consisting of numbered copies, the monetary value of which would make the mandatory deposit of two copies of the best edition of the work burdensome, unfair, or unreasonable.

(d) At any time after publication of a work as provided by subsection (a), the Register of Copyrights may make written demand for the required deposit on any of the persons obligated to make the deposit under subsection (a). Unless deposit is made within three months after the demand is received, the person or persons on whom the demand was made are liable—

(1) to a fine of not more than $250 for each work; and

(2) to pay into a specially designated fund in the Library of Congress the total retail price of the copies or phonorecords demanded, or, if no retail price has been fixed, the reasonable cost to the Library of Congress of acquiring them; and

(3) to pay a fine of $2,500, in addition to any fine or liability imposed under clauses (1) and (2), if such person willfully or repeatedly fails or refuses to comply with such a demand.

(e) With respect to transmission programs that have been fixed and transmitted to the public in the United States but have not been published, the Register of Copyrights shall, after consulting with the Librarian of Congress and other interested organizations and officials, establish regulations governing the acquisition, through deposit or otherwise, of copies or phonorecords of such programs for the collections of the Library of Congress.

(1) The Librarian of Congress shall be permitted, under the standards and conditions set forth in such regulations, to make a fixation of a transmission program directly from a transmission to the public, and to reproduce one copy or phonorecord from such fixation for archival purposes.

(2) Such regulations shall also provide standards and procedures by which the Register of Copyrights may make written demand, upon the owner of the right of transmission in the United States, for the deposit of a copy or phonorecord of a specific transmission program. Such deposit may, at the option of the owner of the right of transmission in the United States, be accomplished by gift, by loan for purposes of reproduction, or by sale at a price not to exceed the cost of reproducing and supplying the copy or phonorecord. The regulations established under this clause shall provide reasonable periods of not less than three months for compliance with a demand, and shall allow for extensions of such periods and adjustments in the scope of the demand or the methods for fulfilling it, as reasonably warranted by the circumstances. Willful failure or refusal to comply with the conditions prescribed by such regulations shall subject the owner of the right of transmission in the United States to liability for an amount, not to exceed the cost of reproducing and supplying the copy or phonorecord in question, to be paid into a specially designated fund in the Library of Congress.

(3) Nothing in this subsection shall be construed to require the making or retention, for purposes of deposit, of any copy or phonorecord of an unpublished transmission program, the transmission of which occurs before the receipt of a specific written demand as provided by clause (2).

(4) No activity undertaken in compliance with regulations prescribed under clauses (1) and (2) of this subsection shall result in liability if intended solely to assist in the acquisition of copies or phonorecords under this subsection.

§408 · Copyright registration in general[9]

(a) Registration Permissive.—At any time during the subsistence of the first term of copyright in any published or unpublished work in which the copyright was secured before January 1, 1978, and during the subsistence of any copyright secured on or after that date, the owner of copyright or of any exclusive right in the work may obtain registration of the copyright claim by delivering to the Copyright Office the deposit specified by this section, together with the application and fee specified by sections 409 and 708. Such registration is not a condition of copyright protection.

(b) Deposit for Copyright Registration.—Except as provided by subsection (c), the material deposited for registration shall include—

(1) in the case of an unpublished work, one complete copy or phonorecord;

(2) in the case of a published work, two complete copies or phonorecords of the best edition;

(3) in the case of a work first published outside the United States, one complete copy or phonorecord as so published;

(4) in the case of a contribution to a collective work, one complete copy or phonorecord of the best edition of the collective work.

Copies or phonorecords deposited for the Library of Congress under section 407 may be used to satisfy the deposit provisions of this section, if they are accompanied by the prescribed application and fee, and by any additional identifying material that the Register may, by regulation, require. The Register shall also prescribe regulations establishing requirements under which copies or phonorecords acquired for the Library of Congress under subsection (e) of section 407, otherwise than by deposit, may be used to satisfy the deposit provisions of this section.

(c) Administrative Classification and Optional Deposit—

(1) The Register of Copyrights is authorized to specify by regulation the administrative classes into which works are to be placed for purposes of deposit and registration, and the nature of the copies or phonorecords to be deposited in the various classes specified. The regulations may require or permit, for particular classes, the deposit of identifying material instead of copies or phonorecords, the deposit of only one copy or phonorecord where two would normally be required, or a single registration for a group of related works. This administrative classification of works has no significance with respect to the subject matter of copyright or the exclusive rights provided by this title.

(2) Without prejudice to the general authority provided under clause (1), the Register of Copyrights shall establish regulations specifically permitting a single registration for a group of works by the same individual author, all first published as contributions to periodicals, including newspapers, within a twelve-month period, on the basis of a single deposit, application, and registration fee, under the following conditions—

(A) if the deposit consists of one copy of the entire issue of the periodical, or of the entire section in the case of a newspaper, in which each contribution was first published; and

(B) if the application identifies each work separately, including the periodical containing it and its date of first publication.

(3) As an alternative to separate renewal registrations under subsection (a) of section 304, a single renewal registration may be made for a group of works by the same individual author, all first published as contributions to periodicals, including newspapers, upon the filing of a single application and fee, under all of the following conditions:

(A) the renewal claimant or claimants, and the basis of claim or claims under section 304(a), is the same for each of the works; and

(B) the works were all copyrighted upon their first publication, either through separate copyright notice and registration or by virtue of a general copyright notice in the periodical issue as a whole; and

(C) the renewal application and fee are received not more than twenty-eight or less than twenty-seven years after the thirty-first day of December of the calendar year in which all of the works were first published; and

(D) the renewal application identifies each work separately, including the periodical containing it and its date of first publication.

(d) CORRECTIONS AND AMPLIFICATIONS.—The Register may also establish, by regulation, formal procedures for the filing of an application for supplementary registration, to correct an error in a copyright registration or to amplify the information given in a registration. Such application shall be accompanied by the fee provided by section 708, and shall clearly identify the registration to be corrected or amplified. The information contained in a supplementary registration augments but does not supersede that contained in the earlier registration.

(e) PUBLISHED EDITION OF PREVIOUSLY REGISTERED WORK.—Registration for the first published edition of a work previously registered in unpublished form may be made even though the work as published is substantially the same as the unpublished version.

(f) PREREGISTRATION OF WORKS BEING PREPARED FOR COMMERCIAL DISTRIBUTION.—

(1) RULEMAKING.—Not later than 180 days after the date of enactment of this subsection, the Register of Copyrights shall issue regulations to establish procedures for preregistration of a work that is being prepared for commercial distribution and has not been published.

(2) CLASS OF WORKS.—The regulations established under paragraph (1) shall permit preregistration for any work that is in a class of works that the Register determines has had a history of infringement prior to authorized commercial distribution.

(3) APPLICATION FOR REGISTRATION.—Not later than 3 months after the first publication of a work preregistered under this subsection, the applicant shall submit to the Copyright Office–

(A) an application for registration of the work;

(B) a deposit; and

(C) the applicable fee.

(4) EFFECT OF UNTIMELY APPLICATION.—An action under this chapter for infringement of a work preregistered under this subsection, in a case in which the infringement commenced no later than 2 months after the first publication of the work, shall be dismissed if the items described in paragraph (3) are not submitted to the Copyright Office in proper form within the earlier of—

(A) 3 months after the first publication of the work; or

(B) 1 month after the copyright owner has learned of the infringement.

§409 · Application for copyright registration[10]

The application for copyright registration shall be made on a form prescribed by the Register of Copyrights and shall include—

(1) the name and address of the copyright claimant;

(2) in the case of a work other than an anonymous or pseudonymous work, the name and nationality or domicile of the author or authors, and, if one or more of the authors is dead, the dates of their deaths;

(3) if the work is anonymous or pseudonymous, the nationality or domicile of the author or authors;

(4) in the case of a work made for hire, a statement to this effect;

(5) if the copyright claimant is not the author, a brief statement of how the claimant obtained ownership of the copyright;

(6) the title of the work, together with any previous or alternative titles under which the work can be identified;

(7) the year in which creation of the work was completed;

(8) if the work has been published, the date and nation of its first publication;

(9) in the case of a compilation or derivative work, an identification of any preexisting work or works that it is based on or incorporates, and a brief, general statement of the additional material covered by the copyright claim being registered; and

(10) any other information regarded by the Register of Copyrights as bearing upon the preparation or identification of the work or the existence, ownership, or duration of the copyright.

If an application is submitted for the renewed and extended term provided for in section 304(a)(3)(A) and an original term registration has not been made, the Register may request information with respect to the existence, ownership, or duration of the copyright for the original term.

§410 · Registration of claim and issuance of certificate

(a) When, after examination, the Register of Copyrights determines that, in accordance with the provisions of this title, the material deposited constitutes copyrightable subject matter and that the other legal and formal requirements of this title have been met, the Register shall register the claim and issue to the applicant a certificate of registration under the seal of the Copyright Office. The certificate shall contain the information given in the application, together with the number and effective date of the registration.

(b) In any case in which the Register of Copyrights determines that, in accordance with the provisions of this title, the material deposited does not constitute copyrightable subject matter or that the claim is invalid for any other reason, the

Register shall refuse registration and shall notify the applicant in writing of the reasons for such refusal.

(c) In any judicial proceedings the certificate of a registration made before or within five years after first publication of the work shall constitute prima facie evidence of the validity of the copyright and of the facts stated in the certificate. The evidentiary weight to be accorded the certificate of a registration made thereafter shall be within the discretion of the court.

(d) The effective date of a copyright registration is the day on which an application, deposit, and fee, which are later determined by the Register of Copyrights or by a court of competent jurisdiction to be acceptable for registration, have all been received in the Copyright Office.

§411 · Registration and civil infringement actions[11]

(a) Except for an action brought for a violation of the rights of the author under section 106A(a), and subject to the provisions of subsection (b), no civil action for infringement of the copyright in any United States work shall be instituted until preregistration or registration of the copyright claim has been made in accordance with this title. In any case, however, where the deposit, application, and fee required for registration have been delivered to the Copyright Office in proper form and registration has been refused, the applicant is entitled to institute a civil action for infringement if notice thereof, with a copy of the complaint, is served on the Register of Copyrights. The Register may, at his or her option, become a party to the action with respect to the issue of registrability of the copyright claim by entering an appearance within sixty days after such service, but the Register's failure to become a party shall not deprive the court of jurisdiction to determine that issue.

(b)(1) A certificate of registration satisfies the requirements of this section and section 412, regardless of whether the certificate contains any inaccurate information, unless—

(A) the inaccurate information was included on the application for copyright registration with knowledge that it was inaccurate; and

(B) the inaccuracy of the information, if known, would have caused the Register of Copyrights to refuse registration.

(2) In any case in which inaccurate information described under paragraph (1) is alleged, the court shall request the Register of Copyrights to advise the court whether the inaccurate information, if known, would have caused the Register of Copyrights to refuse registration.

(3) Nothing in this subsection shall affect any rights, obligations, or requirements of a person related to information contained in a registration certificate,

except for the institution of and remedies in infringement actions under this section and section 412.

(c) In the case of a work consisting of sounds, images, or both, the first fixation of which is made simultaneously with its transmission, the copyright owner may, either before or after such fixation takes place, institute an action for infringement under section 501, fully subject to the remedies provided by sections 502 through 505 and section 510, if, in accordance with requirements that the Register of Copyrights shall prescribe by regulation, the copyright owner—

(1) serves notice upon the infringer, not less than 48 hours before such fixation, identifying the work and the specific time and source of its first transmission, and declaring an intention to secure copyright in the work; and

(2) makes registration for the work, if required by subsection (a), within three months after its first transmission.

§ 412 · Registration as prerequisite to certain remedies for infringement[12]

In any action under this title, other than an action brought for a violation of the rights of the author under section 106A(a), an action for infringement of the copyright of a work that has been preregistered under section 408(f) before the commencement of the infringement and that has an effective date of registration not later than the earlier of 3 months after the first publication of the work or 1 month after the copyright owner has learned of the infringement, or an action instituted under section 411(c), no award of statutory damages or of attorney's fees, as provided by sections 504 and 505, shall be made for—

(1) any infringement of copyright in an unpublished work commenced before the effective date of its registration; or

(2) any infringement of copyright commenced after first publication of the work and before the effective date of its registration, unless such registration is made within three months after the first publication of the work.

Chapter 4 · Notes

1. The Prioritizing Resources and Organization for Intellectual Property Act of 2008 amended the title for section 411 by adding "civil" to it, so that the new title is "Registration and civil infringement actions." Pub. L. No. 110-403, 122 Stat. 4256, 4258.

2. The Berne Convention Implementation Act of 1988 amended section 401 as follows: 1) in subsection (a), by changing the heading to "General Provisions" and by inserting "may be placed on" in lieu of "shall be placed on all"; 2) in subsection (b), by inserting "If a notice

appears on the copies, it" in lieu of "The notice appearing on the copies"; and 3) by adding subsection (d). Pub. L. No. 100-568, 102 Stat. 2853, 2857.

3. The Berne Convention Implementation Act of 1988 amended section 402 as follows: 1) in subsection (a), by changing the heading to "General Provisions" and by inserting "may be placed on" in lieu of "shall be placed on all"; 2) in subsection (b), by inserting "If a notice appears on the phonorecords, it" in lieu of "The notice appearing on the phonorecords"; and 3) by adding subsection (d). Pub. L. No. 100-568, 102 Stat. 2853, 2857.

4. The Berne Convention Implementation Act of 1988 amended section 403 in its entirety. Pub. L. No. 100-568, 102 Stat. 2853, 2858.

5. The Berne Convention Implementation Act of 1988 amended section 404 as follows: 1) in the second sentence of subsection (a), by inserting "to invoke the provisions of section 401(d) or 402(d), as applicable" in lieu of "to satisfy the requirements of sections 401 through 403" and 2) in subsection (b), by inserting "With respect to copies and phonorecords publicly distributed by authority of the copyright owner before the effective date of the Berne Convention Implementation Act of 1988," at the beginning of the sentence. Pub. L. No. 100-568, 102 Stat. 2853, 2858.

6. The Berne Convention Implementation Act of 1988 amended section 405 as follows: 1) in subsection (a), by inserting "With respect to copies and phonorecords publicly distributed by authority of the copyright owner before the effective date of the Berne Convention Implementation Act of 1988, the omission of the copyright notice described in" at the beginning of the first sentence, in lieu of "The omission of the copyright notice prescribed by"; 2) in subsection (b), by inserting after "omitted," in the first sentence, "and which was publicly distributed by authority of the copyright owner before the effective date of the Berne Convention Implementation Act of 1988"; and 3) by amending the section heading to add "on certain copies and phonorecords" at the end thereof. Pub. L. No. 100-568, 102 Stat. 2853, 2858.

7. The Berne Convention Implementation Act of 1988 amended section 406 as follows: 1) in subsection (a), by inserting "With respect to copies and phonorecords publicly distributed by authority of the copyright owner before the effective date of the Berne Convention Implementation Act of 1988," at the beginning of the first sentence; 2) in subsection (b), by inserting "before the effective date of the Berne Convention Implementation Act of 1988" after "distributed"; 3) in subsection (c), by inserting "before the effective date of the Berne Convention Implementation Act of 1988" after "publicly distributed" and by inserting "as in effect on the day before the effective date of the Berne Convention Implementation Act of 1988" after "405"; and 4) by amending the section heading to add "on certain copies and phonorecords" at the end thereof. Pub. L. No. 100-568, 102 Stat. 2853, 2858.

8. The Berne Convention Implementation Act of 1988 amended section 407 by striking out the words "with notice of copyright" in subsection (a). Pub. L. No. 100-568, 102 Stat. 2853, 2859.

9. The Berne Convention Implementation Act of 1988 amended section 408 by deleting "Subject to the provisions of section 405(a)," at the beginning of the second sentence of subsection (a). Pub. L. No. 100-568, 102 Stat. 2853, 2859. That Act also amended section 408(c)(2) by inserting "the following conditions:" in lieu of "all of the following conditions" and by striking subparagraph (A) and by redesignating subparagraphs (B) and (C) as subparagraphs (A) and (B), respectively. *Id.* The Copyright Renewal Act of 1992 amended section 408 by

revising the first sentence of subsection (a), preceding the words "the owner of copyright or of any exclusive right." Pub. L. No. 102-307, 106 Stat. 264, 266.

The Artists' Rights and Theft Prevention Act of 2005 amended section 408 by adding a new subsection (f). Pub. L. No. 109-9, 119 Stat. 218, 221.

10. The Copyright Renewal Act of 1992 amended section 409 by adding the last sentence. Pub. L. No. 102-307, 106 Stat. 264, 266. The Copyright Cleanup, Clarification, and Corrections Act of 2010 amended section 409 to delete subsection (10) and redesignate subsection (11) as (10). Pub. L. No. 111-295, 124 Stat. 3180.

11. The Berne Convention Implementation Act of 1988 amended section 411 as follows: 1) in subsection (a), by inserting "Except for actions for infringement of copyright in Berne Convention works whose country of origin is not the United States, and" before "subject"; 2) in paragraph (b)(2), by inserting ", if required by subsection (a)," after "work"; and 3) by inserting "and infringement actions" in the heading, in lieu of "as prerequisite to infringement suit." Pub. L. No. 100-568, 102 Stat. 2853, 2859.

The Visual Artists Rights Act of 1990 amended section 411(a) by inserting "and an action brought for a violation of the rights of the author under section 106A(a)" after "United States." Pub. L. No. 101-650, 104 Stat. 5089, 5131. In 1997, section 411(b)(1) was amended in its entirety. Pub. L. No. 105-80, 111 Stat. 1529, 1532.

The WIPO Copyright and Performances and Phonograms Treaties Implementation Act of 1998 amended the first sentence in section 411(a) by deleting "actions for infringement of copyright in Berne Convention works whose country of origin is not the United and" and by inserting "United States" after "no action for infringement of the copyright in any." Pub. L. No. 105-304, 112 Stat. 2860, 2863.

The Artists' Rights and Theft Prevention Act of 2005 amended subsection 411(a) by inserting "preregistration" in the first sentence, after "shall be instituted until" in the first sentence. Pub. L. No. 109-9, 119 Stat. 218, 222.

The Prioritizing Resources and Organization for Intellectual Property Act of 2008 amended the title for section 411 by inserting "civil," so that the new title is "Registration and civil infringement actions." Pub. L. No. 110-403, 122 Stat. 4256, 4257. It also amended subsection (a) to insert "civil" before "action" in the first and second sentences. *Id.* It redesignated subsection (b) as subsection (c) and added a new subsection (b). *Id.* at 4257-58. The Act also amended the newly designated subsection (c) to remove the reference to section 509 (which was repealed). *Id.* at 4257-58.

12. The Visual Artists Rights Act of 1990 amended section 412 by inserting "an action brought for a violation of the rights of the author under section 106A(a) or" after "other than." Pub. L. No. 101-650, 104 Stat. 5089, 5131.

The Artists' Rights and Theft Prevention Act of 2005 amended subsection 412 by inserting the clause that follows "section 106A(a)," in the text preceding subparagraph (1). Pub. L. No. 109-9, 119 Stat. 218, 222.

The Prioritizing Resources and Organization for Intellectual Property Act of 2008 amended section 412 by making a conforming amendment to substitute "subsection 411(b)" for "subsection 411(c)." Pub. L. No. 110-403, 122 Stat. 4256, 4258.

Chapter 5

Copyright Infringement and Remedies

§501 · Infringement of copyright[3]

(a) Anyone who violates any of the exclusive rights of the copyright owner as provided by sections 106 through 122 or of the author as provided in section 106A(a), or who imports copies or phonorecords into the United States in violation of section 602, is an infringer of the copyright or right of the author, as the case may be. For purposes of this chapter (other than section 506), any reference to copyright shall be deemed to include the rights conferred by section 106A(a). As used in this subsection, the term "anyone" includes any State, any instrumentality of a State, and any officer or employee of a State or instrumentality of a State acting in his or her official capacity. Any State, and any such instrumentality, officer, or employee, shall be subject to the provisions of this title in the same manner and to the same extent as any nongovernmental entity.

(b) The legal or beneficial owner of an exclusive right under a copyright is entitled, subject to the requirements of section 411, to institute an action for any infringement of that particular right committed while he or she is the owner of it. The court may require such owner to serve written notice of the action with a copy of the complaint upon any person shown, by the records of the Copyright Office or otherwise, to have or claim an interest in the copyright, and shall require that such notice be served upon any person whose interest is likely to be affected by a decision in the case. The court may require the joinder, and shall permit the intervention, of any person having or claiming an interest in the copyright.

(c) For any secondary transmission by a cable system that embodies a performance or a display of a work which is actionable as an act of infringement under subsection (c) of section 111, a television broadcast station holding a copyright or other license to transmit or perform the same version of that work shall, for purposes of subsection (b) of this section, be treated as a legal or beneficial owner if such secondary transmission occurs within the local service area of that television station.

(d) For any secondary transmission by a cable system that is actionable as an act of infringement pursuant to section 111(c)(3), the following shall also have standing to sue: (i) the primary transmitter whose transmission has been altered by the cable system; and (ii) any broadcast station within whose local service area the secondary transmission occurs.

(e) With respect to any secondary transmission that is made by a satellite carrier of a performance or display of a work embodied in a primary transmission and is actionable as an act of infringement under section 119(a)(5), a network station holding a copyright or other license to transmit or perform the same version of that work shall, for purposes of subsection (b) of this section, be treated as a legal or beneficial owner if such secondary transmission occurs within the local service area of that station.

(f)(1) With respect to any secondary transmission that is made by a satellite carrier of a performance or display of a work embodied in a primary transmission and is actionable as an act of infringement under section 122, a television broadcast station holding a copyright or other license to transmit or perform the same version of that work shall, for purposes of subsection (b) of this section, be treated as a legal or beneficial owner if such secondary transmission occurs within the local market of that station.

(2) A television broadcast station may file a civil action against any satellite carrier that has refused to carry television broadcast signals, as required under section 122(a)(2), to enforce that television broadcast station's rights under section 338(a) of the Communications Act of 1934.

§502 · Remedies for infringement: Injunctions

(a) Any court having jurisdiction of a civil action arising under this title may, subject to the provisions of section 1498 of title 28, grant temporary and final injunctions on such terms as it may deem reasonable to prevent or restrain infringement of a copyright.

(b) Any such injunction may be served anywhere in the United States on the person enjoined; it shall be operative throughout the United States and shall be enforceable, by proceedings in contempt or otherwise, by any United States court having jurisdiction of that person. The clerk of the court granting the injunction shall, when requested by any other court in which enforcement of the injunction is sought, transmit promptly to the other court a certified copy of all the papers in the case on file in such clerk's office.

§503 · Remedies for infringement: Impounding and disposition of infringing articles[4]

(a)(1) At any time while an action under this title is pending, the court may order the impounding, on such terms as it may deem reasonable—

(A) of all copies or phonorecords claimed to have been made or used in violation of the exclusive right of the copyright owner;

(B) of all plates, molds, matrices, masters, tapes, film negatives, or other articles by means of which such copies or phonorecords may be reproduced; and

(C) of records documenting the manufacture, sale, or receipt of things involved in any such violation, provided that any records seized under this subparagraph shall be taken into the custody of the court.

(2) For impoundments of records ordered under paragraph (1)(C), the court shall enter an appropriate protective order with respect to discovery and use of any records or information that has been impounded. The protective order shall provide for appropriate procedures to ensure that confidential, private, proprietary, or privileged information contained in such records is not improperly disclosed or used.

(3) The relevant provisions of paragraphs (2) through (11) of section 34(d) of the Trademark Act (15 U.S.C. 1116(d)(2) through (11)) shall extend to any impoundment of records ordered under paragraph (1)(C) that is based upon an ex parte application, notwithstanding the provisions of rule 65 of the Federal Rules of Civil Procedure. Any references in paragraphs (2) through (11) of section 34(d) of the Trademark Act to section 32 of such Act shall be read as references to section 501 of this title, and references to use of a counterfeit mark in connection with the sale, offering for sale, or distribution of goods or services shall be read as references to infringement of a copyright.

(b) As part of a final judgment or decree, the court may order the destruction or other reasonable disposition of all copies or phonorecords found to have been made or used in violation of the copyright owner's exclusive rights, and of all plates, molds, matrices, masters, tapes, film negatives, or other articles by means of which such copies or phonorecords may be reproduced.

§504 · Remedies for infringement: Damages and profits[5]

(a) In General.—Except as otherwise provided by this title, an infringer of copyright is liable for either—

(1) the copyright owner's actual damages and any additional profits of the infringer, as provided by subsection (b); or

(2) statutory damages, as provided by subsection (c).

(b) Actual Damages and Profits.—The copyright owner is entitled to recover the actual damages suffered by him or her as a result of the infringement, and any profits of the infringer that are attributable to the infringement and are not taken into account in computing the actual damages. In establishing the infringer's profits, the copyright owner is required to present proof only of the infringer's gross revenue, and the infringer is required to prove his or her deductible expenses and the elements of profit attributable to factors other than the copyrighted work.

(c) Statutory Damages.—

(1) Except as provided by clause (2) of this subsection, the copyright owner may elect, at any time before final judgment is rendered, to recover, instead of actual damages and profits, an award of statutory damages for all infringements involved in the action, with respect to any one work, for which any one infringer is liable individually, or for which any two or more infringers are li-

able jointly and severally, in a sum of not less than $750 or more than $30,000 as the court considers just. For the purposes of this subsection, all the parts of a compilation or derivative work constitute one work.

(2) In a case where the copyright owner sustains the burden of proving, and the court finds, that infringement was committed willfully, the court in its discretion may increase the award of statutory damages to a sum of not more than $150,000. In a case where the infringer sustains the burden of proving, and the court finds, that such infringer was not aware and had no reason to believe that his or her acts constituted an infringement of copyright, the court in its discretion may reduce the award of statutory damages to a sum of not less than $200. The court shall remit statutory damages in any case where an infringer believed and had reasonable grounds for believing that his or her use of the copyrighted work was a fair use under section 107, if the infringer was: (i) an employee or agent of a nonprofit educational institution, library, or archives acting within the scope of his or her employment who, or such institution, library, or archives itself, which infringed by reproducing the work in copies or phonorecords; or (ii) a public broadcasting entity which or a person who, as a regular part of the nonprofit activities of a public broadcasting entity (as defined in section 118(f)) infringed by performing a published nondramatic literary work or by reproducing a transmission program embodying a performance of such a work.

(3) (A) In a case of infringement, it shall be a rebuttable presumption that the infringement was committed willfully for purposes of determining relief if the violator, or a person acting in concert with the violator, knowingly provided or knowingly caused to be provided materially false contact information to a domain name registrar, domain name registry, or other domain name registration authority in registering, maintaining, or renewing a domain name used in connection with the infringement.

(B) Nothing in this paragraph limits what may be considered willful infringement under this subsection.

(C) For purposes of this paragraph, the term "domain name" has the meaning given that term in section 45 of the Act entitled "An Act to provide for the registration and protection of trademarks used in commerce, to carry out the provisions of certain international conventions, and for other purposes" approved July 5, 1946 (commonly referred to as the "Trademark Act of 1946"; 15 U.S.C. 1127).

(d) Additional Damages in Certain Cases.—In any case in which the court finds that a defendant proprietor of an establishment who claims as a defense that its activities were exempt under section 110(5) did not have reasonable grounds to believe that its use of a copyrighted work was exempt under such section, the plaintiff shall be entitled to, in addition to any award of damages under this section, an additional award of two times the amount of the license fee that the proprietor of the establishment concerned should have paid the plaintiff for such use during the preceding period of up to 3 years.

§505 · Remedies for infringement: Costs and attorney's fees

In any civil action under this title, the court in its discretion may allow the recovery of full costs by or against any party other than the United States or an officer thereof. Except as otherwise provided by this title, the court may also award a reasonable attorney's fee to the prevailing party as part of the costs.

§506 · Criminal offenses[6]

(a) Criminal Infringement.—

(1) In general.—Any person who willfully infringes a copyright shall be punished as provided under section 2319 of title 18, if the infringement was committed—

(A) for purposes of commercial advantage or private financial gain;

(B) by the reproduction or distribution, including by electronic means, during any 180-day period, of 1 or more copies or phonorecords of 1 or more copyrighted works, which have a total retail value of more than $1,000; or

(C) by the distribution of a work being prepared for commercial distribution, by making it available on a computer network accessible to members of the public, if such person knew or should have known that the work was intended for commercial distribution.

(2) Evidence.—For purposes of this subsection, evidence of reproduction or distribution of a copyrighted work, by itself, shall not be sufficient to establish willful infringement of a copyright.

(3) Definition.—In this subsection, the term "work being prepared for commercial distribution" means—

(A) a computer program, a musical work, a motion picture or other audiovisual work, or a sound recording, if, at the time of unauthorized distribution—

(i) the copyright owner has a reasonable expectation of commercial distribution; and

(ii) the copies or phonorecords of the work have not been commercially distributed; or

(B) a motion picture, if, at the time of unauthorized distribution, the motion picture—

(i) has been made available for viewing in a motion picture exhibition facility; and

(ii) has not been made available in copies for sale to the general public in the United States in a format intended to permit viewing outside a motion picture exhibition facility.

(b) Forfeiture, Destruction, and Restitution.—Forfeiture, destruction, and restitution relating to this section shall be subject to section 2323 of title 18, to the extent provided in that section, in addition to any other similar remedies provided by law.

(c) Fraudulent Copyright Notice.—Any person who, with fraudulent intent, places on any article a notice of copyright or words of the same purport that such person knows to be false, or who, with fraudulent intent, publicly distributes or imports for public distribution any article bearing such notice or words that such person knows to be false, shall be fined not more than $2,500.

(d) Fraudulent Removal of Copyright Notice.—Any person who, with fraudulent intent, removes or alters any notice of copyright appearing on a copy of a copyrighted work shall be fined not more than $2,500.

(e) False Representation.—Any person who knowingly makes a false representation of a material fact in the application for copyright registration provided for by section 409, or in any written statement filed in connection with the application, shall be fined not more than $2,500.

(f) Rights of Attribution and Integrity.—Nothing in this section applies to infringement of the rights conferred by section 106A(a).

§507 · Limitations on actions[7]

(a) Criminal Proceedings.—Except as expressly provided otherwise in this title, no criminal proceeding shall be maintained under the provisions of this title unless it is commenced within 5 years after the cause of action arose.

(b) Civil Actions.—No civil action shall be maintained under the provisions of this title unless it is commenced within three years after the claim accrued.

§508 · Notification of filing and determination of actions

(a) Within one month after the filing of any action under this title, the clerks of the courts of the United States shall send written notification to the Register of Copyrights setting forth, as far as is shown by the papers filed in the court, the names and addresses of the parties and the title, author, and registration number of each work involved in the action. If any other copyrighted work is later included in the action by amendment, answer, or other pleading, the clerk shall also send a notification concerning it to the Register within one month after the pleading is filed.

(b) Within one month after any final order or judgment is issued in the case, the clerk of the court shall notify the Register of it, sending with the notification a copy of the order or judgment together with the written opinion, if any, of the court.

(c) Upon receiving the notifications specified in this section, the Register shall make them a part of the public records of the Copyright Office.

§509 · [Repealed][8]

§510 · Remedies for alteration of programming by cable systems[9]

(a) In any action filed pursuant to section 111(c)(3), the following remedies shall be available:

(1) Where an action is brought by a party identified in subsections (b) or (c) of section 501, the remedies provided by sections 502 through 505, and the remedy provided by subsection (b) of this section; and

(2) When an action is brought by a party identified in subsection (d) of section 501, the remedies provided by sections 502 and 505, together with any actual damages suffered by such party as a result of the infringement, and the remedy provided by subsection (b) of this section.

(b) In any action filed pursuant to section 111(c)(3), the court may decree that, for a period not to exceed thirty days, the cable system shall be deprived of the benefit of a statutory license for one or more distant signals carried by such cable system.

§511 · Liability of States, instrumentalities of States, and State officials for infringement of copyright[10]

(a) In General.—Any State, any instrumentality of a State, and any officer or employee of a State or instrumentality of a State acting in his or her official capacity, shall not be immune, under the Eleventh Amendment of the Constitution of the United States or under any other doctrine of sovereign immunity, from suit in Federal Court by any person, including any governmental or nongovernmental entity, for a violation of any of the exclusive rights of a copyright owner provided by sections 106 through 122, for importing copies of phonorecords in violation of section 602, or for any other violation under this title.

(b) REMEDIES.—In a suit described in subsection (a) for a violation described in that subsection, remedies (including remedies both at law and in equity) are available for the violation to the same extent as such remedies are available for such a violation in a suit against any public or private entity other than a State, instrumentality of a State, or officer or employee of a State acting in his or her official capacity. Such remedies include impounding and disposition of infringing articles under section 503, actual damages and profits and statutory damages under section 504, costs and attorney's fees under section 505, and the remedies provided in section 510.

§512 · Limitations on liability relating to material online[11]

(a) TRANSITORY DIGITAL NETWORK COMMUNICATIONS.—A service provider shall not be liable for monetary relief, or, except as provided in subsection (j), for injunctive or other equitable relief, for infringement of copyright by reason of the provider's transmitting, routing, or providing connections for, material through a system or network controlled or operated by or for the service provider, or by reason of the intermediate and transient storage of that material in the course of such transmitting, routing, or providing connections, if—

(1) the transmission of the material was initiated by or at the direction of a person other than the service provider;

(2) the transmission, routing, provision of connections, or storage is carried out through an automatic technical process without selection of the material by the service provider;

(3) the service provider does not select the recipients of the material except as an automatic response to the request of another person;

(4) no copy of the material made by the service provider in the course of such intermediate or transient storage is maintained on the system or network in a manner ordinarily accessible to anyone other than anticipated recipients, and no such copy is maintained on the system or network in a manner ordinarily accessible to such anticipated recipients for a longer period than is reasonably necessary for the transmission, routing, or provision of connections; and

(5) the material is transmitted through the system or network without modification of its content.

(b) SYSTEM CACHING.—

(1) LIMITATION ON LIABILITY.—A service provider shall not be liable for monetary relief, or, except as provided in subsection (j), for injunctive or other equitable relief, for infringement of copyright by reason of the intermediate

and temporary storage of material on a system or network controlled or operated by or for the service provider in a case in which—

(A) the material is made available online by a person other than the service provider;

(B) the material is transmitted from the person described in subparagraph (A) through the system or network to a person other than the person described in subparagraph (A) at the direction of that other person; and

(C) the storage is carried out through an automatic technical process for the purpose of making the material available to users of the system or network who, after the material is transmitted as described in subparagraph (B), request access to the material from the person described in subparagraph (A), if the conditions set forth in paragraph (2) are met.

(2) Conditions.—The conditions referred to in paragraph (1) are that—

(A) the material described in paragraph (1) is transmitted to the subsequent users described in paragraph (1)(C) without modification to its content from the manner in which the material was transmitted from the person described in paragraph (1)(A);

(B) the service provider described in paragraph (1) complies with rules concerning the refreshing, reloading, or other updating of the material when specified by the person making the material available online in accordance with a generally accepted industry standard data communications protocol for the system or network through which that person makes the material available, except that this subparagraph applies only if those rules are not used by the person described in paragraph (1)(A) to prevent or unreasonably impair the intermediate storage to which this subsection applies;

(C) the service provider does not interfere with the ability of technology associated with the material to return to the person described in paragraph (1)(A) the information that would have been available to that person if the material had been obtained by the subsequent users described in paragraph (1)(C) directly from that person, except that this subparagraph applies only if that technology—

(i) does not significantly interfere with the performance of the provider's system or network or with the intermediate storage of the material;

(ii) is consistent with generally accepted industry standard communications protocols; and

(iii) does not extract information from the provider's system or network other than the information that would have been available to the person described in paragraph (1)(A) if the subsequent users had gained access to the material directly from that person;

(D) if the person described in paragraph (1)(A) has in effect a condition that a person must meet prior to having access to the material, such as a condition based on payment of a fee or provision of a password or other information, the service provider permits access to the stored material in significant part only to users of its system or network that have met those conditions and only in accordance with those conditions; and

(E) if the person described in paragraph (1)(A) makes that material available online without the authorization of the copyright owner of the material, the service provider responds expeditiously to remove, or disable access to, the material that is claimed to be infringing upon notification of claimed infringement as described in subsection (c)(3), except that this subparagraph applies only if—

(i) the material has previously been removed from the originating site or access to it has been disabled, or a court has ordered that the material be removed from the originating site or that access to the material on the originating site be disabled; and

(ii) the party giving the notification includes in the notification a statement confirming that the material has been removed from the originating site or access to it has been disabled or that a court has ordered that the material be removed from the originating site or that access to the material on the originating site be disabled.

(c) Information Residing on Systems or Networks at Direction of Users.—

(1) In general.—A service provider shall not be liable for monetary relief, or, except as provided in subsection (j), for injunctive or other equitable relief, for infringement of copyright by reason of the storage at the direction of a user of material that resides on a system or network controlled or operated by or for the service provider, if the service provider—

(A)(i) does not have actual knowledge that the material or an activity using the material on the system or network is infringing;

(ii) in the absence of such actual knowledge, is not aware of facts or circumstances from which infringing activity is apparent; or

(iii) upon obtaining such knowledge or awareness, acts expeditiously to remove, or disable access to, the material;

(B) does not receive a financial benefit directly attributable to the infringing activity, in a case in which the service provider has the right and ability to control such activity; and

(C) upon notification of claimed infringement as described in paragraph (3), responds expeditiously to remove, or disable access to, the material that is claimed to be infringing or to be the subject of infringing activity.

(2) Designated agent.—The limitations on liability established in this subsection apply to a service provider only if the service provider has designated an agent to receive notifications of claimed infringement described

in paragraph (3), by making available through its service, including on its website in a location accessible to the public, and by providing to the Copyright Office, substantially the following information:

(A) the name, address, phone number, and electronic mail address of the agent.

(B) other contact information which the Register of Copyrights may deem appropriate.

The Register of Copyrights shall maintain a current directory of agents available to the public for inspection, including through the Internet, and may require payment of a fee by service providers to cover the costs of maintaining the directory.

(3) ELEMENTS OF NOTIFICATION.—

(A) To be effective under this subsection, a notification of claimed infringement must be a written communication provided to the designated agent of a service provider that includes substantially the following:

(i) A physical or electronic signature of a person authorized to act on behalf of the owner of an exclusive right that is allegedly infringed.

(ii) Identification of the copyrighted work claimed to have been infringed, or, if multiple copyrighted works at a single online site are covered by a single notification, a representative list of such works at that site.

(iii) Identification of the material that is claimed to be infringing or to be the subject of infringing activity and that is to be removed or access to which is to be disabled, and information reasonably sufficient to permit the service provider to locate the material.

(iv) Information reasonably sufficient to permit the service provider to contact the complaining party, such as an address, telephone number, and, if available, an electronic mail address at which the complaining party may be contacted.

(v) A statement that the complaining party has a good faith belief that use of the material in the manner complained of is not authorized by the copyright owner, its agent, or the law.

(vi) A statement that the information in the notification is accurate, and under penalty of perjury, that the complaining party is authorized to act on behalf of the owner of an exclusive right that is allegedly infringed.

(B)(i) Subject to clause (ii), a notification from a copyright owner or from a person authorized to act on behalf of the copyright owner that fails to comply substantially with the provisions of subparagraph (A) shall not be considered under paragraph (1)(A) in determining whether a service provider has actual knowledge or is aware of facts or circumstances from which infringing activity is apparent.

(ii) In a case in which the notification that is provided to the service provider's designated agent fails to comply substantially with all the provisions of subparagraph (A) but substantially complies with clauses (ii), (iii), and (iv) of subparagraph (A), clause (i) of this subparagraph applies only if the service provider promptly attempts to contact the person making the notification or takes other reasonable steps to assist in the receipt of notification that substantially complies with all the provisions of subparagraph (A).

(d) INFORMATION LOCATION TOOLS.—A service provider shall not be liable for monetary relief, or, except as provided in subsection (j), for injunctive or other equitable relief, for infringement of copyright by reason of the provider referring or linking users to an online location containing infringing material or infringing activity, by using information location tools, including a directory, index, reference, pointer, or hypertext link, if the service provider—

(1) (A) does not have actual knowledge that the material or activity is infringing;

(B) in the absence of such actual knowledge, is not aware of facts or circumstances from which infringing activity is apparent; or

(C) upon obtaining such knowledge or awareness, acts expeditiously to remove, or disable access to, the material;

(2) does not receive a financial benefit directly attributable to the infringing activity, in a case in which the service provider has the right and ability to control such activity; and

(3) upon notification of claimed infringement as described in subsection (c)(3), responds expeditiously to remove, or disable access to, the material that is claimed to be infringing or to be the subject of infringing activity, except that, for purposes of this paragraph, the information described in subsection (c)(3)(A)(iii) shall be identification of the reference or link, to material or activity claimed to be infringing, that is to be removed or access to which is to be disabled, and information reasonably sufficient to permit the service provider to locate that reference or link.

(e) LIMITATION ON LIABILITY OF NONPROFIT EDUCATIONAL INSTITUTIONS.—(1) When a public or other nonprofit institution of higher education is a service provider, and when a faculty member or graduate student who is an employee of such institution is performing a teaching or research function, for the purposes of subsections (a) and (b) such faculty member or graduate student shall be considered to be a person other than the institution, and for the purposes of subsections (c) and (d) such faculty member's or graduate student's knowledge or awareness of his or her infringing activities shall not be attributed to the institution, if—

(A) such faculty member's or graduate student's infringing activities do not involve the provision of online access to instructional materials that are or were required or recommended, within the preceding 3-year period, for a course taught at the institution by such faculty member or graduate student;

(B) the institution has not, within the preceding 3-year period, received more than 2 notifications described in subsection (c)(3) of claimed infringement by such faculty member or graduate student, and such notifications of claimed infringement were not actionable under subsection (f); and

(C) the institution provides to all users of its system or network informational materials that accurately describe, and promote compliance with, the laws of the United States relating to copyright.

(2) For the purposes of this subsection, the limitations on injunctive relief contained in subsections (j)(2) and (j)(3), but not those in (j)(1), shall apply.

(f) Misrepresentations.—Any person who knowingly materially misrepresents under this section—

(1) that material or activity is infringing, or

(2) that material or activity was removed or disabled by mistake or misidentification,

shall be liable for any damages, including costs and attorneys' fees, incurred by the alleged infringer, by any copyright owner or copyright owner's authorized licensee, or by a service provider, who is injured by such misrepresentation, as the result of the service provider relying upon such misrepresentation in removing or disabling access to the material or activity claimed to be infringing, or in replacing the removed material or ceasing to disable access to it.

(g) Replacement of Removed or Disabled Material and Limitation on Other Liability.—

(1) No liability for taking down generally.—Subject to paragraph (2), a service provider shall not be liable to any person for any claim based on the service provider's good faith disabling of access to, or removal of, material or activity claimed to be infringing or based on facts or circumstances from which infringing activity is apparent, regardless of whether the material or activity is ultimately determined to be infringing.

(2) Exception.—Paragraph (1) shall not apply with respect to material residing at the direction of a subscriber of the service provider on a system or network controlled or operated by or for the service provider that is removed, or to which access is disabled by the service provider, pursuant to a notice provided under subsection (c)(1)(C), unless the service provider—

(A) takes reasonable steps promptly to notify the subscriber that it has removed or disabled access to the material;

(B) upon receipt of a counter notification described in paragraph (3), promptly provides the person who provided the notification under subsection (c)(1)(C) with a copy of the counter notification, and informs that person that it will replace the removed material or cease disabling access to it in 10 business days; and

(C) replaces the removed material and ceases disabling access to it not less than 10, nor more than 14, business days following receipt of the counter notice, unless its designated agent first receives notice from the person who submitted the notification under subsection (c)(1)(C) that such person has filed an action seeking a court order to restrain the subscriber from engaging in infringing activity relating to the material on the service provider's system or network.

(3) CONTENTS OF COUNTER NOTIFICATION.—To be effective under this subsection, a counter notification must be a written communication provided to the service provider's designated agent that includes substantially the following:

(A) A physical or electronic signature of the subscriber.

(B) Identification of the material that has been removed or to which access has been disabled and the location at which the material appeared before it was removed or access to it was disabled.

(C) A statement under penalty of perjury that the subscriber has a good faith belief that the material was removed or disabled as a result of mistake or misidentification of the material to be removed or disabled.

(D) The subscriber's name, address, and telephone number, and a statement that the subscriber consents to the jurisdiction of Federal District Court for the judicial district in which the address is located, or if the subscriber's address is outside of the United States, for any judicial district in which the service provider may be found, and that the subscriber will accept service of process from the person who provided notification under subsection (c)(1)(C) or an agent of such person.

(4) LIMITATION ON OTHER LIABILITY.—A service provider's compliance with paragraph (2) shall not subject the service provider to liability for copyright infringement with respect to the material identified in the notice provided under subsection (c)(1)(C).

(h) SUBPOENA TO IDENTIFY INFRINGER.—

(1) REQUEST.—A copyright owner or a person authorized to act on the owner's behalf may request the clerk of any United States district court to issue a subpoena to a service provider for identification of an alleged infringer in accordance with this subsection.

(2) CONTENTS OF REQUEST.—The request may be made by filing with the clerk—

(A) a copy of a notification described in subsection (c)(3)(A);

(B) a proposed subpoena; and

(C) a sworn declaration to the effect that the purpose for which the subpoena is sought is to obtain the identity of an alleged infringer and that such information will only be used for the purpose of protecting rights under this title.

(3) Contents of subpoena.—The subpoena shall authorize and order the service provider receiving the notification and the subpoena to expeditiously disclose to the copyright owner or person authorized by the copyright owner information sufficient to identify the alleged infringer of the material described in the notification to the extent such information is available to the service provider.

(4) Basis for granting subpoena.—If the notification filed satisfies the provisions of subsection (c)(3)(A), the proposed subpoena is in proper form, and the accompanying declaration is properly executed, the clerk shall expeditiously issue and sign the proposed subpoena and return it to the requester for delivery to the service provider.

(5) Actions of service provider receiving subpoena.—Upon receipt of the issued subpoena, either accompanying or subsequent to the receipt of a notification described in subsection (c)(3)(A), the service provider shall expeditiously disclose to the copyright owner or person authorized by the copyright owner the information required by the subpoena, notwithstanding any other provision of law and regardless of whether the service provider responds to the notification.

(6) Rules applicable to subpoena.—Unless otherwise provided by this section or by applicable rules of the court, the procedure for issuance and delivery of the subpoena, and the remedies for noncompliance with the subpoena, shall be governed to the greatest extent practicable by those provisions of the Federal Rules of Civil Procedure governing the issuance, service, and enforcement of a subpoena *duces tecum*.

(i) Conditions for Eligibility.—

(1) Accommodation of technology.—The limitations on liability established by this section shall apply to a service provider only if the service provider—

(A) has adopted and reasonably implemented, and informs subscribers and account holders of the service provider's system or network of, a policy that provides for the termination in appropriate circumstances of subscribers and account holders of the service provider's system or network who are repeat infringers; and

(B) accommodates and does not interfere with standard technical measures.

(2) Definition.—As used in this subsection, the term "standard technical measures" means technical measures that are used by copyright owners to identify or protect copyrighted works and—

(A) have been developed pursuant to a broad consensus of copyright owners and service providers in an open, fair, voluntary, multi-industry standards process;

(B) are available to any person on reasonable and nondiscriminatory terms; and

(C) do not impose substantial costs on service providers or substantial burdens on their systems or networks.

(j) Injunctions.—The following rules shall apply in the case of any application for an injunction under section 502 against a service provider that is not subject to monetary remedies under this section:

(1) Scope of relief.—(A) With respect to conduct other than that which qualifies for the limitation on remedies set forth in subsection (a), the court may grant injunctive relief with respect to a service provider only in one or more of the following forms:

(i) An order restraining the service provider from providing access to infringing material or activity residing at a particular online site on the provider's system or network.

(ii) An order restraining the service provider from providing access to a subscriber or account holder of the service provider's system or network who is engaging in infringing activity and is identified in the order, by terminating the accounts of the subscriber or account holder that are specified in the order.

(iii) Such other injunctive relief as the court may consider necessary to prevent or restrain infringement of copyrighted material specified in the order of the court at a particular online location, if such relief is the least burdensome to the service provider among the forms of relief comparably effective for that purpose.

(B) If the service provider qualifies for the limitation on remedies described in subsection (a), the court may only grant injunctive relief in one or both of the following forms:

(i) An order restraining the service provider from providing access to a subscriber or account holder of the service provider's system or network who is using the provider's service to engage in infringing activity and is identified in the order, by terminating the accounts of the subscriber or account holder that are specified in the order.

(ii) An order restraining the service provider from providing access, by taking reasonable steps specified in the order to block access, to a specific, identified, online location outside the United States.

(2) Considerations.—The court, in considering the relevant criteria for injunctive relief under applicable law, shall consider—

(A) whether such an injunction, either alone or in combination with other such injunctions issued against the same service provider under this subsection, would significantly burden either the provider or the operation of the provider's system or network;

(B) the magnitude of the harm likely to be suffered by the copyright owner in the digital network environment if steps are not taken to prevent or restrain the infringement;

(C) whether implementation of such an injunction would be technically feasible and effective, and would not interfere with access to noninfringing material at other online locations; and

(D) whether other less burdensome and comparably effective means of preventing or restraining access to the infringing material are available.

(3) NOTICE AND EX PARTE ORDERS.—Injunctive relief under this subsection shall be available only after notice to the service provider and an opportunity for the service provider to appear are provided, except for orders ensuring the preservation of evidence or other orders having no material adverse effect on the operation of the service provider's communications network.

(k) DEFINITIONS.—

(1) SERVICE PROVIDER.—(A) As used in subsection (a), the term "service provider" means an entity offering the transmission, routing, or providing of connections for digital online communications, between or among points specified by a user, of material of the user's choosing, without modification to the content of the material as sent or received.

(B) As used in this section, other than subsection (a), the term "service provider" means a provider of online services or network access, or the operator of facilities therefor, and includes an entity described in subparagraph (A).

(2) MONETARY RELIEF.—As used in this section, the term "monetary relief" means damages, costs, attorneys' fees, and any other form of monetary payment.

(l) OTHER DEFENSES NOT AFFECTED.—The failure of a service provider's conduct to qualify for limitation of liability under this section shall not bear adversely upon the consideration of a defense by the service provider that the service provider's conduct is not infringing under this title or any other defense.

(m) PROTECTION OF PRIVACY.—Nothing in this section shall be construed to condition the applicability of subsections (a) through (d) on—

(1) a service provider monitoring its service or affirmatively seeking facts indicating infringing activity, except to the extent consistent with a standard technical measure complying with the provisions of subsection (i); or

(2) a service provider gaining access to, removing, or disabling access to material in cases in which such conduct is prohibited by law.

(n) CONSTRUCTION.—Subsections (a), (b), (c), and (d) describe separate and distinct functions for purposes of applying this section. Whether a service provider qualifies for the limitation on liability in any one of those subsections shall be based solely on the criteria in that subsection, and shall not affect a determination of whether that service provider qualifies for the limitations on liability under any other such subsection.

§513 · Determination of reasonable license fees for individual proprietors[12]

In the case of any performing rights society subject to a consent decree which provides for the determination of reasonable license rates or fees to be charged by the performing rights society, notwithstanding the provisions of that consent decree, an individual proprietor who owns or operates fewer than 7 nonpublicly traded establishments in which nondramatic musical works are performed publicly and who claims that any license agreement offered by that performing rights society is unreasonable in its license rate or fee as to that individual proprietor, shall be entitled to determination of a reasonable license rate or fee as follows:

(1) The individual proprietor may commence such proceeding for determination of a reasonable license rate or fee by filing an application in the applicable district court under paragraph (2) that a rate disagreement exists and by serving a copy of the application on the performing rights society. Such proceeding shall commence in the applicable district court within 90 days after the service of such copy, except that such 90-day requirement shall be subject to the administrative requirements of the court.

(2) The proceeding under paragraph (1) shall be held, at the individual proprietor's election, in the judicial district of the district court with jurisdiction over the applicable consent decree or in that place of holding court of a district court that is the seat of the Federal circuit (other than the Court of Appeals for the Federal Circuit) in which the proprietor's establishment is located.

(3) Such proceeding shall be held before the judge of the court with jurisdiction over the consent decree governing the performing rights society. At the discretion of the court, the proceeding shall be held before a special master or magistrate judge appointed by such judge. Should that consent decree provide for the appointment of an advisor or advisors to the court for any purpose, any such advisor shall be the special master so named by the court.

(4) In any such proceeding, the industry rate shall be presumed to have been reasonable at the time it was agreed to or determined by the court. Such presumption shall in no way affect a determination of whether the rate is being correctly applied to the individual proprietor.

(5) Pending the completion of such proceeding, the individual proprietor shall have the right to perform publicly the copyrighted musical compositions in the repertoire of the performing rights society by paying an interim license rate or fee into an interest bearing escrow account with the clerk of the court, subject to retroactive adjustment when a final rate or fee has been determined, in an amount equal to the industry rate, or, in the absence of an industry rate, the amount of the most recent license rate or fee agreed to by the parties.

(6) Any decision rendered in such proceeding by a special master or magistrate judge named under paragraph (3) shall be reviewed by the judge of

the court with jurisdiction over the consent decree governing the performing rights society. Such proceeding, including such review, shall be concluded within 6 months after its commencement.

(7) Any such final determination shall be binding only as to the individual proprietor commencing the proceeding, and shall not be applicable to any other proprietor or any other performing rights society, and the performing rights society shall be relieved of any obligation of nondiscrimination among similarly situated music users that may be imposed by the consent decree governing its operations.

(8) An individual proprietor may not bring more than one proceeding provided for in this section for the determination of a reasonable license rate or fee under any license agreement with respect to any one performing rights society.

(9) For purposes of this section, the term "industry rate" means the license fee a performing rights society has agreed to with, or which has been determined by the court for, a significant segment of the music user industry to which the individual proprietor belongs.

Chapter 5 · Notes

1. See note 8, *infra*.

2. In 1998, two sections 512 were enacted into law. First, on October 17, 1998, the Fairness in Music Licensing Act of 1998 was enacted. This Act amended chapter 5 to add section 512 entitled "Determination of reasonable license fees for individual proprietors." Pub. L. No. 105-298, 112 Stat. 2827, 2831. Second, on October 28, 1998, the Online Copyright Infringement Liability Limitation Act was enacted. This Act amended chapter 5 to add section 512 entitled "Limitations on liability relating to material online." Pub. L. No. 105-304, 112 Stat. 2860, 2877. Consequently, in 1999, a technical correction was enacted to redesignate the section 512 that was entitled "Determination of reasonable license fees for individual proprietors" as section 513. Also, the table of sections was amended to reflect that change. Pub. L. No. 106-44, 113 Stat. 221. See also note 12, *infra*.

3. The Berne Convention Implementation Act of 1988 amended section 501(b) by striking out "sections 205(d) and 411" and inserting in lieu thereof "section 411." Pub. L. No. 100-568, 102 Stat. 2853, 2860. The Satellite Home Viewer Act of 1988 amended section 501 by adding subsection (e). Pub. L. No. 100-667, 102 Stat. 3935, 3957.

In 1990, the Copyright Remedy Clarification Act amended section 501(a) by adding the last two sentences. Pub. L. No. 101-553, 104 Stat. 2749. The Visual Artists Rights Act of 1990 also amended section 501(a) as follows: 1) by inserting "or of the author as provided in section 106A(a)" after "118" and 2) by striking out "copyright." and inserting in lieu thereof "copyright or right of the author, as the case may be. For purposes of this chapter (other than section 506), any reference to copyright shall be deemed to include the rights conferred by section 106A(a)." Pub. L. No. 101-650, 104 Stat. 5089, 5131.

In 1999, a technical correction amended the first sentence in subsection 501(a) by inserting "121" in lieu of "118." Pub. L. No. 106-44, 113 Stat. 221, 222. The Satellite Home Viewer Improvement Act of 1999 amended section 501 by adding a subsection (f) and, in subsection (e), by inserting "performance or display of a work embodied in a primary transmission" in lieu of "primary transmission embodying the performance or display of a work." Pub. L. No. 106-113, 113 Stat. 1501, app. I at 1501A-527 and 544. The Satellite Home Viewer Improvement Act of 1999 states that section 501(f) shall be effective as of July 1, 1999. Pub. L. No. 106-113, 113 Stat. 1501, app. I at 1501A-544.

The Intellectual Property and High Technology Technical Amendments Act of 2002 amended section 501(a) by substituting sections "106 through 122" for "106 through 121." Pub. L. No. 107-273, 116 Stat. 1758, 1909.

4. The Prioritizing Resources and Organization for Intellectual Property Act of 2008 amended section 503 by revising subsection (a) in its entirety. Pub. L. No. 110-403, 122 Stat. 4256, 4258. A technical correction in the Copyright Cleanup, Clarification, and Corrections Act of 2010 amended section 503(a)(1)(B) to substitute "copies or phonorecords" for "copies of phonorecords." Pub. L. No. 111-295, 124 Stat. 3180, 3181.

5. The Berne Convention Implementation Act of 1988 amended section 504(c) as follows: 1) in paragraph (1), by inserting "$500" in lieu of "$250" and by inserting "$20,000" in lieu of "$10,000" and 2) in paragraph (2), by inserting "$100,000" in lieu of "$50,000" and by inserting "$200" in lieu of "$100." Pub. L. No. 100-568, 102 Stat. 2853, 2860. The Digital Theft Deterrence and Copyright Damages Improvement Act of 1999 amended section 504(c), in paragraph (1), by substituting "$750" for "$500" and "$30,000" for "$20,000" and, in paragraph (2), by substituting "$150,000" for "$100,000." Pub. L. No. 106-160, 113 Stat. 1774.

The Fraudulent Online Identity Sanctions Act of 2004 amended section 504(c) by adding a new subparagraph (3). Pub. L. No. 108-482, 118 Stat. 3912, 3916. The Copyright Cleanup, Clarification, and Corrections Act of 2010 amended paragraph 504(c)(2) to change the reference from "subsection (g) of section 118" to "section 118(f)." Pub. L. No. 111-295, 124 Stat. 3180, 3181.

6. The Piracy and Counterfeiting Amendments Act of 1982 amended section 506 by substituting a new subsection (a). Pub. L. No. 97-180, 96 Stat. 91, 93. The Visual Artists Rights Act of 1990 amended section 506 by adding subsection (f). Pub. L. No.101-650, 104 Stat. 5089, 5131. In 1997, the No Electronic Theft (NET) Act again amended section 506 by amending subsection (a) in its entirety. Pub. L. No. 105-147, 111 Stat. 2678. That Act also directed the United States Sentencing Commission to "ensure that the applicable guideline range for a defendant convicted of a crime against intellectual property ... is sufficiently stringent to deter such a crime" and to "ensure that the guidelines provide for consideration of the retail value and quantity of the items with respect to which the crime against intellectual property was committed." Pub. L. No. 105-147, 111 Stat. 2678, 2680. See also note 2 in Appendix H.

The Artists' Rights and Theft Prevention Act of 2005 amended subsection 506(a) in its entirety. Pub. L. No. 109-9, 119 Stat. 218, 220.

The Prioritizing Resources and Organization for Intellectual Property Act of 2008 amended section 506 by revising subsection (b) in its entirety. Pub. L. No. 110-403, 122 Stat. 4256, 4260.

7. In 1997, the No Electronic Theft (NET) Act amended section 507(a) by inserting "5" in lieu of "three." Pub. L. No. 105-147, 111 Stat. 2678.

8. The Prioritizing Resources and Organization for Intellectual Property Act of 2008 repealed section 509. Pub. L. No. 110-403, 122 Stat. 4256, 4260. In lieu of this provision, refer to section 2323, chapter 113 of title 18, *United States Code*, entitled, "Forfeiture, Destruction and Restitution." Section 2323 is included in Appendix H to this volume.

9. The Satellite Home Viewer Improvement Act of 1999 amended the heading for section 510 by substituting "programming" for "programing" and, in subsection (b), by substituting "statutory" for "compulsory." Pub. L. No. 106-113, 113 Stat. 1501, app. I at 1501A-543.

10. In 1990, the Copyright Remedy Clarification Act added section 511. Pub. L. No. 101-553, 104 Stat. 2749. In 1999, a technical correction amended subsection 511(a) by inserting "121" in lieu of "119." Pub. L. No. 106-44, 113 Stat. 221, 222. The Intellectual Property and High Technology Technical Amendments Act of 2002 amended section 511(a) by substituting sections "106 through 122" for "106 through 121." Pub. L. No. 107-273, 116 Stat. 1758, 1909.

11. In 1998, the Online Copyright Infringement Liability Limitation Act added section 512. Pub. L. No. 105-304, 112 Stat. 2860, 2877. In 1999, a technical correction deleted the heading for paragraph (2) of section 512(e), which was "Injunctions." Pub. L. No. 106-44, 113 Stat. 221, 222. The Copyright Cleanup, Clarification, and Corrections Act of 2010 amended the last sentence in paragraph 512(c)(2)(B) by deleting "in both electronic and hard copy formats" after "through the Internet." Pub. L. No. 111-295, 124 Stat. 3180, 3180.

12. The Fairness in Music Licensing Act of 1998 added section 513. Pub. L. No. 105-298, 112 Stat. 2827, 2831. This section was originally designated as section 512. However, because two sections 512 had been enacted into law in 1998, a technical amendment redesignated this as section 513. Pub. L. No. 106-44, 113 Stat. 221. See also note 2, *supra*.

Chapter 6

Importation and Exportation[1]

§601 · [Repealed][4]

§602 · Infringing importation or exportation of copies or phonorecords[5]

(a) Infringing Importation or Exportation.—

(1) Importation.—Importation into the United States, without the authority of the owner of copyright under this title, of copies or phonorecords of a work that have been acquired outside the United States is an infringement of the exclusive right to distribute copies or phonorecords under section 106, actionable under section 501.

(2) Importation or exportation of infringing items.—Importation into the United States or exportation from the United States, without the authority of the owner of copyright under this title, of copies or phonorecords, the making of which either constituted an infringement of copyright, or which would have constituted an infringement of copyright if this title had been applicable, is an infringement of the exclusive right to distribute copies or phonorecords under section 106, actionable under sections 501 and 506.

(3) Exceptions.—This subsection does not apply to—

(A) importation or exportation of copies or phonorecords under the authority or for the use of the Government of the United States or of any State or political subdivision of a State, but not including copies or phonorecords for use in schools, or copies of any audiovisual work imported for purposes other than archival use;

(B) importation or exportation, for the private use of the importer or exporter and not for distribution, by any person with respect to no more than one copy or phonorecord of any one work at any one time, or by any person arriving from outside the United States or departing from the United States with respect to copies or phonorecords forming part of such person's personal baggage; or

(C) importation by or for an organization operated for scholarly, educational, or religious purposes and not for private gain, with respect to no more than one copy of an audiovisual work solely for its archival purposes, and no more than five copies or phonorecords of any other work for its library lending or archival purposes, unless the importation of such copies or phonorecords is part of an activity consisting of systematic reproduction or distribution, engaged in by such organization in violation of the provisions of section 108(g)(2).

(b) Import Prohibition.—In a case where the making of the copies or phonorecords would have constituted an infringement of copyright if this title had been applicable, their importation is prohibited. In a case where the copies or phonorecords were lawfully made, the United States Customs and Border Protection Service has no authority to prevent their importation. In either case, the Secretary of the Treasury is authorized to prescribe, by regulation, a procedure under which any person claiming an interest in the copyright in a particular work may, upon payment of a specified fee, be entitled to notification by the United States Customs and Border Protection Service of the importation of articles that appear to be copies or phonorecords of the work.

§ 603 · Importation prohibitions: Enforcement and disposition of excluded articles[6]

(a) The Secretary of the Treasury and the United States Postal Service shall separately or jointly make regulations for the enforcement of the provisions of this title prohibiting importation.

(b) These regulations may require, as a condition for the exclusion of articles under section 602—

(1) that the person seeking exclusion obtain a court order enjoining importation of the articles; or

(2) that the person seeking exclusion furnish proof, of a specified nature and in accordance with prescribed procedures, that the copyright in which such person claims an interest is valid and that the importation would violate the prohibition in section 602; the person seeking exclusion may also be required to post a surety bond for any injury that may result if the detention or exclusion of the articles proves to be unjustified.

(c) Articles imported in violation of the importation prohibitions of this title are subject to seizure and forfeiture in the same manner as property imported in violation of the customs revenue laws. Forfeited articles shall be destroyed as directed by the Secretary of the Treasury or the court, as the case may be.

Chapter 6 · Notes

1. The Prioritizing Resources and Organization for Intellectual Property Act of 2008 amended the title of Chapter 6 to add "Exportation" to it, so that now the title is "Manufacturing Requirements, Importation, and Exportation." Pub. L. No. 110-403, 122 Stat. 4256, 4259. The Copyright Cleanup, Clarification, and Corrections Act of 2010 amended chapter six by repealing section 601, entitled "Manufacture, importation, and public distribution of certain copies." Pub. L. No. 111-295, 124 Stat. 3180. It also deleted "Manufacturing Requirements" from the beginning of the title for chapter six. *Id.*

2. See note 4, *infra.*

3. The Prioritizing Resources and Organization for Intellectual Property Act of 2008 amended the title of section 602 in the table of contents by adding "Exportation" to it, so that the new title is "Infringing importation or exportation of copies or phonorecords." Pub. L. No. 110-403, 122 Stat. 4256, 4260.

4. In 1982, section 601(a) was amended in the first sentence by substituting "1986" for "1982." Pub. L. No. 97-215, 96 Stat. 178. The Prioritizing Resources and Organization for Intellectual Property Act of 2008 amended the first sentence of subpart 601(b)(2) by inserting "and Border Protection" after "United States Customs." Pub. L. No. 110-403, 122 Stat. 4256, 4260. The Copyright Cleanup, Clarification, and Corrections Act of 2010 repealed section 601. Pub. L. No. 111-295, 124 Stat. 3180.

5. The Prioritizing Resources and Organization for Intellectual Property Act of 2008 amended the title of section 602 by adding "Exportation" to it, so the new title is "Infringing importation or exportation of copies or phonorecords." Pub. L. No. 110-403, 122 Stat. 4256, 4260. The Act also amended section 602(a) by dividing it into paragraphs (1), (2) and (3); by adding paragraph (2); and by adding references to exports throughout. *Id.* at 4259-60. It further amended subsection 602(b) by inserting the subtitle, "Import Prohibition," at the beginning and adding references to the United Stated Customs and Border Protection Service. *Id.* at 4260. The Copyright Cleanup, Clarification, and Corrections Act of 2010 made a conforming amendment to subsection 602(b) to eliminate the reference to section 601, which the Act had repealed, by deleting at the end of the second sentence "unless the provisions of section 601 are applicable." Pub. L. No. 111-295, 124 Stat. 3180, 3181.

6. The Anticounterfeiting Consumer Protection Act of 1996 amended the last sentence of section 603(c) by deleting the semicolon and all text immediately following the words "as the case may be." Pub. L. No. 104-153, 110 Stat. 1386, 1388.

Chapter 7[1]

Copyright Office

§701 · The Copyright Office: General responsibilities and organization[2]

(a) All administrative functions and duties under this title, except as otherwise specified, are the responsibility of the Register of Copyrights as director of the Copyright Office of the Library of Congress. The Register of Copyrights, together with the subordinate officers and employees of the Copyright Office, shall be appointed by the Librarian of Congress, and shall act under the Librarian's general direction and supervision.

(b) In addition to the functions and duties set out elsewhere in this chapter, the Register of Copyrights shall perform the following functions:

(1) Advise Congress on national and international issues relating to copyright, other matters arising under this title, and related matters.

(2) Provide information and assistance to Federal departments and agencies and the Judiciary on national and international issues relating to copyright, other matters arising under this title, and related matters.

(3) Participate in meetings of international intergovernmental organizations and meetings with foreign government officials relating to copyright, other matters arising under this title, and related matters, including as a member of United States delegations as authorized by the appropriate Executive branch authority.

(4) Conduct studies and programs regarding copyright, other matters arising under this title, and related matters, the administration of the Copyright Office, or any function vested in the Copyright Office by law, including educational programs conducted cooperatively with foreign intellectual property offices and international intergovernmental organizations.

(5) Perform such other functions as Congress may direct, or as may be appropriate in furtherance of the functions and duties specifically set forth in this title.

(c) The Register of Copyrights shall adopt a seal to be used on and after January 1, 1978, to authenticate all certified documents issued by the Copyright Office.

(d) The Register of Copyrights shall make an annual report to the Librarian of Congress of the work and accomplishments of the Copyright Office during the previous fiscal year. The annual report of the Register of Copyrights shall be published separately and as a part of the annual report of the Librarian of Congress.

(e) Except as provided by section 706(b) and the regulations issued thereunder, all actions taken by the Register of Copyrights under this title are subject to the provisions of the Administrative Procedure Act of June 11, 1946, as amended (c. 324, 60 Stat. 237, title 5, United States Code, Chapter 5, Subchapter II and Chapter 7).

(f) The Register of Copyrights shall be compensated at the rate of pay in effect for level III of the Executive Schedule under section 5314 of title 5.[3] The Librarian of Congress shall establish not more than four positions for Associate

Registers of Copyrights, in accordance with the recommendations of the Register of Copyrights. The Librarian shall make appointments to such positions after consultation with the Register of Copyrights. Each Associate Register of Copyrights shall be paid at a rate not to exceed the maximum annual rate of basic pay payable for GS-18 of the General Schedule under section 5332 of title 5.

§702 · Copyright Office regulations[4]

The Register of Copyrights is authorized to establish regulations not inconsistent with law for the administration of the functions and duties made the responsibility of the Register under this title. All regulations established by the Register under this title are subject to the approval of the Librarian of Congress.

§703 · Effective date of actions in Copyright Office

In any case in which time limits are prescribed under this title for the performance of an action in the Copyright Office, and in which the last day of the prescribed period falls on a Saturday, Sunday, holiday, or other nonbusiness day within the District of Columbia or the Federal Government, the action may be taken on the next succeeding business day, and is effective as of the date when the period expired.

§704 · Retention and disposition of articles deposited in Copyright Office[5]

(a) Upon their deposit in the Copyright Office under sections 407 and 408, all copies, phonorecords, and identifying material, including those deposited in connection with claims that have been refused registration, are the property of the United States Government.

(b) In the case of published works, all copies, phonorecords, and identifying material deposited are available to the Library of Congress for its collections, or for exchange or transfer to any other library. In the case of unpublished works, the Library is entitled, under regulations that the Register of Copyrights shall prescribe, to select any deposits for its collections or for transfer to the National Archives of the United States or to a Federal records center, as defined in section 2901 of title 44.

(c) The Register of Copyrights is authorized, for specific or general categories of works, to make a facsimile reproduction of all or any part of the material deposited under section 408, and to make such reproduction a part of the

Copyright Office records of the registration, before transferring such material to the Library of Congress as provided by subsection (b), or before destroying or otherwise disposing of such material as provided by subsection (d).

(d) Deposits not selected by the Library under subsection (b), or identifying portions or reproductions of them, shall be retained under the control of the Copyright Office, including retention in Government storage facilities, for the longest period considered practicable and desirable by the Register of Copyrights and the Librarian of Congress. After that period it is within the joint discretion of the Register and the Librarian to order their destruction or other disposition; but, in the case of unpublished works, no deposit shall be knowingly or intentionally destroyed or otherwise disposed of during its term of copyright unless a facsimile reproduction of the entire deposit has been made a part of the Copyright Office records as provided by subsection (c).

(e) The depositor of copies, phonorecords, or identifying material under section 408, or the copyright owner of record, may request retention, under the control of the Copyright Office, of one or more of such articles for the full term of copyright in the work. The Register of Copyrights shall prescribe, by regulation, the conditions under which such requests are to be made and granted, and shall fix the fee to be charged under section 708(a) if the request is granted.

§705 · Copyright Office records: Preparation, maintenance, public inspection, and searching[6]

(a) The Register of Copyrights shall ensure that records of deposits, registrations, recordations, and other actions taken under this title are maintained, and that indexes of such records are prepared.

(b) Such records and indexes, as well as the articles deposited in connection with completed copyright registrations and retained under the control of the Copyright Office, shall be open to public inspection.

(c) Upon request and payment of the fee specified by section 708, the Copyright Office shall make a search of its public records, indexes, and deposits, and shall furnish a report of the information they disclose with respect to any particular deposits, registrations, or recorded documents.

§706 · Copies of Copyright Office records

(a) Copies may be made of any public records or indexes of the Copyright Office; additional certificates of copyright registration and copies of any public records or indexes may be furnished upon request and payment of the fees specified by section 708.

(b) Copies or reproductions of deposited articles retained under the control of the Copyright Office shall be authorized or furnished only under the conditions specified by the Copyright Office regulations.

§707 · Copyright Office forms and publications

(a) Catalog of Copyright Entries.—The Register of Copyrights shall compile and publish at periodic intervals catalogs of all copyright registrations. These catalogs shall be divided into parts in accordance with the various classes of works, and the Register has discretion to determine, on the basis of practicability and usefulness, the form and frequency of publication of each particular part.

(b) Other Publications.—The Register shall furnish, free of charge upon request, application forms for copyright registration and general informational material in connection with the functions of the Copyright Office. The Register also has the authority to publish compilations of information, bibliographies, and other material he or she considers to be of value to the public.

(c) Distribution of Publications.—All publications of the Copyright Office shall be furnished to depository libraries as specified under section 1905 of title 44, and, aside from those furnished free of charge, shall be offered for sale to the public at prices based on the cost of reproduction and distribution.

§708 · Copyright Office fees[7]

(a) Fees.—Fees shall be paid to the Register of Copyrights—

(1) on filing each application under section 408 for registration of a copyright claim or for a supplementary registration, including the issuance of a certificate of registration if registration is made;

(2) on filing each application for registration of a claim for renewal of a subsisting copyright under section 304(a), including the issuance of a certificate of registration if registration is made;

(3) for the issuance of a receipt for a deposit under section 407;

(4) for the recordation, as provided by section 205, of a transfer of copyright ownership or other document;

(5) for the filing, under section 115(b), of a notice of intention to obtain a compulsory license;

(6) for the recordation, under section 302(c), of a statement revealing the identity of an author of an anonymous or pseudonymous work, or for the recordation, under section 302(d), of a statement relating to the death of an author;

(7) for the issuance, under section 706, of an additional certificate of registration;

(8) for the issuance of any other certification;

(9) for the making and reporting of a search as provided by section 705, and for any related services;

(10) on filing a statement of account based on secondary transmissions of primary transmissions pursuant to section 119 or 122; and

(11) on filing a statement of account based on secondary transmissions of primary transmissions pursuant to section 111.

The Register is authorized to fix fees for other services, including the cost of preparing copies of Copyright Office records, whether or not such copies are certified, based on the cost of providing the service. Fees established under paragraphs (10) and (11) shall be reasonable and may not exceed one-half of the cost necessary to cover reasonable expenses incurred by the Copyright Office for the collection and administration of the statements of account and any royalty fees deposited with such statements.

(b) Adjustment of Fees.—The Register of Copyrights may, by regulation, adjust the fees for the services specified in paragraphs (1) through (9) of subsection (a) in the following manner:[8]

(1) The Register shall conduct a study of the costs incurred by the Copyright Office for the registration of claims, the recordation of documents, and the provision of services. The study shall also consider the timing of any adjustment in fees and the authority to use such fees consistent with the budget.

(2) The Register may, on the basis of the study under paragraph (1), and subject to paragraph (5), adjust fees to not more than that necessary to cover the reasonable costs incurred by the Copyright Office for the services described in paragraph (1), plus a reasonable inflation adjustment to account for any estimated increase in costs.

(3) Any fee established under paragraph (2) shall be rounded off to the nearest dollar, or for a fee less than $12, rounded off to the nearest 50 cents.

(4) Fees established under this subsection shall be fair and equitable and give due consideration to the objectives of the copyright system.

(5) If the Register determines under paragraph (2) that fees should be adjusted, the Register shall prepare a proposed fee schedule and submit the schedule with the accompanying economic analysis to the Congress. The fees proposed by the Register may be instituted after the end of 120 days after the schedule is submitted to the Congress unless, within that 120-day period, a law is enacted stating in substance that the Congress does not approve the schedule.

(c) The fees prescribed by or under this section are applicable to the United States Government and any of its agencies, employees, or officers, but the Register of Copyrights has discretion to waive the requirement of this subsection in occasional or isolated cases involving relatively small amounts.

(d) (1) Except as provided in paragraph (2), all fees received under this section shall be deposited by the Register of Copyrights in the Treasury of the United

States and shall be credited to the appropriations for necessary expenses of the Copyright Office. Such fees that are collected shall remain available until expended. The Register may, in accordance with regulations that he or she shall prescribe, refund any sum paid by mistake or in excess of the fee required by this section.

(2) In the case of fees deposited against future services, the Register of Copyrights shall request the Secretary of the Treasury to invest in interest-bearing securities in the United States Treasury any portion of the fees that, as determined by the Register, is not required to meet current deposit account demands. Funds from such portion of fees shall be invested in securities that permit funds to be available to the Copyright Office at all times if they are determined to be necessary to meet current deposit account demands. Such investments shall be in public debt securities with maturities suitable to the needs of the Copyright Office, as determined by the Register of Copyrights, and bearing interest at rates determined by the Secretary of the Treasury, taking into consideration current market yields on outstanding marketable obligations of the United States of comparable maturities.

(3) The income on such investments shall be deposited in the Treasury of the United States and shall be credited to the appropriations for necessary expenses of the Copyright Office.

§709 · Delay in delivery caused by disruption of postal or other services

In any case in which the Register of Copyrights determines, on the basis of such evidence as the Register may by regulation require, that a deposit, application, fee, or any other material to be delivered to the Copyright Office by a particular date, would have been received in the Copyright Office in due time except for a general disruption or suspension of postal or other transportation or communications services, the actual receipt of such material in the Copyright Office within one month after the date on which the Register determines that the disruption or suspension of such services has terminated, shall be considered timely.

Chapter 7 · Notes

1. The Work Made for Hire and Copyright Corrections Act of 2000 amended the table of sections for chapter 7 by deleting section 710, entitled, "Reproduction for use of the blind and physically handicapped: Voluntary licensing forms and procedures." Pub. L. No. 106-379, 114 Stat. 1444, 1445.

2. The Copyright Fees and Technical Amendments Act of 1989 amended section 701 by adding subsection (e). Pub. L. No. 101-319, 104 Stat. 290. In 1998, the Digital Millennium Copyright Act amended section 701 by adding a new subsection (b), redesignating former subsections (b) through (e) as (c) through (f) respectively, and, in the new subsection (f), by substituting "III" for "IV" and "5314" for "5315." Pub. L. No. 105-304, 112 Stat. 2860, 2887.

3. Title 5 of the *United States Code* is entitled "Government Organization and Employees."

4. Copyright Office regulations are published in the *Federal Register* and in title 37, chapter II, of the *Code of Federal Regulations.*

5. The Copyright Cleanup, Clarification, and Corrections Act of 2010 amended the last sentence of section 704(e) to substitute "section 708(a)" for "section 708(a)(10)." Pub. L. No. 111-295, 124 Stat. 3180, 3181.

6. The Work Made for Hire and Copyright Corrections Act of 2000 amended section 705 by rewriting paragraph (a). Pub. L. No. 106-379, 114 Stat. 1444, 1445.

7. The Copyright Fees and Technical Amendments Act of 1989 amended section 708 by substituting a new subsection (a), by redesignating subsections (b) and (c) as subsections (c) and (d), respectively, and by adding a new subsection (b). Pub. L. No. 101-318, 104 Stat. 287. The Act states that these amendments "shall take effect 6 months after the date of the enactment of this Act" and shall apply to:

(A) claims to original, supplementary, and renewal copyright received for registration, and to items received for recordation in the Copyright Office, on or after such effective date, and

(B) other requests for services received on or after such effective date, or received before such effective date for services not yet rendered as of such date.

With respect to prior claims, the Act states that claims to original, supplementary, and renewal copyright received for registration and items received for recordation in acceptable form in the Copyright Office before the above mentioned effective date, and requests for services which are rendered before such effective date "shall be governed by section 708 of title 17, United States Code, as in effect before such effective date." Pub. L. No. 101-318, 104 Stat. 287, 288.

The Copyright Renewal Act of 1992 amended paragraph (2) of section 708(a) by striking the words "in its first term" and by substituting "$20" in lieu of "$12." Pub. L. No. 102-307, 106 Stat. 264, 266.

In 1997, section 708 was amended by rewriting subsections (b) and (d) in their entirety. Pub. L. No. 105-80, 111 Stat. 1529, 1532.

The Work Made for Hire and Copyright Corrections Act of 2000 amended section 708 by rewriting subsection (a), by substituting new language for the first sentence in subsection (b) and by substituting "adjustment" for "increase" in paragraph (b)(1), the word "adjust" for "increase" in paragraph (b)(2) and the word "adjusted" for "increased" in paragraph (b)(5). Pub. L. No. 106-379, 114 Stat. 1444, 1445. The Act also stated that "The fees under section 708(a) of title 17, United States Code, on the date of the enactment of this Act shall be the fees in effect under section 708(a) of such title on the day before such date of enactment."

The Satellite Television Extension and Localism Act of 2010 amended subsection 708(a) by adding new paragraphs (10) and (11) and by adding the last sentence. Pub. L. No. 111-175, 124 Stat. 1218, 1244-45.

8. The current fees may be found in the *Code of Federal Regulations*, at 37 CFR §201.3, as authorized by Pub. L. No. 105-80, 111 Stat. 1529, 1532. In Pub. L. No. 105-80, Congress amended section 708(b) to require that the Register of Copyrights establish fees by regulation rather than by codifying them in title 17, *United States Code*, as was previously done.

Chapter 8[1]

Proceedings by Copyright Royalty Judges

§801 · Copyright Royalty Judges; appointment and functions[2]

(a) APPOINTMENT.—The Librarian of Congress shall appoint 3 full-time Copyright Royalty Judges, and shall appoint 1 of the 3 as the Chief Copyright Royalty Judge. The Librarian shall make appointments to such positions after consultation with the Register of Copyrights.

(b) FUNCTIONS.—Subject to the provisions of this chapter, the functions of the Copyright Royalty Judges shall be as follows:

(1) To make determinations and adjustments of reasonable terms and rates of royalty payments as provided in sections 112(e), 114, 115, 116, 118, 119, and 1004. The rates applicable under sections 114(f)(1)(B), 115, and 116 shall be calculated to achieve the following objectives:

(A) To maximize the availability of creative works to the public.

(B) To afford the copyright owner a fair return for his or her creative work and the copyright user a fair income under existing economic conditions.

(C) To reflect the relative roles of the copyright owner and the copyright user in the product made available to the public with respect to relative creative contribution, technological contribution, capital investment, cost, risk, and contribution to the opening of new markets for creative expression and media for their communication.

(D) To minimize any disruptive impact on the structure of the industries involved and on generally prevailing industry practices.

(2) To make determinations concerning the adjustment of the copyright royalty rates under section 111 solely in accordance with the following provisions:

(A) The rates established by section 111(d)(1)(B) may be adjusted to reflect—

(i) national monetary inflation or deflation; or

(ii) changes in the average rates charged cable subscribers for the basic service of providing secondary transmissions to maintain the real constant dollar level of the royalty fee per subscriber which existed as of the date of October 19, 1976,

except that—

(I) if the average rates charged cable system subscribers for the basic service of providing secondary transmissions are changed so that the average rates exceed national monetary inflation, no change in the rates established by section 111(d)(1)(B) shall be permitted; and

(II) no increase in the royalty fee shall be permitted based on any reduction in the average number of distant signal equivalents per subscriber.

The Copyright Royalty Judges may consider all factors relating to the maintenance of such level of payments, including, as an extenuating factor, whether the industry has been restrained by subscriber rate regulating authorities from increasing the rates for the basic service of providing secondary transmissions.

(B) In the event that the rules and regulations of the Federal Communications Commission are amended at any time after April 15, 1976, to permit the carriage by cable systems of additional television broadcast signals beyond the local service area of the primary transmitters of such signals, the royalty rates established by section 111(d)(1)(B) may be adjusted to ensure that the rates for the additional distant signal equivalents resulting from such carriage are reasonable in the light of the changes effected by the amendment to such rules and regulations. In determining the reasonableness of rates proposed following an amendment of Federal Communications Commission rules and regulations, the Copyright Royalty Judges shall consider, among other factors, the economic impact on copyright owners and users; except that no adjustment in royalty rates shall be made under this subparagraph with respect to any distant signal equivalent or fraction thereof represented by—

(i) carriage of any signal permitted under the rules and regulations of the Federal Communications Commission in effect on April 15, 1976, or the carriage of a signal of the same type (that is, independent, network, or noncommercial educational) substituted for such permitted signal; or

(ii) a television broadcast signal first carried after April 15, 1976, pursuant to an individual waiver of the rules and regulations of the Federal Communications Commission, as such rules and regulations were in effect on April 15, 1976.

(C) In the event of any change in the rules and regulations of the Federal Communications Commission with respect to syndicated and sports program exclusivity after April 15, 1976, the rates established by section 111(d)(1)(B) may be adjusted to assure that such rates are reasonable in light of the changes to such rules and regulations, but any such adjustment shall apply only to the affected television broadcast signals carried on those systems affected by the change.

(D) The gross receipts limitations established by section 111(d)(1)(C) and (D) shall be adjusted to reflect national monetary inflation or deflation or changes in the average rates charged cable system subscribers for the basic service of providing secondary transmissions to maintain the real constant dollar value of the exemption provided by such section, and the royalty rate specified therein shall not be subject to adjustment.

(3)(A) To authorize the distribution, under sections 111, 119, and 1007, of those royalty fees collected under sections 111, 119, and 1005, as the case may be, to the extent that the Copyright Royalty Judges have found that the distribution of such fees is not subject to controversy.

(B) In cases where the Copyright Royalty Judges determine that controversy exists, the Copyright Royalty Judges shall determine the distribution of such fees, including partial distributions, in accordance with section 111, 119, or 1007, as the case may be.

(C) Notwithstanding section 804(b)(8), the Copyright Royalty Judges, at any time after the filing of claims under section 111, 119, or 1007, may, upon motion of one or more of the claimants and after publication in the Federal Register of a request for responses to the motion from interested claimants, make a partial distribution of such fees, if, based upon all responses received during the 30-day period beginning on the date of such publication, the Copyright Royalty Judges conclude that no claimant entitled to receive such fees has stated a reasonable objection to the partial distribution, and all such claimants—

(i) agree to the partial distribution;

(ii) sign an agreement obligating them to return any excess amounts to the extent necessary to comply with the final determination on the distribution of the fees made under subparagraph (B);

(iii) file the agreement with the Copyright Royalty Judges; and

(iv) agree that such funds are available for distribution.

(D) The Copyright Royalty Judges and any other officer or employee acting in good faith in distributing funds under subparagraph (C) shall not be held liable for the payment of any excess fees under subparagraph (C). The Copyright Royalty Judges shall, at the time the final determination is made, calculate any such excess amounts.

(4) To accept or reject royalty claims filed under sections 111, 119, and 1007, on the basis of timeliness or the failure to establish the basis for a claim.

(5) To accept or reject rate adjustment petitions as provided in section 804 and petitions to participate as provided in section 803(b) (1) and (2).

(6) To determine the status of a digital audio recording device or a digital audio interface device under sections 1002 and 1003, as provided in section 1010.

(7)(A) To adopt as a basis for statutory terms and rates or as a basis for the distribution of statutory royalty payments, an agreement concerning such matters reached among some or all of the participants in a proceeding at any time during the proceeding, except that—

(i) the Copyright Royalty Judges shall provide to those that would be bound by the terms, rates, or other determination set by any agreement in a proceeding to determine royalty rates an opportunity to comment on the agreement and shall provide to participants in the proceeding under section 803(b)(2) that would be bound by the terms, rates, or other determination set by the agreement an opportunity to comment on the agreement and object to its adoption as a basis for statutory terms and rates; and

(ii) the Copyright Royalty Judges may decline to adopt the agreement as a basis for statutory terms and rates for participants that are not parties to the agreement, if any participant described in clause (i) objects to the agreement and the Copyright Royalty Judges conclude, based on the record before them if one exists, that the agreement does not provide a reasonable basis for setting statutory terms or rates.

(B) License agreements voluntarily negotiated pursuant to section 112(e)(5), 114(f)(3), 115(c)(3)(E)(i), 116(c), or 118(b)(2) that do not result in statutory terms and rates shall not be subject to clauses (i) and (ii) of subparagraph (A).

(C) Interested parties may negotiate and agree to, and the Copyright Royalty Judges may adopt, an agreement that specifies as terms notice and recordkeeping requirements that apply in lieu of those that would otherwise apply under regulations.

(8) To perform other duties, as assigned by the Register of Copyrights within the Library of Congress, except as provided in section 802(g), at times when Copyright Royalty Judges are not engaged in performing the other duties set forth in this section.

(c) Rulings.—The Copyright Royalty Judges may make any necessary procedural or evidentiary rulings in any proceeding under this chapter and may, before commencing a proceeding under this chapter, make any such rulings that would apply to the proceedings conducted by the Copyright Royalty Judges.

(d) Administrative Support.—The Librarian of Congress shall provide the Copyright Royalty Judges with the necessary administrative services related to proceedings under this chapter.

(e) Location in Library of Congress.—The offices of the Copyright Royalty Judges and staff shall be in the Library of Congress.

(f) Effective Date of Actions.—On and after the date of the enactment of the Copyright Royalty and Distribution Reform Act of 2004, in any case in which time limits are prescribed under this title for performance of an action with or by the Copyright Royalty Judges, and in which the last day of the prescribed period falls on a Saturday, Sunday, holiday, or other nonbusiness day within the District of Columbia or the Federal Government, the action may be taken on the next succeeding business day, and is effective as of the date when the period expired.

§802 · Copyright Royalty Judgeships; staff[3]

(a) Qualifications of Copyright Royalty Judges.—

(1) In general.—Each Copyright Royalty Judge shall be an attorney who has at least 7 years of legal experience. The Chief Copyright Royalty Judge shall have at least 5 years of experience in adjudications, arbitrations, or court trials. Of the other 2 Copyright Royalty Judges, 1 shall have significant knowledge of copyright law, and the other shall have significant

knowledge of economics. An individual may serve as a Copyright Royalty Judge only if the individual is free of any financial conflict of interest under subsection (h).

(2) Definition.—In this subsection, the term "adjudication" has the meaning given that term in section 551 of title 5, but does not include mediation.

(b) Staff.—The Chief Copyright Royalty Judge shall hire 3 full-time staff members to assist the Copyright Royalty Judges in performing their functions.

(c) Terms.—The individual first appointed as the Chief Copyright Royalty Judge shall be appointed to a term of 6 years, and of the remaining individuals first appointed as Copyright Royalty Judges, 1 shall be appointed to a term of 4 years, and the other shall be appointed to a term of 2 years. Thereafter, the terms of succeeding Copyright Royalty Judges shall each be 6 years. An individual serving as a Copyright Royalty Judge may be reappointed to subsequent terms. The term of a Copyright Royalty Judge shall begin when the term of the predecessor of that Copyright Royalty Judge ends. When the term of office of a Copyright Royalty Judge ends, the individual serving that term may continue to serve until a successor is selected.

(d) Vacancies or Incapacity.—

(1) Vacancies.—If a vacancy should occur in the position of Copyright Royalty Judge, the Librarian of Congress shall act expeditiously to fill the vacancy, and may appoint an interim Copyright Royalty Judge to serve until another Copyright Royalty Judge is appointed under this section. An individual appointed to fill the vacancy occurring before the expiration of the term for which the predecessor of that individual was appointed shall be appointed for the remainder of that term.

(2) Incapacity.—In the case in which a Copyright Royalty Judge is temporarily unable to perform his or her duties, the Librarian of Congress may appoint an interim Copyright Royalty Judge to perform such duties during the period of such incapacity.

(e) Compensation.—

(1) Judges.—The Chief Copyright Royalty Judge shall receive compensation at the rate of basic pay payable for level AL-1 for administrative law judges pursuant to section 5372(b) of title 5, and each of the other two Copyright Royalty Judges shall receive compensation at the rate of basic pay payable for level AL-2 for administrative law judges pursuant to such section. The compensation of the Copyright Royalty Judges shall not be subject to any regulations adopted by the Office of Personnel Management pursuant to its authority under section 5376(b)(1) of title 5.

(2) Staff members.—Of the staff members appointed under subsection (b)—

(A) the rate of pay of 1 staff member shall be not more than the basic rate of pay payable for level 10 of GS-15 of the General Schedule;

(B) the rate of pay of 1 staff member shall be not less than the basic rate of pay payable for GS-13 of the General Schedule and not more than the basic rate of pay payable for level 10 of GS-14 of such Schedule; and

(C) the rate of pay for the third staff member shall be not less than the basic rate of pay payable for GS-8 of the General Schedule and not more than the basic rate of pay payable for level 10 of GS-11 of such Schedule.

(3) Locality pay.—All rates of pay referred to under this subsection shall include locality pay.

(f) Independence of Copyright Royalty Judge.—

(1) In making determinations.—

(A) In general.—(i) Subject to subparagraph (B) and clause (ii) of this subparagraph, the Copyright Royalty Judges shall have full independence in making determinations concerning adjustments and determinations of copyright royalty rates and terms, the distribution of copyright royalties, the acceptance or rejection of royalty claims, rate adjustment petitions, and petitions to participate, and in issuing other rulings under this title, except that the Copyright Royalty Judges may consult with the Register of Copyrights on any matter other than a question of fact.

(ii) One or more Copyright Royalty Judges may, or by motion to the Copyright Royalty Judges, any participant in a proceeding may, request from the Register of Copyrights an interpretation of any material questions of substantive law that relate to the construction of provisions of this title and arise in the course of the proceeding. Any request for a written interpretation shall be in writing and on the record, and reasonable provision shall be made to permit participants in the proceeding to comment on the material questions of substantive law in a manner that minimizes duplication and delay. Except as provided in subparagraph (B), the Register of Copyrights shall deliver to the Copyright Royalty Judges a written response within 14 days after the receipt of all briefs and comments from the participants. The Copyright Royalty Judges shall apply the legal interpretation embodied in the response of the Register of Copyrights if it is timely delivered, and the response shall be included in the record that accompanies the final determination. The authority under this clause shall not be construed to authorize the Register of Copyrights to provide an interpretation of questions of procedure before the Copyright Royalty Judges, the ultimate adjustments and determinations of copyright royalty rates and terms, the ultimate distribution of copyright royalties, or the acceptance or rejection of royalty claims, rate adjustment petitions, or petitions to participate in a proceeding.

(B) Novel questions.—(i) In any case in which a novel material question of substantive law concerning an interpretation of those provisions of this title that are the subject of the proceeding is presented, the Copyright

Royalty Judges shall request a decision of the Register of Copyrights, in writing, to resolve such novel question. Reasonable provision shall be made for comment on such request by the participants in the proceeding, in such a way as to minimize duplication and delay. The Register of Copyrights shall transmit his or her decision to the Copyright Royalty Judges within 30 days after the Register of Copyrights receives all of the briefs or comments of the participants. Such decision shall be in writing and included by the Copyright Royalty Judges in the record that accompanies their final determination. If such a decision is timely delivered to the Copyright Royalty Judges, the Copyright Royalty Judges shall apply the legal determinations embodied in the decision of the Register of Copyrights in resolving material questions of substantive law.

(ii) In clause (i), a "novel question of law" is a question of law that has not been determined in prior decisions, determinations, and rulings described in section 803(a).

(C) Consultation.—Notwithstanding the provisions of subparagraph (A), the Copyright Royalty Judges shall consult with the Register of Copyrights with respect to any determination or ruling that would require that any act be performed by the Copyright Office, and any such determination or ruling shall not be binding upon the Register of Copyrights.

(D) Review of legal conclusions by the Register of Copyrights.—The Register of Copyrights may review for legal error the resolution by the Copyright Royalty Judges of a material question of substantive law under this title that underlies or is contained in a final determination of the Copyright Royalty Judges. If the Register of Copyrights concludes, after taking into consideration the views of the participants in the proceeding, that any resolution reached by the Copyright Royalty Judges was in material error, the Register of Copyrights shall issue a written decision correcting such legal error, which shall be made part of the record of the proceeding. The Register of Copyrights shall issue such written decision not later than 60 days after the date on which the final determination by the Copyright Royalty Judges is issued. Additionally, the Register of Copyrights shall cause to be published in the Federal Register such written decision, together with a specific identification of the legal conclusion of the Copyright Royalty Judges that is determined to be erroneous. As to conclusions of substantive law involving an interpretation of the statutory provisions of this title, the decision of the Register of Copyrights shall be binding as precedent upon the Copyright Royalty Judges in subsequent proceedings under this chapter. When a decision has been rendered pursuant to this subparagraph, the Register of Copyrights may, on the basis of and in accordance with such decision, intervene as of right in any appeal of a final determination of the Copyright Royalty Judges pursuant to section

803(d) in the United States Court of Appeals for the District of Columbia Circuit. If, prior to intervening in such an appeal, the Register of Copyrights gives notification to, and undertakes to consult with, the Attorney General with respect to such intervention, and the Attorney General fails, within a reasonable period after receiving such notification, to intervene in such appeal, the Register of Copyrights may intervene in such appeal in his or her own name by any attorney designated by the Register of Copyrights for such purpose. Intervention by the Register of Copyrights in his or her own name shall not preclude the Attorney General from intervening on behalf of the United States in such an appeal as may be otherwise provided or required by law.

(E) Effect on judicial review.—Nothing in this section shall be interpreted to alter the standard applied by a court in reviewing legal determinations involving an interpretation or construction of the provisions of this title or to affect the extent to which any construction or interpretation of the provisions of this title shall be accorded deference by a reviewing court.

(2) Performance appraisals.—

(A) In general.—Notwithstanding any other provision of law or any regulation of the Library of Congress, and subject to subparagraph (B), the Copyright Royalty Judges shall not receive performance appraisals.

(B) Relating to sanction or removal.—To the extent that the Librarian of Congress adopts regulations under subsection (h) relating to the sanction or removal of a Copyright Royalty Judge and such regulations require documentation to establish the cause of such sanction or removal, the Copyright Royalty Judge may receive an appraisal related specifically to the cause of the sanction or removal.

(g) Inconsistent Duties Barred.—No Copyright Royalty Judge may undertake duties that conflict with his or her duties and responsibilities as a Copyright Royalty Judge.

(h) Standards of Conduct.—The Librarian of Congress shall adopt regulations regarding the standards of conduct, including financial conflict of interest and restrictions against ex parte communications, which shall govern the Copyright Royalty Judges and the proceedings under this chapter.

(i) Removal or Sanction.—The Librarian of Congress may sanction or remove a Copyright Royalty Judge for violation of the standards of conduct adopted under subsection (h), misconduct, neglect of duty, or any disqualifying physical or mental disability. Any sanction or removal may be made only after notice and opportunity for a hearing, but the Librarian of Congress may suspend the Copyright Royalty Judge during the pendency of such hearing. The Librarian shall appoint an interim Copyright Royalty Judge during the period of any such suspension.

§ 803 · Proceedings of Copyright Royalty Judges[4]

(a) Proceedings.—

(1) In general.—The Copyright Royalty Judges shall act in accordance with this title, and to the extent not inconsistent with this title, in accordance with subchapter II of chapter 5 of title 5, in carrying out the purposes set forth in section 801. The Copyright Royalty Judges shall act in accordance with regulations issued by the Copyright Royalty Judges and the Librarian of Congress, and on the basis of a written record, prior determinations and interpretations of the Copyright Royalty Tribunal, Librarian of Congress, the Register of Copyrights, copyright arbitration royalty panels (to the extent those determinations are not inconsistent with a decision of the Librarian of Congress or the Register of Copyrights), and the Copyright Royalty Judges (to the extent those determinations are not inconsistent with a decision of the Register of Copyrights that was timely delivered to the Copyright Royalty Judges pursuant to section 802(f)(1) (A) or (B), or with a decision of the Register of Copyrights pursuant to section 802(f)(1)(D)), under this chapter, and decisions of the court of appeals under this chapter before, on, or after the effective date of the Copyright Royalty and Distribution Reform Act of 2004.

(2) Judges acting as panel and individually.—The Copyright Royalty Judges shall preside over hearings in proceedings under this chapter en banc. The Chief Copyright Royalty Judge may designate a Copyright Royalty Judge to preside individually over such collateral and administrative proceedings, and over such proceedings under paragraphs (1) through (5) of subsection (b), as the Chief Judge considers appropriate.

(3) Determinations.—Final determinations of the Copyright Royalty Judges in proceedings under this chapter shall be made by majority vote. A Copyright Royalty Judge dissenting from the majority on any determination under this chapter may issue his or her dissenting opinion, which shall be included with the determination.

(b) Procedures.—

(1) Initiation.—

(A) Call for petitions to participate.—(i) The Copyright Royalty Judges shall cause to be published in the Federal Register notice of commencement of proceedings under this chapter, calling for the filing of petitions to participate in a proceeding under this chapter for the purpose of making the relevant determination under section 111, 112, 114, 115, 116, 118, 119, 1004, or 1007, as the case may be—

(I) promptly upon a determination made under section 804(a);

(II) by no later than January 5 of a year specified in paragraph (2) of section 804(b) for the commencement of proceedings;

(III) by no later than January 5 of a year specified in subparagraph (A) or (B) of paragraph (3) of section 804(b) for the commencement of proceedings, or as otherwise provided in subparagraph (A) or (C) of such paragraph for the commencement of proceedings;

(IV) as provided under section 804(b)(8); or

(V) by no later than January 5 of a year specified in any other provision of section 804(b) for the filing of petitions for the commencement of proceedings, if a petition has not been filed by that date, except that the publication of notice requirement shall not apply in the case of proceedings under section 111 that are scheduled to commence in 2005.

(ii) Petitions to participate shall be filed by no later than 30 days after publication of notice of commencement of a proceeding under clause (i), except that the Copyright Royalty Judges may, for substantial good cause shown and if there is no prejudice to the participants that have already filed petitions, accept late petitions to participate at any time up to the date that is 90 days before the date on which participants in the proceeding are to file their written direct statements. Notwithstanding the preceding sentence, petitioners whose petitions are filed more than 30 days after publication of notice of commencement of a proceeding are not eligible to object to a settlement reached during the voluntary negotiation period under paragraph (3), and any objection filed by such a petitioner shall not be taken into account by the Copyright Royalty Judges.

(B) Petitions to participate.—Each petition to participate in a proceeding shall describe the petitioner's interest in the subject matter of the proceeding. Parties with similar interests may file a single petition to participate.

(2) Participation in general.—Subject to paragraph (4), a person may participate in a proceeding under this chapter, including through the submission of briefs or other information, only if—

(A) that person has filed a petition to participate in accordance with paragraph (1) (either individually or as a group under paragraph (1)(B));

(B) the Copyright Royalty Judges have not determined that the petition to participate is facially invalid;

(C) the Copyright Royalty Judges have not determined, sua sponte or on the motion of another participant in the proceeding, that the person lacks a significant interest in the proceeding; and

(D) the petition to participate is accompanied by either—

(i) in a proceeding to determine royalty rates, a filing fee of $150; or

(ii) in a proceeding to determine distribution of royalty fees—

(I) a filing fee of $150; or

(II) a statement that the petitioner (individually or as a group) will not seek a distribution of more than $1000, in which case the amount distributed to the petitioner shall not exceed $1000.

(3) Voluntary negotiation period.—

(A) Commencement of proceedings.—

(i) Rate adjustment proceeding.—Promptly after the date for filing of petitions to participate in a proceeding, the Copyright Royalty Judges shall make available to all participants in the proceeding a list of such participants and shall initiate a voluntary negotiation period among the participants.

(ii) Distribution proceeding.—Promptly after the date for filing of petitions to participate in a proceeding to determine the distribution of royalties, the Copyright Royalty Judges shall make available to all participants in the proceeding a list of such participants. The initiation of a voluntary negotiation period among the participants shall be set at a time determined by the Copyright Royalty Judges.

(B) Length of proceedings.—The voluntary negotiation period initiated under subparagraph (A) shall be 3 months.

(C) Determination of subsequent proceedings.—At the close of the voluntary negotiation proceedings, the Copyright Royalty Judges shall, if further proceedings under this chapter are necessary, determine whether and to what extent paragraphs (4) and (5) will apply to the parties.

(4) Small claims procedure in distribution proceedings.—

(A) In general.—If, in a proceeding under this chapter to determine the distribution of royalties, the contested amount of a claim is $10,000 or less, the Copyright Royalty Judges shall decide the controversy on the basis of the filing of the written direct statement by the participant, the response by any opposing participant, and 1 additional response by each such party.

(B) Bad faith inflation of claim.—If the Copyright Royalty Judges determine that a participant asserts in bad faith an amount in controversy in excess of $10,000 for the purpose of avoiding a determination under the procedure set forth in subparagraph (A), the Copyright Royalty Judges shall impose a fine on that participant in an amount not to exceed the difference between the actual amount distributed and the amount asserted by the participant.

(5) Paper proceedings.—The Copyright Royalty Judges in proceedings under this chapter may decide, sua sponte or upon motion of a participant, to determine issues on the basis of the filing of the written direct statement by the participant, the response by any opposing participant, and one additional response by each such participant. Prior to making such decision to proceed on such a paper record only, the Copyright Royalty Judges shall offer to all parties to the proceeding the opportunity to comment on the decision. The procedure under this paragraph—

(A) shall be applied in cases in which there is no genuine issue of material fact, there is no need for evidentiary hearings, and all participants in the proceeding agree in writing to the procedure; and

(B) may be applied under such other circumstances as the Copyright Royalty Judges consider appropriate.

(6) Regulations.—

(A) In general.—The Copyright Royalty Judges may issue regulations to carry out their functions under this title. All regulations issued by the Copyright Royalty Judges are subject to the approval of the Librarian of Congress and are subject to judicial review pursuant to chapter 7 of title 5, except as set forth in subsection (d). Not later than 120 days after Copyright Royalty Judges or interim Copyright Royalty Judges, as the case may be, are first appointed after the enactment of the Copyright Royalty and Distribution Reform Act of 2004, such judges shall issue regulations to govern proceedings under this chapter.

(B) Interim regulations.—Until regulations are adopted under subparagraph (A), the Copyright Royalty Judges shall apply the regulations in effect under this chapter on the day before the effective date of the Copyright Royalty and Distribution Reform Act of 2004, to the extent such regulations are not inconsistent with this chapter, except that functions carried out under such regulations by the Librarian of Congress, the Register of Copyrights, or copyright arbitration royalty panels that, as of such date of enactment, are to be carried out by the Copyright Royalty Judges under this chapter, shall be carried out by the Copyright Royalty Judges under such regulations.

(C) Requirements.—Regulations issued under subparagraph (A) shall include the following:

(i) The written direct statements and written rebuttal statements of all participants in a proceeding under paragraph (2) shall be filed by a date specified by the Copyright Royalty Judges, which, in the case of written direct statements, may be not earlier than 4 months, and not later than 5 months, after the end of the voluntary negotiation period under paragraph (3). Notwithstanding the preceding sentence, the Copyright Royalty Judges may allow a participant in a proceeding to file an amended written direct statement based on new information received during the discovery process, within 15 days after the end of the discovery period specified in clause (iv).

(ii)(I) Following the submission to the Copyright Royalty Judges of written direct statements and written rebuttal statements by the participants in a proceeding under paragraph (2), the Copyright Royalty Judges, after taking into consideration the views of the participants in the proceeding, shall determine a schedule for conducting and completing discovery.

(II) In this chapter, the term "written direct statements" means witness statements, testimony, and exhibits to be presented in the proceedings, and such other information that is necessary to establish terms and rates, or the distribution of royalty payments, as the case may be, as set forth in regulations issued by the Copyright Royalty Judges.

(iii) Hearsay may be admitted in proceedings under this chapter to the extent deemed appropriate by the Copyright Royalty Judges.

(iv) Discovery in connection with written direct statements shall be permitted for a period of 60 days, except for discovery ordered by the Copyright Royalty Judges in connection with the resolution of motions, orders, and disputes pending at the end of such period. The Copyright Royalty Judges may order a discovery schedule in connection with written rebuttal statements.

(v) Any participant under paragraph (2) in a proceeding under this chapter to determine royalty rates may request of an opposing participant nonprivileged documents directly related to the written direct statement or written rebuttal statement of that participant. Any objection to such a request shall be resolved by a motion or request to compel production made to the Copyright Royalty Judges in accordance with regulations adopted by the Copyright Royalty Judges. Each motion or request to compel discovery shall be determined by the Copyright Royalty Judges, or by a Copyright Royalty Judge when permitted under subsection (a)(2). Upon such motion, the Copyright Royalty Judges may order discovery pursuant to regulations established under this paragraph.

(vi)(I) Any participant under paragraph (2) in a proceeding under this chapter to determine royalty rates may, by means of written motion or on the record, request of an opposing participant or witness other relevant information and materials if, absent the discovery sought, the Copyright Royalty Judges' resolution of the proceeding would be substantially impaired. In determining whether discovery will be granted under this clause, the Copyright Royalty Judges may consider—

(aa) whether the burden or expense of producing the requested information or materials outweighs the likely benefit, taking into account the needs and resources of the participants, the importance of the issues at stake, and the probative value of the requested information or materials in resolving such issues;

(bb) whether the requested information or materials would be unreasonably cumulative or duplicative, or are obtainable from another source that is more convenient, less burdensome, or less expensive; and

(cc) whether the participant seeking discovery has had ample opportunity by discovery in the proceeding or by other means to obtain the information sought.

(II) This clause shall not apply to any proceeding scheduled to commence after December 31, 2010.

(vii) In a proceeding under this chapter to determine royalty rates, the participants entitled to receive royalties shall collectively be permitted to take no more than 10 depositions and secure responses to no more than 25 interrogatories, and the participants obligated to pay royalties shall collectively be permitted to take no more than 10 depositions and secure responses to no more than 25 interrogatories. The Copyright Royalty Judges shall resolve any disputes among similarly aligned participants to allocate the number of depositions or interrogatories permitted under this clause.

(viii) The rules and practices in effect on the day before the effective date of the Copyright Royalty and Distribution Reform Act of 2004, relating to discovery in proceedings under this chapter to determine the distribution of royalty fees, shall continue to apply to such proceedings on and after such effective date.

(ix) In proceedings to determine royalty rates, the Copyright Royalty Judges may issue a subpoena commanding a participant or witness to appear and give testimony, or to produce and permit inspection of documents or tangible things, if the Copyright Royalty Judges' resolution of the proceeding would be substantially impaired by the absence of such testimony or production of documents or tangible things. Such subpoena shall specify with reasonable particularity the materials to be produced or the scope and nature of the required testimony. Nothing in this clause shall preclude the Copyright Royalty Judges from requesting the production by a nonparticipant of information or materials relevant to the resolution by the Copyright Royalty Judges of a material issue of fact.

(x) The Copyright Royalty Judges shall order a settlement conference among the participants in the proceeding to facilitate the presentation of offers of settlement among the participants. The settlement conference shall be held during a 21-day period following the 60-day discovery period specified in clause (iv) and shall take place outside the presence of the Copyright Royalty Judges.

(xi) No evidence, including exhibits, may be submitted in the written direct statement or written rebuttal statement of a participant without a sponsoring witness, except where the Copyright Royalty Judges have taken official notice, or in the case of incorporation by reference of past records, or for good cause shown.

(c) Determination of Copyright Royalty Judges.—

(1) Timing.—The Copyright Royalty Judges shall issue their determination in a proceeding not later than 11 months after the conclusion of the 21-day settlement conference period under subsection (b)(6)(C)(x), but, in the case of a proceeding to determine successors to rates or terms that expire on a specified date, in no event later than 15 days before the expiration of the then current statutory rates and terms.

(2) Rehearings.—

(A) In general.—The Copyright Royalty Judges may, in exceptional cases, upon motion of a participant in a proceeding under subsection (b)(2), order a rehearing, after the determination in the proceeding is issued under paragraph (1), on such matters as the Copyright Royalty Judges determine to be appropriate.

(B) Timing for filing motion.—Any motion for a rehearing under subparagraph (A) may only be filed within 15 days after the date on which the Copyright Royalty Judges deliver to the participants in the proceeding their initial determination.

(C) Participation by opposing party not required.—In any case in which a rehearing is ordered, any opposing party shall not be required to participate in the rehearing, except that nonparticipation may give rise to the limitations with respect to judicial review provided for in subsection (d)(1).

(D) No negative inference.—No negative inference shall be drawn from lack of participation in a rehearing.

(E) Continuity of rates and terms.—(i) If the decision of the Copyright Royalty Judges on any motion for a rehearing is not rendered before the expiration of the statutory rates and terms that were previously in effect, in the case of a proceeding to determine successors to rates and terms that expire on a specified date, then—

(I) the initial determination of the Copyright Royalty Judges that is the subject of the rehearing motion shall be effective as of the day following the date on which the rates and terms that were previously in effect expire; and

(II) in the case of a proceeding under section 114(f)(1)(C) or 114(f)(2)(C), royalty rates and terms shall, for purposes of section 114(f)(4)(B), be deemed to have been set at those rates and terms contained in the initial determination of the Copyright Royalty Judges that is the subject of the rehearing motion, as of the date of that determination.

(ii) The pendency of a motion for a rehearing under this paragraph shall not relieve persons obligated to make royalty payments who would be affected by the determination on that motion from providing the statements of account and any reports of use, to the extent required, and paying the royalties required under the relevant determination or regulations.

(iii) Notwithstanding clause (ii), whenever royalties described in clause (ii) are paid to a person other than the Copyright Office, the entity designated by the Copyright Royalty Judges to which such royalties are paid by the copyright user (and any successor thereto) shall, within 60 days after the motion for rehearing is resolved or, if the motion is granted, within 60 days after the rehearing is concluded, return any excess amounts previously paid to the extent necessary to comply with the final determination of royalty rates by the Copyright Royalty Judges. Any underpayment of royalties resulting from a rehearing shall be paid within the same period.

(3) Contents of determination.—A determination of the Copyright Royalty Judges shall be supported by the written record and shall set forth the findings of fact relied on by the Copyright Royalty Judges. Among other terms adopted in a determination, the Copyright Royalty Judges may specify notice and recordkeeping requirements of users of the copyrights at issue that apply in lieu of those that would otherwise apply under regulations.

(4) Continuing jurisdiction.—The Copyright Royalty Judges may issue an amendment to a written determination to correct any technical or clerical errors in the determination or to modify the terms, but not the rates, of royalty payments in response to unforeseen circumstances that would frustrate the proper implementation of such determination. Such amendment shall be set forth in a written addendum to the determination that shall be distributed to the participants of the proceeding and shall be published in the Federal Register.

(5) Protective order.—The Copyright Royalty Judges may issue such orders as may be appropriate to protect confidential information, including orders excluding confidential information from the record of the determination that is published or made available to the public, except that any terms or rates of royalty payments or distributions may not be excluded.

(6) Publication of determination.—By no later than the end of the 60-day period provided in section 802(f)(1)(D), the Librarian of Congress shall cause the determination, and any corrections thereto, to be published in the Federal Register. The Librarian of Congress shall also publicize the determination and corrections in such other manner as the Librarian considers appropriate, including, but not limited to, publication on the Internet. The Librarian of Congress shall also make the determination, corrections, and the accompanying record available for public inspection and copying.

(7) Late payment.—A determination of the Copyright Royalty Judges may include terms with respect to late payment, but in no way shall such terms prevent the copyright holder from asserting other rights or remedies provided under this title.

(d) Judicial Review.—

(1) Appeal.—Any determination of the Copyright Royalty Judges under subsection (c) may, within 30 days after the publication of the determination in the Federal Register, be appealed, to the United States Court of Appeals for the District of Columbia Circuit, by any aggrieved participant in the proceeding under subsection (b)(2) who fully participated in the proceeding and who would be bound by the determination. Any participant that did not participate in a rehearing may not raise any issue that was the subject of that rehearing at any stage of judicial review of the hearing determination. If no appeal is brought within that 30-day period, the determination of the Copyright Royalty Judges shall be final, and the royalty fee or determination with respect to the distribution of fees, as the case may be, shall take effect as set forth in paragraph (2).

(2) Effect of rates.—

(A) Expiration on specified date.—When this title provides that the royalty rates and terms that were previously in effect are to expire on a specified date, any adjustment or determination by the Copyright Royalty Judges of successor rates and terms for an ensuing statutory license period shall be effective as of the day following the date of expiration of the rates and terms that were previously in effect, even if the determination of the Copyright Royalty Judges is rendered on a later date. A licensee shall be obligated to continue making payments under the rates and terms previously in effect until such time as rates and terms for the successor period are established. Whenever royalties pursuant to this section are paid to a person other than the Copyright Office, the entity designated by the Copyright Royalty Judges to which such royalties are paid by the copyright user (and any successor thereto) shall, within 60 days after the final determination of the Copyright Royalty Judges establishing rates and terms for a successor period or the exhaustion of all rehearings or appeals of such determination, if any, return any excess amounts previously paid to the extent necessary to comply with the final determination of royalty rates. Any underpayment of royalties by a copyright user shall be paid to the entity designated by the Copyright Royalty Judges within the same period.

(B) Other cases.—In cases where rates and terms have not, prior to the inception of an activity, been established for that particular activity under the relevant license, such rates and terms shall be retroactive to the inception of activity under the relevant license covered by such rates and terms. In other cases where rates and terms do not expire on a specified date, successor rates and terms shall take effect on the first day of the second month that begins after the publication of the determination of the Copyright Royalty Judges in the Federal Register, except as otherwise provided in this title, or by the Copyright Royalty Judges, or as agreed by the participants in a proceeding that would be bound by the rates and terms. Except as otherwise provided in this title, the rates and terms, to the extent applicable, shall remain in effect until such successor rates and terms become effective.

(C) Obligation to make payments.—

(i) The pendency of an appeal under this subsection shall not relieve persons obligated to make royalty payments under section 111, 112, 114, 115, 116, 118, 119, or 1003, who would be affected by the determination on appeal, from–

(I) providing the applicable statements of account and report of use; and

(II) paying the royalties required under the relevant determination or regulations.

(ii) Notwithstanding clause (i), whenever royalties described in clause (i) are paid to a person other than the Copyright Office, the entity designated by the Copyright Royalty Judges to which such royalties are paid by the copyright user (and any successor thereto) shall, within 60 days after the final resolution of the appeal, return any excess amounts previously paid (and interest thereon, if ordered pursuant to paragraph (3)) to the extent necessary to comply with the final determination of royalty rates on appeal. Any underpayment of royalties resulting from an appeal (and interest thereon, if ordered pursuant to paragraph (3)) shall be paid within the same period.

(3) Jurisdiction of court.—Section 706 of title 5 shall apply with respect to review by the court of appeals under this subsection. If the court modifies or vacates a determination of the Copyright Royalty Judges, the court may enter its own determination with respect to the amount or distribution of royalty fees and costs, and order the repayment of any excess fees, the payment of any underpaid fees, and the payment of interest pertaining respectively thereto, in accordance with its final judgment. The court may also vacate the determination of the Copyright Royalty Judges and remand the case to the Copyright Royalty Judges for further proceedings in accordance with subsection (a).

(e) Administrative Matters.—

(1) Deduction of costs of Library of Congress and Copyright Office from filing fees.—

(A) Deduction from filing fees.—The Librarian of Congress may, to the extent not otherwise provided under this title, deduct from the filing fees collected under subsection (b) for a particular proceeding under this chapter the reasonable costs incurred by the Librarian of Congress, the Copyright Office, and the Copyright Royalty Judges in conducting that proceeding, other than the salaries of the Copyright Royalty Judges and the 3 staff members appointed under section 802(b).

(B) AUTHORIZATION OF APPROPRIATIONS.—There are authorized to be appropriated such sums as may be necessary to pay the costs incurred under this chapter not covered by the filing fees collected under subsection (b). All funds made available pursuant to this subparagraph shall remain available until expended.

(2) POSITIONS REQUIRED FOR ADMINISTRATION OF COMPULSORY LICENSING.—Section 307 of the Legislative Branch Appropriations Act, 1994, shall not apply to employee positions in the Library of Congress that are required to be filled in order to carry out section 111, 112, 114, 115, 116, 118, or 119 or chapter 10.

§804 · Institution of proceedings[5]

(a) FILING OF PETITION.—With respect to proceedings referred to in paragraphs (1) and (2) of section 801(b) concerning the determination or adjustment of royalty rates as provided in sections 111, 112, 114, 115, 116, 118, 119, and 1004, during the calendar years specified in the schedule set forth in subsection (b), any owner or user of a copyrighted work whose royalty rates are specified by this title, or are established under this chapter before or after the enactment of the Copyright Royalty and Distribution Reform Act of 2004, may file a petition with the Copyright Royalty Judges declaring that the petitioner requests a determination or adjustment of the rate. The Copyright Royalty Judges shall make a determination as to whether the petitioner has such a significant interest in the royalty rate in which a determination or adjustment is requested. If the Copyright Royalty Judges determine that the petitioner has such a significant interest, the Copyright Royalty Judges shall cause notice of this determination, with the reasons for such determination, to be published in the Federal Register, together with the notice of commencement of proceedings under this chapter. With respect to proceedings under paragraph (1) of section 801(b) concerning the determination or adjustment of royalty rates as provided in sections 112 and 114, during the calendar years specified in the schedule set forth in subsection (b), the Copyright Royalty Judges shall cause notice of commencement of proceedings under this chapter to be published in the Federal Register as provided in section 803(b)(1)(A).

(b) TIMING OF PROCEEDINGS.—

(1) SECTION 111 PROCEEDINGS.—(A) A petition described in subsection (a) to initiate proceedings under section 801(b)(2) concerning the adjustment of royalty rates under section 111 to which subparagraph (A) or (D) of section

801(b)(2) applies may be filed during the year 2015 and in each subsequent fifth calendar year.

(B) In order to initiate proceedings under section 801(b)(2) concerning the adjustment of royalty rates under section 111 to which subparagraph (B) or (C) of section 801(b)(2) applies, within 12 months after an event described in either of those subsections, any owner or user of a copyrighted work whose royalty rates are specified by section 111, or by a rate established under this chapter before or after the enactment of the Copyright Royalty and Distribution Reform Act of 2004, may file a petition with the Copyright Royalty Judges declaring that the petitioner requests an adjustment of the rate. The Copyright Royalty Judges shall then proceed as set forth in subsection (a) of this section. Any change in royalty rates made under this chapter pursuant to this subparagraph may be reconsidered in the year 2015, and each fifth calendar year thereafter, in accordance with the provisions in section 801(b)(2) (B) or (C), as the case may be. A petition for adjustment of rates established by section 111(d)(1)(B) as a result of a change in the rules and regulations of the Federal Communications Commission shall set forth the change on which the petition is based.

(C) Any adjustment of royalty rates under section 111 shall take effect as of the first accounting period commencing after the publication of the determination of the Copyright Royalty Judges in the Federal Register, or on such other date as is specified in that determination.

(2) Certain section 112 proceedings.—Proceedings under this chapter shall be commenced in the year 2007 to determine reasonable terms and rates of royalty payments for the activities described in section 112(e)(1) relating to the limitation on exclusive rights specified by section 114(d)(1)(C)(iv), to become effective on January 1, 2009. Such proceedings shall be repeated in each subsequent fifth calendar year.

(3) Section 114 and corresponding 112 proceedings.—

(A) For eligible nonsubscription services and new subscription services.—Proceedings under this chapter shall be commenced as soon as practicable after the date of enactment of the Copyright Royalty and Distribution Reform Act of 2004 to determine reasonable terms and rates of royalty payments under sections 114 and 112 for the activities of eligible nonsubscription transmission services and new subscription services, to be effective for the period beginning on January 1, 2006, and ending on December 31, 2010. Such proceedings shall next be commenced in January 2009 to determine reasonable terms and rates of royalty payments, to become effective on January 1, 2011. Thereafter, such proceedings shall be repeated in each subsequent fifth calendar year.

(B) For preexisting subscription and satellite digital audio radio services.—Proceedings under this chapter shall be commenced in January 2006 to determine reasonable terms and rates of royalty payments under sections 114 and 112 for the activities of preexisting subscription services, to be effective during the period beginning on January 1, 2008, and ending on December 31, 2012, and preexisting satellite digital audio radio services, to be effective during the period beginning on January 1, 2007, and ending on December 31, 2012. Such proceedings shall next be commenced in 2011 to determine reasonable terms and rates of royalty payments, to become effective on January 1, 2013. Thereafter, such proceedings shall be repeated in each subsequent fifth calendar year.

(C)(i) Notwithstanding any other provision of this chapter, this subparagraph shall govern proceedings commenced pursuant to section 114(f)(1)(C) and 114(f)(2)(C) concerning new types of services.

(ii) Not later than 30 days after a petition to determine rates and terms for a new type of service is filed by any copyright owner of sound recordings, or such new type of service, indicating that such new type of service is or is about to become operational, the Copyright Royalty Judges shall issue a notice for a proceeding to determine rates and terms for such service.

(iii) The proceeding shall follow the schedule set forth in subsections (b), (c), and (d) of section 803, except that—

(I) the determination shall be issued by not later than 24 months after the publication of the notice under clause (ii); and

(II) the decision shall take effect as provided in subsections (c)(2) and (d)(2) of section 803 and section 114(f)(4)(B)(ii) and (C).

(iv) The rates and terms shall remain in effect for the period set forth in section 114(f)(1)(C) or 114(f)(2)(C), as the case may be.

(4) Section 115 proceedings.—A petition described in subsection (a) to initiate proceedings under section 801(b)(1) concerning the adjustment or determination of royalty rates as provided in section 115 may be filed in the year 2006 and in each subsequent fifth calendar year, or at such other times as the parties have agreed under section 115(c)(3) (B) and (C).

(5) Section 116 proceedings.—(A) A petition described in subsection (a) to initiate proceedings under section 801(b) concerning the determination of royalty rates and terms as provided in section 116 may be filed at any time within 1 year after negotiated licenses authorized by section 116 are terminated or expire and are not replaced by subsequent agreements.

(B) If a negotiated license authorized by section 116 is terminated or expires and is not replaced by another such license agreement which provides permission to use a quantity of musical works not substantially smaller than the quantity of such works performed on coin-operated phonorecord players during the 1-year period ending March 1, 1989, the Copyright Royalty Judges shall, upon petition filed under paragraph (1) within 1 year after such termination or expiration, commence a proceeding to promptly establish an interim royalty rate or rates for the public performance by means of a coin-operated phonorecord player of nondramatic musical works embodied in phonorecords which had been subject to the terminated or expired negotiated license agreement. Such rate or rates shall be the same as the last such rate or rates and shall remain in force until the conclusion of proceedings by the Copyright Royalty Judges, in accordance with section 803, to adjust the royalty rates applicable to such works, or until superseded by a new negotiated license agreement, as provided in section 116(b).

(6) Section 118 proceedings.—A petition described in subsection (a) to initiate proceedings under section 801(b)(1) concerning the determination of reasonable terms and rates of royalty payments as provided in section 118 may be filed in the year 2006 and in each subsequent fifth calendar year.

(7) Section 1004 proceedings.—A petition described in subsection (a) to initiate proceedings under section 801(b)(1) concerning the adjustment of reasonable royalty rates under section 1004 may be filed as provided in section 1004(a)(3).

(8) Proceedings concerning distribution of royalty fees.—With respect to proceedings under section 801(b)(3) concerning the distribution of royalty fees in certain circumstances under section 111, 119, or 1007, the Copyright Royalty Judges shall, upon a determination that a controversy exists concerning such distribution, cause to be published in the Federal Register notice of commencement of proceedings under this chapter.

§805 · General rule for voluntarily negotiated agreements

Any rates or terms under this title that—

(1) are agreed to by participants to a proceeding under section 803(b)(3),

(2) are adopted by the Copyright Royalty Judges as part of a determination under this chapter, and

(3) are in effect for a period shorter than would otherwise apply under a determination pursuant to this chapter,

shall remain in effect for such period of time as would otherwise apply under such determination, except that the Copyright Royalty Judges shall adjust the rates pursuant to the voluntary negotiations to reflect national monetary inflation during the additional period the rates remain in effect.

Chapter 8 · Notes

1. The Copyright Royalty and Distribution Reform Act of 2004 amended chapter 8 in its entirety. Pub. L. No. 108-419, 118 Stat. 2341.

In 2006, the Copyright Royalty Judges Program Technical Corrections Act amended chapter 8 throughout. Pub. L. No. 109-303, 120 Stat. 1478. Section 6 of that Act states, "Except as provided under subsection (b), this Act and the amendments made by this Act shall be effective as if included in the Copyright Royalty and Distribution Reform Act of 2004." *Id.* at 1483.

2. In 2006, the Copyright Royalty Judges Program Technical Corrections Act amended section 801 by inserting a comma after "119" in the first sentence of subsection (b)(1) and by adding a new subsection (f) at the end. Pub. L. No. 109-303, 120 Stat. 1478. It also amended the language in 803(b)(3)(C) that preceded (i) and substituted "the" for "such" in (i). *Id.* at 1483.

3. In 2006, the Copyright Royalty Judges Program Technical Corrections Act amended 802(f)(1)(A)(i) by substituting "subparagraph (B) and clause (ii) of this subparagraph" for "clause (ii) of this subparagraph and subparagraph (B),"; by amending (f)(1)(A)(ii) in its entirety; and by inserting a comma after "undertakes to consult with" in the seventh sentence of (f)(1)(D). Pub. L. No. 109-303, 120 Stat. 1478-79.

4. The Satellite Home Viewer Extension and Reauthorization Act of 2004 amended section 803(b)(1)(A)(i)(V) by inserting at the end, "except that in the case of proceedings under section 111 that are scheduled to commence in 2005, such notice may not be published." Pub. L. No. 108-447, 118 Stat. 2809, 3393, 3409.

In 2006, the Copyright Royalty Judges Program Technical Corrections Act amended paragraph 803(a)(1) by inserting a new sentence at the beginning and by amending the second sentence. Pub. L. No. 109-303, 120 Stat. 1478, 1479. It amended (b)(1)(A)(i)(V) by inserting "the publication of notice requirement shall not apply" prior to "in the case of" and deleting from the end of the sentence "such notice may not be published." *Id.* It amended (b)(2)(A) by deleting from the end "together with a filing fee of $150" and by adding a new clause (D). *Id.* at 1479-80. It amended (b)(3)(A) by changing the heading and adding the text for (ii). *Id.* at 1480. It amended (b)(4)(A) by deleting the last sentence. *Id.* It amended the first sentence of (b)(6)(C)(i) by inserting "and written rebuttal statements" after "direct statements" and inserting "in the case of written direct statements" after "Copyright Royalty Judge." *Id.* It entirely amended (b)(6)(C)(ii)(I), iv, and x. *Id.* It amended (c)(2)(B) by deleting "concerning rates and terms" at the end of the sentence; (c)(4) by deleting "with the approval of the Register of Copyrights" in the first sentence after "Copyright Royalty Judges;" and (c)(7) by making a technical correction to add "the" before "Copyright Royalty Judges." *Id.* It amended (d)(2)C)(i)(I) by inserting "applicable" before "statements of account" and deleting "any" before "reports of use." *Id.* at 1481. It amended (d)(3) by inserting a new sentence at the beginning and by deleting "pursuant to section 706 of title 5" at the beginning of what was previously the first sentence, now the second sentence. *Id.*

The Copyright Cleanup, Clarification, and Corrections Act of 2010 amended subparagraph 803(b)(6)(A) by revising the second sentence in its entirety. Pub. L. No. 111-295, 124 Stat. 3180, 3181.

5. In 2006, the Copyright Royalty Judges Program Technical Corrections Act amended paragraph 804(b)(1)(B) by substituting "801(b)(2)(B) or (C)" for "801(b)(3)(B) or (C)" in the third sentence. Pub. L. No. 109-303, 120 Stat. 1478, 1481. It amended (b)(3)(A) by substituting "date of enactment" for "effective date" and (b)(3)(C)(i) and (ii) by making technical corrections to correct grammatical errors. *Id.*

The Satellite Television Extension and Localism Act of 2010 amended paragraphs 804(b)(1)(A) and (B) by substituting "2015" for "2005." Pub. L. No. 111-175, 124 Stat. 1218, 1238.

Chapter 9[1]

Protection of Semiconductor Chip Products

§901 · Definitions

(a) As used in this chapter—

(1) a "semiconductor chip product" is the final or intermediate form of any product—

(A) having two or more layers of metallic, insulating, or semiconductor material, deposited or otherwise placed on, or etched away or otherwise removed from, a piece of semiconductor material in accordance with a predetermined pattern; and

(B) intended to perform electronic circuitry functions;

(2) a "mask work" is a series of related images, however fixed or encoded—

(A) having or representing the predetermined, three-dimensional pattern of metallic, insulating, or semiconductor material present or removed from the layers of a semiconductor chip product; and

(B) in which series the relation of the images to one another is that each image has the pattern of the surface of one form of the semiconductor chip product;

(3) a mask work is "fixed" in a semiconductor chip product when its embodiment in the product is sufficiently permanent or stable to permit the mask work to be perceived or reproduced from the product for a period of more than transitory duration;

(4) to "distribute" means to sell, or to lease, bail, or otherwise transfer, or to offer to sell, lease, bail, or otherwise transfer;

(5) to "commercially exploit" a mask work is to distribute to the public for commercial purposes a semiconductor chip product embodying the mask work; except that such term includes an offer to sell or transfer a semiconductor chip product only when the offer is in writing and occurs after the mask work is fixed in the semiconductor chip product;

(6) the "owner" of a mask work is the person who created the mask work, the legal representative of that person if that person is deceased or under a legal incapacity, or a party to whom all the rights under this chapter of such person or representative are transferred in accordance with section 903(b); except that, in the case of a work made within the scope of a person's employment, the owner is the employer for whom the person created the mask work or a party to whom all the rights under this chapter of the employer are transferred in accordance with section 903(b);

(7) an "innocent purchaser" is a person who purchases a semiconductor chip product in good faith and without having notice of protection with respect to the semiconductor chip product;

(8) having "notice of protection" means having actual knowledge that, or reasonable grounds to believe that, a mask work is protected under this chapter; and

(9) an "infringing semiconductor chip product" is a semiconductor chip product which is made, imported, or distributed in violation of the exclusive rights of the owner of a mask work under this chapter.

(b) For purposes of this chapter, the distribution or importation of a product incorporating a semiconductor chip product as a part thereof is a distribution or importation of that semiconductor chip product.

§902 · Subject matter of protection[3]

(a)(1) Subject to the provisions of subsection (b), a mask work fixed in a semiconductor chip product, by or under the authority of the owner of the mask work, is eligible for protection under this chapter if—

(A) on the date on which the mask work is registered under section 908, or is first commercially exploited anywhere in the world, whichever occurs first, the owner of the mask work is (i) a national or domiciliary of the United States, (ii) a national, domiciliary, or sovereign authority of a foreign nation that is a party to a treaty affording protection to mask works to which the United States is also a party, or (iii) a stateless person, wherever that person may be domiciled;

(B) the mask work is first commercially exploited in the United States; or

(C) the mask work comes within the scope of a Presidential proclamation issued under paragraph (2).

(2) Whenever the President finds that a foreign nation extends, to mask works of owners who are nationals or domiciliaries of the United States protection (A) on substantially the same basis as that on which the foreign nation extends protection to mask works of its own nationals and domiciliaries and mask works first commercially exploited in that nation, or (B) on substantially the same basis as provided in this chapter, the President may by proclamation extend protection under this chapter to mask works (i) of owners who are, on the date on which the mask works are registered under section 908, or the date on which the mask works are first commercially exploited anywhere in the world, whichever occurs first, nationals, domiciliaries, or sovereign authorities of that nation, or (ii) which are first commercially exploited in that nation. The President may revise, suspend, or revoke any such proclamation or impose any conditions or limitations on protection extended under any such proclamation.

(b) Protection under this chapter shall not be available for a mask work that—

(1) is not original; or

(2) consists of designs that are staple, commonplace, or familiar in the semiconductor industry, or variations of such designs, combined in a way that, considered as a whole, is not original.

(c) In no case does protection under this chapter for a mask work extend to any idea, procedure, process, system, method of operation, concept, principle, or discovery, regardless of the form in which it is described, explained, illustrated, or embodied in such work.

§903 · Ownership, transfer, licensing, and recordation

(a) The exclusive rights in a mask work subject to protection under this chapter belong to the owner of the mask work.

(b) The owner of the exclusive rights in a mask work may transfer all of those rights, or license all or less than all of those rights, by any written instrument signed by such owner or a duly authorized agent of the owner. Such rights may be transferred or licensed by operation of law, may be bequeathed by will, and may pass as personal property by the applicable laws of intestate succession.

(c)(1) Any document pertaining to a mask work may be recorded in the Copyright Office if the document filed for recordation bears the actual signature of the person who executed it, or if it is accompanied by a sworn or official certification that it is a true copy of the original, signed document. The Register of Copyrights shall, upon receipt of the document and the fee specified pursuant to section 908(d), record the document and return it with a certificate of recordation. The recordation of any transfer or license under this paragraph gives all persons constructive notice of the facts stated in the recorded document concerning the transfer or license.

(2) In any case in which conflicting transfers of the exclusive rights in a mask work are made, the transfer first executed shall be void as against a subsequent transfer which is made for a valuable consideration and without notice of the first transfer, unless the first transfer is recorded in accordance with paragraph (1) within three months after the date on which it is executed, but in no case later than the day before the date of such subsequent transfer.

(d) Mask works prepared by an officer or employee of the United States Government as part of that person's official duties are not protected under this chapter, but the United States Government is not precluded from receiving and holding exclusive rights in mask works transferred to the Government under subsection (b).

§904 · Duration of protection

(a) The protection provided for a mask work under this chapter shall commence on the date on which the mask work is registered under section 908, or the date on which the mask work is first commercially exploited anywhere in the world, whichever occurs first.

(b) Subject to subsection (c) and the provisions of this chapter, the protection provided under this chapter to a mask work shall end ten years after the date on which such protection commences under subsection (a).

(c) All terms of protection provided in this section shall run to the end of the calendar year in which they would otherwise expire.

§905 · Exclusive rights in mask works

The owner of a mask work provided protection under this chapter has the exclusive rights to do and to authorize any of the following:

(1) to reproduce the mask work by optical, electronic, or any other means;

(2) to import or distribute a semiconductor chip product in which the mask work is embodied; and

(3) to induce or knowingly to cause another person to do any of the acts described in paragraphs (1) and (2).

§906 · Limitation on exclusive rights: reverse engineering; first sale

(a) Notwithstanding the provisions of section 905, it is not an infringement of the exclusive rights of the owner of a mask work for—

(1) a person to reproduce the mask work solely for the purpose of teaching, analyzing, or evaluating the concepts or techniques embodied in the mask work or the circuitry, logic flow, or organization of components used in the mask work; or

(2) a person who performs the analysis or evaluation described in paragraph (1) to incorporate the results of such conduct in an original mask work which is made to be distributed.

(b) Notwithstanding the provisions of section 905(2), the owner of a particular semiconductor chip product made by the owner of the mask work, or by any person authorized by the owner of the mask work, may import, distribute, or otherwise dispose of or use, but not reproduce, that particular semiconductor chip product without the authority of the owner of the mask work.

§907 · Limitation on exclusive rights: innocent infringement

(a) Notwithstanding any other provision of this chapter, an innocent purchaser of an infringing semiconductor chip product—

(1) shall incur no liability under this chapter with respect to the importation or distribution of units of the infringing semiconductor chip product that occurs before the innocent purchaser has notice of protection with respect to the mask work embodied in the semiconductor chip product; and

(2) shall be liable only for a reasonable royalty on each unit of the infringing semiconductor chip product that the innocent purchaser imports or distributes after having notice of protection with respect to the mask work embodied in the semiconductor chip product.

(b) The amount of the royalty referred to in subsection (a)(2) shall be determined by the court in a civil action for infringement unless the parties resolve the issue by voluntary negotiation, mediation, or binding arbitration.

(c) The immunity of an innocent purchaser from liability referred to in subsection (a)(1) and the limitation of remedies with respect to an innocent purchaser referred to in subsection (a)(2) shall extend to any person who directly or indirectly purchases an infringing semiconductor chip product from an innocent purchaser.

(d) The provisions of subsections (a), (b), and (c) apply only with respect to those units of an infringing semiconductor chip product that an innocent purchaser purchased before having notice of protection with respect to the mask work embodied in the semiconductor chip product.

§908 · Registration of claims of protection

(a) The owner of a mask work may apply to the Register of Copyrights for registration of a claim of protection in a mask work. Protection of a mask work under this chapter shall terminate if application for registration of a claim of protection in the mask work is not made as provided in this chapter within two years after the date on which the mask work is first commercially exploited anywhere in the world.

(b) The Register of Copyrights shall be responsible for all administrative functions and duties under this chapter. Except for section 708, the provisions of chapter 7 of this title relating to the general responsibilities, organization, regulatory authority, actions, records, and publications of the Copyright Office shall apply to this chapter, except that the Register of Copyrights may make such changes as may be necessary in applying those provisions to this chapter.

(c) The application for registration of a mask work shall be made on a form prescribed by the Register of Copyrights. Such form may require any information regarded by the Register as bearing upon the preparation or identification of the mask work, the existence or duration of protection of the mask work under this chapter, or ownership of the mask work. The application shall be accompanied by the fee set pursuant to subsection (d) and the identifying material specified pursuant to such subsection.

(d) The Register of Copyrights shall by regulation set reasonable fees for the filing of applications to register claims of protection in mask works under this chapter, and for other services relating to the administration of this chapter or the rights under this chapter, taking into consideration the cost of providing those services, the benefits of a public record, and statutory fee schedules under this title. The Register shall also specify the identifying material to be deposited in connection with the claim for registration.

(e) If the Register of Copyrights, after examining an application for registration, determines, in accordance with the provisions of this chapter, that the application relates to a mask work which is entitled to protection under this chapter, then the Register shall register the claim of protection and issue to the applicant a certificate of registration of the claim of protection under the seal of the Copyright Office. The effective date of registration of a claim of protection shall be the date on which an application, deposit of identifying material, and fee, which are determined by the Register of Copyrights or by a court of competent jurisdiction to be acceptable for registration of the claim, have all been received in the Copyright Office.

(f) In any action for infringement under this chapter, the certificate of registration of a mask work shall constitute prima facie evidence (1) of the facts stated in the certificate, and (2) that the applicant issued the certificate has met the requirements of this chapter, and the regulations issued under this chapter, with respect to the registration of claims.

(g) Any applicant for registration under this section who is dissatisfied with the refusal of the Register of Copyrights to issue a certificate of registration under this section may seek judicial review of that refusal by bringing an action for such review in an appropriate United States district court not later than sixty days after the refusal. The provisions of chapter 7 of title 5 shall apply to such judicial review. The failure of the Register of Copyrights to issue a certificate of registration within four months after an application for registration is filed shall be deemed to be a refusal to issue a certificate of registration for purposes of this subsection and section 910(b)(2), except that, upon a showing of good cause, the district court may shorten such four-month period.

§909 · Mask work notice[4]

(a) The owner of a mask work provided protection under this chapter may affix notice to the mask work, and to masks and semiconductor chip products embodying the mask work, in such manner and location as to give reasonable notice of such protection. The Register of Copyrights shall prescribe by regulation, as examples, specific methods of affixation and positions of notice for purposes of this section, but these specifications shall not be considered exhaustive. The affixation of such notice is not a condition of protection under this chapter, but shall constitute prima facie evidence of notice of protection.

(b) The notice referred to in subsection (a) shall consist of—

(1) the words "mask work", the symbol *M*, or the symbol Ⓜ (the letter M in a circle); and

(2) the name of the owner or owners of the mask work or an abbreviation by which the name is recognized or is generally known.

§910 · Enforcement of exclusive rights[5]

(a) Except as otherwise provided in this chapter, any person who violates any of the exclusive rights of the owner of a mask work under this chapter, by conduct in or affecting commerce, shall be liable as an infringer of such rights. As used in this subsection, the term "any person" includes any State, any instrumentality of a State, and any officer or employee of a State or instrumentality of a State acting in his or her official capacity. Any State, and any such instrumentality, officer, or employee, shall be subject to the provisions of this chapter in the same manner and to the same extent as any nongovernmental entity.

(b)(1) The owner of a mask work protected under this chapter, or the exclusive licensee of all rights under this chapter with respect to the mask work, shall, after a certificate of registration of a claim of protection in that mask work has been issued under section 908, be entitled to institute a civil action for any infringement with respect to the mask work which is committed after the commencement of protection of the mask work under section 904(a).

(2) In any case in which an application for registration of a claim of protection in a mask work and the required deposit of identifying material and fee have been received in the Copyright Office in proper form and registration of the mask work has been refused, the applicant is entitled to institute a civil action for infringement under this chapter with respect to the mask work if notice of the action, together with a copy of the complaint, is served on the Register of Copyrights, in accordance with the Federal Rules of Civil Procedure. The Register may, at his or her option, become a party to the action with respect to the issue of whether the claim of protection is eligible for registration by entering an appearance within sixty days after such service, but the failure of the Register to become a party to the action shall not deprive the court of jurisdiction to determine that issue.

(c)(1) The Secretary of the Treasury and the United States Postal Service shall separately or jointly issue regulations for the enforcement of the rights set forth in section 905 with respect to importation. These regulations may require, as a condition for the exclusion of articles from the United States, that the person seeking exclusion take any one or more of the following actions:

(A) Obtain a court order enjoining, or an order of the International Trade Commission under section 337 of the Tariff Act of 1930 excluding, importation of the articles.

(B) Furnish proof that the mask work involved is protected under this chapter and that the importation of the articles would infringe the rights in the mask work under this chapter.

(C) Post a surety bond for any injury that may result if the detention or exclusion of the articles proves to be unjustified.

(2) Articles imported in violation of the rights set forth in section 905 are subject to seizure and forfeiture in the same manner as property imported in violation of the customs laws. Any such forfeited articles shall be destroyed as directed by the Secretary of the Treasury or the court, as the case may be, except that the articles may be returned to the country of export whenever it is shown to the satisfaction of the Secretary of the Treasury that the importer had no reasonable grounds for believing that his or her acts constituted a violation of the law.

§911 · Civil actions[6]

(a) Any court having jurisdiction of a civil action arising under this chapter may grant temporary restraining orders, preliminary injunctions, and permanent injunctions on such terms as the court may deem reasonable to prevent or restrain infringement of the exclusive rights in a mask work under this chapter.

(b) Upon finding an infringer liable, to a person entitled under section 910(b)(1) to institute a civil action, for an infringement of any exclusive right under this chapter, the court shall award such person actual damages suffered by the person as a result of the infringement. The court shall also award such person the infringer's profits that are attributable to the infringement and are not taken into account in computing the award of actual damages. In establishing the infringer's profits, such person is required to present proof only of the infringer's gross revenue, and the infringer is required to prove his or her deductible expenses and the elements of profit attributable to factors other than the mask work.

(c) At any time before final judgment is rendered, a person entitled to institute a civil action for infringement may elect, instead of actual damages and profits as provided by subsection (b), an award of statutory damages for all infringements involved in the action, with respect to any one mask work for which any one infringer is liable individually, or for which any two or more infringers are liable jointly and severally, in an amount not more than $250,000 as the court considers just.

(d) An action for infringement under this chapter shall be barred unless the action is commenced within three years after the claim accrues.

(e)(1) At any time while an action for infringement of the exclusive rights in a mask work under this chapter is pending, the court may order the impounding, on such terms as it may deem reasonable, of all semiconductor chip products, and any drawings, tapes, masks, or other products by means of which such products may be reproduced, that are claimed to have been made, imported, or used in violation of those exclusive rights. Insofar as practicable, applications for orders under this paragraph shall be heard and determined in the same manner as an application for a temporary restraining order or preliminary injunction.

(2) As part of a final judgment or decree, the court may order the destruction or other disposition of any infringing semiconductor chip products, and any masks, tapes, or other articles by means of which such products may be reproduced.

(f) In any civil action arising under this chapter, the court in its discretion may allow the recovery of full costs, including reasonable attorneys' fees, to the prevailing party.

(g)(1) Any State, any instrumentality of a State, and any officer or employee of a State or instrumentality of a State acting in his or her official capacity, shall not be immune, under the Eleventh Amendment of the Constitution of the United States or under any other doctrine of sovereign immunity, from suit in Federal court by any person, including any governmental or nongovernmental entity, for a violation of any of the exclusive rights of the owner of a mask work under this chapter, or for any other violation under this chapter.

(2) In a suit described in paragraph (1) for a violation described in that paragraph, remedies (including remedies both at law and in equity) are available for the violation to the same extent as such remedies are available for such a violation in a suit against any public or private entity other than a State, instrumentality of a State, or officer or employee of a State acting in his or her official capacity. Such remedies include actual damages and profits under subsection (b), statutory damages under subsection (c), impounding and disposition of infringing articles under subsection (e), and costs and attorney's fees under subsection (f).

§912 · Relation to other laws[7]

(a) Nothing in this chapter shall affect any right or remedy held by any person under chapters 1 through 8 or 10 of this title, or under title 35.

(b) Except as provided in section 908(b) of this title, references to "this title" or "title 17" in chapters 1 through 8 or 10 of this title shall be deemed not to apply to this chapter.

(c) The provisions of this chapter shall preempt the laws of any State to the extent those laws provide any rights or remedies with respect to a mask work which are equivalent to those rights or remedies provided by this chapter, except that such preemption shall be effective only with respect to actions filed on or after January 1, 1986.

(d) Notwithstanding subsection (c), nothing in this chapter shall detract from any rights of a mask work owner, whether under Federal law (exclusive of this chapter) or under the common law or the statutes of a State, heretofore or hereafter declared or enacted, with respect to any mask work first commercially exploited before July 1, 1983.

§913 · Transitional provisions

(a) No application for registration under section 908 may be filed, and no civil action under section 910 or other enforcement proceeding under this chapter may be instituted, until sixty days after the date of the enactment of this chapter.

(b) No monetary relief under section 911 may be granted with respect to any conduct that occurred before the date of the enactment of this chapter, except as provided in subsection (d).

(c) Subject to subsection (a), the provisions of this chapter apply to all mask works that are first commercially exploited or are registered under this chapter, or both, on or after the date of the enactment of this chapter.

(d)(1) Subject to subsection (a), protection is available under this chapter to any mask work that was first commercially exploited on or after July 1, 1983, and before the date of the enactment of this chapter, if a claim of protection in the mask work is registered in the Copyright Office before July 1, 1985, under section 908.

(2) In the case of any mask work described in paragraph (1) that is provided protection under this chapter, infringing semiconductor chip product units manufactured before the date of the enactment of this chapter may, without liability under sections 910 and 911, be imported into or distributed in the United States, or both, until two years after the date of registration of the mask work under section 908, but only if the importer or distributor, as the case may be, first pays or offers to pay the reasonable royalty referred to in section 907(a)(2) to the mask work owner, on all such units imported or distributed, or both, after the date of the enactment of this chapter.

(3) In the event that a person imports or distributes infringing semiconductor chip product units described in paragraph (2) of this subsection without first paying or offering to pay the reasonable royalty specified in such paragraph, or if the person refuses or fails to make such payment, the mask work owner shall be entitled to the relief provided in sections 910 and 911.

§914 · International transitional provisions[8]

(a) Notwithstanding the conditions set forth in subparagraphs (A) and (C) of section 902(a)(1) with respect to the availability of protection under this chapter to nationals, domiciliaries, and sovereign authorities of a foreign nation, the Secretary of Commerce may, upon the petition of any person, or upon the Secretary's own motion, issue an order extending protection under this chapter to such foreign nationals, domiciliaries, and sovereign authorities if the Secretary finds—

(1) that the foreign nation is making good faith efforts and reasonable progress toward—

(A) entering into a treaty described in section 902(a)(1)(A); or

(B) enacting or implementing legislation that would be in compliance with subparagraph (A) or (B) of section 902(a)(2); and

(2) that the nationals, domiciliaries, and sovereign authorities of the foreign nation, and persons controlled by them, are not engaged in the misappropriation, or unauthorized distribution or commercial exploitation, of mask works; and

(3) that issuing the order would promote the purposes of this chapter and international comity with respect to the protection of mask works.

(b) While an order under subsection (a) is in effect with respect to a foreign nation, no application for registration of a claim for protection in a mask work under this chapter may be denied solely because the owner of the mask work is a national, domiciliary, or sovereign authority of that foreign nation, or solely because the mask work was first commercially exploited in that foreign nation.

(c) Any order issued by the Secretary of Commerce under subsection (a) shall be effective for such a period as the Secretary designates in the order, except that no such order may be effective after that date on which the authority of the Secretary of Commerce terminates under subsection (e). The effective date of any such order shall also be designated in the order. In the case of an order issued upon the petition of a person, such effective date may be no earlier than the date on which the Secretary receives such petition.

(d)(1) Any order issued under this section shall terminate if—

(A) the Secretary of Commerce finds that any of the conditions set forth in paragraphs (1), (2), and (3) of subsection (a) no longer exist; or

(B) mask works of nationals, domiciliaries, and sovereign authorities of that foreign nation or mask works first commercially exploited in that foreign nation become eligible for protection under subparagraph (A) or (C) of section 902(a)(1).

(2) Upon the termination or expiration of an order issued under this section, registrations of claims of protection in mask works made pursuant to that order shall remain valid for the period specified in section 904.

(e) The authority of the Secretary of Commerce under this section shall commence on the date of the enactment of this chapter, and shall terminate on July 1, 1995.

(f) (1) The Secretary of Commerce shall promptly notify the Register of Copyrights and the Committees on the Judiciary of the Senate and the House of Representatives of the issuance or termination of any order under this section, together with a statement of the reasons for such action. The Secretary shall also publish such notification and statement of reasons in the Federal Register.

(2) Two years after the date of the enactment of this chapter, the Secretary of Commerce, in consultation with the Register of Copyrights, shall transmit to the Committees on the Judiciary of the Senate and the House of Representatives a report on the actions taken under this section and on the current status of international recognition of mask work protection. The report shall include such recommendation for modifications of the protection accorded under this chapter to mask works owned by nationals, domiciliaries, or sovereign authorities of foreign nations as the Secretary, in consultation with the Register of Copyrights, considers would promote the purposes of this chapter and international comity with respect to mask work protection. Not later than July 1, 1994, the Secretary of Commerce, in consultation with the Register of Copyrights, shall transmit to the Committees on the Judiciary of the Senate and the House of Representatives a report updating the matters contained in the report transmitted under the preceding sentence.

Chapter 9 · Notes

1. In 1984, the Semiconductor Chip Protection Act amended title 17 of the *United States Code* to add a new chapter 9 entitled "Protection of Semiconductor Chip Products." Pub. L. No. 98-620, 98 Stat. 3335, 3347.

2. In 1997, the heading for section 903 in the table of sections was changed from "Ownership and Transfer" to "Ownership, transfer, licensure, and recordation." Pub. L. No. 105-80, 111 Stat. 1529, 1535. The Intellectual Property and High Technology Technical Amendments Act of 2002 amended the heading for section 903 in the table of sections for chapter 9 by substituting "licensing" for "licensure." Pub. L. No. 107-273, 116 Stat. 1758, 1910.

3. In 1987, section 902 was amended by adding the last sentence in subsection (a)(2). Pub. L. No. 100-159, 101 Stat. 899, 900.

4. In 1997, section 909 was amended by correcting misspellings in subsection (b)(1). Pub. L. No. 105-80, 111 Stat. 1529, 1535.

5. In 1990, the Copyright Remedy Clarification Act amended section 910 by adding the last two sentences to subsection (a). Pub. L. No. 101-553, 104 Stat. 2749, 2750. In 1997, a technical correction amended section 910(a) by capitalizing the first word of the second sentence. Pub. L. No. 105-80, 111 Stat. 1529 1535.

6. In 1990, the Copyright Remedy Clarification Act amended section 911 by adding subsection (g). Pub. L. No. 101-553, 104 Stat. 2749, 2750.

7. In 1988, the Judicial Improvements and Access to Justice Act amended section 912 by deleting subsection (d) and redesignating subsection (e) as subsection (d). Pub. L. No. 100-702, 102 Stat. 4642, 4672. The Audio Home Recording Act of 1992 amended section 912 by inserting "or 10" after "8" in subsections (a) and (b). Pub. L. No. 102-563, 106 Stat. 4237, 4248.

8. In 1987, section 914 was amended in subsection (e) by inserting "on July 1, 1991" in lieu of "three years after such date of enactment" and by adding the last sentence to subsection (f)(2). Pub. L. No. 100-159, 101 Stat. 899. The Semiconductor International Protection Extension Act of 1991 amended section 914 by inserting "or implementing" after "enacting" in the first sentence of subsection (a)(1)(B), by changing the date in subsection (e) to "July 1, 1995" and by changing the date in the last sentence of subsection (f)(2) to "July 1, 1994." Pub. L. No. 102-64, 105 Stat. 320.

On July 1, 1995, section 914 expired as required by subsection (e). It was rendered largely unnecessary upon the entry into force on January 1, 1995, of the Agreement on Trade-Related Aspects of Intellectual Property Rights (TRIPs) (Annex 1C to the World Trade Organization (WTO) Agreement). Part II, section 6, of TRIPs protects semiconductor chip products and was the basis for Presidential Proclamation No. 6780, March 23, 1995, under section 902(a)(2) extending protection to all present and future WTO members (146 countries as of April 4, 2003), as of January 1, 1996. See Appendix M.

For a discussion of Congressional findings regarding extending protection to semiconductor chip products of foreign entities, see Pub. L. No. 100-159, 101 Stat. 899, and the Semiconductor International Protection Extension Act of 1991, Pub. L. No. 102-64, 105 Stat. 320.

Chapter 10[1]

Digital Audio Recording Devices and Media

Subchapter A—Definitions

§1001 · Definitions

As used in this chapter, the following terms have the following meanings:

(1) A "digital audio copied recording" is a reproduction in a digital recording format of a digital musical recording, whether that reproduction is made directly from another digital musical recording or indirectly from a transmission.

(2) A "digital audio interface device" is any machine or device that is designed specifically to communicate digital audio information and related interface data to a digital audio recording device through a nonprofessional interface.

(3) A "digital audio recording device" is any machine or device of a type commonly distributed to individuals for use by individuals, whether or not included with or as part of some other machine or device, the digital recording function of which is designed or marketed for the primary purpose of, and that is capable of, making a digital audio copied recording for private use, except for—

(A) professional model products, and

(B) dictation machines, answering machines, and other audio recording equipment that is designed and marketed primarily for the creation of sound recordings resulting from the fixation of nonmusical sounds.

(4)(A) A "digital audio recording medium" is any material object in a form commonly distributed for use by individuals, that is primarily marketed or most commonly used by consumers for the purpose of making digital audio copied recordings by use of a digital audio recording device.

(B) Such term does not include any material object—

(i) that embodies a sound recording at the time it is first distributed by the importer or manufacturer; or

(ii) that is primarily marketed and most commonly used by consumers either for the purpose of making copies of motion pictures or other audiovisual works or for the purpose of making copies of nonmusical literary works, including computer programs or data bases.

(5)(A) A "digital musical recording" is a material object—

(i) in which are fixed, in a digital recording format, only sounds, and material, statements, or instructions incidental to those fixed sounds, if any, and

(ii) from which the sounds and material can be perceived, reproduced, or otherwise communicated, either directly or with the aid of a machine or device.

(B) A "digital musical recording" does not include a material object—

(i) in which the fixed sounds consist entirely of spoken word recordings, or

(ii) in which one or more computer programs are fixed, except that a digital musical recording may contain statements or instructions constituting the fixed sounds and incidental material, and statements or instructions to be used directly or indirectly in order to bring about the perception, reproduction, or communication of the fixed sounds and incidental material.

(C) For purposes of this paragraph—

(i) a "spoken word recording" is a sound recording in which are fixed only a series of spoken words, except that the spoken words may be accompanied by incidental musical or other sounds, and

(ii) the term "incidental" means related to and relatively minor by comparison.

(6) "Distribute" means to sell, lease, or assign a product to consumers in the United States, or to sell, lease, or assign a product in the United States for ultimate transfer to consumers in the United States.

(7) An "interested copyright party" is—

(A) the owner of the exclusive right under section 106(1) of this title to reproduce a sound recording of a musical work that has been embodied in a digital musical recording or analog musical recording lawfully made under this title that has been distributed;

(B) the legal or beneficial owner of, or the person that controls, the right to reproduce in a digital musical recording or analog musical recording a musical work that has been embodied in a digital musical recording or analog musical recording lawfully made under this title that has been distributed;

(C) a featured recording artist who performs on a sound recording that has been distributed; or

(D) any association or other organization—

(i) representing persons specified in subparagraph (A), (B), or (C), or

(ii) engaged in licensing rights in musical works to music users on behalf of writers and publishers.

(8) To "manufacture" means to produce or assemble a product in the United States. A "manufacturer" is a person who manufactures.

(9) A "music publisher" is a person that is authorized to license the reproduction of a particular musical work in a sound recording.

(10) A "professional model product" is an audio recording device that is designed, manufactured, marketed, and intended for use by recording professionals in the ordinary course of a lawful business, in accordance with such requirements as the Secretary of Commerce shall establish by regulation.

(11) The term "serial copying" means the duplication in a digital format of a copyrighted musical work or sound recording from a digital reproduction of a digital musical recording. The term "digital reproduction of a digital musical recording" does not include a digital musical recording as distributed, by authority of the copyright owner, for ultimate sale to consumers.

(12) The "transfer price" of a digital audio recording device or a digital audio recording medium—

(A) is, subject to subparagraph (B)—

(i) in the case of an imported product, the actual entered value at United States Customs (exclusive of any freight, insurance, and applicable duty), and

(ii) in the case of a domestic product, the manufacturer's transfer price (FOB the manufacturer, and exclusive of any direct sales taxes or excise taxes incurred in connection with the sale); and

(B) shall, in a case in which the transferor and transferee are related entities or within a single entity, not be less than a reasonable arms-length price under the principles of the regulations adopted pursuant to section 482 of the Internal Revenue Code of 1986, or any successor provision to such section.

(13) A "writer" is the composer or lyricist of a particular musical work.

Subchapter B—Copying Controls

§1002 · Incorporation of copying controls

(a) Prohibition on Importation, Manufacture, and Distribution.—No person shall import, manufacture, or distribute any digital audio recording device or digital audio interface device that does not conform to—

(1) the Serial Copy Management System;

(2) a system that has the same functional characteristics as the Serial Copy Management System and requires that copyright and generation status information be accurately sent, received, and acted upon between devices using the system's method of serial copying regulation and devices using the Serial Copy Management System; or

(3) any other system certified by the Secretary of Commerce as prohibiting unauthorized serial copying.

(b) Development of Verification Procedure.—The Secretary of Commerce shall establish a procedure to verify, upon the petition of an interested party, that a system meets the standards set forth in subsection (a)(2).

(c) Prohibition on Circumvention of the System.—No person shall import, manufacture, or distribute any device, or offer or perform any service, the primary purpose or effect of which is to avoid, bypass, remove, deactivate, or otherwise circumvent any program or circuit which implements, in whole or in part, a system described in subsection (a).

(d) Encoding of Information on Digital Musical Recordings.—

(1) Prohibition on encoding inaccurate information.—No person shall encode a digital musical recording of a sound recording with inaccurate information relating to the category code, copyright status, or generation status of the source material for the recording.

(2) Encoding of copyright status not required.—Nothing in this chapter requires any person engaged in the importation or manufacture of digital musical recordings to encode any such digital musical recording with respect to its copyright status.

(e) Information Accompanying Transmission in Digital Format.—Any person who transmits or otherwise communicates to the public any sound recording in digital format is not required under this chapter to transmit or otherwise communicate the information relating to the copyright status of the sound recording. Any such person who does transmit or otherwise communicate such copyright status information shall transmit or communicate such information accurately.

Subchapter C—Royalty Payments

§1003 · Obligation to make royalty payments

(a) Prohibition on Importation and Manufacture.—No person shall import into and distribute, or manufacture and distribute, any digital audio recording device or digital audio recording medium unless such person records the notice specified by this section and subsequently deposits the statements of account and applicable royalty payments for such device or medium specified in section 1004.

(b) Filing of Notice.—The importer or manufacturer of any digital audio recording device or digital audio recording medium, within a product category or utilizing a technology with respect to which such manufacturer or importer has not previously filed a notice under this subsection, shall file with the Register of Copyrights a notice with respect to such device or medium, in such form and content as the Register shall prescribe by regulation.

(c) Filing of Quarterly and Annual Statements of Account.—

(1) Generally.—Any importer or manufacturer that distributes any digital audio recording device or digital audio recording medium that it manufactured or imported shall file with the Register of Copyrights, in such form

and content as the Register shall prescribe by regulation, such quarterly and annual statements of account with respect to such distribution as the Register shall prescribe by regulation.

(2) CERTIFICATION, VERIFICATION, AND CONFIDENTIALITY.—Each such statement shall be certified as accurate by an authorized officer or principal of the importer or manufacturer. The Register shall issue regulations to provide for the verification and audit of such statements and to protect the confidentiality of the information contained in such statements. Such regulations shall provide for the disclosure, in confidence, of such statements to interested copyright parties.

(3) ROYALTY PAYMENTS.—Each such statement shall be accompanied by the royalty payments specified in section 1004.

§1004 · Royalty payments[2]

(a) DIGITAL AUDIO RECORDING DEVICES.—

(1) AMOUNT OF PAYMENT.—The royalty payment due under section 1003 for each digital audio recording device imported into and distributed in the United States, or manufactured and distributed in the United States, shall be 2 percent of the transfer price. Only the first person to manufacture and distribute or import and distribute such device shall be required to pay the royalty with respect to such device.

(2) CALCULATION FOR DEVICES DISTRIBUTED WITH OTHER DEVICES.—With respect to a digital audio recording device first distributed in combination with one or more devices, either as a physically integrated unit or as separate components, the royalty payment shall be calculated as follows:

(A) If the digital audio recording device and such other devices are part of a physically integrated unit, the royalty payment shall be based on the transfer price of the unit, but shall be reduced by any royalty payment made on any digital audio recording device included within the unit that was not first distributed in combination with the unit.

(B) If the digital audio recording device is not part of a physically integrated unit and substantially similar devices have been distributed separately at any time during the preceding 4 calendar quarters, the royalty payment shall be based on the average transfer price of such devices during those 4 quarters.

(C) If the digital audio recording device is not part of a physically integrated unit and substantially similar devices have not been distributed separately at any time during the preceding 4 calendar quarters, the royalty payment shall be based on a constructed price reflecting the proportional value of such device to the combination as a whole.

(3) LIMITS ON ROYALTIES.—Notwithstanding paragraph (1) or (2), the amount of the royalty payment for each digital audio recording device shall not be less than $1 nor more than the royalty maximum. The royalty maximum shall be $8 per device, except that in the case of a physically integrated unit containing more than 1 digital audio recording device, the royalty maximum for such unit shall be $12. During the 6th year after the effective date of this chapter, and not more than once each year thereafter, any interested copyright party may petition the Copyright Royalty Judges to increase the royalty maximum and, if more than 20 percent of the royalty payments are at the relevant royalty maximum, the Copyright Royalty Judges shall prospectively increase such royalty maximum with the goal of having no more than 10 percent of such payments at the new royalty maximum; however the amount of any such increase as a percentage of the royalty maximum shall in no event exceed the percentage increase in the Consumer Price Index during the period under review.

(b) DIGITAL AUDIO RECORDING MEDIA.—The royalty payment due under section 1003 for each digital audio recording medium imported into and distributed in the United States, or manufactured and distributed in the United States, shall be 3 percent of the transfer price. Only the first person to manufacture and distribute or import and distribute such medium shall be required to pay the royalty with respect to such medium.

§1005 · Deposit of royalty payments and deduction of expenses[3]

The Register of Copyrights shall receive all royalty payments deposited under this chapter and, after deducting the reasonable costs incurred by the Copyright Office under this chapter, shall deposit the balance in the Treasury of the United States as offsetting receipts, in such manner as the Secretary of the Treasury directs. All funds held by the Secretary of the Treasury shall be invested in interest-bearing United States securities for later distribution with interest under section 1007. The Register may, in the Register's discretion, 4 years after the close of any calendar year, close out the royalty payments account for that calendar year, and may treat any funds remaining in such account and any subsequent deposits that would otherwise be attributable to that calendar year as attributable to the succeeding calendar year.

§1006 · Entitlement to royalty payments[4]

(a) INTERESTED COPYRIGHT PARTIES.—The royalty payments deposited pursuant to section 1005 shall, in accordance with the procedures specified in section 1007, be distributed to any interested copyright party—

(1) whose musical work or sound recording has been—

(A) embodied in a digital musical recording or an analog musical recording lawfully made under this title that has been distributed, and

(B) distributed in the form of digital musical recordings or analog musical recordings or disseminated to the public in transmissions, during the period to which such payments pertain; and

(2) who has filed a claim under section 1007.

(b) ALLOCATION OF ROYALTY PAYMENTS TO GROUPS.—The royalty payments shall be divided into 2 funds as follows:

(1) THE SOUND RECORDINGS FUND.—66⅔ percent of the royalty payments shall be allocated to the Sound Recordings Fund. 2⅝ percent of the royalty payments allocated to the Sound Recordings Fund shall be placed in an escrow account managed by an independent administrator jointly appointed by the interested copyright parties described in section 1001(7)(A) and the American Federation of Musicians (or any successor entity) to be distributed to nonfeatured musicians (whether or not members of the American Federation of Musicians or any successor entity) who have performed on sound recordings distributed in the United States. 1⅜ percent of the royalty payments allocated to the Sound Recordings Fund shall be placed in an escrow account managed by an independent administrator jointly appointed by the interested copyright parties described in section 1001(7)(A) and the American Federation of Television and Radio Artists (or any successor entity) to be distributed to nonfeatured vocalists (whether or not members of the American Federation of Television and Radio Artists or any successor entity) who have performed on sound recordings distributed in the United States. 40 percent of the remaining royalty payments in the Sound Recordings Fund shall be distributed to the interested copyright parties described in section 1001(7)(C), and 60 percent of such remaining royalty payments shall be distributed to the interested copyright parties described in section 1001(7)(A).

(2) THE MUSICAL WORKS FUND.—

(A) 33⅓ percent of the royalty payments shall be allocated to the Musical Works Fund for distribution to interested copyright parties described in section 1001(7)(B).

(B)(i) Music publishers shall be entitled to 50 percent of the royalty payments allocated to the Musical Works Fund.

(ii) Writers shall be entitled to the other 50 percent of the royalty payments allocated to the Musical Works Fund.

(c) ALLOCATION OF ROYALTY PAYMENTS WITHIN GROUPS.—If all interested copyright parties within a group specified in subsection (b) do not agree on a voluntary proposal for the distribution of the royalty payments within each group, the Copyright Royalty Judges shall, pursuant to the procedures specified under section 1007(c), allocate royalty payments under this section based on the extent to which, during the relevant period—

(1) for the Sound Recordings Fund, each sound recording was distributed in the form of digital musical recordings or analog musical recordings; and

(2) for the Musical Works Fund, each musical work was distributed in the form of digital musical recordings or analog musical recordings or disseminated to the public in transmissions.

§1007 · Procedures for distributing royalty payments[5]

(a) Filing of Claims and Negotiations.—

(1) Filing of claims.—During the first 2 months of each calendar year, every interested copyright party seeking to receive royalty payments to which such party is entitled under section 1006 shall file with the Copyright Royalty Judges a claim for payments collected during the preceding year in such form and manner as the Copyright Royalty Judges shall prescribe by regulation.

(2) Negotiations.—Notwithstanding any provision of the antitrust laws, for purposes of this section interested copyright parties within each group specified in section 1006(b) may agree among themselves to the proportionate division of royalty payments, may lump their claims together and file them jointly or as a single claim, or may designate a common agent, including any organization described in section 1001(7)(D), to negotiate or receive payment on their behalf; except that no agreement under this subsection may modify the allocation of royalties specified in section 1006(b).

(b) Distribution of Payments in the Absence of a Dispute.—After the period established for the filing of claims under subsection (a), in each year, the Copyright Royalty Judges shall determine whether there exists a controversy concerning the distribution of royalty payments under section 1006(c). If the Copyright Royalty Judges determine that no such controversy exists, the Copyright Royalty Judges shall, within 30 days after such determination, authorize the distribution of the royalty payments as set forth in the agreements regarding the distribution of royalty payments entered into pursuant to subsection (a). The Librarian of Congress shall, before such royalty payments are distributed, deduct the reasonable administrative costs incurred under this section.

(c) Resolution of Disputes.—If the Copyright Royalty Judges find the existence of a controversy, the Copyright Royalty Judges shall, pursuant to chapter 8 of this title, conduct a proceeding to determine the distribution of royalty payments. During the pendency of such a proceeding, the Copyright Royalty Judges shall withhold from distribution an amount sufficient to satisfy all claims with respect to which a controversy exists, but shall, to the extent feasible, authorize the distribution of any amounts that are not in controversy. The Librarian of

Congress shall, before such royalty payments are distributed, deduct the reasonable administrative costs incurred under this section.

Subchapter D — Prohibition on Certain Infringement Actions, Remedies, and Arbitration

§1008 · Prohibition on certain infringement actions

No action may be brought under this title alleging infringement of copyright based on the manufacture, importation, or distribution of a digital audio recording device, a digital audio recording medium, an analog recording device, or an analog recording medium, or based on the noncommercial use by a consumer of such a device or medium for making digital musical recordings or analog musical recordings.

§1009 · Civil remedies

(a) Civil Actions.—Any interested copyright party injured by a violation of section 1002 or 1003 may bring a civil action in an appropriate United States district court against any person for such violation.

(b) Other Civil Actions.—Any person injured by a violation of this chapter may bring a civil action in an appropriate United States district court for actual damages incurred as a result of such violation.

(c) Powers of the Court.—In an action brought under subsection (a), the court—

(1) may grant temporary and permanent injunctions on such terms as it deems reasonable to prevent or restrain such violation;

(2) in the case of a violation of section 1002, or in the case of an injury resulting from a failure to make royalty payments required by section 1003, shall award damages under subsection (d);

(3) in its discretion may allow the recovery of costs by or against any party other than the United States or an officer thereof; and

(4) in its discretion may award a reasonable attorney's fee to the prevailing party.

(d) Award of Damages.—

(1) Damages for section 1002 or 1003 violations.—

(A) Actual damages.—

(i) In an action brought under subsection (a), if the court finds that a violation of section 1002 or 1003 has occurred, the court shall award to the complaining party its actual damages if the complaining party elects such damages at any time before final judgment is entered.

(ii) In the case of section 1003, actual damages shall constitute the royalty payments that should have been paid under section 1004 and deposited under section 1005. In such a case, the court, in its discretion, may award an additional amount of not to exceed 50 percent of the actual damages.

(B) Statutory damages for section 1002 violations.—

(i) Device.—A complaining party may recover an award of statutory damages for each violation of section 1002(a) or (c) in the sum of not more than $2,500 per device involved in such violation or per device on which a service prohibited by section 1002(c) has been performed, as the court considers just.

(ii) Digital musical recording.—A complaining party may recover an award of statutory damages for each violation of section 1002(d) in the sum of not more than $25 per digital musical recording involved in such violation, as the court considers just.

(iii) Transmission.—A complaining party may recover an award of damages for each transmission or communication that violates section 1002(e) in the sum of not more than $10,000, as the court considers just.

(2) Repeated violations.—In any case in which the court finds that a person has violated section 1002 or 1003 within 3 years after a final judgment against that person for another such violation was entered, the court may increase the award of damages to not more than double the amounts that would otherwise be awarded under paragraph (1), as the court considers just.

(3) Innocent violations of section 1002.—The court in its discretion may reduce the total award of damages against a person violating section 1002 to a sum of not less than $250 in any case in which the court finds that the violator was not aware and had no reason to believe that its acts constituted a violation of section 1002.

(e) Payment of Damages.—Any award of damages under subsection (d) shall be deposited with the Register pursuant to section 1005 for distribution to interested copyright parties as though such funds were royalty payments made pursuant to section 1003.

(f) Impounding of Articles.—At any time while an action under subsection (a) is pending, the court may order the impounding, on such terms as it deems reasonable, of any digital audio recording device, digital musical recording, or device specified in section 1002(c) that is in the custody or control of the alleged violator and that the court has reasonable cause to believe does not comply with, or was involved in a violation of, section 1002.

(g) Remedial Modification and Destruction of Articles.—In an action brought under subsection (a), the court may, as part of a final judgment or decree finding a violation of section 1002, order the remedial modification or the destruction of any digital audio recording device, digital musical recording, or device specified in section 1002(c) that—

(1) does not comply with, or was involved in a violation of, section 1002, and

(2) is in the custody or control of the violator or has been impounded under subsection (f).

§1010 · Determination of certain disputes[6]

(a) Scope of Determination.—Before the date of first distribution in the United States of a digital audio recording device or a digital audio interface device, any party manufacturing, importing, or distributing such device, and any interested copyright party may mutually agree to petition the Copyright Royalty Judges to determine whether such device is subject to section 1002, or the basis on which royalty payments for such device are to be made under section 1003.

(b) Initiation of Proceedings.—The parties under subsection (a) shall file the petition with the Copyright Royalty Judges requesting the commencement of a proceeding. Within 2 weeks after receiving such a petition, the Chief Copyright Royalty Judge shall cause notice to be published in the Federal Register of the initiation of the proceeding.

(c) Stay of Judicial Proceedings.—Any civil action brought under section 1009 against a party to a proceeding under this section shall, on application of one of the parties to the proceeding, be stayed until completion of the proceeding.

(d) Proceeding.—The Copyright Royalty Judges shall conduct a proceeding with respect to the matter concerned, in accordance with such procedures as the Copyright Royalty Judges may adopt. The Copyright Royalty Judges shall act on the basis of a fully documented written record. Any party to the proceeding may submit relevant information and proposals to the Copyright Royalty Judges. The parties to the proceeding shall each bear their respective costs of participation.

(e) Judicial Review.—Any determination of the Copyright Royalty Judges under subsection (d) may be appealed, by a party to the proceeding, in accordance with section 803(d) of this title. The pendency of an appeal under this subsection shall not stay the determination of the Copyright Royalty Judges. If the court modifies the determination of the Copyright Royalty Judges, the court shall have jurisdiction to enter its own decision in accordance with its final judgment. The court may further vacate the determination of the Copyright Royalty Judges and remand the case for proceedings as provided in this section.

Chapter 10 · Notes

1. The Audio Home Recording Act of 1992 added chapter 10, entitled "Digital Audio Recording Devices and Media," to title 17. Pub. L. No. 102-563, 106 Stat. 4237.

2. The Copyright Royalty Tribunal Reform Act of 1993 amended section 1004(a)(3) by substituting "Librarian of Congress" in lieu of "Copyright Royalty Tribunal," where appropriate. Pub. L. No. 103-198, 107 Stat. 2304, 2312.

The Copyright Royalty and Distribution Reform Act of 2004 amended paragraph 1004(a)(3) by substituting "Copyright Royalty Judges" in lieu of "Librarian of Congress," wherever it appeared. Pub. L. No. 108-419, 118 Stat. 2341, 2368.

3. The Copyright Royalty Tribunal Reform Act of 1993 amended section 1005 by striking the last sentence which began "The Register shall submit to the Copyright Royalty Tribunal." Pub. L. No. 103-198, 107 Stat. 2304, 2312.

4. The Copyright Royalty Tribunal Reform Act of 1993 amended section 1006(c) by substituting "Librarian of Congress" in lieu of "Copyright Royalty Tribunal," where appropriate. Pub. L. No. 103-198, 107 Stat. 2304, 2312. In 1997, section 1006(b)(1) was amended to insert "Federation of Television" in lieu of "Federation Television" wherever it appeared. Pub. L. No. 105-80, 111 Stat. 1529, 1535.

The Copyright Royalty and Distribution Reform Act of 2004 amended subsection 1006(c) by substituting "Copyright Royalty Judges" for "Librarian of Congress shall convene a copyright arbitration royalty panel which" in matter preceding paragraph (1). Pub. L. No. 108-419, 118 Stat. 2341, 2368.

5. The Copyright Royalty Tribunal Reform Act of 1993 amended section 1007 by substituting "Librarian of Congress" in lieu of "Copyright Royalty Tribunal" or "Tribunal," where appropriate, by amending the first sentence in subsection (c) and by inserting "the reasonable administrative costs incurred by the Librarian" in the last sentence of subsection (c), in lieu of "its reasonable administrative costs." Pub. L. No. 103-198, 107 Stat. 2304, 2312.

In 1997, section 1007 was amended, in subsection (a)(1), by inserting "calendar year 1992" in lieu of "the calendar year in which this chapter takes effect" and, in subsection (b), by inserting "1992" in lieu of "the year in which this section takes effect," and also in subsection (b), by inserting "After" in lieu of "Within 30 days after." Pub. L. No. 105-80, 111 Stat. 1529, 1534 and 1535.

The Copyright Royalty and Distribution Reform Act of 2004 Act amended paragraph 1007(a)(1) and subsections (b) and (c) in their entirety. Pub. L. No. 108-419, 118 Stat. 2341, 2368.

In 2006, the Copyright Royalty Judges Program Technical Corrections Act amended subsections 1007(b) and (c) by making technical and conforming amendments to correct references to the Copyright Royalty Board and deleting "Librarian of Congress," where appropriate. Pub. L. No. 109-303, 120 Stat. 1478, 1483.

6. The Copyright Royalty Tribunal Reform Act of 1993 amended section 1010 by substituting "Librarian of Congress" in lieu of "Copyright Royalty Tribunal" or "Tribunal," where appropriate, and by inserting "Librarian's" in lieu of "its." Pub. L. No. 103-198, 107 Stat. 2304, 2312. That Act, which established copyright arbitration royalty panels, states that "[a]ll royalty rates and all determinations with respect to the proportionate division of compulsory

license fees among copyright claimants, whether made by the Copyright Royalty Tribunal, or by voluntary agreement, before the effective date set forth in subsection (a) [December 17, 1993] shall remain in effect until modified by voluntary agreement or pursuant to the amendments made by this Act." Pub. L. No. 103-198, 107 Stat. 2304, 2313.

The Copyright Royalty and Distribution Reform Act of 2004 Act amended section 1010 in its entirety. Pub. L. No. 108-419, 118 Stat. 2341, 2368.

Chapter 11[1]

Sound Recordings and Music Videos

§1101 · Unauthorized fixation and trafficking in sound recordings and music videos

(a) UNAUTHORIZED ACTS.—Anyone who, without the consent of the performer or performers involved—

(1) fixes the sounds or sounds and images of a live musical performance in a copy or phonorecord, or reproduces copies or phonorecords of such a performance from an unauthorized fixation,

(2) transmits or otherwise communicates to the public the sounds or sounds and images of a live musical performance, or

(3) distributes or offers to distribute, sells or offers to sell, rents or offers to rent, or traffics in any copy or phonorecord fixed as described in paragraph (1), regardless of whether the fixations occurred in the United States,

shall be subject to the remedies provided in sections 502 through 505, to the same extent as an infringer of copyright.

(b) DEFINITION.—As used in this section, the term "traffic in" means transport, transfer, or otherwise dispose of, to another, as consideration for anything of value, or make or obtain control of with intent to transport, transfer, or dispose of.

(c) APPLICABILITY.—This section shall apply to any act or acts that occur on or after the date of the enactment of the Uruguay Round Agreements Act.

(d) STATE LAW NOT PREEMPTED.—Nothing in this section may be construed to annul or limit any rights or remedies under the common law or statutes of any State.

Chapter 11 · Note

1. In 1994, the Uruguay Round Agreements Act added chapter 11, entitled "Sound Recordings and Music Videos," to title 17. Pub. L. No. 103-465, 108 Stat. 4809, 4974.

Chapter 12[1]

Copyright Protection and Management Systems

§1201 · Circumvention of copyright protection systems[2]

(a) VIOLATIONS REGARDING CIRCUMVENTION OF TECHNOLOGICAL MEASURES.—(1)(A) No person shall circumvent a technological measure that effectively controls access to a work protected under this title. The prohibition contained in the preceding sentence shall take effect at the end of the 2-year period beginning on the date of the enactment of this chapter.

(B) The prohibition contained in subparagraph (A) shall not apply to persons who are users of a copyrighted work which is in a particular class of works, if such persons are, or are likely to be in the succeeding 3-year period, adversely affected by virtue of such prohibition in their ability to make noninfringing uses of that particular class of works under this title, as determined under subparagraph (C).

(C) During the 2-year period described in subparagraph (A), and during each succeeding 3-year period, the Librarian of Congress, upon the recommendation of the Register of Copyrights, who shall consult with the Assistant Secretary for Communications and Information of the Department of Commerce and report and comment on his or her views in making such recommendation, shall make the determination in a rulemaking proceeding for purposes of subparagraph (B) of whether persons who are users of a copyrighted work are, or are likely to be in the succeeding 3-year period, adversely affected by the prohibition under subparagraph (A) in their ability to make noninfringing uses under this title of a particular class of copyrighted works. In conducting such rulemaking, the Librarian shall examine—

(i) the availability for use of copyrighted works;

(ii) the availability for use of works for nonprofit archival, preservation, and educational purposes;

(iii) the impact that the prohibition on the circumvention of technological measures applied to copyrighted works has on criticism, comment, news reporting, teaching, scholarship, or research;

(iv) the effect of circumvention of technological measures on the market for or value of copyrighted works; and

(v) such other factors as the Librarian considers appropriate.

(D) The Librarian shall publish any class of copyrighted works for which the Librarian has determined, pursuant to the rulemaking conducted under subparagraph (C), that noninfringing uses by persons who are users of a copyrighted work are, or are likely to be, adversely affected, and the prohibition contained in subparagraph (A) shall not apply to such users with respect to such class of works for the ensuing 3-year period.

(E) Neither the exception under subparagraph (B) from the applicability of the prohibition contained in subparagraph (A), nor any determination made in a rulemaking conducted under subparagraph (C), may be used as a defense in any action to enforce any provision of this title other than this paragraph.

(2) No person shall manufacture, import, offer to the public, provide, or otherwise traffic in any technology, product, service, device, component, or part thereof, that—

(A) is primarily designed or produced for the purpose of circumventing a technological measure that effectively controls access to a work protected under this title;

(B) has only limited commercially significant purpose or use other than to circumvent a technological measure that effectively controls access to a work protected under this title; or

(C) is marketed by that person or another acting in concert with that person with that person's knowledge for use in circumventing a technological measure that effectively controls access to a work protected under this title.

(3) As used in this subsection—

(A) to "circumvent a technological measure" means to descramble a scrambled work, to decrypt an encrypted work, or otherwise to avoid, bypass, remove, deactivate, or impair a technological measure, without the authority of the copyright owner; and

(B) a technological measure "effectively controls access to a work" if the measure, in the ordinary course of its operation, requires the application of information, or a process or a treatment, with the authority of the copyright owner, to gain access to the work.

(b) Additional Violations.—(1) No person shall manufacture, import, offer to the public, provide, or otherwise traffic in any technology, product, service, device, component, or part thereof, that—

(A) is primarily designed or produced for the purpose of circumventing protection afforded by a technological measure that effectively protects a right of a copyright owner under this title in a work or a portion thereof;

(B) has only limited commercially significant purpose or use other than to circumvent protection afforded by a technological measure that effectively protects a right of a copyright owner under this title in a work or a portion thereof; or

(C) is marketed by that person or another acting in concert with that person with that person's knowledge for use in circumventing protection afforded by a technological measure that effectively protects a right of a copyright owner under this title in a work or a portion thereof.

(2) As used in this subsection—

(A) to "circumvent protection afforded by a technological measure" means avoiding, bypassing, removing, deactivating, or otherwise impairing a technological measure; and

(B) a technological measure "effectively protects a right of a copyright owner under this title" if the measure, in the ordinary course of its operation, prevents, restricts, or otherwise limits the exercise of a right of a copyright owner under this title.

(c) Other Rights, Etc., Not Affected.—(1) Nothing in this section shall affect rights, remedies, limitations, or defenses to copyright infringement, including fair use, under this title.

(2) Nothing in this section shall enlarge or diminish vicarious or contributory liability for copyright infringement in connection with any technology, product, service, device, component, or part thereof.

(3) Nothing in this section shall require that the design of, or design and selection of parts and components for, a consumer electronics, telecommunications, or computing product provide for a response to any particular technological measure, so long as such part or component, or the product in which such part or component is integrated, does not otherwise fall within the prohibitions of subsection (a)(2) or (b)(1).

(4) Nothing in this section shall enlarge or diminish any rights of free speech or the press for activities using consumer electronics, telecommunications, or computing products.

(d) Exemption for Nonprofit Libraries, Archives, and Educational Institutions.—(1) A nonprofit library, archives, or educational institution which gains access to a commercially exploited copyrighted work solely in order to make a good faith determination of whether to acquire a copy of that work for the sole purpose of engaging in conduct permitted under this title shall not be in violation of subsection (a)(1)(A). A copy of a work to which access has been gained under this paragraph—

(A) may not be retained longer than necessary to make such good faith determination; and

(B) may not be used for any other purpose.

(2) The exemption made available under paragraph (1) shall only apply with respect to a work when an identical copy of that work is not reasonably available in another form.

(3) A nonprofit library, archives, or educational institution that willfully for the purpose of commercial advantage or financial gain violates paragraph (1)—

(A) shall, for the first offense, be subject to the civil remedies under section 1203; and

(B) shall, for repeated or subsequent offenses, in addition to the civil remedies under section 1203, forfeit the exemption provided under paragraph (1).

(4) This subsection may not be used as a defense to a claim under subsection (a)(2) or (b), nor may this subsection permit a nonprofit library, archives, or educational institution to manufacture, import, offer to the public, provide,

or otherwise traffic in any technology, product, service, component, or part thereof, which circumvents a technological measure.

(5) In order for a library or archives to qualify for the exemption under this subsection, the collections of that library or archives shall be—

(A) open to the public; or

(B) available not only to researchers affiliated with the library or archives or with the institution of which it is a part, but also to other persons doing research in a specialized field.

(e) Law Enforcement, Intelligence, and Other Government Activities.—This section does not prohibit any lawfully authorized investigative, protective, information security, or intelligence activity of an officer, agent, or employee of the United States, a State, or a political subdivision of a State, or a person acting pursuant to a contract with the United States, a State, or a political subdivision of a State. For purposes of this subsection, the term "information security" means activities carried out in order to identify and address the vulnerabilities of a government computer, computer system, or computer network.

(f) Reverse Engineering.—(1) Notwithstanding the provisions of subsection (a)(1)(A), a person who has lawfully obtained the right to use a copy of a computer program may circumvent a technological measure that effectively controls access to a particular portion of that program for the sole purpose of identifying and analyzing those elements of the program that are necessary to achieve interoperability of an independently created computer program with other programs, and that have not previously been readily available to the person engaging in the circumvention, to the extent any such acts of identification and analysis do not constitute infringement under this title.

(2) Notwithstanding the provisions of subsections (a)(2) and (b), a person may develop and employ technological means to circumvent a technological measure, or to circumvent protection afforded by a technological measure, in order to enable the identification and analysis under paragraph (1), or for the purpose of enabling interoperability of an independently created computer program with other programs, if such means are necessary to achieve such interoperability, to the extent that doing so does not constitute infringement under this title.

(3) The information acquired through the acts permitted under paragraph (1), and the means permitted under paragraph (2), may be made available to others if the person referred to in paragraph (1) or (2), as the case may be, provides such information or means solely for the purpose of enabling interoperability of an independently created computer program with other programs, and to the extent that doing so does not constitute infringement under this title or violate applicable law other than this section.

(4) For purposes of this subsection, the term "interoperability" means the ability of computer programs to exchange information, and of such programs mutually to use the information which has been exchanged.

(g) Encryption Research.—

(1) Definitions.—For purposes of this subsection—

(A) the term "encryption research" means activities necessary to identify and analyze flaws and vulnerabilities of encryption technologies applied to copyrighted works, if these activities are conducted to advance the state of knowledge in the field of encryption technology or to assist in the development of encryption products; and

(B) the term "encryption technology" means the scrambling and descrambling of information using mathematical formulas or algorithms.

(2) Permissible acts of encryption research.—Notwithstanding the provisions of subsection (a)(1)(A), it is not a violation of that subsection for a person to circumvent a technological measure as applied to a copy, phonorecord, performance, or display of a published work in the course of an act of good faith encryption research if—

(A) the person lawfully obtained the encrypted copy, phonorecord, performance, or display of the published work;

(B) such act is necessary to conduct such encryption research;

(C) the person made a good faith effort to obtain authorization before the circumvention; and

(D) such act does not constitute infringement under this title or a violation of applicable law other than this section, including section 1030 of title 18 and those provisions of title 18 amended by the Computer Fraud and Abuse Act of 1986.

(3) Factors in determining exemption.—In determining whether a person qualifies for the exemption under paragraph (2), the factors to be considered shall include—

(A) whether the information derived from the encryption research was disseminated, and if so, whether it was disseminated in a manner reasonably calculated to advance the state of knowledge or development of encryption technology, versus whether it was disseminated in a manner that facilitates infringement under this title or a violation of applicable law other than this section, including a violation of privacy or breach of security;

(B) whether the person is engaged in a legitimate course of study, is employed, or is appropriately trained or experienced, in the field of encryption technology; and

(C) whether the person provides the copyright owner of the work to which the technological measure is applied with notice of the findings and documentation of the research, and the time when such notice is provided.

(4) Use of technological means for research activities.—Notwithstanding the provisions of subsection (a)(2), it is not a violation of that subsection for a person to—

(A) develop and employ technological means to circumvent a technological measure for the sole purpose of that person performing the acts of good faith encryption research described in paragraph (2); and

(B) provide the technological means to another person with whom he or she is working collaboratively for the purpose of conducting the acts of good faith encryption research described in paragraph (2) or for the purpose of having that other person verify his or her acts of good faith encryption research described in paragraph (2).

(5) Report to Congress.—Not later than 1 year after the date of the enactment of this chapter, the Register of Copyrights and the Assistant Secretary for Communications and Information of the Department of Commerce shall jointly report to the Congress on the effect this subsection has had on—

(A) encryption research and the development of encryption technology;

(B) the adequacy and effectiveness of technological measures designed to protect copyrighted works; and

(C) protection of copyright owners against the unauthorized access to their encrypted copyrighted works.

The report shall include legislative recommendations, if any.

(h) Exceptions Regarding Minors.—In applying subsection (a) to a component or part, the court may consider the necessity for its intended and actual incorporation in a technology, product, service, or device, which—

(1) does not itself violate the provisions of this title; and

(2) has the sole purpose to prevent the access of minors to material on the Internet.

(i) Protection of Personally Identifying Information.—

(1) Circumvention permitted.—Notwithstanding the provisions of subsection (a)(1)(A), it is not a violation of that subsection for a person to circumvent a technological measure that effectively controls access to a work protected under this title, if—

(A) the technological measure, or the work it protects, contains the capability of collecting or disseminating personally identifying information reflecting the online activities of a natural person who seeks to gain access to the work protected;

(B) in the normal course of its operation, the technological measure, or the work it protects, collects or disseminates personally identifying information about the person who seeks to gain access to the work protected, without providing conspicuous notice of such collection or dissemination to such person, and without providing such person with the capability to prevent or restrict such collection or dissemination;

(C) the act of circumvention has the sole effect of identifying and disabling the capability described in subparagraph (A), and has no other effect on the ability of any person to gain access to any work; and

(D) the act of circumvention is carried out solely for the purpose of preventing the collection or dissemination of personally identifying information about a natural person who seeks to gain access to the work protected, and is not in violation of any other law.

(2) INAPPLICABILITY TO CERTAIN TECHNOLOGICAL MEASURES.—This subsection does not apply to a technological measure, or a work it protects, that does not collect or disseminate personally identifying information and that is disclosed to a user as not having or using such capability.

(j) SECURITY TESTING.—

(1) DEFINITION.—For purposes of this subsection, the term "security testing" means accessing a computer, computer system, or computer network, solely for the purpose of good faith testing, investigating, or correcting, a security flaw or vulnerability, with the authorization of the owner or operator of such computer, computer system, or computer network.

(2) PERMISSIBLE ACTS OF SECURITY TESTING.—Notwithstanding the provisions of subsection (a)(1)(A), it is not a violation of that subsection for a person to engage in an act of security testing, if such act does not constitute infringement under this title or a violation of applicable law other than this section, including section 1030 of title 18 and those provisions of title 18 amended by the Computer Fraud and Abuse Act of 1986.

(3) FACTORS IN DETERMINING EXEMPTION.—In determining whether a person qualifies for the exemption under paragraph (2), the factors to be considered shall include—

(A) whether the information derived from the security testing was used solely to promote the security of the owner or operator of such computer, computer system or computer network, or shared directly with the developer of such computer, computer system, or computer network; and

(B) whether the information derived from the security testing was used or maintained in a manner that does not facilitate infringement under this title or a violation of applicable law other than this section, including a violation of privacy or breach of security.

(4) USE OF TECHNOLOGICAL MEANS FOR SECURITY TESTING.—Notwithstanding the provisions of subsection (a)(2), it is not a violation of that subsection for a person to develop, produce, distribute or employ technological means for the sole purpose of performing the acts of security testing described in subsection (2), provided such technological means does not otherwise violate section (a)(2).

(k) CERTAIN ANALOG DEVICES AND CERTAIN TECHNOLOGICAL MEASURES.—

(1) CERTAIN ANALOG DEVICES.—

(A) Effective 18 months after the date of the enactment of this chapter, no person shall manufacture, import, offer to the public, provide or otherwise traffic in any—

(i) VHS format analog video cassette recorder unless such recorder conforms to the automatic gain control copy control technology;

(ii) 8mm format analog video cassette camcorder unless such camcorder conforms to the automatic gain control technology;

(iii) Beta format analog video cassette recorder, unless such recorder conforms to the automatic gain control copy control technology, except that this requirement shall not apply until there are 1,000 Beta format analog video cassette recorders sold in the United States in any one calendar year after the date of the enactment of this chapter;

(iv) 8mm format analog video cassette recorder that is not an analog video cassette camcorder, unless such recorder conforms to the automatic gain control copy control technology, except that this requirement shall not apply until there are 20,000 such recorders sold in the United States in any one calendar year after the date of the enactment of this chapter; or

(v) analog video cassette recorder that records using an NTSC format video input and that is not otherwise covered under clauses (i) through (iv), unless such device conforms to the automatic gain control copy control technology.

(B) Effective on the date of the enactment of this chapter, no person shall manufacture, import, offer to the public, provide or otherwise traffic in—

(i) any VHS format analog video cassette recorder or any 8mm format analog video cassette recorder if the design of the model of such recorder has been modified after such date of enactment so that a model of recorder that previously conformed to the automatic gain control copy control technology no longer conforms to such technology; or

(ii) any VHS format analog video cassette recorder, or any 8mm format analog video cassette recorder that is not an 8mm analog video cassette camcorder, if the design of the model of such recorder has been modified after such date of enactment so that a model of recorder that previously conformed to the four-line colorstripe copy control technology no longer conforms to such technology.

Manufacturers that have not previously manufactured or sold a VHS format analog video cassette recorder, or an 8mm format analog cassette recorder, shall be required to conform to the four-line colorstripe copy control technology in the initial model of any such recorder manufactured after the date of the enactment of this chapter, and thereafter to continue conforming to the four-line colorstripe copy control technology. For purposes of this subparagraph, an analog video cassette recorder "conforms to" the four-line colorstripe copy control technology if it records a signal that, when played back by the playback function of that recorder in the normal viewing mode, exhibits, on a reference display device, a display containing distracting visible lines through portions of the viewable picture.

(2) Certain encoding restrictions.—No person shall apply the automatic gain control copy control technology or colorstripe copy control technology to prevent or limit consumer copying except such copying—

(A) of a single transmission, or specified group of transmissions, of live events or of audiovisual works for which a member of the public has exercised choice in selecting the transmissions, including the content of the transmissions or the time of receipt of such transmissions, or both, and as to which such member is charged a separate fee for each such transmission or specified group of transmissions;

(B) from a copy of a transmission of a live event or an audiovisual work if such transmission is provided by a channel or service where payment is made by a member of the public for such channel or service in the form of a subscription fee that entitles the member of the public to receive all of the programming contained in such channel or service;

(C) from a physical medium containing one or more prerecorded audiovisual works; or

(D) from a copy of a transmission described in subparagraph (A) or from a copy made from a physical medium described in subparagraph (C).

In the event that a transmission meets both the conditions set forth in subparagraph (A) and those set forth in subparagraph (B), the transmission shall be treated as a transmission described in subparagraph (A).

(3) Inapplicability.—This subsection shall not—

(A) require any analog video cassette camcorder to conform to the automatic gain control copy control technology with respect to any video signal received through a camera lens;

(B) apply to the manufacture, importation, offer for sale, provision of, or other trafficking in, any professional analog video cassette recorder; or

(C) apply to the offer for sale or provision of, or other trafficking in, any previously owned analog video cassette recorder, if such recorder was legally manufactured and sold when new and not subsequently modified in violation of paragraph (1)(B).

(4) Definitions.—For purposes of this subsection:

(A) An "analog video cassette recorder" means a device that records, or a device that includes a function that records, on electromagnetic tape in an analog format the electronic impulses produced by the video and audio portions of a television program, motion picture, or other form of audiovisual work.

(B) An "analog video cassette camcorder" means an analog video cassette recorder that contains a recording function that operates through a camera lens and through a video input that may be connected with a television or other video playback device.

(C) An analog video cassette recorder "conforms" to the automatic gain control copy control technology if it—

(i) detects one or more of the elements of such technology and does not record the motion picture or transmission protected by such technology; or

(ii) records a signal that, when played back, exhibits a meaningfully distorted or degraded display.

(D) The term "professional analog video cassette recorder" means an analog video cassette recorder that is designed, manufactured, marketed, and intended for use by a person who regularly employs such a device for a lawful business or industrial use, including making, performing, displaying, distributing, or transmitting copies of motion pictures on a commercial scale.

(E) The terms "VHS format," "8mm format," "Beta format," "automatic gain control copy control technology," "colorstripe copy control technology," "four-line version of the colorstripe copy control technology," and "NTSC" have the meanings that are commonly understood in the consumer electronics and motion picture industries as of the date of the enactment of this chapter.

(5) Violations.—Any violation of paragraph (1) of this subsection shall be treated as a violation of subsection (b)(1) of this section. Any violation of paragraph (2) of this subsection shall be deemed an "act of circumvention" for the purposes of section 1203(c)(3)(A) of this chapter.

§1202 · Integrity of copyright management information[3]

(a) False Copyright Management Information.—No person shall knowingly and with the intent to induce, enable, facilitate, or conceal infringement—

(1) provide copyright management information that is false, or

(2) distribute or import for distribution copyright management information that is false.

(b) Removal or Alteration of Copyright Management Information.—No person shall, without the authority of the copyright owner or the law—

(1) intentionally remove or alter any copyright management information,

(2) distribute or import for distribution copyright management information knowing that the copyright management information has been removed or altered without authority of the copyright owner or the law, or

(3) distribute, import for distribution, or publicly perform works, copies of works, or phonorecords, knowing that copyright management information has been removed or altered without authority of the copyright owner or the law,

knowing, or, with respect to civil remedies under section 1203, having reasonable grounds to know, that it will induce, enable, facilitate, or conceal an infringement of any right under this title.

(c) Definition.—As used in this section, the term "copyright management information" means any of the following information conveyed in connection with copies or phonorecords of a work or performances or displays of a work, including in digital form, except that such term does not include any personally identifying information about a user of a work or of a copy, phonorecord, performance, or display of a work:

(1) The title and other information identifying the work, including the information set forth on a notice of copyright.

(2) The name of, and other identifying information about, the author of a work.

(3) The name of, and other identifying information about, the copyright owner of the work, including the information set forth in a notice of copyright.

(4) With the exception of public performances of works by radio and television broadcast stations, the name of, and other identifying information about, a performer whose performance is fixed in a work other than an audiovisual work.

(5) With the exception of public performances of works by radio and television broadcast stations, in the case of an audiovisual work, the name of, and other identifying information about, a writer, performer, or director who is credited in the audiovisual work.

(6) Terms and conditions for use of the work.

(7) Identifying numbers or symbols referring to such information or links to such information.

(8) Such other information as the Register of Copyrights may prescribe by regulation, except that the Register of Copyrights may not require the provision of any information concerning the user of a copyrighted work.

(d) Law Enforcement, Intelligence, and Other Government Activities.—This section does not prohibit any lawfully authorized investigative, protective, information security, or intelligence activity of an officer, agent, or employee of the United States, a State, or a political subdivision of a State, or a person acting pursuant to a contract with the United States, a State, or a political subdivision of a State. For purposes of this subsection, the term "information security" means activities carried out in order to identify and address the vulnerabilities of a government computer, computer system, or computer network.

(e) Limitations on Liability.—

(1) Analog transmissions.—In the case of an analog transmission, a person who is making transmissions in its capacity as a broadcast station, or as a cable system, or someone who provides programming to such station or system, shall not be liable for a violation of subsection (b) if—

(A) avoiding the activity that constitutes such violation is not technically feasible or would create an undue financial hardship on such person; and

(B) such person did not intend, by engaging in such activity, to induce, enable, facilitate, or conceal infringement of a right under this title.

(2) Digital transmissions.—

(A) If a digital transmission standard for the placement of copyright management information for a category of works is set in a voluntary, consensus standard-setting process involving a representative cross-section of broadcast stations or cable systems and copyright owners of a category of works that are intended for public performance by such stations or systems, a person identified in paragraph (1) shall not be liable for a violation of subsection (b) with respect to the particular copyright management information addressed by such standard if—

(i) the placement of such information by someone other than such person is not in accordance with such standard; and

(ii) the activity that constitutes such violation is not intended to induce, enable, facilitate, or conceal infringement of a right under this title.

(B) Until a digital transmission standard has been set pursuant to subparagraph (A) with respect to the placement of copyright management information for a category of works, a person identified in paragraph (1) shall not be liable for a violation of subsection (b) with respect to such copyright management information, if the activity that constitutes such violation is not intended to induce, enable, facilitate, or conceal infringement of a right under this title, and if—

(i) the transmission of such information by such person would result in a perceptible visual or aural degradation of the digital signal; or

(ii) the transmission of such information by such person would conflict with—

(I) an applicable government regulation relating to transmission of information in a digital signal;

(II) an applicable industry-wide standard relating to the transmission of information in a digital signal that was adopted by a voluntary consensus standards body prior to the effective date of this chapter; or

(III) an applicable industry-wide standard relating to the transmission of information in a digital signal that was adopted in a voluntary, consensus standards-setting process open to participation by a representative cross-section of broadcast stations or cable systems and copyright owners of a category of works that are intended for public performance by such stations or systems.

(3) Definitions.—As used in this subsection—

(A) the term "broadcast station" has the meaning given that term in section 3 of the Communications Act of 1934 (47 U.S.C. 153); and

(B) the term "cable system" has the meaning given that term in section 602 of the Communications Act of 1934 (47 U.S.C. 522).

§1203 · Civil remedies[4]

(a) Civil Actions.—Any person injured by a violation of section 1201 or 1202 may bring a civil action in an appropriate United States district court for such violation.

(b) Powers of the Court.—In an action brought under subsection (a), the court—

(1) may grant temporary and permanent injunctions on such terms as it deems reasonable to prevent or restrain a violation, but in no event shall impose a prior restraint on free speech or the press protected under the 1st amendment to the Constitution;

(2) at any time while an action is pending, may order the impounding, on such terms as it deems reasonable, of any device or product that is in the custody or control of the alleged violator and that the court has reasonable cause to believe was involved in a violation;

(3) may award damages under subsection (c);

(4) in its discretion may allow the recovery of costs by or against any party other than the United States or an officer thereof;

(5) in its discretion may award reasonable attorney's fees to the prevailing party; and

(6) may, as part of a final judgment or decree finding a violation, order the remedial modification or the destruction of any device or product involved in the violation that is in the custody or control of the violator or has been impounded under paragraph (2).

(c) Award of Damages.—

(1) In general.—Except as otherwise provided in this title, a person committing a violation of section 1201 or 1202 is liable for either—

(A) the actual damages and any additional profits of the violator, as provided in paragraph (2), or

(B) statutory damages, as provided in paragraph (3).

(2) Actual damages.—The court shall award to the complaining party the actual damages suffered by the party as a result of the violation, and any profits of the violator that are attributable to the violation and are not taken into account in computing the actual damages, if the complaining party elects such damages at any time before final judgment is entered.

(3) Statutory damages.—(A) At any time before final judgment is entered, a complaining party may elect to recover an award of statutory damages for each violation of section 1201 in the sum of not less than $200 or more than $2,500 per act of circumvention, device, product, component, offer, or performance of service, as the court considers just.

(B) At any time before final judgment is entered, a complaining party may elect to recover an award of statutory damages for each violation of section 1202 in the sum of not less than $2,500 or more than $25,000.

(4) REPEATED VIOLATIONS.—In any case in which the injured party sustains the burden of proving, and the court finds, that a person has violated section 1201 or 1202 within three years after a final judgment was entered against the person for another such violation, the court may increase the award of damages up to triple the amount that would otherwise be awarded, as the court considers just.

(5) INNOCENT VIOLATIONS.—

(A) IN GENERAL.—The court in its discretion may reduce or remit the total award of damages in any case in which the violator sustains the burden of proving, and the court finds, that the violator was not aware and had no reason to believe that its acts constituted a violation.

(B) NONPROFIT LIBRARY, ARCHIVES, EDUCATIONAL INSTITUTIONS, OR PUBLIC BROADCASTING ENTITIES.—

(i) DEFINITION.—In this subparagraph, the term "public broadcasting entity" has the meaning given such term under section 118(f).

(ii) IN GENERAL.—In the case of a nonprofit library, archives, educational institution, or public broadcasting entity, the court shall remit damages in any case in which the library, archives, educational institution, or public broadcasting entity sustains the burden of proving, and the court finds, that the library, archives, educational institution, or public broadcasting entity was not aware and had no reason to believe that its acts constituted a violation.

§1204 · Criminal offenses and penalties[5]

(a) IN GENERAL.—Any person who violates section 1201 or 1202 willfully and for purposes of commercial advantage or private financial gain—

(1) shall be fined not more than $500,000 or imprisoned for not more than 5 years, or both, for the first offense; and

(2) shall be fined not more than $1,000,000 or imprisoned for not more than 10 years, or both, for any subsequent offense.

(b) LIMITATION FOR NONPROFIT LIBRARY, ARCHIVES, EDUCATIONAL INSTITUTION, OR PUBLIC BROADCASTING ENTITY.—Subsection (a) shall not apply to a nonprofit library, archives, educational institution, or public broadcasting entity (as defined under section 118(f)).

(c) STATUTE OF LIMITATIONS.—No criminal proceeding shall be brought under this section unless such proceeding is commenced within five years after the cause of action arose.

§1205 · Savings clause

Nothing in this chapter abrogates, diminishes, or weakens the provisions of, nor provides any defense or element of mitigation in a criminal prosecution or civil action under, any Federal or State law that prevents the violation of the privacy of an individual in connection with the individual's use of the Internet.

Chapter 12 · Notes

1. The WIPO Copyright and Performances and Phonograms Treaties Implementation Act of 1998 added chapter 12, entitled "Copyright Protection and Management Systems," to title 17. Pub. L. No. 105-304, 112 Stat. 2860, 2863. The WIPO Copyright and Performances and Phonograms Treaties Implementation Act of 1998 is title I of the Digital Millennium Copyright Act. Pub. L. No. 105-304, 112 Stat. 2860.

2. The Satellite Home Viewer Improvement Act of 1999 amended section 1201(a)(1)(C) by deleting "on the record." Pub. L. No. 106-113, 113 Stat. 1501, app. I at 1501A-594.

3. In 1999, section 1202 was amended by inserting "category of works" for "category or works," in subsection (e)(2)(B). Pub. L. No. 106-44, 113 Stat. 221, 222.

4. The Satellite Home Viewer Improvement Act of 1999 amended section 1203(c)(5)(B) in its entirety. Pub. L. No. 106-113, 113 Stat. 1501, app. I at 1501A-593. The Copyright Cleanup, Clarification, and Corrections Act of 2010 amended subparagraph 1203(c)(5)(B)(i) to substitute "section 118(f)" for "section 118(g)." Pub. L. No. 111-295, 124 Stat. 3180, 3181.

5. The Satellite Home Viewer Improvement Act of 1999 amended section 1204(b) in its entirety. Pub. L. No. 106-113, 113 Stat. 1501, app. I at 1501A-593. The Copyright Cleanup, Clarification, and Corrections Act of 2010 amended subsection 1204(b) to substitute "section 118(f)" for "section 118(g)." Pub. L. No. 111-295, 124 Stat. 3180, 3181.

Chapter 13[1]

Protection of Original Designs

§1301 · Designs protected[2]

(a) Designs Protected.—

(1) In general.—The designer or other owner of an original design of a useful article which makes the article attractive or distinctive in appearance to the purchasing or using public may secure the protection provided by this chapter upon complying with and subject to this chapter.

(2) Vessel features.—The design of a vessel hull, deck, or combination of a hull and deck, including a plug or mold, is subject to protection under this chapter, notwithstanding section 1302(4).

(3) Exceptions.—Department of Defense rights in a registered design under this chapter, including the right to build to such registered design, shall be determined solely by operation of section 2320 of title 10 or by the instrument under which the design was developed for the United States Government.

(b) Definitions.—For the purpose of this chapter, the following terms have the following meanings:

(1) A design is "original" if it is the result of the designer's creative endeavor that provides a distinguishable variation over prior work pertaining to similar articles which is more than merely trivial and has not been copied from another source.

(2) A "useful article" is a vessel hull or deck, including a plug or mold, which in normal use has an intrinsic utilitarian function that is not merely to portray the appearance of the article or to convey information. An article which normally is part of a useful article shall be deemed to be a useful article.

(3) A "vessel" is a craft—

(A) that is designed and capable of independently steering a course on or through water through its own means of propulsion; and

(B) that is designed and capable of carrying and transporting one or more passengers.

(4) A 'hull' is the exterior frame or body of a vessel, exclusive of the deck, superstructure, masts, sails, yards, rigging, hardware, fixtures, and other attachments.

(5) A "plug" means a device or model used to make a mold for the purpose of exact duplication, regardless of whether the device or model has an intrinsic utilitarian function that is not only to portray the appearance of the product or to convey information.

(6) A "mold" means a matrix or form in which a substance for material is used, regardless of whether the matrix or form has an intrinsic utilitarian function that is not only to portray the appearance of the product or to convey information.

(7) A 'deck' is the horizontal surface of a vessel that covers the hull, including exterior cabin and cockpit surfaces and exclusive of masts, sails, yards, rigging, hardware, fixtures, and other attachments.

§1302 · Designs not subject to protection[3]

Protection under this chapter shall not be available for a design that is—

(1) not original;

(2) staple or commonplace, such as a standard geometric figure, a familiar symbol, an emblem, or a motif, or another shape, pattern, or configuration which has become standard, common, prevalent, or ordinary;

(3) different from a design excluded by paragraph (2) only in insignificant details or in elements which are variants commonly used in the relevant trades;

(4) dictated solely by a utilitarian function of the article that embodies it; or

(5) embodied in a useful article that was made public by the designer or owner in the United States or a foreign country more than 2 years before the date of the application for registration under this chapter.

§1303 · Revisions, adaptations, and rearrangements

Protection for a design under this chapter shall be available notwithstanding the employment in the design of subject matter excluded from protection under section 1302 if the design is a substantial revision, adaptation, or rearrangement of such subject matter. Such protection shall be independent of any subsisting protection in subject matter employed in the design, and shall not be construed as securing any right to subject matter excluded from protection under this chapter or as extending any subsisting protection under this chapter.

§1304 · Commencement of protection

The protection provided for a design under this chapter shall commence upon the earlier of the date of publication of the registration under section 1313(a) or the date the design is first made public as defined by section 1310(b).

§1305 · Term of protection

(a) In General.—Subject to subsection (b), the protection provided under this chapter for a design shall continue for a term of 10 years beginning on the date of the commencement of protection under section 1304.

(b) Expiration.—All terms of protection provided in this section shall run to the end of the calendar year in which they would otherwise expire.

(c) Termination of Rights.—Upon expiration or termination of protection in a particular design under this chapter, all rights under this chapter in the design shall terminate, regardless of the number of different articles in which the design may have been used during the term of its protection.

§1306 · Design notice

(a) Contents of Design Notice.—

(1) Whenever any design for which protection is sought under this chapter is made public under section 1310(b), the owner of the design shall, subject to the provisions of section 1307, mark it or have it marked legibly with a design notice consisting of—

(A) the words "Protected Design", the abbreviation "Prot'd Des.", or the letter "D" within a circle, Ⓓ, or the symbol "*D*";

(B) the year of the date on which protection for the design commenced; and

(C) the name of the owner, an abbreviation by which the name can be recognized, or a generally accepted alternative designation of the owner.

Any distinctive identification of the owner may be used for purposes of subparagraph (C) if it has been recorded by the Administrator before the design marked with such identification is registered.

(2) After registration, the registration number may be used instead of the elements specified in subparagraphs (B) and (C) of paragraph (1).

(b) Location of Notice.—The design notice shall be so located and applied as to give reasonable notice of design protection while the useful article embodying the design is passing through its normal channels of commerce.

(c) Subsequent Removal of Notice.—When the owner of a design has complied with the provisions of this section, protection under this chapter shall not be affected by the removal, destruction, or obliteration by others of the design notice on an article.

§1307 · Effect of omission of notice

(a) Actions with Notice.—Except as provided in subsection (b), the omission of the notice prescribed in section 1306 shall not cause loss of the protection under this chapter or prevent recovery for infringement under this chapter against any person who, after receiving written notice of the design protection, begins an undertaking leading to infringement under this chapter.

(b) Actions without Notice.—The omission of the notice prescribed in section 1306 shall prevent any recovery under section 1323 against a person who began an undertaking leading to infringement under this chapter before receiving written notice of the design protection. No injunction shall be issued under this chapter with respect to such undertaking unless the owner of the design reimburses that person for any reasonable expenditure or contractual obligation in connection with such undertaking that was incurred before receiving written notice of the design protection, as the court in its discretion directs. The burden of providing written notice of design protection shall be on the owner of the design.

§1308 · Exclusive rights

The owner of a design protected under this chapter has the exclusive right to—

(1) make, have made, or import, for sale or for use in trade, any useful article embodying that design; and

(2) sell or distribute for sale or for use in trade any useful article embodying that design.

§1309 · Infringement

(a) Acts of Infringement.—Except as provided in subsection (b), it shall be infringement of the exclusive rights in a design protected under this chapter for any person, without the consent of the owner of the design, within the United States and during the term of such protection, to—

(1) make, have made, or import, for sale or for use in trade, any infringing article as defined in subsection (e); or

(2) sell or distribute for sale or for use in trade any such infringing article.

(b) Acts of Sellers and Distributors.—A seller or distributor of an infringing article who did not make or import the article shall be deemed to have infringed on a design protected under this chapter only if that person—

(1) induced or acted in collusion with a manufacturer to make, or an importer to import such article, except that merely purchasing or giving an order to purchase such article in the ordinary course of business shall not of itself

constitute such inducement or collusion; or

(2) refused or failed, upon the request of the owner of the design, to make a prompt and full disclosure of that person's source of such article, and that person orders or reorders such article after receiving notice by registered or certified mail of the protection subsisting in the design.

(c) Acts without Knowledge.—It shall not be infringement under this section to make, have made, import, sell, or distribute, any article embodying a design which was created without knowledge that a design was protected under this chapter and was copied from such protected design.

(d) Acts in Ordinary Course of Business.—A person who incorporates into that person's product of manufacture an infringing article acquired from others in the ordinary course of business, or who, without knowledge of the protected design embodied in an infringing article, makes or processes the infringing article for the account of another person in the ordinary course of business, shall not be deemed to have infringed the rights in that design under this chapter except under a condition contained in paragraph (1) or (2) of subsection (b). Accepting an order or reorder from the source of the infringing article shall be deemed ordering or reordering within the meaning of subsection (b)(2).

(e) Infringing Article Defined.—As used in this section, an "infringing article" is any article the design of which has been copied from a design protected under this chapter, without the consent of the owner of the protected design. An infringing article is not an illustration or picture of a protected design in an advertisement, book, periodical, newspaper, photograph, broadcast, motion picture, or similar medium. A design shall not be deemed to have been copied from a protected design if it is original and not substantially similar in appearance to a protected design.

(f) Establishing Originality.—The party to any action or proceeding under this chapter who alleges rights under this chapter in a design shall have the burden of establishing the design's originality whenever the opposing party introduces an earlier work which is identical to such design, or so similar as to make prima facie showing that such design was copied from such work.

(g) Reproduction for Teaching or Analysis.—It is not an infringement of the exclusive rights of a design owner for a person to reproduce the design in a useful article or in any other form solely for the purpose of teaching, analyzing, or evaluating the appearance, concepts, or techniques embodied in the design, or the function of the useful article embodying the design.

§1310 · Application for registration

(a) Time Limit for Application for Registration.—Protection under this chapter shall be lost if application for registration of the design is not made within 2 years after the date on which the design is first made public.

(b) When Design Is Made Public.—A design is made public when an existing useful article embodying the design is anywhere publicly exhibited, publicly distributed, or offered for sale or sold to the public by the owner of the design or with the owner's consent.

(c) Application by Owner of Design.—Application for registration may be made by the owner of the design.

(d) Contents of Application.—The application for registration shall be made to the Administrator and shall state—

(1) the name and address of the designer or designers of the design;

(2) the name and address of the owner if different from the designer;

(3) the specific name of the useful article embodying the design;

(4) the date, if any, that the design was first made public, if such date was earlier than the date of the application;

(5) affirmation that the design has been fixed in a useful article; and

(6) such other information as may be required by the Administrator.

The application for registration may include a description setting forth the salient features of the design, but the absence of such a description shall not prevent registration under this chapter.

(e) Sworn Statement.—The application for registration shall be accompanied by a statement under oath by the applicant or the applicant's duly authorized agent or representative, setting forth, to the best of the applicant's knowledge and belief—

(1) that the design is original and was created by the designer or designers named in the application;

(2) that the design has not previously been registered on behalf of the applicant or the applicant's predecessor in title; and

(3) that the applicant is the person entitled to protection and to registration under this chapter.

If the design has been made public with the design notice prescribed in section 1306, the statement shall also describe the exact form and position of the design notice.

(f) Effect of Errors.—(1) Error in any statement or assertion as to the utility of the useful article named in the application under this section, the design of which is sought to be registered, shall not affect the protection secured under this chapter.

(2) Errors in omitting a joint designer or in naming an alleged joint designer shall not affect the validity of the registration, or the actual ownership or the protection of the design, unless it is shown that the error occurred with deceptive intent.

(g) Design Made in Scope of Employment.—In a case in which the design was made within the regular scope of the designer's employment and individual authorship of the design is difficult or impossible to ascribe and the application so states, the name and address of the employer for whom the design was made may be stated instead of that of the individual designer.

(h) Pictorial Representation of Design.—The application for registration shall be accompanied by two copies of a drawing or other pictorial representation of the useful article embodying the design, having one or more views, adequate to show the design, in a form and style suitable for reproduction, which shall be deemed a part of the application.

(i) Design in More than One Useful Article.—If the distinguishing elements of a design are in substantially the same form in different useful articles, the design shall be protected as to all such useful articles when protected as to one of them, but not more than one registration shall be required for the design.

(j) Application for More than One Design.—More than one design may be included in the same application under such conditions as may be prescribed by the Administrator. For each design included in an application the fee prescribed for a single design shall be paid.

§1311 · Benefit of earlier filing date in foreign country

An application for registration of a design filed in the United States by any person who has, or whose legal representative or predecessor or successor in title has, previously filed an application for registration of the same design in a foreign country which extends to designs of owners who are citizens of the United States, or to applications filed under this chapter, similar protection to that provided under this chapter shall have that same effect as if filed in the United States on the date on which the application was first filed in such foreign country, if the application in the United States is filed within 6 months after the earliest date on which any such foreign application was filed.

§1312 · Oaths and acknowledgments

(a) In General.—Oaths and acknowledgments required by this chapter—

(1) may be made—

(A) before any person in the United States authorized by law to administer oaths; or

(B) when made in a foreign country, before any diplomatic or consular officer of the United States authorized to administer oaths, or before any official authorized to administer oaths in the foreign country concerned, whose authority shall be proved by a certificate of a diplomatic or consular officer of the United States; and

(2) shall be valid if they comply with the laws of the State or country where made.

(b) Written Declaration in Lieu of Oath.—(1) The Administrator may by rule prescribe that any document which is to be filed under this chapter in the Office of the Administrator and which is required by any law, rule, or other regulation to be under oath, may be subscribed to by a written declaration in such form as the Administrator may prescribe, and such declaration shall be in lieu of the oath otherwise required.

(2) Whenever a written declaration under paragraph (1) is used, the document containing the declaration shall state that willful false statements are punishable by fine or imprisonment, or both, pursuant to section 1001 of title 18, and may jeopardize the validity of the application or document or a registration resulting therefrom.

§1313 · Examination of application and issue or refusal of registration[4]

(a) Determination of Registrability of Design; Registration.—Upon the filing of an application for registration in proper form under section 1310, and upon payment of the fee prescribed under section 1316, the Administrator shall determine whether or not the application relates to a design which on its face appears to be subject to protection under this chapter, and, if so, the Register shall register the design. Registration under this subsection shall be announced by publication. The date of registration shall be the date of publication.

(b) Refusal to Register; Reconsideration.—If, in the judgment of the Administrator, the application for registration relates to a design which on its face is not subject to protection under this chapter, the Administrator shall send to the applicant a notice of refusal to register and the grounds for the refusal. Within 3 months after the date on which the notice of refusal is sent, the applicant may, by written request, seek reconsideration of the application. After consideration of such a request, the Administrator shall either register the design or send to the applicant a notice of final refusal to register.

(c) Application to Cancel Registration.—Any person who believes he or she is or will be damaged by a registration under this chapter may, upon payment of the prescribed fee, apply to the Administrator at any time to cancel the registration on the ground that the design is not subject to protection under this chapter, stating the reasons for the request. Upon receipt of an application for cancellation, the Administrator shall send to the owner of the design, as shown in the records of the Office of the Administrator, a notice of the application, and the owner shall have a period of 3 months after the date on which such notice is mailed in which to present arguments to the Administrator for support of the validity of the registration. The Administrator shall also have the authority to establish, by regulation, conditions under which the opposing parties may appear and be heard in support of their arguments. If, after the periods provided for the presentation of arguments have expired, the Administrator determines that the applicant for cancellation has established that the design is not subject to protection under this chapter, the Administrator shall order the registration stricken from the record. Cancellation under this subsection shall be announced by publication, and notice of the Administrator's final determination with respect to any application for cancellation shall be sent to the applicant and to the owner of record. Costs of the cancellation procedure under this subsection shall be borne by the nonprevailing party or parties, and the Administrator shall have the authority to assess and collect such costs.

§1314 · Certification of registration

Certificates of registration shall be issued in the name of the United States under the seal of the Office of the Administrator and shall be recorded in the official records of the Office. The certificate shall state the name of the useful article, the date of filing of the application, the date of registration, and the date the design was made public, if earlier than the date of filing of the application, and shall contain a reproduction of the drawing or other pictorial representation of the design. If a description of the salient features of the design appears in the application, the description shall also appear in the certificate. A certificate of registration shall be admitted in any court as prima facie evidence of the facts stated in the certificate.

§1315 · Publication of announcements and indexes

(a) Publications of the Administrator.—The Administrator shall publish lists and indexes of registered designs and cancellations of designs and may also publish the drawings or other pictorial representations of registered designs for sale or other distribution.

(b) File of Representatives of Registered Designs.—The Administrator shall establish and maintain a file of the drawings or other pictorial representations of registered designs. The file shall be available for use by the public under such conditions as the Administrator may prescribe.

§1316 · Fees

The Administrator shall by regulation set reasonable fees for the filing of applications to register designs under this chapter and for other services relating to the administration of this chapter, taking into consideration the cost of providing these services and the benefit of a public record.

§1317 · Regulations

The Administrator may establish regulations for the administration of this chapter.

§1318 · Copies of records

Upon payment of the prescribed fee, any person may obtain a certified copy of any official record of the Office of the Administrator that relates to this chapter. That copy shall be admissible in evidence with the same effect as the original.

§1319 · Correction of errors in certificates

The Administrator may, by a certificate of correction under seal, correct any error in a registration incurred through the fault of the Office, or, upon payment of the required fee, any error of a clerical or typographical nature occurring in good faith but not through the fault of the Office. Such registration, together with the certificate, shall thereafter have the same effect as if it had been originally issued in such corrected form.

§1320 · Ownership and transfer[5]

(a) Property Right in Design.—The property right in a design subject to protection under this chapter shall vest in the designer, the legal representatives of a deceased designer or of one under legal incapacity, the employer for whom the designer created the design in the case of a design made within the regular scope of the designer's employment, or a person to whom the rights of the designer or of such employer have been transferred. The person in whom the property right is vested shall be considered the owner of the design.

(b) Transfer of Property Right.—The property right in a registered design, or a design for which an application for registration has been or may be filed, may be assigned, granted, conveyed, or mortgaged by an instrument in writing, signed by the owner, or may be bequeathed by will.

(c) Oath or Acknowledgment of Transfer.—An oath or acknowledgment under section 1312 shall be prima facie evidence of the execution of an assignment, grant, conveyance, or mortgage under subsection (b).

(d) Recordation of Transfer.—An assignment, grant, conveyance, or mortgage under subsection (b) shall be void as against any subsequent purchaser or mortgagee for a valuable consideration, unless it is recorded in the Office of the Administrator within 3 months after its date of execution or before the date of such subsequent purchase or mortgage.

§1321 · Remedy for infringement

(a) In General.—The owner of a design is entitled, after issuance of a certificate of registration of the design under this chapter, to institute an action for any infringement of the design.

(b) Review of Refusal to Register.—(1) Subject to paragraph (2), the owner of a design may seek judicial review of a final refusal of the Administrator to register the design under this chapter by bringing a civil action, and may in the same action, if the court adjudges the design subject to protection under this chapter, enforce the rights in that design under this chapter.

(2) The owner of a design may seek judicial review under this section if—

(A) the owner has previously duly filed and prosecuted to final refusal an application in proper form for registration of the design;

(B) the owner causes a copy of the complaint in the action to be delivered to the Administrator within 10 days after the commencement of the action; and

(C) the defendant has committed acts in respect to the design which would constitute infringement with respect to a design protected under this chapter.

(c) Administrator as Party to Action.—The Administrator may, at the Administrator's option, become a party to the action with respect to the issue of registrability of the design claim by entering an appearance within 60 days after being served with the complaint, but the failure of the Administrator to become a party shall not deprive the court of jurisdiction to determine that issue.

(d) Use of Arbitration to Resolve Dispute.—The parties to an infringement dispute under this chapter, within such time as may be specified by the Administrator by regulation, may determine the dispute, or any aspect of the dispute, by arbitration. Arbitration shall be governed by title 9. The parties shall give notice of any arbitration award to the Administrator, and such award shall, as between the parties to the arbitration, be dispositive of the issues to which it relates. The arbitration award shall be unenforceable until such notice is given. Nothing in this subsection shall preclude the Administrator from determining whether a design is subject to registration in a cancellation proceeding under section 1313(c).

§1322 · Injunctions

(a) In General.—A court having jurisdiction over actions under this chapter may grant injunctions in accordance with the principles of equity to prevent infringement of a design under this chapter, including, in its discretion, prompt relief by temporary restraining orders and preliminary injunctions.

(b) Damages for Injunctive Relief Wrongfully Obtained.—A seller or distributor who suffers damage by reason of injunctive relief wrongfully obtained under this section has a cause of action against the applicant for such injunctive relief and may recover such relief as may be appropriate, including damages for lost profits, cost of materials, loss of good will, and punitive damages in instances where the injunctive relief was sought in bad faith, and, unless the court finds extenuating circumstances, reasonable attorney's fees.

§1323 · Recovery for infringement

(a) Damages.—Upon a finding for the claimant in an action for infringement under this chapter, the court shall award the claimant damages adequate to compensate for the infringement. In addition, the court may increase the damages to such amount, not exceeding $50,000 or $1 per copy, whichever is greater, as the court determines to be just. The damages awarded shall constitute compensation and not a penalty. The court may receive expert testimony as an aid to the determination of damages.

(b) Infringer's Profits.—As an alternative to the remedies provided in subsection (a), the court may award the claimant the infringer's profits resulting from the sale of the copies if the court finds that the infringer's sales are reasonably related to the use of the claimant's design. In such a case, the claimant shall be required to prove only the amount of the infringer's sales and the infringer shall be required to prove its expenses against such sales.

(c) Statute of Limitations.—No recovery under subsection (a) or (b) shall be had for any infringement committed more than 3 years before the date on which the complaint is filed.

(d) Attorney's Fees.—In an action for infringement under this chapter, the court may award reasonable attorney's fees to the prevailing party.

(e) Disposition of Infringing and Other Articles.—The court may order that all infringing articles, and any plates, molds, patterns, models, or other means specifically adapted for making the articles, be delivered up for destruction or other disposition as the court may direct.

§1324 · Power of court over registration

In any action involving the protection of a design under this chapter, the court, when appropriate, may order registration of a design under this chapter or the cancellation of such a registration. Any such order shall be certified by the court to the Administrator, who shall make an appropriate entry upon the record.

§1325 · Liability for action on registration fraudulently obtained

Any person who brings an action for infringement knowing that registration of the design was obtained by a false or fraudulent representation materially affecting the rights under this chapter, shall be liable in the sum of $10,000, or such part of that amount as the court may determine. That amount shall be to compensate the defendant and shall be charged against the plaintiff and paid to the defendant, in addition to such costs and attorney's fees of the defendant as may be assessed by the court.

§1326 · Penalty for false marking

(a) In General.—Whoever, for the purpose of deceiving the public, marks upon, applies to, or uses in advertising in connection with an article made, used, distributed, or sold, a design which is not protected under this chapter, a design notice specified in section 1306, or any other words or symbols importing that the design is protected under this chapter, knowing that the design is not so protected, shall pay a civil fine of not more than $500 for each such offense.

(b) Suit by Private Persons.—Any person may sue for the penalty established by subsection (a), in which event one-half of the penalty shall be awarded to the person suing and the remainder shall be awarded to the United States.

§1327 · Penalty for false representation

Whoever knowingly makes a false representation materially affecting the rights obtainable under this chapter for the purpose of obtaining registration of a design under this chapter shall pay a penalty of not less than $500 and not more than $1,000, and any rights or privileges that individual may have in the design under this chapter shall be forfeited.

§1328 · Enforcement by Treasury and Postal Service

(a) Regulations.—The Secretary of the Treasury and the United States Postal Service shall separately or jointly issue regulations for the enforcement of the rights set forth in section 1308 with respect to importation. Such regulations may require, as a condition for the exclusion of articles from the United States, that the person seeking exclusion take any one or more of the following actions:

(1) Obtain a court order enjoining, or an order of the International Trade Commission under section 337 of the Tariff Act of 1930 excluding, importation of the articles.

(2) Furnish proof that the design involved is protected under this chapter and that the importation of the articles would infringe the rights in the design under this chapter.

(3) Post a surety bond for any injury that may result if the detention or exclusion of the articles proves to be unjustified.

(b) Seizure and Forfeiture.—Articles imported in violation of the rights set forth in section 1308 are subject to seizure and forfeiture in the same manner as property imported in violation of the customs laws. Any such forfeited articles shall be destroyed as directed by the Secretary of the Treasury or the court, as the case may be, except that the articles may be returned to the country of export whenever it is shown to the satisfaction of the Secretary of the Treasury that the importer had no reasonable grounds for believing that his or her acts constituted a violation of the law.

§1329 · Relation to design patent law

The issuance of a design patent under title 35, United States Code, for an original design for an article of manufacture shall terminate any protection of the original design under this chapter.

§1330 · Common law and other rights unaffected

Nothing in this chapter shall annul or limit—

(1) common law or other rights or remedies, if any, available to or held by any person with respect to a design which has not been registered under this chapter; or

(2) any right under the trademark laws or any right protected against unfair competition.

§1331 · Administrator; Office of the Administrator

In this chapter, the "Administrator" is the Register of Copyrights, and the "Office of the Administrator" and the "Office" refer to the Copyright Office of the Library of Congress.

§1332 · No retroactive effect

Protection under this chapter shall not be available for any design that has been made public under section 1310(b) before the effective date of this chapter.[6]

Chapter 13 · Notes

1. In 1998, the Vessel Hull Design Protection Act added chapter 13, entitled "Protection of Original Designs," to title 17. Pub. L. No. 105-304, 112 Stat. 2860, 2905. The Vessel Hull Design Protection Act is title V of the Digital Millennium Copyright Act, Pub. L. No. 105-304, 112 Stat. 2860, 2905.

2. The Satellite Home Viewer Improvement Act of 1999 amended section 1301(b)(3) in its entirety. Pub. L. No. 106-113, 113 Stat. 1501, app. I at 1501A-593.

The Vessel Hull Design Protection Amendments of 2008 amended subsection 1301(a) by revising the definition of vessel hulls in subpart (2) and by providing an exception for the U.S. Department of Defense in a new subpart (3). Pub. L. No. 110-434, 122 Stat. 4972. It also amended subsection 301(b) by revising the definitions of useful article in subpart (2) and hull in subpart (4) and by adding a definition for deck in new subpart (7). *Id.*

3. In 1999, section 1302(5) was amended to substitute "2 years" in lieu of "1 year." Pub. L. No. 106-44, 113 Stat. 221, 222.

4. The Satellite Home Viewer Improvement Act of 1999 amended section 1313(c) by adding at the end thereof the last sentence, which begins "Costs of the cancellation procedure." Pub. L. No. 106-113, 113 Stat. 1501, app. I at 1501A-594.

5. In 1999, section 1320 was amended to change the spelling in the heading of subsection (c) from "acknowledgement" to "acknowledgment." Pub. L. No. 106-44, 113 Stat. 221, 222.

6. The effective date of chapter 13 is October 28, 1998. See section 505 of the Digital Millennium Copyright Act, which appears in Appendix B.

Appendices

RELATED INTERNATIONAL PROVISIONS

Appendix A

The Copyright Act of 1976[1]

Title I — General Revision of Copyright Law

* * * * * * *

Transitional and Supplementary Provisions

SEC. 102. This Act becomes effective on January 1, 1978, except as otherwise expressly provided by this Act, including provisions of the first section of this Act. The provisions of sections 118, 304(b), and chapter 8 of title 17, as amended by the first section of this Act, take effect upon enactment of this Act.[2]

SEC. 103. This Act does not provide copyright protection for any work that goes into the public domain before January 1, 1978. The exclusive rights, as provided by section 106 of title 17 as amended by the first section of this Act, to reproduce a work in phonorecords and to distribute phonorecords of the work, do not extend to any nondramatic musical work copyrighted before July 1, 1909.

SEC. 104. All proclamations issued by the President under section 1(e) or 9(b) of title 17 as it existed on December 31, 1977, or under previous copyright statutes of the United States, shall continue in force until terminated, suspended, or revised by the President.

SEC. 105. (a)(1) Section 505 of title 44 is amended to read as follows:

> "**§ 505. Sale of duplicate plates**
>
> "The Public Printer shall sell, under regulations of the Joint Committee on Printing to persons who may apply, additional or duplicate stereotype or electrotype plates from which a Government publication is printed, at a price not to exceed the cost of composition, the metal, and making to the Government, plus 10 per centum, and the full amount of the price shall be paid when the order is filed.".

(2) The item relating to section 505 in the sectional analysis at the beginning of chapter 5 of title 44, is amended to read as follows:

> "505. Sale of duplicate plates.".

(b) Section 2113 of title 44 is amended to read as follows:

[To assist the reader, section 2113 of title 44, now designated section 2117, appears in Appendix J, *infra*, as currently amended.]

(c) In section 1498(b) of title 28, the phrase "section 101(b) of title 17" is amended to read "section 504(c) of title 17".

(d) Section 543(a)(4) of the Internal Revenue Code of 1954, as amended, is amended by striking out "(other than by reason of section 2 or 6 thereof)".

(e) Section 3202(a) of title 39 is amended by striking out clause (5). Section 3206 of title 39 is amended by deleting the words "subsections (b) and (c)" and inserting "subsection (b)" in subsection (a), and by deleting subsection (c). Section 3206(d) is renumbered (c).

(f) Subsection (a) of section 6 of the Standard Reference Data Act (15 U.S.C. 290e) is amended by deleting the phrase "section 8" and inserting in lieu thereof the phrase "section 105".[3]

(g) Section 131 of title 2 is amended by deleting the phrase "deposit to secure copyright," and inserting in lieu thereof the phrase "acquisition of material under the copyright law,".

SEC. 106. In any case where, before January 1, 1978, a person has lawfully made parts of instruments serving to reproduce mechanically a copyrighted work under the compulsory license provisions of section 1(e) of title 17 as it existed on December 31, 1977, such person may continue to make and distribute such parts embodying the same mechanical reproduction without obtaining a new compulsory license under the terms of section 115 of title 17 as amended by the first section of this Act. However, such parts made on or after January 1, 1978, constitute phonorecords and are otherwise subject to the provisions of said section 115.

SEC. 107. In the case of any work in which an ad interim copyright is subsisting or is capable of being secured on December 31, 1977, under section 22 of title 17 as it existed on that date, copyright protection is hereby extended to endure for the term or terms provided by section 304 of title 17 as amended by the first section of this Act.

SEC. 108. The notice provisions of sections 401 through 403 of title 17 as amended by the first section of this Act apply to all copies or phonorecords publicly distributed on or after January 1, 1978. However, in the case of a work published before January 1, 1978, compliance with the notice provisions of title 17 either as it existed on December 31, 1977, or as amended by the first section of this Act, is adequate with respect to copies publicly distributed after December 31, 1977.

SEC. 109. The registration of claims to copyright for which the required deposit, application, and fee were received in the Copyright Office before January 1, 1978, and the recordation of assignments of copyright or other instruments received in the Copyright Office before January 1, 1978, shall be made in accordance with title 17 as it existed on December 31, 1977.

SEC. 110. The demand and penalty provisions of section 14 of title 17 as it existed on December 31, 1977, apply to any work in which copyright has been secured by publication with notice of copyright on or before that date, but any deposit and registration made after that date in response to a demand under that section shall be made in accordance with the provisions of title 17 as amended by the first section of this Act.

SEC. 111. Section 2318 of title 18 of the United States Code is amended to read as follows:

[To assist the reader, section 2318 of title 18, as currently amended, along with related criminal provisions, appears in Appendix H, *infra*.]

SEC. 112. All causes of action that arose under title 17 before January 1, 1978, shall be governed by title 17 as it existed when the cause of action arose.

SEC. 113. (a) The Librarian of Congress (hereinafter referred to as the "Librarian") shall establish and maintain in the Library of Congress a library to be known as the American Television and Radio Archives (hereinafter referred to as the "Archives"). The purpose of the Archives shall be to preserve a permanent record of the television and radio programs which are the heritage of the people of the United States and to provide access to such programs to historians and scholars without encouraging or causing copyright infringement.

(1) The Librarian, after consultation with interested organizations and individuals, shall determine and place in the Archives such copies and phonorecords of television and radio programs transmitted to the public in the United States and in other countries which are of present or potential public or cultural interest, historical significance, cognitive value, or otherwise worthy of preservation, including copies and phonorecords of published and unpublished transmission programs—

(A) acquired in accordance with sections 407 and 408 of title 17 as amended by the first section of this Act; and

(B) transferred from the existing collections of the Library of Congress; and

(C) given to or exchanged with the Archives by other libraries, archives, organizations, and individuals; and

(D) purchased from the owner thereof.

(2) The Librarian shall maintain and publish appropriate catalogs and indexes of the collections of the Archives, and shall make such collections available for study and research under the conditions prescribed under this section.

(b) Notwithstanding the provisions of section 106 of title 17 as amended by the first section of this Act, the Librarian is authorized with respect to a transmission program which consists of a regularly scheduled newscast or on-the-spot coverage of news events and, under standards and conditions that the Librarian shall prescribe by regulation—

(1) to reproduce a fixation of such a program, in the same or another tangible form, for the purposes of preservation or security or for distribution under the conditions of clause (3) of this subsection; and

(2) to compile, without abridgment or any other editing, portions of such fixations according to subject matter, and to reproduce such compilations for the purpose of clause (1) of this subsection; and

(3) to distribute a reproduction made under clause (1) or (2) of this subsection—

(A) by loan to a person engaged in research; and

(B) for deposit in a library or archives which meets the requirements of section 108(a) of title 17 as amended by the first section of this Act,

in either case for use only in research and not for further reproduction or performance.

(c) The Librarian or any employee of the Library who is acting under the authority of this section shall not be liable in any action for copyright infringement committed by any other person unless the Librarian or such employee knowingly participated in the act of infringement committed by such person. Nothing in this section shall be construed to excuse or limit liability under title 17 as amended by the first section of this Act for any act not authorized by that title or this section, or for any act performed by a person not authorized to act under that title or this section.

(d) This section may be cited as the "American Television and Radio Archives Act".

SEC. 114. There are hereby authorized to be appropriated such funds as may be necessary to carry out the purposes of this Act.

SEC. 115. If any provision of title 17, as amended by the first section of this Act, is declared unconstitutional, the validity of the remainder of this title is not affected.

Appendix A · Notes

1. This appendix contains the Transitional and Supplementary Provisions of the Copyright Act of 1976, Pub. L. No. 94-533, 90 Stat. 2541, that do not amend title 17 of the *United States Code*.

2. The Copyright Act of 1976 was enacted on October 19, 1976.

3. The Intellectual Property and High Technology Technical Amendments Act of 2002 amended section 105(f) by substituting "section 6 of the Standard Reference Data Act (15 U.S.C. 290e)" for "section 290(e) of title 15." Pub. L. No. 107-273, 116 Stat. 1758, 1910.

Appendix B

The Digital Millennium Copyright Act of 1998[1]

Section 1 · Short Title.

This Act may be cited as the "Digital Millennium Copyright Act".

Title I—WIPO Treaties Implementation

Sec. 101 · Short Title.

This title may be cited as the "WIPO Copyright and Performances and Phonograms Treaties Implementation Act of 1998".

* * * * * * *

Sec. 105 · Effective Date.

(a) In General.—Except as otherwise provided in this title, this title and the amendments made by this title shall take effect on the date of the enactment of this Act.

(b) Amendments Relating to Certain International Agreements.—(1) The following shall take effect upon the entry into force of the WIPO Copyright Treaty with respect to the United States:

(A) Paragraph (5) of the definition of "international agreement" contained in section 101 of title 17, United States Code, as amended by section 102(a)(4) of this Act.

(B) The amendment made by section 102(a)(6) of this Act.

(C) Subparagraph (C) of section 104A(h)(1) of title 17, United States Code, as amended by section 102(c)(1) of this Act.

(D) Subparagraph (C) of section 104A(h)(3) of title 17, United States Code, as amended by section 102(c)(2) of this Act.

(2) The following shall take effect upon the entry into force of the WIPO Performances and Phonograms Treaty with respect to the United States:

(A) Paragraph (6) of the definition of "international agreement" contained in section 101 of title 17, United States Code, as amended by section 102(a)(4) of this Act.

(B) The amendment made by section 102(a)(7) of this Act.

(C) The amendment made by section 102(b)(2) of this Act.

(D) Subparagraph (D) of section 104A(h)(1) of title 17, United States Code, as amended by section 102(c)(1) of this Act.

(E) Subparagraph (D) of section 104A(h)(3) of title 17, United States Code, as amended by section 102(c)(2) of this Act.

(F) The amendments made by section 102(c)(3) of this Act.

* * * * * * *

Title II—Online Copyright Infringement Liability Limitation

Sec. 201 · Short Title.

This title may be cited as the "Online Copyright Infringement Liability Limitation Act".

* * * * * * *

Sec. 203 · Effective Date.

This title and the amendments made by this title shall take effect on the date of the enactment of this Act.

* * * * * * *

Title IV—Miscellaneous Provisions

Sec. 401 · Provisions Relating to the Commissioner of Patents and Trademarks and the Register of Copyrights

(a) Compensation.—(1) Section 3(d) of title 35, United States Code, is amended by striking "prescribed by law for Assistant Secretaries of Commerce" and inserting "in effect for level III of the Executive Schedule under section 5314 of title 5, United States Code".

* * * * * * *

(3) Section 5314 of title 5, United States Code, is amended by adding at the end the following:

"Assistant Secretary of Commerce and Commissioner of Patents and Trademarks.

"Register of Copyrights.".

* * * * * * *

Sec. 405 · Scope of Exclusive Rights in Sound Recordings; Ephemeral Recordings.

(a) Scope of Exclusive Rights in Sound Recordings.

* * * * * * *

(5) The amendment made by paragraph (2)(B)(i)(III) of this subsection shall be deemed to have been enacted as part of the Digital Performance Right in Sound Recordings Act of 1995, and the publication of notice of proceedings under section 114(f)(1) of title 17, United States Code, as in effect upon the effective date of that Act, for the determination of royalty payments shall be deemed to have been made for the period beginning on the effective date of that Act and ending on December 1, 2001.

(6) The amendments made by this subsection do not annul, limit, or otherwise impair the rights that are preserved by section 114 of title 17, United States Code, including the rights preserved by subsections (c), (d)(4), and (i) of such section.

* * * * * * *

(c) Scope of Section 112(a) of Title 17 Not Affected.—

Nothing in this section or the amendments made by this section shall affect the scope of section 112(a) of title 17, United States Code, or the entitlement of any person to an exemption thereunder.

* * * * * * *

Sec. 406 · Assumption of Contractual Obligations Related to Transfers of Rights in Motion Pictures.

(a) In General.—Part VI of title 28, United States Code, is amended by adding at the end the following new chapter:

"Chapter 180—Assumption of Certain Contractual Obligations

"Sec. 4001. Assumption of contractual obligations related to transfers of rights in motion pictures.

"§4001. Assumption of contractual obligations related to transfers of rights in motion pictures

"(a) Assumption of Obligations.—(1) In the case of a transfer of copyright ownership under United States law in a motion picture (as the terms 'transfer of copyright ownership' and 'motion picture' are defined in section 101 of title 17) that is produced subject to 1 or more collective bargaining agreements negotiated under the laws of the United States, if the transfer is executed on or after the effective date of this chapter and is not limited to public performance rights, the transfer instrument shall be deemed to incorporate the assumption agreements applicable to the copyright ownership being transferred that are required by the applicable collective bargaining agreement, and the transferee shall be subject to the obligations under each such assumption agreement to make residual payments and provide related notices, accruing after the effective date of the transfer and applicable to the exploitation of the rights transferred, and any remedies under each such assumption agreement for breach of those obligations, as those obligations and remedies are set forth in the applicable collective bargaining agreement, if—

"(A) the transferee knows or has reason to know at the time of the transfer that such collective bargaining agreement was or will be applicable to the motion picture; or

"(B) in the event of a court order confirming an arbitration award against the transferor under the collective bargaining agreement, the transferor does not have the financial ability to satisfy the award within 90 days after the order is issued.

"(2) For purposes of paragraph (1)(A), 'knows or has reason to know' means any of the following:

"(A) Actual knowledge that the collective bargaining agreement was or will be applicable to the motion picture.

"(B)(i) Constructive knowledge that the collective bargaining agreement was or will be applicable to the motion picture, arising from recordation of a document pertaining to copyright in the motion picture under section 205 of title 17 or from publication, at a site available to the public online that is operated by the relevant union, of information that identifies the motion picture as subject to a collective bargaining agreement with that union, if the site permits commercially reasonable verification of the date on which the information was available for access.

"(ii) Clause (i) applies only if the transfer referred to in subsection (a)(1) occurs—

"(I) after the motion picture is completed, or

"(II) before the motion picture is completed and—

"(aa) within 18 months before the filing of an application for copyright registration for the motion picture under section 408 of title 17, or

"(bb) if no such application is filed, within 18 months before the first publication of the motion picture in the United States.

"(C) Awareness of other facts and circumstances pertaining to a particular transfer from which it is apparent that the collective bargaining agreement was or will be applicable to the motion picture.

"(b) Scope of Exclusion of Transfers of Public Performance Rights.—For purposes of this section, the exclusion under subsection (a) of transfers of copyright ownership in a motion picture that are limited to public performance rights includes transfers to a terrestrial broadcast station, cable system, or programmer to the extent that the station, system, or programmer is functioning as an exhibitor of the motion picture, either by exhibiting the motion picture on its own network, system, service, or station, or by initiating the transmission of an exhibition that is carried on another network, system, service, or station. When a terrestrial broadcast station, cable system, or programmer, or other transferee, is also functioning otherwise as a distributor or as a producer of the motion picture, the public performance exclusion does not affect any obligations imposed on the transferee to the extent that it is engaging in such functions.

"(c) Exclusion for Grants of Security Interests.—Subsection (a) shall not apply to—

"(1) a transfer of copyright ownership consisting solely of a mortgage, hypothecation, or other security interest; or

"(2) a subsequent transfer of the copyright ownership secured by the security interest described in paragraph (1) by or under the authority of the secured party, including a transfer through the exercise of the secured party's rights or remedies as a secured party, or by a subsequent transferee.

The exclusion under this subsection shall not affect any rights or remedies under law or contract.

"(d) Deferral Pending Resolution of Bona Fide Dispute.—A transferee on which obligations are imposed under subsection (a) by virtue of paragraph (1) of that subsection may elect to defer performance of such obligations that are subject to a bona fide dispute between a union and a prior transferor until that dispute is resolved, except that such deferral shall not stay accrual of any union claims due under an applicable collective bargaining agreement.

"(e) Scope of Obligations Determined by Private Agreement.—Nothing in this section shall expand or diminish the rights, obligations, or remedies of any person under the collective bargaining agreements or assumption agreements referred to in this section.

"(f) Failure to Notify.—If the transferor under subsection (a) fails to notify the transferee under subsection (a) of applicable collective bargaining obligations before the execution of the transfer instrument, and subsection (a) is made applicable to the transferee solely by virtue of subsection (a)(1)(B), the transferor shall be liable to the transferee for any damages suffered by the transferee as a result of the failure to notify.

"(g) Determination of Disputes and Claims.—Any dispute concerning the application of subsections (a) through (f) shall be determined by an action in United States district court, and the court in its discretion may allow the recovery of full costs by or against any party and may also award a reasonable attorney's fee to the prevailing party as part of the costs.

"(h) Study.—The Comptroller General, in consultation with the Register of Copyrights, shall conduct a study of the conditions in the motion picture industry that gave rise to this section, and the impact of this section on the motion picture industry. The Comptroller General shall report the findings of the study to the Congress within 2 years after the effective date of this chapter.".

* * * * * * *

Sec. 407 · Effective Date.

Except as otherwise provided in this title, this title and the amendments made by this title shall take effect on the date of the enactment of this Act.

* * * * * * *

Title V—Protection of Certain Original Designs

Sec. 501 · Short Title.

This Act may be referred to as the "Vessel Hull Design Protection Act".

* * * * * * *

Sec. 505 · Effective Date.[2]

The amendments made by sections 502 and 503 shall take effect on the date of the enactment of this Act.[3]

Appendix B · Notes

1. This appendix contains provisions from the Digital Millennium Copyright Act (DMCA), Pub. L. No. 105-304, 112 Stat. 2860, that do not amend title 17 of the *United States Code*.

2. The Intellectual Property and Communications Omnibus Reform Act of 1999 amended section 505 by deleting everything at the end of the sentence, after "Act." Pub. L. No. 106-113, 113 Stat. 1501, app. I at 1501A-521, 593.

3. Section 502 of the DMCA added chapter 13 to title 17 of the *United States Code*. Section 503 made conforming amendments. The date of enactment of this Act is October 28, 1998.

Appendix C

The Copyright Royalty and Distribution Reform Act of 2004[1]

Section 1 · Short Title.

This Act may be cited as the "Copyright Royalty and Distribution Reform Act of 2004".

Sec. 2 · Reference.

Except as otherwise expressly provided, whenever in this Act an amendment or repeal is expressed in terms of an amendment to, or repeal of, a section or other provision, the reference shall be considered to be made to a section or other provision of title 17, United States Code.

* * * * * * *

Sec. 6 · Effective Date and Transition Provisions.[2]

(a) Effective Date.—This Act and the amendments made by this Act shall take effect 6 months after the date of enactment of this Act, except that the Librarian of Congress shall appoint 1 or more interim Copyright Royalty Judges under section 802(d) of title 17, United States Code, as amended by this Act, within 90 days after such date of enactment to carry out the functions of the Copyright Royalty Judges under title 17, United States Code, to the extent that Copyright Royalty Judges provided for in section 801(a) of title 17, United States Code, as amended by this Act, have not been appointed before the end of that 90-day period.

(b) Transition Provisions.—

(1) In general.—Subject to paragraphs (2) and (3), the amendments made by this Act shall not affect any proceedings commenced, petitions filed, or voluntary agreements entered into before the effective date provided in subsection (a) under the provisions of title 17, United States Code, as amended by this Act, and pending on such effective date. Such proceedings shall continue, determinations made in such proceedings, and appeals taken therefrom, as if this Act had not been enacted, and shall continue in effect until modified under title 17, United States Code, as amended by this Act. Such petitions filed and voluntary agreements entered into shall remain in effect as if this Act had not been enacted. For purposes of this paragraph, the Librarian of Congress may determine whether a proceeding has commenced. The Librarian of Congress may terminate any proceeding commenced before the effective date provided in subsection (a) pursuant to chapter 8 of title 17, United

States Code, and any proceeding so terminated shall become null and void. In such cases, the Copyright Royalty Judges may initiate a new proceeding in accordance with regulations adopted pursuant to section 803(b)(6) of title 17, United States Code.

(2) CERTAIN ROYALTY RATE PROCEEDINGS.—Notwithstanding paragraph (1), the amendments made by this Act shall not affect proceedings to determine royalty rates pursuant to section 119(c) of title 17, United States Code, that are commenced before January 31, 2006.

(3) PENDING PROCEEDINGS.—Notwithstanding paragraph (1), any proceedings to establish or adjust rates and terms for the statutory licenses under section 114(f)(2) or 112(e) of title 17, United States Code, for a statutory period commencing on or after January 1, 2005, shall be terminated upon the date of enactment of this Act and shall be null and void. The rates and terms in effect under section 114(f)(2) or 112(e) of title 17, United States Code, on December 31, 2004, for new subscription services, eligible nonsubscription services, and services exempt under section 114(d)(1)(C)(iv) of such title, and the rates and terms published in the Federal Register under the authority of the Small Webcaster Settlement Act of 2002 (17 U.S.C. 114 note; Public Law 107-321) (including the amendments made by that Act) for the years 2003 through 2004, as well as any notice and recordkeeping provisions adopted pursuant thereto, shall remain in effect until the later of the first applicable effective date for successor terms and rates specified in section 804(b) (2) or (3)(A) of title 17, United States Code, or such later date as the parties may agree or the Copyright Royalty Judges may establish. For the period commencing January 1, 2005, an eligible small webcaster or a noncommercial webcaster, as defined in the regulations published by the Register of Copyrights pursuant to the Small Webcaster Settlement Act of 2002 (17 U.S.C. 114 note; Public Law 107-321) (including the amendments made by that Act), may elect to be subject to the rates and terms published in those regulations by complying with the procedures governing the election process set forth in those regulations not later than the first date on which the webcaster would be obligated to make a royalty payment for such period. Until successor terms and rates have been established for the period commencing January 1, 2006, licensees shall continue to make royalty payments at the rates and on the terms previously in effect, subject to retroactive adjustment when successor rates and terms for such services are established.

(4) INTERIM PROCEEDINGS.—Notwithstanding subsection (a), as soon as practicable after the date of enactment of this Act, the Copyright Royalty Judges or interim Copyright Royalty Judges shall publish the notice described in section 803(b)(1)(A) of title 17, United States Code, as amended by this Act, to initiate a proceeding to establish or adjust rates and terms for the statutory licenses under section 114(f)(2) or 112(e) of title 17, United States

Code, for new subscription services and eligible nonsubscription services for the period commencing January 1, 2006. The Copyright Royalty Judges or Interim Copyright Royalty Judges are authorized to cause that proceeding to take place as provided in subsection (b) of section 803 of that title within the time periods set forth in that subsection. Notwithstanding section 803(c)(1) of that title, the Copyright Royalty Judges shall not be required to issue their determination in that proceeding before the expiration of the statutory rates and terms in effect on December 31, 2004.

(c) EXISTING APPROPRIATIONS.—Any funds made available in an appropriations Act to carry out chapter 8 of title 17, United States Code, shall be available to the extent necessary to carry out this section.

Appendix C · Notes

1. This appendix contains provisions from the Copyright Royalty and Distribution Reform Act of 2004, Pub. L. No. 108-419, 118 Stat. 2341, that do not amend title 17 of the *United States Code.*

2. In 2006, the Copyright Royalty Judges Program Technical Corrections Act amended section 6(b)(1) by substituting "effective date provided in subsection (a)" for "date of enactment of this Act" in the third sentence. Pub. L. No. 109-303, 120 Stat. 1478, 1483.

Appendix D

The Satellite Home Viewer Extension and Reauthorization Act of 2004[1]

* * * * * * *

Title IX—Satellite Home Viewer Extension and Reauthorization Act of 2004

Section 1 · Short Titles; Table of Contents.

(a) SHORT TITLES.—This title may be cited as the "Satellite Home Viewer Extension and Reauthorization Act of 2004" or the "W. J. (Billy) Tauzin Satellite Television Act of 2004".

* * * * * * *

Title I—Statutory License for Satellite Carriers

Sec. 101 · Extension of Authority.

(a) IN GENERAL.—Section 4(a) of the Satellite Home Viewer Act of 1994 (17 U.S.C. 119 note; Public Law 103-369; 108 Stat. 3481) is amended by striking "'December 31, 2004" and inserting "'December 31, 2009".

(b) EXTENSION FOR CERTAIN SUBSCRIBERS.—Section 119(e) of title 17, United States Code, is amended by striking "'December 31, 2004" and inserting "'December 31, 2009".

* * * * * * *

Sec. 106 · Effect on Certain Proceedings.

Nothing in this title shall modify any remedy imposed on a party that is required by the judgment of a court in any action that was brought before May 1, 2004, against that party for a violation of section 119 of title 17, United States Code.

* * * * * * *

Sec. 109 · Study.

No later than June 30, 2008, the Register of Copyrights shall report to the Committee on the Judiciary of the House of Representatives and the Committee on the Judiciary of the Senate the Register's findings and recommendations on the operation and revision of the statutory licenses under sections 111, 119, and 122 of title 17, United States Code. The report shall include, but not be limited to, the following:

(1) A comparison of the royalties paid by licensees under such sections, including historical rates of increases in these royalties, a comparison between the royalties under each such section and the prices paid in the marketplace for comparable programming.

(2) An analysis of the differences in the terms and conditions of the licenses under such sections, an analysis of whether these differences are required or justified by historical, technological, or regulatory differences that affect the satellite and cable industries, and an analysis of whether the cable or satellite industry is placed in a competitive disadvantage due to these terms and conditions.

(3) An analysis of whether the licenses under such sections are still justified by the bases upon which they were originally created.

(4) An analysis of the correlation, if any, between the royalties, or lack thereof, under such sections and the fees charged to cable and satellite subscribers, addressing whether cable and satellite companies have passed to subscribers any savings realized as a result of the royalty structure and amounts under such sections.

(5) An analysis of issues that may arise with respect to the application of the licenses under such sections to the secondary transmissions of the primary transmissions of network stations and superstations that originate as digital signals, including issues that relate to the application of the unserved household limitations under section 119 of title 17, United States Code, and to the determination of royalties of cable systems and satellite carriers.

Appendix D · Note

1. This appendix contains provisions from the Satellite Home Viewer Extension and Reauthorization Act of 2004, Title IX, Division J of the Consolidated Appropriations Act, 2005, Pub. L. No. 108-447, 118 Stat. 2809, 3393, that do not amend title 17 of the *United States Code.*

Appendix E

The Intellectual Property Protection and Courts Amendments Act of 2004[1]

Section 1 · Short Title.

This Act may be cited as the "Intellectual Property Protection and Courts Amendments Act of 2004".

Title I—Anti-counterfeiting Provisions

Sec. 101 · Short Title.

This title may be cited as the "'Anti-counterfeiting Amendments Act of 2004".

* * * * * * *

Sec. 103 · Other Rights Not Affected.

(a) CHAPTERS 5 AND 12 OF TITLE 17; ELECTRONIC TRANSMISSIONS.—The amendments made by this title—

(1) shall not enlarge, diminish, or otherwise affect any liability or limitations on liability under sections 512, 1201 or 1202 of title 17, United States Code; and

(2) shall not be construed to apply—

(A) in any case, to the electronic transmission of a genuine certificate, licensing document, registration card, similar labeling component, or documentation or packaging described in paragraph (4) or (5) of section 2318(b) of title 18, United States Code, as amended by this title; and

(B) in the case of a civil action under section 2318(f) of title 18, United States Code, to the electronic transmission of a counterfeit label or counterfeit documentation or packaging defined in paragraph (1) or (6) of section 2318(b) of title 18, United States Code.

(b) FAIR USE.—The amendments made by this title shall not affect the fair use, under section 107 of title 17, United States Code, of a genuine certificate, licensing document, registration card, similar labeling component, or documentation or packaging described in paragraph (4) or (5) of section 2318(b) of title 18, United States Code, as amended by this title.

Title II—Fraudulent Online Identity Sanctions

Sec. 201 · Short Title.

This title may be cited as the "'Fraudulent Online Identity Sanctions Act".

* * * * * * *

Sec. 205 · Construction.

(a) Free Speech and Press.—Nothing in this title shall enlarge or diminish any rights of free speech or of the press for activities related to the registration or use of domain names.

(b) Discretion of Courts in Determining Relief.—Nothing in this title shall restrict the discretion of a court in determining damages or other relief to be assessed against a person found liable for the infringement of intellectual property rights.

(c) Discretion of Courts in Determining Terms of Imprisonment.—Nothing in this title shall be construed to limit the discretion of a court to determine the appropriate term of imprisonment for an offense under applicable law.

Appendix E · Note

1. This appendix contains provisions from the Intellectual Property Protection and Courts Amendments Act of 2004, Pub. L. No. 108-482, 118 Stat. 3912, that do not amend title 17 of the *United States Code.*

Appendix F

The Prioritizing Resources and Organization for Intellectual Property Act of 2008[1]

Section 1 · Short Title; Table of Contents.

(a) Short Title.—This Act may be cited as the "Prioritizing Resources and Organization for Intellectual Property Act of 2008".

* * * * * * *

Sec. 2 · Reference.

Any reference in this Act to the "Trademark Act of 1946" refers to the Act entitled "An Act to provide for the registration of trademarks used in commerce, to carry out the provisions of certain international conventions, and for other purposes", approved July 5, 1946 (15 U.S.C. 1051 et seq.).

Sec. 3 · Definition.

In this Act, the term "United States person" means—

(1) any United States resident or national,

(2) any domestic concern (including any permanent domestic establishment of any foreign concern), and

(3) any foreign subsidiary or affiliate (including any permanent foreign establishment) of any domestic concern that is controlled in fact by such domestic concern,

except that such term does not include an individual who resides outside the United States and is employed by an individual or entity other than an individual or entity described in paragraph (1), (2), or (3).

Title I—Enhancements to Civil Intellectual Property Laws

* * * * * * *

Sec. 102 · Civil Remedies for Infringement.

* * * * * * *

(b) Protective Order for Seized Records.—Section 34(d)(7) of the Trademark Act (15 U.S.C. 1116(d)(7)) is amended to read as follows:

"(7) Any materials seized under this subsection shall be taken into the custody of the court. For seizures made under this section, the court shall enter an appropriate protective order with respect to discovery and use of any records or information that has been seized. The protective order shall provide for appropriate procedures to ensure that confidential, private, proprietary, or privileged information contained in such records is not improperly disclosed or used.

Sec. 103 · Treble Damages in Counterfeiting Cases.

Section 35(b) of the Trademark Act of 1946 (15 U.S.C. 1117(b)) is amended to read as follows:

"(b) In assessing damages under subsection (a) for any violation of section 32(1)(a) of this Act or section 220506 of title 36, United States Code, in a case involving use of a counterfeit mark or designation (as defined in section 34(d) of this Act), the court shall, unless the court finds extenuating circumstances, enter judgment for three times such profits or damages, whichever amount is greater, together with a reasonable attorney's fee, if the violation consists of—

"(1) intentionally using a mark or designation, knowing such mark or designation is a counterfeit mark (as defined in section 34(d) of this Act), in connection with the sale, offering for sale, or distribution of goods or services; or

"(2) providing goods or services necessary to the commission of a violation specified in paragraph (1), with the intent that the recipient of the goods or services would put the goods or services to use in committing the violation.

In such a case, the court may award prejudgment interest on such amount at an annual interest rate established under section 6621(a)(2) of the Internal Revenue Code of 1986, beginning on the date of the service of the claimant's pleadings setting forth the claim for such entry of judgment and ending on the date such entry is made, or for such shorter time as the court considers appropriate.".

Sec. 104 · Statutory Damages in Counterfeiting Cases.

Section 35(c) of the Trademark Act of 1946 (15 U.S.C. 1117) is amended—

(1) in paragraph (1)—

(A) by striking "$500" and inserting "$1,000"; and

(B) by striking "$100,000" and inserting "$200,000"; and

(2) in paragraph (2), by striking "$1,000,000" and inserting "$2,000,000".

* * * * * * *

Title II—Enhancements to Criminal Intellectual Property Laws

* * * * * * *

Sec. 205. Trafficking in Counterfeit Goods or Services.

(a) In General.—Section 2320 of title 18, United States Code, is amended—

(1) in subsection (a)—

(A) by striking "WHOEVER" and inserting "OFFENSE.—"

"(1) IN GENERAL.—Whoever;";

(B) by moving the remaining text 2 ems to the right; and

(C) by adding at the end the following:

"(2) SERIOUS BODILY HARM OR DEATH.—

"(A) SERIOUS BODILY HARM.—If the offender knowingly or recklessly causes or attempts to cause serious bodily injury from conduct in violation of paragraph (1), the penalty shall be a fine under this title or imprisonment for not more than 20 years, or both.

"(B) DEATH.—If the offender knowingly or recklessly causes or attempts to cause death from conduct in violation of paragraph (1), the penalty shall be a fine under this title or imprisonment for any term of years or for life, or both."; and

(2) by adding at the end the following:

"(h) TRANSSHIPMENT AND EXPORTATION.—No goods or services, the trafficking in of which is prohibited by this section, shall be transshipped through or exported from the United States. Any such transshipment or exportation shall be deemed a violation of section 42 of an Act to provide for the registration of trademarks used in commerce, to carry out the provisions of certain international conventions, and for other purposes, approved July 5, 1946 (commonly referred to as the 'Trademark Act of 1946' or the 'Lanham Act').".

(b) FORFEITURE AND DESTRUCTION OF PROPERTY; RESTITUTION.—Section 2320(b) of title 18, United States Code, is amended to read as follows:

"(b) FORFEITURE AND DESTRUCTION OF PROPERTY; RESTITUTION.—Forfeiture, destruction, and restitution relating to this section shall be subject to section 2323, to the extent provided in that section, in addition to any other similar remedies provided by law.".

Sec. 206 · Forfeiture, Destruction, and Restitution.

* * * * * * *

(b) TECHNICAL AND CONFORMING AMENDMENT.—The table of sections for chapter 113 of title 18, United States Code, is amended by adding at the end the following:

"Sec. 2323 · Forfeiture, destruction, and restitution.".

Sec. 207 · Forfeiture Under Economic Espionage Act.

Section 1834 of title 18, United States Code, is amended to read as follows:

"Sec. 1834 · Criminal Forfeiture.

"Forfeiture, destruction, and restitution relating to this chapter shall be subject to section 2323, to the extent provided in that section, in addition to any other similar remedies provided by law.

* * * * * * *

Sec. 209 · Technical and Conforming Amendments.

* * * * * * *

(b) Other Amendments.—Section 596(c)(2)(c) of the Tariff Act of 1950 (19 U.S.C. 1595a(c)(2)(c)) is amended by striking "or 509".

Title III—Coordination and Strategic Planning of Federal Effort Against Counterfeiting and Infringement

Sec. 301 · Intellectual Property Enforcement Coordinator.

(a) Intellectual Property Enforcement Coordinator.—The President shall appoint, by and with the advice and consent of the Senate, an Intellectual Property Enforcement Coordinator (in this title referred to as the "IPEC") to serve within the Executive Office of the President. As an exercise of the rule-making power of the Senate, any nomination of the IPEC submitted to the Senate for confirmation, and referred to a committee, shall be referred to the Committee on the Judiciary.

(b) Duties of IPEC.—

(1) In general.—The IPEC shall—

(A) chair the interagency intellectual property enforcement advisory committee established under subsection (b)(3)(A);

(B) coordinate the development of the Joint Strategic Plan against counterfeiting and infringement by the advisory committee under section 303;

(C) assist, at the request of the departments and agencies listed in subsection (b)(3)(A), in the implementation of the Joint Strategic Plan;

(D) facilitate the issuance of policy guidance to departments and agencies on basic issues of policy and interpretation, to the extent necessary to assure the coordination of intellectual property enforcement policy and consistency with other law;

(E) report to the President and report to Congress, to the extent consistent with law, regarding domestic and international intellectual property enforcement programs;

(F) report to Congress, as provided in section 304, on the implementation of the Joint Strategic Plan, and make recommendations, if any and as appropriate, to Congress for improvements in Federal intellectual property laws and enforcement efforts; and

(G) carry out such other functions as the President may direct.

(2) LIMITATION ON AUTHORITY.—The IPEC may not control or direct any law enforcement agency, including the Department of Justice, in the exercise of its investigative or prosecutorial authority.

(3) ADVISORY COMMITTEE.—

(A) ESTABLISHMENT.—There is established an interagency intellectual property enforcement advisory committee composed of the IPEC, who shall chair the committee, and the following members:

(i) Senate-confirmed representatives of the following departments and agencies who are involved in intellectual property enforcement, and who are, or are appointed by, the respective heads of those departments and agencies:

(I) The Office of Management and Budget.

(II) Relevant units within the Department of Justice, including the Federal Bureau of Investigation and the Criminal Division.

(III) The United States Patent and Trademark Office and other relevant units of the Department of Commerce.

(IV) The Office of the United States Trade Representative.

(V) The Department of State, the United States Agency for International Development, and the Bureau of International Narcotics Law Enforcement.

(VI) The Department of Homeland Security, United States Customs and Border Protection, and United States Immigration and Customs Enforcement.

(VII) The Food and Drug Administration of the Department of Health and Human Services.

(VIII) The Department of Agriculture.

(IX) Any such other agencies as the President determines to be substantially involved in the efforts of the Federal Government to combat counterfeiting and infringement.

(ii) The Register of Copyrights, or a senior representative of the United States Copyright Office appointed by the Register of Copyrights.

(B) FUNCTIONS.—The advisory committee established under subparagraph (A) shall develop the Joint Strategic Plan against counterfeiting and infringement under section 303.

Sec. 302 · Definition.

For purposes of this title, the term "intellectual property enforcement" means matters relating to the enforcement of laws protecting copyrights, patents, trademarks, other forms of intellectual property, and trade secrets, both in the United

States and abroad, including in particular matters relating to combating counterfeit and infringing goods.

Sec. 303 · Joint Strategic Plan.

(a) Purpose.—The objectives of the Joint Strategic Plan against counterfeiting and infringement that is referred to in section 301(b)(1)(B) (in this section referred to as the "joint strategic plan") are the following:

(1) Reducing counterfeit and infringing goods in the domestic and international supply chain.

(2) Identifying and addressing structural weaknesses, systemic flaws, or other unjustified impediments to effective enforcement action against the financing, production, trafficking, or sale of counterfeit or infringing goods, including identifying duplicative efforts to enforce, investigate, and prosecute intellectual property crimes across the Federal agencies and Departments that comprise the Advisory Committee and recommending how such duplicative efforts may be minimized. Such recommendations may include recommendations on how to reduce duplication in personnel, materials, technologies, and facilities utilized by the agencies and Departments responsible for the enforcement, investigation, or prosecution of intellectual property crimes.

(3) Ensuring that information is identified and shared among the relevant departments and agencies, to the extent permitted by law, including requirements relating to confidentiality and privacy, and to the extent that such sharing of information is consistent with Department of Justice and other law enforcement protocols for handling such information, to aid in the objective of arresting and prosecuting individuals and entities that are knowingly involved in the financing, production, trafficking, or sale of counterfeit or infringing goods.

(4) Disrupting and eliminating domestic and international counterfeiting and infringement networks.

(5) Strengthening the capacity of other countries to protect and enforce intellectual property rights, and reducing the number of countries that fail to enforce laws preventing the financing, production, trafficking, and sale of counterfeit and infringing goods.

(6) Working with other countries to establish international standards and policies for the effective protection and enforcement of intellectual property rights.

(7) Protecting intellectual property rights overseas by—

(A) working with other countries and exchanging information with appropriate law enforcement agencies in other countries relating to individuals and entities involved in the financing, production, trafficking, or sale of counterfeit and infringing goods;

(B) ensuring that the information referred to in subparagraph (A) is provided to appropriate United States law enforcement agencies in order to assist, as warranted, enforcement activities in cooperation with appropriate law enforcement agencies in other countries; and

(C) building a formal process for consulting with companies, industry associations, labor unions, and other interested groups in other countries with respect to intellectual property enforcement.

(b) Timing.—Not later than 12 months after the date of the enactment of this Act, and not later than December 31 of every third year thereafter, the IPEC shall submit the joint strategic plan to the Committee on the Judiciary and the Committee on Appropriations of the Senate, and to the Committee on the Judiciary and the Committee on Appropriations of the House of Representatives.

(c) Responsibility of the IPEC.—During the development of the joint strategic plan, the IPEC—

(1) shall provide assistance to, and coordinate the meetings and efforts of, the appropriate officers and employees of departments and agencies represented on the advisory committee appointed under section 301(b)(3) who are involved in intellectual property enforcement; and

(2) may consult with private sector experts in intellectual property enforcement in furtherance of providing assistance to the members of the advisory committee appointed under section 301(b)(3).

(d) Responsibilities of Other Departments and Agencies.—In the development and implementation of the joint strategic plan, the heads of the departments and agencies identified under section 301(b)(3) shall—

(1) designate personnel with expertise and experience in intellectual property enforcement matters to work with the IPEC and other members of the advisory committee; and

(2) share relevant department or agency information with the IPEC and other members of the advisory committee, including statistical information on the enforcement activities of the department or agency against counterfeiting or infringement, and plans for addressing the joint strategic plan, to the extent permitted by law, including requirements relating to confidentiality and privacy, and to the extent that suchsharing of information is consistent with Department of Justice and other law enforcement protocols for handling such information.

(e) Contents of the Joint Strategic Plan.—Each joint strategic plan shall include the following:

(1) A description of the priorities identified for carrying out the objectives in the joint strategic plan, including activities of the Federal Government relating to intellectual property enforcement.

(2) A description of the means to be employed to achieve the priorities, including the means for improving the efficiency and effectiveness of the Federal Government's enforcement efforts against counterfeiting and infringement.

(3) Estimates of the resources necessary to fulfill the priorities identified under paragraph (1).

(4) The performance measures to be used to monitor results under the joint strategic plan during the following year.

(5) An analysis of the threat posed by violations of intellectual property rights, including the costs to the economy of the United States resulting from violations of intellectual property laws, and the threats to public health and safety created by counterfeiting and infringement.

(6) An identification of the departments and agencies that will be involved in implementing each priority under paragraph (1).

(7) A strategy for ensuring coordination among the departments and agencies identified under paragraph (6), which will facilitate oversight by the executive branch of, and accountability among, the departments and agencies responsible for carrying out the strategy.

(8) Such other information as is necessary to convey the costs imposed on the United States economy by, and the threats to public health and safety created by, counterfeiting and infringement, and those steps that the Federal Government intends to take over the period covered by the succeeding joint strategic plan to reduce those costs and counter those threats.

(f) Enhancing Enforcement Efforts of Foreign Governments.—The joint strategic plan shall include programs to provide training and technical assistance to foreign governments for the purpose of enhancing the efforts of such governments to enforce laws against counterfeiting and infringement. With respect to such programs, the joint strategic plan shall—

(1) seek to enhance the efficiency and consistency with which Federal resources are expended, and seek to minimize duplication, overlap, or inconsistency of efforts;

(2) identify and give priority to those countries where programs of training and technical assistance can be carried out most effectively and with the greatest benefit to reducing counterfeit and infringing products in the United States market, to protecting the intellectual property rights of United States persons and their licensees, and to protecting the interests of United States persons otherwise harmed by violations of intellectual property rights in those countries;

(3) in identifying the priorities under paragraph (2), be guided by the list of countries identified by the United StatesTrade Representative under section 182(a) of the Trade Act of 1974 (19 U.S.C. 2242(a)); and

(4) develop metrics to measure the effectiveness of the Federal Government's efforts to improve the laws and enforcement practices of foreign governments against counterfeiting and infringement.

(g) Dissemination of the Joint Strategic Plan.—The joint strategic plan shall be posted for public access on the website of the White House, and shall be disseminated to the public through such other means as the IPEC may identify.

Sec. 304 · Reporting.

(a) Annual Report.—Not later than December 31 of each calendar year beginning in 2009, the IPEC shall submit a report on the activities of the advisory committee during the preceding fiscal year. The annual report shall be submitted to Congress, and disseminated to the people of the United States, in the manner specified in subsections (b) and (g) of section 303.

(b) Contents.—The report required by this section shall include the following:

(1) The progress made on implementing the strategic plan and on the progress toward fulfillment of the priorities identified under section 303(e)(1).

(2) The progress made in efforts to encourage Federal, State, and local government departments and agencies to accord higher priority to intellectual property enforcement.

(3) The progress made in working with foreign countries to investigate, arrest, and prosecute entities and individuals involved in the financing, production, trafficking, and sale of counterfeit and infringing goods.

(4) The manner in which the relevant departments and agencies are working together and sharing information to strengthen intellectual property enforcement.

(5) An assessment of the successes and shortcomings of the efforts of the Federal Government, including departments and agencies represented on the committee established under section 301(b)(3).

(6) Recommendations, if any and as appropriate, for any changes in enforcement statutes, regulations, or funding levels that the advisory committee considers would significantly improve the effectiveness or efficiency of the effort of the Federal Government to combat counterfeiting and infringement and otherwise strengthen intellectual property enforcement, including through the elimination or consolidation of duplicative programs or initiatives.

(7) The progress made in strengthening the capacity of countries to protect and enforce intellectual property rights.

(8) The successes and challenges in sharing with other countries information relating to intellectual property enforcement.

(9) The progress made under trade agreements and treaties to protect intellectual property rights of United States persons and their licensees.

(10) The progress made in minimizing duplicative efforts, materials, facilities, and procedures of the Federal agencies and Departments responsible for the enforcement, investigation, or prosecution of intellectual property crimes.

(11) Recommendations, if any and as appropriate, on how to enhance the efficiency and consistency with which Federal funds and resources are expended to enforce, investigate, or prosecute intellectual property crimes, including the extent to which the agencies and Departments responsible for the enforcement, investigation, or prosecution of intellectual property crimes have utilized existing personnel, materials, technologies, and facilities.

Sec. 305 · Savings and Repeals.

(a) Transition From NIPLECC to IPEC.—

(1) Repeal of niplecc.—Section 653 of the Treasury and General Government Appropriations Act, 2000 (15 U.S.C. 1128) is repealed effective upon confirmation of the IPEC by the Senate and publication of such appointment in the Congressional Record.

(2) Continuity of performance of duties.—Upon confirmation by the Senate, and notwithstanding paragraph (1), the IPEC may use the services and personnel of the National Intellectual Property Law Enforcement Coordination Council, for such time as is reasonable, to perform any functions or duties which in the discretion of the IPEC are necessary to facilitate the orderly transition of any functions or duties transferred from the Council to the IPEC pursuant to any provision of this Act or any amendment made by this Act.

(b) Current Authorities Not Affected.—Except as provided in subsection (a), nothing in this title shall alter the authority of any department or agency of the United States (including any independent agency) that relates to—

(1) the investigation and prosecution of violations of laws that protect intellectual property rights;

(2) the administrative enforcement, at the borders of the United States, of laws that protect intellectual property rights; or

(3) the United States trade agreements program or international trade.

(c) Rules of Construction.—Nothing in this title—

(1) shall derogate from the powers, duties, and functions of any of the agencies, departments, or other entities listed or included under section 301(b)(3)(A); and

(2) shall be construed to transfer authority regarding the control, use, or allocation of law enforcement resources, or the initiation or prosecution of individual cases or types of cases, from the responsible law enforcement department or agency.

Sec. 306 · Authorization of Appropriations.

(a) In General.—There are authorized to be appropriated for each fiscal year such sums as may be necessary to carry out this title.

Title IV—Department of Justice Programs

Sec. 401 · Local Law Enforcement Grants.

(a) Authorization.—Section 2 of the Computer Crime Enforcement Act (42 U.S.C. 3713) is amended—

(1) in subsection (b), by inserting after "computer crime" each place it appears the following: ", including infringement of copyrighted works over the Internet"; and

(2) in subsection (e)(1), relating to authorization of appropriations, by striking "fiscal years 2001 through 2004" and inserting "fiscal years 2009 through 2013".

(b) Grants.—The Office of Justice Programs of the Department of Justice may make grants to eligible State or local law enforcement entities, including law enforcement agencies of municipal governments and public educational institutions, for training, prevention, enforcement, and prosecution of intellectual property theft and infringement crimes (in this subsection referred to as "IP-TIC grants"), in accordance with the following:

(1) Use of IP-TIC grant amounts.—IP-TIC grants may be used to establish and develop programs to do the following with respect to the enforcement of State and local true name and address laws and State and local criminal laws on anti-infringement, anti-counterfeiting, and unlawful acts with respect to goods by reason of their protection by a patent, trademark, service mark, trade secret, or other intellectual property right under State or Federal law:

(A) Assist State and local law enforcement agencies in enforcing those laws, including by reimbursing State and local entities for expenses incurred in performing enforcement operations, such as overtime payments and storage fees for seized evidence.

(B) Assist State and local law enforcement agencies in educating the public to prevent, deter, and identify violations of those laws.

(C) Educate and train State and local law enforcement officers and prosecutors to conduct investigations and forensic analyses of evidence and prosecutions in matters involving those laws.

(D) Establish task forces that include personnel from State or local law enforcement entities, or both, exclusively to conduct investigations and forensic analyses of evidence and prosecutions in matters involving those laws

(E) Assist State and local law enforcement officers and prosecutors in acquiring computer and other equipment to conduct investigations and forensic analyses of evidence in matters involving those laws.

(F) Facilitate and promote the sharing, with State and local law enforcement officers and prosecutors, of the expertise and information of Federal law enforcement agencies about the investigation, analysis, and prosecution of matters involving those laws and criminal infringement of copyrighted works, including the use of multijurisdictional task forces.

(2) Eligibility.—To be eligible to receive an IP-TIC grant, a State or local government entity shall provide to the Attorney General, in addition to the information regularly required to be provided under the Financial Guide issued by the Office of Justice Programs and any other information required of Department of Justice's grantees—

(A) assurances that the State in which the government entity is located has in effect laws described in paragraph (1);

(B) an assessment of the resource needs of the State or local government entity applying for the grant, including information on the need for reimbursements of base salaries and overtime costs, storage fees, and other expenditures to improve the investigation, prevention, or enforcement of laws described in paragraph (1); and

(C) a plan for coordinating the programs funded under this section with other federally funded technical assistance and training programs, including directly funded local programs such as the Edward Byrne Memorial Justice Assistance Grant Program authorized by subpart 1 of part E of title I of the Omnibus Crime Control and Safe Streets Act of 1968 (42 U.S.C. 3750 et seq.).

(3) Matching funds.—The Federal share of an IP-TIC grant may not exceed 50 percent of the costs of the program or proposal funded by the IP-TIC grant.

(4) Authorization of appropriations.—

(A) Authorization.—There is authorized to be appropriated to carry out this subsection the sum of $25,000,000 for each of fiscal years 2009 through 2013.

(B) Limitation.—Of the amount made available to carry out this subsection in any fiscal year, not more than 3 percent may be used by the Attorney General for salaries and administrative expenses.

Sec. 402 · Improved Investigative and Forensic Resources for Enforcement of Laws Related to Intellectual Property Crimes.

(a) In General.—Subject to the availability of appropriations to carry out this subsection, the Attorney General, in consultation with the Director of the

Federal Bureau of Investigation, shall, with respect to crimes related to the theft of intellectual property—

(1) ensure that there are at least 10 additional operational agents of the Federal Bureau of Investigation designated to support the Computer Crime and Intellectual Property Section of the Criminal Division of the Department of Justice in the investigation and coordination of intellectual property crimes;

(2) ensure that any Computer Hacking and Intellectual Property Crime Unit in the Department of Justice is supported by at least 1 agent of the Federal Bureau of Investigation (in addition to any agent supporting such unit as of the date of the enactment of this Act) to support such unit for the purpose of investigating or prosecuting intellectual property crimes;

(3) ensure that all Computer Hacking and Intellectual Property Crime Units located at an office of a United States Attorney are assigned at least 2 Assistant United States Attorneys responsible for investigating and prosecuting computer hacking or intellectual property crimes; and

(4) ensure the implementation of a regular and comprehensive training program—

(A) the purpose of which is to train agents of the Federal Bureau of Investigation in the investigation and prosecution of such crimes and the enforcement of laws related to intellectual property crimes; and

(B) that includes relevant forensic training related to investigating and prosecuting intellectual property crimes.

(b) Organized Crime Plan.—Subject to the availability of appropriations to carry out this subsection, and not later than 180 days after the date of the enactment of this Act, the Attorney General, through the United States Attorneys' Offices, the Computer Crime and Intellectual Property section, and the Organized Crime and Racketeering section of the Department of Justice, and in consultation with the Federal Bureau of Investigation and other Federal law enforcement agencies, such as the Department of Homeland Security, shall create and implement a comprehensive, long-range plan to investigate and prosecute international organized crime syndicates engaging in or supporting crimes relating to the theft of intellectual property.

(c) Authorization.—There are authorized to be appropriated to carry out this section $10,000,000 for each of fiscal years 2009 through 2013.

Sec. 403 · Additional Funding for Resources to Investigate and Prosecute Intellectual Property Crimes and Other Criminal Activity Involving Computers.

(a) Additional Funding for Resources.—

(1) Authorization.—In addition to amounts otherwise authorized for resources to investigate and prosecute intellectual property crimes and other criminal activity involving computers, there are authorized to be appropriated for each of the fiscal years 2009 through 2013—

(A) $10,000,000 to the Director of the Federal Bureau of Investigation; and

(B) $10,000,000 to the Attorney General for the Criminal Division of the Department of Justice.

(2) AVAILABILITY.—Any amounts appropriated under paragraph (1) shall remain available until expended.

(b) USE OF ADDITIONAL FUNDING.—Funds made available under subsection (a) shall be used by the Director of the Federal Bureau of Investigation and the Attorney General, for the Federal Bureau of Investigation and the Criminal Division of the Department of Justice, respectively, to—

(1) hire and train law enforcement officers to—

(A) investigate intellectual property crimes and other crimes committed through the use of computers and other information technology, including through the use of the Internet; and

(B) assist in the prosecution of such crimes; and

(2) enable relevant units of the Department of Justice, including units responsible for investigating computer hacking or intellectual property crimes, to procure advanced tools of forensic science and expert computer forensic assistance, including from non-governmental entities, to investigate, prosecute, and study such crimes.

Sec. 404 · Annual Reports.

(a) REPORT OF THE ATTORNEY GENERAL.—Not later than 1 year after the date of the enactment of this Act, and annually thereafter, the Attorney General shall submit a report to Congress on actions taken to carry out this title. The initial report required under this subsection shall be submitted by May 1, 2009. All subsequent annual reports shall be submitted by May 1st of each fiscal year thereafter. The report required under this subsection may be submitted as part of the annual performance report of the Department of Justice, and shall include the following:

(1) With respect to grants issued under section 401, the number and identity of State and local law enforcement grant applicants, the number of grants issued, the dollar value of each grant, including a break down of such value showing how the recipient used the funds, the specific purpose of each grant, and the reports from recipients of the grants on the efficacy of the program supported by the grant. The Department of Justice shall use the information provided by the grant recipients to produce a statement for each individual grant. Such statement shall state whether each grantee has accomplished the purposes of the grant as established in section 401(b). Those grantees not in compliance with the requirements of this title shall be subject, but not limited to, sanctions as described in the Financial Guide issued by the Office of Justice Programs at the Department of Justice.

(2) With respect to the additional agents of the Federal Bureau of Investigation authorized under paragraphs (1) and (2) of section 402(a), the number of investigations and actions in which such agents were engaged, the type of each action, the resolution of each action, and any penalties imposed in each action.

(3) With respect to the training program authorized under section 402(a)(4), the number of agents of the Federal Bureau of Investigation participating in such program, the elements of the training program, and the subject matters covered by the program.

(4) With respect to the organized crime plan authorized under section 402(b), the number of organized crime investigations and prosecutions resulting from such plan.

(5) With respect to the authorizations under section 403—

(A) the number of law enforcement officers hired and the number trained;

(B) the number and type of investigations and prosecutions resulting from the hiring and training of such law enforcement officers;

(C) the defendants involved in any such prosecutions;

(D) any penalties imposed in each such successful prosecution;

(E) the advanced tools of forensic science procured to investigate, prosecute, and study computer hacking or intellectual property crimes; and

(F) the number and type of investigations and prosecutions in such tools were used.

(6) Any other information that the Attorney General may consider relevant to inform Congress on the effective use of the resources authorized under sections 401, 402, and 403.

(7) A summary of the efforts, activities, and resources the Department of Justice has allocated to the enforcement, investigation, and prosecution of intellectual property crimes, including—

(A) a review of the policies and efforts of the Department of Justice related to the prevention and investigation of intellectual property crimes, including efforts at the Office of Justice Programs, the Criminal Division of the Department of Justice, the Executive Office of United States Attorneys, the Office of the Attorney General, the Office of the Deputy Attorney General, the Office of Legal Policy, and any other agency or bureau of the Department of Justice whose activities relate to intellectual property;

(B) a summary of the overall successes and failures of such policies and efforts;

(C) a review of the investigative and prosecution activity of the Department of Justice with respect to intellectual property crimes, including—

(i) the number of investigations initiated related to such crimes;

(ii) the number of arrests related to such crimes; and

(iii) the number of prosecutions for such crimes, including—

(I) the number of defendants involved in such prosecutions;

(II) whether the prosecution resulted in a conviction; and

(III) the sentence and the statutory maximum for such crime, as well as the average sentence imposed for such crime; and

(D) a Department-wide assessment of the staff, financial resources, and other resources (such as time, technology, and training) devoted to the enforcement, investigation, and prosecution of intellectual property crimes, including the number of investigators, prosecutors, and forensic specialists dedicated to investigating and prosecuting intellectual property crimes.

(8) A summary of the efforts, activities, and resources that the Department of Justice has taken to—

(A) minimize duplicating the efforts, materials, facilities, and procedures of any other Federal agency responsible for the enforcement, investigation, or prosecution of intellectual property crimes; and

(B) enhance the efficiency and consistency with which Federal funds and resources are expended to enforce, investigate, or prosecute intellectual property crimes, including the extent to which the Department has utilized existing personnel, materials, technologies, and facilities.

(b) Initial Report of the Attorney General.—The first report required to be submitted by the Attorney General under subsection (a) shall include a summary of the efforts, activities, and resources the Department of Justice has allocated in the 5 years prior to the date of enactment of this Act, as well as the 1-year period following such date of enactment, to the enforcement, investigation, and prosecution of intellectual property crimes, including—

(1) a review of the policies and efforts of the Department of Justice related to the prevention and investigation of intellectual property crimes, including efforts at the Office of Justice Programs, the Criminal Division of the Department of Justice, the Executive Office of United States Attorneys, the Office of the Attorney General, the Office of the Deputy Attorney General, the Office of Legal Policy, and any other agency or bureau of the Department of Justice whose activities relate to intellectual property;

(2) a summary of the overall successes and failures of such policies and efforts;

(3) a review of the investigative and prosecution activity of the Department of Justice with respect to intellectual property crimes, including—

(A) the number of investigations initiated related to such crimes;

(B) the number of arrests related to such crimes; and

(C) the number of prosecutions for such crimes, including—

(i) the number of defendants involved in such prosecutions;

(ii) whether the prosecution resulted in a conviction; and

(iii) the sentence and the statutory maximum for such crime, as well as the average sentence imposed for such crime; and

(4) a Department-wide assessment of the staff, financial resources, and other resources (such as time, technology, and training) devoted to the enforcement, investigation, and prosecution of intellectual property crimes, including the number of investigators, prosecutors, and forensic specialists dedicated to investigating and prosecuting intellectual property crimes.

(c) Report of the FBI.—Not later than 1 year after the date of the enactment of this Act, and annually thereafter, the Director of the Federal Bureau of Investigation shall submit a report to Congress on actions taken to carry out this title. The initial report required under this subsection shall be submitted by May 1, 2009. All subsequent annual reports shall be submitted by May 1st of each fiscal year thereafter. The report required under this subsection may be submitted as part of the annual performance report of the Department of Justice, and shall include—

(1) a review of the policies and efforts of the Bureau related to the prevention and investigation of intellectual property crimes;

(2) a summary of the overall successes and failures of such policies and efforts;

(3) a review of the investigative and prosecution activity of the Bureau with respect to intellectual property crimes, including—

(A) the number of investigations initiated related to such crimes;

(B) the number of arrests related to such crimes; and

(C) the number of prosecutions for such crimes, including—

(i) the number of defendants involved in such prosecutions;

(ii) whether the prosecution resulted in a conviction; and

(iii) the sentence and the statutory maximum for such crime, as well as the average sentence imposed for such crime; and

(4) a Bureau-wide assessment of the staff, financial resources, and other resources (such as time, technology, and training) devoted to the enforcement, investigation, and prosecution of intellectual property crimes, including the number of investigators, prosecutors, and forensic specialists dedicated to investigating and prosecuting intellectual property crimes.

(d) Initial Report of the FBI.—The first report required to be submitted by the Director of the Federal Bureau of Investigation under subsection (c) shall include a summary of the efforts, activities, and resources the Federal Bureau of Investigation has allocated in the 5 years prior to the date of enactment of this Act, as well as the 1-year period following such date of enactment to the enforcement, investigation, and prosecution of intellectual property crimes, including—

(1) a review of the policies and efforts of the Bureau related to the prevention and investigation of intellectual property crimes;

(2) a summary of the overall successes and failures of such policies and efforts;

(3) a review of the investigative and prosecution activity of the Bureau with respect to intellectual property crimes, including—

(A) the number of investigations initiated related to such crimes;

(B) the number of arrests related to such crimes; and

(C) the number of prosecutions for such crimes, including—

(i) the number of defendants involved in such prosecutions;

(ii) whether the prosecution resulted in a conviction; and

(iii) the sentence and the statutory maximum for such crime, as well as the average sentence imposed for such crime; and

(4) a Bureau-wide assessment of the staff, financial resources, and other resources (such as time, technology, and training) devoted to the enforcement, investigation, and prosecution of intellectual property crimes, including the number of investigators, prosecutors, and forensic specialists dedicated to investigating and prosecuting intellectual property crimes.

Title V—Miscellaneous

Sec. 501 · GAO Study on Protection of Intellectual Property of Manufacturers.

(a) Study.—The Comptroller General of the United States shall conduct a study to help determine how the Federal Government could better protect the intellectual property of manufacturers by quantification of the impacts of imported and domestic counterfeit goods on—

(1) the manufacturing industry in the United States; and

(2) the overall economy of the United States.

(b) Contents.—In conducting the study required under subsection (a), the Comptroller General shall examine—

(1) the extent that counterfeit manufactured goods are actively being trafficked in and imported into the United States;

(2) the impacts on domestic manufacturers in the United States of current law regarding defending intellectual property, including patent, trademark, and copyright protections;

(3) the nature and scope of current statutory law and case law regarding protecting trade dress from being illegally copied;

(4) the extent which such laws are being used to investigate and prosecute acts of trafficking in counterfeit manufactured goods;

(5) any effective practices or procedures that are protecting all types of intellectual property; and

(6) any changes to current statutes or rules that would need to be implemented to more effectively protect the intellectual property rights of manufacturers.

(c) Report.—Not later than 1 year after the date of the enactment of this Act, the Comptroller General shall submit to Congress a report on the results of the study required under subsection (a).

Sec. 502 · GAO Audit and Report on Nonduplication and Efficiency.

Not later than 2 years after the date of enactment of this Act, the Comptroller General shall conduct an audit and submit a report to the Committee on the Judiciary of the Senate and to the Committee on the Judiciary of the House of Representatives on—

(1) the efforts, activities, and actions of the Intellectual Property Enforcement Coordinator and the Attorney General in achieving the goals and purposes of this Act, as well as in carrying out any responsibilities or duties assigned to each such individual or agency under this Act;

(2) any possible legislative, administrative, or regulatory changes that Comptroller General recommends be taken by or on behalf of the Intellectual Property Enforcement Coordinator or the Attorney General to better achieve such goals and purposes, and to more effectively carry out such responsibilities and duties;

(3) the effectiveness of any actions taken and efforts made by the Intellectual Property Enforcement Coordinator and the Attorney General to—

(A) minimize duplicating the efforts, materials, facilities, and procedures of any other Federal agency responsible for the enforcement, investigation, or prosecution of intellectual property crimes; and

(B) enhance the efficiency and consistency with which Federal funds and resources are expended to enforce, investigate, or prosecute intellectual property crimes, including whether the IPEC has utilized existing personnel, materials, technologies, and facilities, such as the National Intellectual Property Rights Coordination Center established at the Department of Homeland Security; and

(4) any actions or efforts that the Comptroller General recommends be taken by or on behalf of the Intellectual Property Enforcement Coordinator and the Attorney General to reduce duplication of efforts and increase the efficiency and consistency with which Federal funds and resources are expended to enforce, investigate, or prosecute intellectual property crimes.

Sec. 503 · Sense of Congress.

It is the sense of Congress that—

(1) the United States intellectual property industries have created millions of high-skill, high-paying United States jobs and pay billions of dollars in annual United States tax revenues;

(2) the United States intellectual property industries continue to represent a major source of creativity and innovation, business start-ups, skilled job creation, exports, economic growth, and competitiveness;

(3) counterfeiting and infringement results in billions of dollars in lost revenue for United States companies each year and even greater losses to the United States economy in terms of reduced job growth, exports, and competitiveness;

(4) the growing number of willful violations of existing Federal criminal laws involving counterfeiting and infringement by actors in the United States and, increasingly, by foreign-based individuals and entities is a serious threat to the long-term vitality of the United States economy and the future competitiveness of United States industry;

(5) terrorists and organized crime utilize piracy, counterfeiting, and infringement to fund some of their activities;

(6) effective criminal enforcement of the intellectual property laws against violations in all categories of works should be among the highest priorities of the Attorney General;

(7) with respect to all crimes related to the theft of intellectual property, the Attorney General shall give priority to cases with a nexus to terrorism and organized crime; and

(8) with respect to criminal counterfeiting and infringement of computer software, including those by foreign-owned or foreign-controlled entities, the Attorney General should give priority to cases—

(A) involving the willful theft of intellectual property for purposes of commercial advantage or private financial gain;

(B) where the theft of intellectual property is central to the sustainability and viability of the commercial activity of the enterprise (or subsidiary) involved in the violation;

(C) where the counterfe ited or infringing goods or services enables the enterprise to unfairly compete against the legitimate rights holder; or

(D) where there is actual knowledge of the theft of intellectual property by the directors or officers of the enterprise.

Appendix F · Note

1. This appendix contains provisions from the Prioritizing Resources and Organization for Intellectual Property Act of 2008, Pub. L. No. 110-403, 122 Stat. 4256, that do not amend title 17 of the *United States Code*.

Appendix G

The Satellite Television Extension and Localism Act of 2010[1]

Section 1 · Short Title; Table of Contents.

(a) Short Title.—This Act may be cited as the "Satellite Television Extension and Localism Act of 2010".

* * * * * * *

Title I—Statutory Licenses

* * * * * * *

Sec. 104 · Modifications to Cable System Secondary Transmission Rights Under Section 111.

* * * * * * *

(d) Effective Date of New Royalty Fee Rates.—The royalty fee rates established in section 111(d)(1)(B) of title 17, United States Code, as amended by subsection (c)(1)(C) of this section, shall take effect commencing with the first accounting period occurring in 2010.

* * * * * * *

(f) Timing of Section 111 Proceedings.—

* * * * * * *

(h) Effective Date with Respect to Multicast Streams.—

(1) In general.—Subject to paragraphs (2) and (3), the amendments made by this section, to the extent such amendments assign a distant signal equivalent value to the secondary transmission of the multicast stream of a primary transmitter, shall take effect on the date of the enactment of this Act.

(2) Delayed applicability.—

(A) Secondary transmissions of a multicast stream beyond the local service area of its primary transmitter before 2010 act.—In any case in which a cable system was making secondary transmissions of a multicast stream beyond the local service area of its primary transmitter before the date of the enactment of this Act, a distant signal equivalent value (referred to in paragraph (1)) shall not be assigned to secondary transmissions of such multicast stream that are made on or before June 30, 2010.

(B) MULTICAST STREAMS SUBJECT TO PREEXISTING WRITTEN AGREEMENTS FOR THE SECONDARY TRANSMISSION OF SUCH STREAMS.—In any case in which the secondary transmission of a multicast stream of a primary transmitter is the subject of a written agreement entered into on or before June 30, 2009, between a cable system or an association representing the cable system and a primary transmitter or an association representing the primary transmitter, a distant signal equivalent value (referred to in paragraph (1)) shall not be assigned to secondary transmissions of such multicast stream beyond the local service area of its primary transmitter that are made on or before the date on which such written agreement expires.

(C) NO REFUNDS OR OFFSETS FOR PRIOR STATEMENTS OF ACCOUNT.—A cable system that has reported secondary transmissions of a multicast stream beyond the local service area of its primary transmitter on a statement of account deposited under section 111 of title 17, United States Code, before the date of the enactment of this Act shall not be entitled to any refund, or offset, of royalty fees paid on account of such secondary transmissions of such multicast stream.

(3) DEFINITIONS.—In this subsection, the terms "cable system", "secondary transmission", "multicast stream", and "local service area of a primary transmitter" have the meanings given those terms in section 111(f) of title 17, United States Code, as amended by this section.

* * * * * * *

Sec. 107. Termination of license.

(a) TERMINATION.—Section 119 of title 17, United States Code, as amended by this Act, shall cease to be effective on December 31, 2014.

(b) CONFORMING AMENDMENT.—Section 1003(a)(2)(A) of Public Law 111–118 (17 U.S.C. 119 note) is repealed.

Sec. 108. Construction.

Nothing in section 111, 119, or 122 of title 17, United States Code, including the amendments made to such sections by this title, shall be construed to affect the meaning of any terms under the Communications Act of 1934, except to the extent that such sections are specifically cross-referenced in such Act or the regulations issued thereunder.

Appendix G Note

1. This appendix contains provisions from the Satellite Television Extension and Localism Act of 2010, Pub. L. No. 111-175, 124 Stat. 1218, that do not amend title 17 of the *United States Code*.

Appendix H

Title 18—Crimes and Criminal Procedure, U.S. Code

Part I—Crimes
Chapter 113—Stolen Property

* * * * * * *

§ 2318 · Trafficking in counterfeit labels, illicit labels, or counterfeit documentation or packaging[1]

(a) (1) Whoever, in any of the circumstances described in subsection (c), knowingly traffics in—

(A) a counterfeit label or illicit label affixed to, enclosing, or accompanying, or designed to be affixed to, enclose, or accompany—

(i) a phonorecord;

(ii) a copy of a computer program;

(iii) a copy of a motion picture or other audiovisual work;

(iv) a copy of a literary work;

(v) a copy of a pictorial, graphic, or sculptural work;

(vi) a work of visual art; or

(vii) documentation or packaging; or

(B) counterfeit documentation or packaging, shall be fined under this title or imprisoned for not more than 5 years, or both.

(b) As used in this section—

(1) the term "counterfeit label" means an identifying label or container that appears to be genuine, but is not;

(2) the term "traffic" has the same meaning as in section 2320(e) of this title;

(3) the terms "copy", "phonorecord", "motion picture", "computer program", "audiovisual work", "literary work", "pictorial, graphic, or sculptural work", "sound recording", "work of visual art", and "copyright owner" have, respectively, the meanings given those terms in section 101 (relating to definitions) of title 17;

(4) the term "illicit label" means a genuine certificate, licensing document, registration card, or similar labeling component—

(A) that is used by the copyright owner to verify that a phonorecord, a copy of a computer program, a copy of a motion picture or other audiovisual work, a copy of a literary work, a copy of a pictorial, graphic, or sculptural work, a work of visual art, or documentation or packaging is not counterfeit or infringing of any copyright; and

(B) that is, without the authorization of the copyright owner—

(i) distributed or intended for distribution not in connection with the copy, phonorecord, or work of visual art to which such labeling component was intended to be affixed by the respective copyright owner; or

(ii) in connection with a genuine certificate or licensing document, knowingly falsified in order to designate a higher number of licensed users or copies than authorized by the copyright owner, unless that certificate or document is used by the copyright owner solely for the purpose of monitoring or tracking the copyright owner's distribution channel and not for the purpose of verifying that a copy or phonorecord is noninfringing;

(5) the term "documentation or packaging" means documentation or packaging, in physical form, for a phonorecord, copy of a computer program, copy of a motion picture or other audiovisual work, copy of a literary work, copy of a pictorial, graphic, or sculptural work, or work of visual art; and

(6) the term "counterfeit documentation or packaging" means documentation or packaging that appears to be genuine, but is not.

(c) The circumstances referred to in subsection (a) of this section are—

(1) the offense is committed within the special maritime and territorial jurisdiction of the United States; or within the special aircraft jurisdiction of the United States (as defined in section 46501 of title 49);

(2) the mail or a facility of interstate or foreign commerce is used or intended to be used in the commission of the offense;

(3) the counterfeit label or illicit label is affixed to, encloses, or accompanies, or is designed to be affixed to, enclose, or accompany—

(A) a phonorecord of a copyrighted sound recording or copyrighted musical work;

(B) a copy of a copyrighted computer program;

(C) a copy of a copyrighted motion picture or other audiovisual work;

(D) a copy of a literary work;

(E) a copy of a pictorial, graphic, or sculptural work;

(F) a work of visual art; or

(G) copyrighted documentation or packaging; or

(4) the counterfeited documentation or packaging is copyrighted.

(d) Forfeiture and Destruction of Property; Restitution.—Forfeiture, destruction, and restitution relating to this section shall be subject to section 2323, to the extent provided in that section, in addition to any other similar remedies provided by law.

(e) Civil Remedies.—

(1) In general.—Any copyright owner who is injured, or is threatened with injury, by a violation of subsection (a) may bring a civil action in an appropriate United States district court.

(2) Discretion of court.—In any action brought under paragraph (1), the court—

(A) may grant 1 or more temporary or permanent injunctions on such terms as the court determines to be reasonable to prevent or restrain a violation of subsection (a);

(B) at any time while the action is pending, may order the impounding, on such terms as the court determines to be reasonable, of any article that is in the custody or control of the alleged violator and that the court has reasonable cause to believe was involved in a violation of subsection (a); and

(C) may award to the injured party—

(i) reasonable attorney fees and costs; and

(ii)(I) actual damages and any additional profits of the violator, as provided in paragraph (3); or

(II) statutory damages, as provided in paragraph (4).

(3) Actual damages and profits.—

(A) In general.—The injured party is entitled to recover—

(i) the actual damages suffered by the injured party as a result of a violation of subsection (a), as provided in subparagraph (B) of this paragraph; and

(ii) any profits of the violator that are attributable to a violation of subsection (a) and are not taken into account in computing the actual damages.

(B) Calculation of damages.—The court shall calculate actual damages by multiplying—

(i) the value of the phonorecords, copies, or works of visual art which are, or are intended to be, affixed with, enclosed in, or accompanied by any counterfeit labels, illicit labels, or counterfeit documentation or packaging, by

(ii) the number of phonorecords, copies, or works of visual art which are, or are intended to be, affixed with, enclosed in, or accompanied by any counterfeit labels, illicit labels, or counterfeit documentation or packaging.

(C) Definition.—For purposes of this paragraph, the "value" of a phonorecord, copy, or work of visual art is—

(i) in the case of a copyrighted sound recording or copyrighted musical work, the retail value of an authorized phonorecord of that sound recording or musical work;

(ii) in the case of a copyrighted computer program, the retail value of an authorized copy of that computer program;

(iii) in the case of a copyrighted motion picture or other audiovisual work, the retail value of an authorized copy of that motion picture or audiovisual work;

(iv) in the case of a copyrighted literary work, the retail value of an authorized copy of that literary work;

(v) in the case of a pictorial, graphic, or sculptural work, the retail value of an authorized copy of that work; and

(vi) in the case of a work of visual art, the retail value of that work.

(4) Statutory damages.—The injured party may elect, at any time before final judgment is rendered, to recover, instead of actual damages and profits, an award of statutory damages for each violation of subsection (a) in a sum of not less than $2,500 or more than $25,000, as the court considers appropriate.

(5) Subsequent violation.—The court may increase an award of damages under this subsection by 3 times the amount that would otherwise be awarded, as the court considers appropriate, if the court finds that a person has subsequently violated subsection (a) within 3 years after a final judgment was entered against that person for a violation of that subsection.

(6) Limitation on actions.—A civil action may not be commenced under this section unless it is commenced within 3 years after the date on which the claimant discovers the violation of subsection (a).

§ 2319 · *Criminal infringement of a copyright*[2]

(a) Any person who violates section 506(a) (relating to criminal offenses) of title 17 shall be punished as provided in subsections (b), (c), and (d) and such penalties shall be in addition to any other provisions of title 17 or any other law.

(b) Any person who commits an offense under section 506(a)(1)(A) of title 17—

(1) shall be imprisoned not more than 5 years, or fined in the amount set forth in this title, or both, if the offense consists of the reproduction or distribution, including by electronic means, during any 180-day period, of at least 10 copies or phonorecords, of 1 or more copyrighted works, which have a total retail value of more than $2,500;

(2) shall be imprisoned not more than 10 years, or fined in the amount set forth in this title, or both, if the offense is a felony and is a second or subsequent offense under subsection (a); and

(3) shall be imprisoned not more than 1 year, or fined in the amount set forth in this title, or both, in any other case.

(c) Any person who commits an offense under section 506(a)(1)(B) of title 17—

(1) shall be imprisoned not more than 3 years, or fined in the amount set forth in this title, or both, if the offense consists of the reproduction or distribution of 10 or more copies or phonorecords of 1 or more copyrighted works, which have a total retail value of $2,500 or more;

(2) shall be imprisoned not more than 6 years, or fined in the amount set forth in this title, or both, if the offense is a felony and is a second or subsequent offense under subsection (a); and

(3) shall be imprisoned not more than 1 year, or fined in the amount set forth in this title, or both, if the offense consists of the reproduction or distribution of 1 or more copies or phonorecords of 1 or more copyrighted works, which have a total retail value of more than $1,000.

(d) Any person who commits an offense under section 506(a)(1)(C) of title 17—

(1) shall be imprisoned not more than 3 years, fined under this title, or both;

(2) shall be imprisoned not more than 5 years, fined under this title, or both, if the offense was committed for purposes of commercial advantage or private financial gain;

(3) shall be imprisoned not more than 6 years, fined under this title, or both, if the offense is a felony and is a second or subsequent offense under subsection (a); and

(4) shall be imprisoned not more than 10 years, fined under this title, or both, if the offense is a felony and is a second or subsequent offense under paragraph (2).

(e) (1) During preparation of the presentence report pursuant to Rule 32(c) of the Federal Rules of Criminal Procedure, victims of the offense shall be permitted to submit, and the probation officer shall receive, a victim impact statement that identifies the victim of the offense and the extent and scope of the injury and loss suffered by the victim, including the estimated economic impact of the offense on that victim.

(2) Persons permitted to submit victim impact statements shall include—

(A) producers and sellers of legitimate works affected by conduct involved in the offense;

(B) holders of intellectual property rights in such works; and

(C) the legal representatives of such producers, sellers, and holders.

(f) As used in this section—

(1) the terms "phonorecord" and "copies" have, respectively, the meanings set forth in section 101 (relating to definitions) of title 17;

(2) the terms "reproduction" and "distribution" refer to the exclusive rights of a copyright owner under clauses (1) and (3) respectively of section 106 (relating to exclusive rights in copyrighted works), as limited by sections 107 through 122, of title 17;

(3) the term "financial gain" has the meaning given the term in section 101 of title 17; and

(4) the term "work being prepared for commercial distribution" has the meaning given the term in section 506(a) of title 17.

§ 2319A · *Unauthorized fixation of and trafficking in sound recordings and music videos of live musical performances*[3]

(a) OFFENSE.—Whoever, without the consent of the performer or performers involved, knowingly and for purposes of commercial advantage or private financial gain—

(1) fixes the sounds or sounds and images of a live musical performance in a copy or phonorecord, or reproduces copies or phonorecords of such a performance from an unauthorized fixation;

(2) transmits or otherwise communicates to the public the sounds or sounds and images of a live musical performance; or

(3) distributes or offers to distribute, sells or offers to sell, rents or offers to rent, or traffics in any copy or phonorecord fixed as described in paragraph (1), regardless of whether the fixations occurred in the United States;

shall be imprisoned for not more than 5 years or fined in the amount set forth in this title, or both, or if the offense is a second or subsequent offense, shall be imprisoned for not more than 10 years or fined in the amount set forth in this title, or both.

(b) FORFEITURE AND DESTRUCTION OF PROPERTY; RESTITUTION.—Forfeiture, destruction, and restitution relating to this section shall be subject to section 2323, to the extent provided in that section, in addition to any other similar remedies provided by law.

(c) SEIZURE AND FORFEITURE.—If copies or phonorecords of sounds or sounds and images of a live musical performance are fixed outside of the United States without the consent of the performer or performers involved, such copies or phonorecords are subject to seizure and forfeiture in the United States in the same manner as property imported in violation of the customs laws. The Secretary of Homeland Security shall issue regulations by which any performer may, upon payment of a specified fee, be entitled to notification by United States Customs and Border Protection of the importation of copies or phonorecords that appear to consist of unauthorized fixations of the sounds or sounds and images of a live musical performance.

(d) VICTIM IMPACT STATEMENT.—

(1) During preparation of the presentence report pursuant to Rule 32(c) of the Federal Rules of Criminal Procedure, victims of the offense shall be permitted to submit, and the probation officer shall receive, a victim impact statement that identifies the victim of the offense and the extent and scope of

the injury and loss suffered by the victim, including the estimated economic impact of the offense on that victim.

(2) Persons permitted to submit victim impact statements shall include—

(A) producers and sellers of legitimate works affected by conduct involved in the offense;

(B) holders of intellectual property rights in such works; and

(C) the legal representatives of such producers, sellers, and holders.

(e) Definitions.—As used in this section—

(1) the terms "copy", "fixed", "musical work", "phonorecord", "reproduce", "sound recordings", and "transmit" mean those terms within the meaning of title 17; and

(2) the term "traffic" has the same meaning as in section 2320(e) of this title.

(f) Applicability.—This section shall apply to any Act or Acts that occur on or after the date of the enactment of the Uruguay Round Agreements Act.[4]

§ 2319B · *Unauthorized recording of motion pictures in a motion picture exhibition facility*[5]

(a) Offense.—Any person who, without the authorization of the copyright owner, knowingly uses or attempts to use an audiovisual recording device to transmit or make a copy of a motion picture or other audiovisual work protected under title 17, or any part thereof, from a performance of such work in a motion picture exhibition facility, shall—

(1) be imprisoned for not more than 3 years, fined under this title, or both; or

(2) if the offense is a second or subsequent offense, be imprisoned for no more than 6 years, fined under this title, or both.

The possession by a person of an audiovisual recording device in a motion picture exhibition facility may be considered as evidence in any proceeding to determine whether that person committed an offense under this subsection, but shall not, by itself, be sufficient to support a conviction of that person for such offense.

(b) Forfeiture and Destruction of Property; Restitution.—Forfeiture, destruction, and restitution relating to this section shall be subject to section 2323, to the extent provided in that section, in addition to any other similar remedies provided by law.

(c) Authorized Activities.—This section does not prevent any lawfully authorized investigative, protective, or intelligence activity by an officer, agent, or employee of the United States, a State, or a political subdivision of a State, or by a person acting under a contract with the United States, a State, or a political subdivision of a State.

(d) Immunity for Theaters.—With reasonable cause, the owner or lessee of a motion picture exhibition facility where a motion picture or other audiovisual work is being exhibited, the authorized agent or employee of such owner or lessee, the licensor of the motion picture or other audiovisual work being exhibited, or the agent or employee of such licensor—

(1) may detain, in a reasonable manner and for a reasonable time, any person suspected of a violation of this section with respect to that motion picture or audiovisual work for the purpose of questioning or summoning a law enforcement officer; and

(2) shall not be held liable in any civil or criminal action arising out of a detention under paragraph (1).

(e) Victim Impact Statement.—

(1) In general.—During the preparation of the presentence report under rule 32(c) of the Federal Rules of Criminal Procedure, victims of an offense under this section shall be permitted to submit to the probation officer a victim impact statement that identifies the victim of the offense and the extent and scope of the injury and loss suffered by the victim, including the estimated economic impact of the offense on that victim.

(2) Contents.—A victim impact statement submitted under this subsection shall include—

(A) producers and sellers of legitimate works affected by conduct involved in the offense;

(B) holders of intellectual property rights in the works described in subparagraph (A); and

(C) the legal representatives of such producers, sellers, and holders.

(f) State Law Not Preempted.—Nothing in this section may be construed to annul or limit any rights or remedies under the laws of any State.

(g) Definitions.—In this section, the following definitions shall apply:

(1) Title 17 definitions.—The terms "audiovisual work", "copy", "copyright owner", "motion picture", "motion picture exhibition facility", and "transmit" have, respectively, the meanings given those terms in section 101 of title 17.

(2) Audiovisual recording device.—The term "audiovisual recording device" means a digital or analog photographic or video camera, or any other technology or device capable of enabling the recording or transmission of a copyrighted motion picture or other audiovisual work, or any part thereof, regardless of whether audiovisual recording is the sole or primary purpose of the device.

* * * * * * *

§ 2323 · *Forfeiture, destruction, and restitution.*[6]

(a) Civil Forfeiture.—

(1) Property subject to forfeiture.—The following property is subject to forfeiture to the United States Government:

(A) Any article, the making or trafficking of which is, prohibited under section 506 of title 17, or section 2318, 2319, 2319A, 2319B, or 2320, or chapter 90, of this title.

(B) Any property used, or intended to be used, in any manner or part to commit or facilitate the commission of an offense referred to in subparagraph (A).

(C) Any property constituting or derived from any proceeds obtained directly or indirectly as a result of the commission of an offense referred to in subparagraph (A).

(2) PROCEDURES.—The provisions of chapter 46 relating to civil forfeitures shall extend to any seizure or civil forfeiture under this section. For seizures made under this section, the court shall enter an appropriate protective order with respect to discovery and use of any records or information that has been seized. The protective order shall provide for appropriate procedures to ensure that confidential, private, proprietary, or privileged information contained in such records is not improperly disclosed or used. At the conclusion of the forfeiture proceedings, unless otherwise requested by an agency of the United States, the court shall order that any property forfeited under paragraph (1) be destroyed, or otherwise disposed of according to law.

(b) CRIMINAL FORFEITURE.—

(1) PROPERTY SUBJECT TO FORFEITURE.—The court, in imposing sentence on a person convicted of an offense under section 506 of title 17, or section 2318, 2319, 2319A, 2319B, or 2320, or chapter 90, of this title, shall order, in addition to any other sentence imposed, that the person forfeit to the United States Government any property subject to forfeiture under subsection (a) for that offense.

(2) PROCEDURES.—

(A) IN GENERAL.—The forfeiture of property under paragraph (1), including any seizure and disposition of the property and any related judicial or administrative proceeding, shall be governed by the procedures set forth in section 413 of the Comprehensive Drug Abuse Prevention and Control Act of 1970 (21 U.S.C. 853), other than subsection (d) of that section.

(B) DESTRUCTION.—At the conclusion of the forfeiture proceedings, the court, unless otherwise requested by an agency of the United States shall order that any—

(i) forfeited article or component of an article bearing or consisting of a counterfeit mark be destroyed or otherwise disposed of according to law; and

(ii) infringing items or other property described in subsection (a)(1)(A) and forfeited under paragraph (1) of this subsection be destroyed or otherwise disposed of according to law.

(c) Restitution.—When a person is convicted of an offense under section 506 of title 17 or section 2318, 2319, 2319A, 2319B, or 2320, or chapter 90, of this title, the court, pursuant to sections 3556, 3663A, and 3664 of this title, shall order the person to pay restitution to any victim of the offense as an offense against property referred to in section 3663A(c)(1)(A)(ii) of this title.

Appendix H · Notes

1. In 1962, section 2318, entitled "Transportation, sale, or receipt of phonograph records bearing forged or counterfeit labels," was added to title 18 of the *United States Code*. Pub. L. No. 87-773, 76 Stat. 775. In 1974, section 2318 was amended to change the penalties. Pub. L. No. 93-573, 88 Stat. 1873. The Copyright Act of 1976 revised section 2318 with an amendment in the nature of a substitute. Pub. L. No. 94-553, 90 Stat. 2541, 2600. The Piracy and Counterfeiting Amendments Act of 1982 again revised section 2318 with an amendment in the nature of a substitute that included a new title, "Trafficking in counterfeit labels for phonorecords, and copies of motion pictures or other audiovisual works." Pub. L. No. 97-180, 96 Stat. 91. The Crime Control Act of 1990 made a technical amendment to section 2318 to delete the comma after "phonorecords" in the title. Pub. L. No. 101-647, 104 Stat. 4789, 4928. In 1994, section 2318(c)(1) was amended by inserting "section 46501 of title 49" in lieu of "section 101 of the Federal Aviation Act of 1958. Pub. L. No. 103-272, 108 Stat. 745, 1374. The Violent Crime Control and Law Enforcement Act of 1994 amended section 2318(a) by inserting "under this title" in lieu of "not more than $250,000." Pub. L. No. 103-322, 108 Stat. 1796, 2148. (As provided in 18 *U.S.C.* section 3571, the maximum fine for an individual is $250,000, and the maximum fine for an organization is $500,000.)

The Anticounterfeiting Consumer Protection Act of 1996 amended section 2318 by changing the title, by amending subsection (a) to insert "a computer program or documentation" through to "knowingly traffics in counterfeit documentation or packaging for a computer program" in lieu of "a motion picture or other audiovisual work" and by amending subsection (b)(3) to insert "computer program" after "motion picture." Pub. L. No. 104-153, 110 Stat. 1386. The Act also amended section 2318(c) by inserting "a copy of a copyrighted computer program or copyrighted documentation or packaging for a computer program" into paragraph (3) and by adding paragraph (4). *Id.* at 1387.

The Anti-counterfeiting Amendments Act of 2004 amended section 2318 by changing its title, by amending subsection 2318(a) in its entirety; and by amending paragraph 2318(c)(3) in its entirety. Pub. L. No. 108-482, 118 Stat. 3912-3913. It amended paragraph 2318(c)(4) by deleting "for a computer program" after "packaging." *Id.* at 3914. It amended subsection 2318(d) by inserting "or illicit labels" after "counterfeit labels," wherever it appears and by inserting the text at the end of the sentence, after "such labels affixed." *Id.* The Act also added a new subsection (f). *Id.*

The Protecting American Goods and Services Act of 2005 amended section 2318(b)(2) in its entirety to make the definition for "traffic" the same as in 18 *U.S.C.* § 2320(e). Pub. L. No. 109-181, 120 Stat. 285, 288. The Act simultaneously amended § 2320(e)(2) to define traffic as "to transport, transfer, or otherwise dispose of, to another, for purposes of commercial advantage or private financial gain, or to make, import, export, obtain control of, or possess, with intent to so transport, transfer, or otherwise dispose of." *Id.*

The Prioritizing Resources and Organization for Intellectual Property Act of 2008 amended section 2318 by revising the section designations for subpart (a), by revising subsection (d) in its entirety and by deleting (e) and redesignating (f) as the new (e). Pub. L. No. 110-403, 122 Stat. 4256, 4261. The Copyright Cleanup, Clarification, and Corrections Act of 2010 amended paragraph 2318(e)(6) by inserting "this" before "section." Pub. L. No. 111-295, 124 Stat. 3180, 3182.

2. The Piracy and Counterfeiting Amendments Act of 1982 added section 2319 to title 18 of the *United States Code*. This section was entitled "Criminal infringement of a copyright." Pub. L. No. 97-180, 96 Stat. 91, 92. In 1992, section 2319 was amended by substituting a new subsection (b), by deleting "sound recording," "motion picture" and "audiovisual work" from subsection (c)(1) and by substituting "120" for "118" in subsection (c)(2). Pub. L. No. 102-561, 106 Stat. 4233. In 1997, a technical amendment corrected the spelling of "last" in subsection (b)(1) to "least." Pub. L. No. 105-80, 111 Stat. 1529, 1536.

In 1997, the No Electronic Theft Act amended section 2319 of title 18 as follows: 1) in subsection (a) by inserting "and (c)" after "subsection (b),"; 2) in subsection (b), in the matter preceding paragraph (1), by inserting "section 506(a)(1) of title 17" in lieu of "subsection (a) of this section,"; 3) in subsection (b)(1) by inserting "including by electronic means" and by inserting "which have a total retail value" in lieu of "with a retail value," 4) by redesignating subsection (c) as subsection (e); and 5) by adding new subsections (c) and (d). Pub. L. No. 105-147, 111 Stat. 2678. The Act also directed the United States Sentencing Commission to "ensure that the applicable guideline range for a defendant convicted of a crime against intellectual property ... is sufficiently stringent to deter such a crime" and to "ensure that the guidelines provide for consideration of the retail value and quantity of the items with respect to which the crime against intellectual property was committed." *Id.* See also note 6, chapter 5, *supra*.

The Intellectual Property and High Technology Technical Amendments Act of 2002 amended paragraph (2) of section 2319(e) by substituting sections "107 through 122" for "107 through 120." Pub. L. No. 107-273, 116 Stat. 1758, 1910.

The Artists' Rights and Theft Prevention Act of 2005 amended the beginning of the first sentence of 5 *U.S.C.* 2319(a) by substituting "Any person who" in lieu of "Whoever." Pub. L. No. 109-9, 119 Stat. 218, 220-221. It amended subsection 2319(a) by substituting "subsections (b), (c) and (d)" in lieu of "subsections (b) and (c). *Id.* at 221. It amended the first line of subsection 2319(b) by inserting "section 506(a)(1)(A)" in lieu of "section 506(a)(1). *Id.* The Act amended the first line of subsection 2319(c) by inserting "section 506(a)(1)(B) of title 17" in lieu of "section 506(a)(2) of title 17, United States Code." *Id.* It also amended subsection (e) by adding a new paragraph (3). *Id.* Finally, the Act amended section 2319 by adding a new subsection (d) and redesignating the following subsections accordingly, as (e) and (f). *Id.*

The Prioritizing Resources and Organization for Intellectual Property Act of 2008 amended paragraph 2319(b)(2) by inserting "is a felony" after "offense" and by deleting "subsection (a)" and inserting "paragraph (1)." Pub. L. No. 110-403, 122 Stat. 4256, 4263. It also amended paragraphs 2319(c)(2), (d)(3) and (d)(4) by making similar changes. *Id.* at 4263-64.

3. In 1994, the Uruguay Round Agreements Act added section 2319A to title 18 of the *United States Code*. This section was entitled "Unauthorized fixation of and trafficking in

sound recordings and music videos of live musical performances." Pub. L. No. 103-465, 108 Stat. 4809, 4974. In 1997, the No Electronic Theft Act amended section 2319A by redesignating subsections (d) and (e) as subsections (e) and (f), respectively, and by adding subsection (d). Pub. L. No. 105-147, 111 Stat. 2678. See also note 2, *supra*, regarding the United States Sentencing Commission.

The Protecting American Goods and Services Act of 2005 amended section 2319A(e)(2) in its entirety to make the definition for "traffic" the same as in 18 *U.S.C.* section 2320(e). Pub. L. No. 109-181, 120 Stat. 285, 288. The Act simultaneously amended section 2320(e)(2) to define traffic as "to transport, transfer, or otherwise dispose of, to another, for purposes of commercial advantage or private financial gain, or to make, import, export, obtain control of, or possess, with intent to so transport, transfer, or otherwise dispose of." *Id.*

The Prioritizing Resources and Organization for Intellectual Property Act of 2008 amended section 2319A by revising subsection (b) in its entirety and by substituting a new sentence for the last sentence in subsection (c). Pub. L. No. 110-403, 122 Stat. 4256, 4261.

4. The Uruguay Round Agreements Act was enacted on December 8, 1994.

5. The Artists' Rights and Theft Prevention Act of 2005 added a new section 2319B to title 5 of the *United States Code*. Pub. L. No. 109-9, 119 Stat. 218.6. The Prioritizing Resources and Organization for Intellectual Property Act of 2008 amended subsection 2319(b)(2) in its entirety. Pub. L. No. 110-403, 122 Stat. 4256, 4261.

6. The Prioritizing Resources and Organization for Intellectual Property Act of 2008 amended chapter 113 of title 18, *United States Code*, by adding a new section 2323, "Forfeiture, Destruction, and Restitution." Pub. L. No. 110-403, 122 Stat. 4256, 4262-63. Section 2323 replaces section 509 of title 17, *United States Code*, which was repealed. *Id.* at 122 Stat. 4260.

Appendix I

Title 28—Judiciary and Judicial Procedure, U.S. Code

Part IV—Jurisdiction and Venue
Chapter 85—District Courts; Jurisdiction

* * * * * * *

§ 1338 · Patents, plant variety protection, copyrights, mask works, designs, trademarks, and unfair competition[1]

(a) The district courts shall have original jurisdiction of any civil action arising under any Act of Congress relating to patents, plant variety protection, copyrights and trademarks. Such jurisdiction shall be exclusive of the courts of the states in patent, plant variety protection and copyright cases.

(b) The district courts shall have original jurisdiction of any civil action asserting a claim of unfair competition when joined with a substantial and related claim under the copyright, patent, plant variety protection or trademark laws.

(c) Subsections (a) and (b) apply to exclusive rights in mask works under chapter 9 of title 17, and to exclusive rights in designs under chapter 13 of title 17, to the same extent as such subsections apply to copyrights.

Chapter 87—District Courts; Venue

* * * * * * *

§ 1400 · Patents and copyrights, mask works, and designs[2]

* * * * * * *

(a) Civil actions, suits, or proceedings arising under any Act of Congress relating to copyrights or exclusive rights in mask works or designs may be instituted in the district in which the defendant or his agent resides or may be found.

(b) Any civil action for patent infringement may be brought in the judicial district where the defendant resides, or where the defendant has committed acts of infringement and has a regular and established place of business.

* * * * * * *

Chapter 91—United States Court of Federal Claims

* * * * * * *

§1498 · *Patent and copyright cases*[3]

* * * * * * *

(b) Hereafter, whenever the copyright in any work protected under the copyright laws of the United States shall be infringed by the United States, by a corporation owned or controlled by the United States, or by a contractor, subcontractor, or any person, firm, or corporation acting for the Government and with the authorization or consent of the Government, the exclusive action which may be brought for such infringement shall be an action by the copyright owner against the United States in the Court of Federal Claims for the recovery of his reasonable and entire compensation as damages for such infringement, including the minimum statutory damages as set forth in section 504(c) of title 17, United States Code: Provided, That a Government employee shall have a right of action against the Government under this subsection except where he was in a position to order, influence, or induce use of the copyrighted work by the Government: Provided, however, That this subsection shall not confer a right of action on any copyright owner or any assignee of such owner with respect to any copyrighted work prepared by a person while in the employment or service of the United States, where the copyrighted work was prepared as a part of the official functions of the employee, or in the preparation of which Government time, material, or facilities were used: And provided further, That before such action against the United States has been instituted the appropriate corporation owned or controlled by the United States or the head of the appropriate department or agency of the Government, as the case may be, is authorized to enter into an agreement with the copyright owner in full settlement and compromise for the damages accruing to him by reason of such infringement and to settle the claim administratively out of available appropriations.

Except as otherwise provided by law, no recovery shall be had for any infringement of a copyright covered by this subsection committed more than three years prior to the filing of the complaint or counterclaim for infringement in the action, except that the period between the date of receipt of a written claim for compensation by the Department or agency of the Government or corporation owned or controlled by the United States, as the case may be, having authority to settle such claim and the date of mailing by the Government of a notice to the claimant that his claim has been denied shall not be counted as a part of the three years, unless suit is brought before the last-mentioned date.

(c) The provisions of this section shall not apply to any claim arising in a foreign country.

* * * * * * *

(e) Subsections (b) and (c) of this section apply to exclusive rights in mask works under chapter 9 of title 17, and to exclusive rights in designs under chapter 13 of title 17, to the same extent as such subsections apply to copyrights.

Appendix I · Notes

1. In 1948, section 1338, entitled "Patents, copyrights, trademarks, and unfair competition," was added to title 28 of the *United States Code*. Pub. L. No. 773, 62 Stat. 869, 931. In 1970, the title of section 1338 and the text of subsection (b) were amended to insert "plant variety protection " after "patent." Pub. L. No. 91-577, 84 Stat. 1542, 1559. In 1988, the Judicial Improvements and Access to Justice Act amended section 1338 by adding "mask works" to the title and by adding subsection (c). Pub. L. No. 100-702, 102 Stat. 4642, 4671. In 1998, the Digital Millennium Copyright Act (DMCA) amended the title by inserting "designs," after "mask works." Pub. L. No. 105-304, 112 Stat. 2860, 2917. The DMCA also amended subsection (c) by inserting ", and to exclusive rights in designs under chapter 13 of title 17," after "chapter 9 of title 17." *Id.* In 1999, the Anticybersquatting Consumer Protection Act amended section 1338 throughout to change "trade-mark" and "trade-marks" to "trademark" and "trademarks," respectively. Pub. L. No. 106-113, 113 Stat. 1501, 1501A-551, app. I.

2. In 1948, section 1400, entitled "Patents and copyrights," was added to title 28 of the *United States Code*. Pub. L. No. 773, 62 Stat. 869, 936. In 1988, the Judicial Improvements and Access to Justice Act amended subsection (a) by inserting "or exclusive rights in mask works" after "copyrights." Pub. L. No. 100-702, 102 Stat. 4642, 4671. In 1998, the Digital Millennium Copyright Act (DMCA) amended subsection (a) to insert "or designs" after "mask works." Pub. L. No. 105-304, 112 Stat. 2860, 2917. The DMCA also amended the section heading to "Patents and copyrights, mask works, and designs." This amendment included a period at the end, after "designs." In 1999, a technical amendment deleted the period. Pub. L. No. 106-44, 113 Stat. 221, 223.

3. In 1960, section 1498 of the *United States Code* was amended to add subsections (b) and (c). Pub. L. No. 86-726, 74 Stat. 855. The Copyright Act of 1976 amended section 1498(b) to insert "section 504(c) of title 17" in lieu of "section 101(b) of title 17." Pub. L. No. 94-553, 90 Stat. 2541, 2599. The Federal Courts Improvement Act of 1982 amended section 1498(a) to insert "United States Claims Court" in lieu of "Court of Claims" and, in subsections (b) and (d), to insert "Claims Court" in lieu of "Court of Claims," wherever it appeared. Pub. L. No. 97-164, 96 Stat. 25, 40. In 1988, the Judicial Improvements and Access to Justice Act amended section 1498 by adding subsection (e). Pub. L. No. 100-702, 102 Stat. 4642, 4671. The Federal Courts Administration Act of 1992 amended section 1498 by inserting "United States Court of Federal Claims" in lieu of "United States Claims Court," wherever it appeared, and by

inserting "Court of Federal Claims" in lieu of "Claims Court," wherever it appeared. Pub. L. No. 102-572, 106 Stat. 4506, 4516. In 1997, the No Electronic Theft (NET) Act amended section 1498(b) to insert "action which may be brought for such infringement shall be an action by the copyright owner" in lieu of "remedy of the owner of such copyright shall be by action." Pub. L. No. 105-147, 111 Stat. 2678, 2680. In 1998, the Digital Millennium Copyright Act amended subsection (e) by inserting, ", and to exclusive rights in designs under chapter 13 of title 17," after "chapter 9 of title 17." Pub. L. No. 105-304, 112 Stat. 2860, 2917.

Appendix J

Title 44—Public Printing and Documents, U.S. Code

Chapter 21—National Archives and Records Administration

* * * * * * *

§ 2117 · Limitation on liability[1]

When letters and other intellectual productions (exclusive of patented material, published works under copyright protection, and unpublished works for which copyright registration has been made) come into the custody or possession of the Archivist, the United States or its agents are not liable for infringement of copyright or analogous rights arising out of use of the materials for display, inspection, research, reproduction, or other purposes.

Appendix J · Note

1. In 1968, this section, originally designated as section 2113, which is entitled "Limitation on liability," was added to title 44 of the *United States Code*. Pub. L. No. 90-620, 82 Stat. 1238, 1291. The 1976 Copyright Act amended section 2113 in its entirety. Pub. L. No. 94-553, 90 Stat. 2541, 2599. The National Archives and Records Administration Act of 1984 amended section 2113 by redesignating it as section 2117 and by inserting "Archivist" in lieu of "Administrator of General Services." Pub. L. No. 98-497, 98 Stat. 2280 and 2286.

Appendix K

The Berne Convention Implementation Act of 1988[1]

Sec. 1 · Short Title and References to Title 17, United States Code.

(a) Short Title.—This Act, may be cited as the "Berne Convention Implementation Act of 1988".

(b) References to Title 17, United States Code.—Whenever in this Act an amendment or repeal is expressed in terms of an amendment to or a repeal of a section or other provision, the reference shall be considered to be made to a section or other provision of title 17, United States Code.

Sec. 2 · Declarations.

The Congress makes the following declarations:

(1) The Convention for the Protection of Literary and Artistic Works, signed at Berne, Switzerland, on September 9, 1886, and all acts, protocols, and revisions thereto (hereafter in this Act referred to as the "Berne Convention") are not self-executing under the Constitution and laws of the United States.

(2) The obligations of the United States under the Berne Convention may be performed only pursuant to appropriate domestic law.

(3) The amendments made by this Act, together with the law as it exists on the date of the enactment of this Act, satisfy the obligations of the United States in adhering to the Berne Convention and no further rights or interests shall be recognized or created for that purpose.

Sec. 3 · Construction of the Berne Convention.

(a) Relationship with Domestic Law.—The provisions of the Berne Convention—

(1) shall be given effect under title 17, as amended by this Act, and any other relevant provision of Federal or State law, including the common law; and

(2) shall not be enforceable in any action brought pursuant to the provisions of the Berne Convention itself.

(b) Certain Rights Not Affected.—The provisions of the Berne Convention, the adherence of the United States thereto, and satisfaction of United States obligations thereunder, do not expand or reduce any right of an author of a work, whether claimed under Federal, State, or the common law—

(1) to claim authorship of the work; or

(2) to object to any distortion, mutilation, or other modification of, or other derogatory action in relation to, the work, that would prejudice the author's honor or reputation.

* * * * * * *

Sec. 12 · Works in the public domain.

Title 17, United States Code, as amended by this Act, does not provide copyright protection for any work that is in the public domain in the United States.

Sec. 13 · Effective date: effect on pending cases.

(a) EFFECTIVE DATE.—This Act and the amendments made by this Act take effect on the date on which the Berne Convention (as defined in section 101 of title 17, United States Code) enters into force with respect to the United States.[2]

(b) EFFECT ON PENDING CASES.—Any cause of action arising under title 17, United States Code, before the effective date of this Act shall be governed by the provisions of such title as in effect when the cause of action arose.

Appendix K · Notes

1. This appendix consists of provisions of the Berne Convention Implementation Act of 1988, Pub. L. No. 100-568, 102 Stat. 2853, that do not amend title 17 of the *United States Code.*

2. The Berne Convention entered into force in the United States on March 1, 1989.

Appendix L

The Uruguay Round Agreements Act of 1994[1]

Sec. 1. Short Title and Table of Contents

(a) SHORT TITLE.—This act may be cited as the "Uruguay Round Agreements Act".

* * * * * * *

Sec. 2. Definitions.

For purposes of this Act:

(1) GATT 1947; GATT 1994—

(A) GATT 1947—The term "GATT 1947" means the General Agreement on Tariffs and Trade, dated October 30, 1947, annexed to the Final Act Adopted at the Conclusion of the Second Session of the Preparatory Committee of the United Nations Conference on Trade and Employment, as subsequently rectified, amended, or modified by the terms of legal instruments which have entered into force before the date of entry into force of the WTO Agreement.

(B) GATT 1994—The term "GATT 1994" means the General Agreement on Tariffs and Trade annexed to the WTO Agreement.

(2) HTS—The term "HTS" means the Harmonized Tariff Schedule of the United States.

(3) INTERNATIONAL TRADE COMMISSION.—The term "International Trade Commission" means the United States International Trade Commission.

(4) MULTILATERAL TRADE AGREEMENT.—The term "multilateral trade agreement" means an agreement described in section 101(d) of this Act (other than an agreement described in paragraph (17) or (18) of such section).

(5) SCHEDULE XX.—The term "Schedule XX" means Schedule XX—United States of America annexed to the Marrakesh Protocol to the GATT 1994.

(6) TRADE REPRESENTATIVE.—The term "Trade Representative" means the United States Trade Representative.

(7) URUGUAY ROUND AGREEMENTS.—The term "Uruguay Round Agreements" means the agreements approved by the Congress under section 101(a)(1).

(8) WORLD TRADE ORGANIZATION AND WTO.—The terms "World Trade Organization" and "WTO" mean the organization established pursuant to the WTO Agreement.

(9) WTO AGREEMENT.—The term "WTO Agreement" means the Agreement Establishing the World Trade Organization entered into on April 15, 1994.

(10) WTO MEMBER AND WTO MEMBER COUNTRY.—The terms "WTO member" and "WTO member country" mean a state, or separate customs territory (within the meaning of Article XII of the WTO Agreement), with respect to which the United States applies the WTO Agreement.

Title I—Approval of, and General Provisions Relating to, the Uruguay Round Agreements
Subtitle A—Approval of Agreements and Related Provisions

Sec. 101 · Approval and entry into force of the Uruguay Round Agreements.

(a) APPROVAL OF AGREEMENTS AND STATEMENT OF ADMINISTRATIVE ACTION.—Pursuant to section 1103 of the Omnibus Trade and Competitiveness Act of 1988 (19 U.S.C. 2903) and section 151 of the Trade Act of 1974 (19 U.S.C. 2191), the Congress approves—

(1) the trade agreements described in subsection (d) resulting from the Uruguay Round of multilateral trade negotiations under the auspices of the General Agreement on Tariffs and Trade, entered into on April 15, 1994, and submitted to the Congress on September 27, 1994; and

(2) the statement of administrative action proposed to implement the agreements that was submitted to the Congress on September 27, 1994.

(b) ENTRY INTO FORCE.—At such time as the President determines that a sufficient number of foreign countries are accepting the obligations of the Uruguay Round Agreements, in accordance with article XIV of the WTO Agreement, to ensure the effective operation of, and adequate benefits for the United States under, those Agreements, the President may accept the Uruguay Round Agreements and implement article VIII of the WTO Agreement.

(c) AUTHORIZATION OF APPROPRIATIONS.—There are authorized to be appropriated annually such sums as may be necessary for the payment by the United States of its share of the expenses of the WTO.

(d) TRADE AGREEMENTS TO WHICH THIS ACT APPLIES.—Subsection (a) applies to the WTO Agreement and to the following agreements annexed to that Agreement:

(1) The General Agreement on Tariffs and Trade 1994.

(2) The Agreement on Agriculture.

(3) The Agreement on the Application of Sanitary and Phytosanitary Measures.

(4) The Agreement on Textiles and Clothing.

(5) The Agreement on Technical Barriers to Trade.

(6) The Agreement on Trade-Related Investment Measures.

(7) The Agreement on Implementation of Article VI of the General Agreement on Tariffs and Trade 1994.

(8) The Agreement on Implementation of Article VII of the General Agreement on Tariffs and Trade 1994.

(9) The Agreement on Preshipment Inspection.

(10) The Agreement on Rules of Origin.

(11) The Agreement on Import Licensing Procedures.

(12) The Agreement on Subsidies and Countervailing Measures.

(13) The Agreement on Safeguards.

(14) The General Agreement on Trade in Services.

(15) The Agreement on Trade-Related Aspects of Intellectual Property Rights.

(16) The Understanding on Rules and Procedures Governing the Settlement of Disputes.

(17) The Agreement on Government Procurement.

(18) The International Bovine Meat Agreement.

Sec. 102 · Relationship of the agreements to United States law and state law.

(a) RELATIONSHIP OF AGREEMENTS TO UNITED STATES LAW.—

(1) UNITED STATES LAW TO PREVAIL IN CONFLICT.—No provision of any of the Uruguay Round Agreements, nor the application of any such provision to any person or circumstance, that is inconsistent with any law of the United States shall have effect.

(2) CONSTRUCTION.—Nothing in this Act shall be construed

(A) to amend or modify any law of the United States, including any law relating to—

(i) the protection of human, animal, or plant life or health,

(ii) the protection of the environment, or

(iii) worker safety, or

(B) to limit any authority conferred under any law of the United States, including section 301 of the Trade Act of 1974,

unless specifically provided for in this Act.

(b) RELATIONSHIP OF AGREEMENTS TO STATE LAW.—

(1) FEDERAL–STATE CONSULTATION.—

(A) IN GENERAL.—Upon the enactment of this Act, the President shall, through the intergovernmental policy advisory committees on trade established under section 306(c)(2)(A) of the Trade and Tariff Act of 1984 (19 U.S.C. 2114c(2)(A)), consult with the States for the purpose of achieving conformity of State laws and practices with the Uruguay Round Agreements.

(B) FEDERAL–STATE CONSULTATION PROCESS.—The Trade Representative shall establish within the Office of the United States Trade Representative a Federal–State consultation process for addressing issues relating to the

Uruguay Round Agreements that directly relate to, or will potentially have a direct effect on, the States. The Federal–State consultation process shall include procedures under which—

(i) the States will be informed on a continuing basis of matters under the Uruguay Round Agreements that directly relate to, or will potentially have a direct impact on, the States;

(ii) the States will be provided an opportunity to submit, on a continuing basis, to the Trade Representative information and advice with respect to matters referred to in clause (i); and

(iii) the Trade Representative will take into account the information and advice received from the States under clause (ii) when formulating United States positions regarding matters referred to in clause (i).

The Federal Advisory Committee Act (5 U.S.C. App.) shall not apply to the Federal–State consultation process established by this paragraph.

(C) FEDERAL–STATE COOPERATION IN WTO DISPUTE SETTLEMENT.—

(i) When a WTO member requests consultations with the United States under Article 4 of the Understanding on Rules and Procedures Governing the Settlement of Disputes referred to in section 101(d)(16) (hereafter in this subsection referred to as the "Dispute Settlement Understanding") concerning whether the law of a State is inconsistent with the obligations undertaken by the United States in any of the Uruguay Round Agreements, the Trade Representative shall notify the Governor of the State or the Governor's designee, and the chief legal officer of the jurisdiction whose law is the subject of the consultations, as soon as possible after the request is received, but in no event later than 7 days thereafter.

(ii) Not later than 30 days after receiving such a request for consultations, the Trade Representative shall consult with representatives of the State concerned regarding the matter. If the consultations involve the laws of a large number of States, the Trade Representative may consult with an appropriate group of representatives of the States concerned, as determined by those States.

(iii) The Trade Representative shall make every effort to ensure that the State concerned is involved in the development of the position of the United States at each stage of the consultations and each subsequent stage of dispute settlement proceedings regarding the matter. In particular, the Trade Representative shall—

(I) notify the State concerned not later than 7 days after a WTO member requests the establishment of a dispute settlement panel or gives notice of the WTO member's decision to appeal a report by a dispute settlement panel regarding the matter; and

(II) provide the State concerned with the opportunity to advise and assist the Trade Representative in the preparation of factual information and argumentation for any written or oral presentations by the United States in consultations or in proceedings of a panel or the Appellate Body regarding the matter.

(iv) If a dispute settlement panel or the Appellate Body finds that the law of a State is inconsistent with any of the Uruguay Round Agreements, the Trade Representative shall consult with the State concerned in an effort to develop a mutually agreeable response to the report of the panel or the Appellate Body and shall make every effort to ensure that the State concerned is involved in the development of the United States position regarding the response.

(D) Notice to States Regarding Consultations on Foreign Subcentral Government Laws.—

(i) Subject to clause (ii), the Trade Representative shall, at least 30 days before making a request for consultations under Article 4 of the Dispute Settlement Understanding regarding a subcentral government measure of another WTO member, notify, and solicit the views of, appropriate representatives of each State regarding the matter.

(ii) In exigent circumstances clause (i) shall not apply, in which case the Trade Representative shall notify the appropriate representatives of each State not later than 3 days after making the request for consultations referred to in clause (i).

(2) Legal Challenge.—

(A) In General.—No State law, or the application of such a State law, may be declared invalid as to any person or circumstance on the ground that the provision or application is inconsistent with any of the Uruguay Round Agreements, except in an action brought by the United States for the purpose of declaring such law or application invalid.

(B) Procedures Governing Action.—In any action described in subparagraph (A) that is brought by the United States against a State or any subdivision thereof

(i) a report of a dispute settlement panel or the Appellate Body convened under the Dispute Settlement Understanding regarding the State law, or the law of any political subdivision thereof, shall not be considered as binding or otherwise accorded deference;

(ii) the United States shall have the burden of proving that the law that is the subject of the action, or the application of that law, is inconsistent with the agreement in question;

(iii) any State whose interests may be impaired or impeded in the action shall have the unconditional right to intervene in the action as a party, and the United States shall be entitled to amend its complaint to include a claim or cross-claim concerning the law of a State that so intervenes; and

(iv) any State law that is declared invalid shall not be deemed to have been invalid in its application during any period before the court's judgment becomes final and all timely appeals, including discretionary review, of such judgment are exhausted.

(C) Reports to Congressional Committees.—At least 30 days before the United States brings an action described in subparagraph (A), the Trade Representative shall provide a report to the Committee on Ways and Means of the House of Representatives and the Committee on Finance of the Senate—

(i) describing the proposed action;

(ii) describing efforts by the Trade Representative to resolve the matter with the State concerned by other means; and

(iii) if the State law was the subject of consultations under the Dispute Settlement Understanding, certifying that the Trade Representative has substantially complied with the requirements of paragraph (1)(C) in connection with the matter.

Following the submission of the report, and before the action is brought, the Trade Representative shall consult with the committees referred to in the preceding sentence concerning the matter.

(3) Definition of State Law.—For purposes of this subsection—

(A) the term "State law" includes—

(i) any law of a political subdivision of a State; and

(ii) any State law regulating or taxing the business of insurance; and

(B) the terms "dispute settlement panel" and "Appellate Body" have the meanings given those terms in section 121.

(c) Effect of Agreement with Respect to Private Remedies.—

(1) Limitations.—No person other than the United States—

(A) shall have any cause of action or defense under any of the Uruguay Round Agreements or by virtue of congressional approval of such an agreement, or

(B) may challenge, in any action brought under any provision of law, any action or inaction by any department, agency, or other instrumentality of the United States, any State, or any political subdivision of a State on the ground that such action or inaction is inconsistent with such agreement.

(2) Intent of Congress.—It is the intention of the Congress through paragraph (1) to occupy the field with respect to any cause of action or defense under or in connection with any of the Uruguay Round Agreements, including by precluding any person other than the United States from bringing any action against any State or political subdivision thereof or raising any defense to the application of State law under or in connection with any of the Uruguay Round Agreements—

(A) on the basis of a judgment obtained by the United States in an action brought under any such agreement; or

(B) on any other basis.

(d) Statement of Administrative Action.—The statement of administrative action approved by the Congress under section 101(a) shall be regarded as an authoritative expression by the United States concerning the interpretation and application of the Uruguay Round Agreements and this Act in any judicial proceeding in which a question arises concerning such interpretation or application.

Sec. 103 · Implementing actions in anticipation of entry into force; regulations.

(a) Implementing Actions.—After the date of the enactment of this Act—

(1) the President may proclaim such actions, and

(2) other appropriate officers of the United States Government may issue such regulations,

as may be necessary to ensure that any provision of this Act, or amendment made by this Act, that takes effect on the date any of the Uruguay Round Agreements enters into force with respect to the United States is appropriately implemented on such date. Such proclamation or regulation may not have an effective date earlier than the date of entry into force with respect to the United States of the agreement to which the proclamation or regulation relates.

(b) Regulations.—Any interim regulation necessary or appropriate to carry out any action proposed in the statement of administrative action approved under section 101(a) to implement an agreement described in section 101(d)(7), (12), or (13) shall be issued not later than 1 year after the date on which the agreement enters into force with respect to the United States.

Appendix L · Note

1. This appendix consists of provisions of the Uruguay Round Agreements Act, Pub. L. No. 103-465, 108 Stat. 4809, that do not amend title 17 of the *United States Code.*

Appendix M

GATT/Trade-Related Aspects of Intellectual Property Rights (TRIPs) Agreement, Part II[1]

* * * * * * *

Section 6: Layout-Designs (Topographies) of Integrated Circuits

* * * * * * *

Article 35 · Relation to IPIC Treaty

Members agree to provide protection to the layout-designs (topographies) of integrated circuits (hereinafter referred to as "layout-designs") in accordance with Articles 2–7 (other than paragraph 3 of Article 6), Article 12 and paragraph 3 of Article 16 of the Treaty on Intellectual Property in Respect of Integrated Circuits and, in addition, to comply with the following provisions.

Article 36 · Scope of the Protection

Subject to the provisions of paragraph 1 of Article 37 below, Members shall consider unlawful the following acts if performed without the authorization of the right holder:[2] importing, selling, or otherwise distributing for commercial purposes a protected layout-design, an integrated circuit in which a protected layout-design is incorporated, or an article incorporating such an integrated circuit only insofar as it continues to contain an unlawfully reproduced layout-design.

Article 37 · Acts Not Requiring the Authorization of the Right Holder[3]

1. Notwithstanding Article 36 above, no Member shall consider unlawful the performance of any of the acts referred to in that Article in respect of an integrated circuit incorporating an unlawfully reproduced layout-design or any article incorporating such an integrated circuit where the person performing or ordering such acts did not know and had no reasonable ground to know, when acquiring the integrated circuit or article incorporating such an integrated circuit, that it incorporated an unlawfully reproduced layout-design. Members shall provide that, after the time that such person has received sufficient notice that the layout-design was unlawfully reproduced, he may perform any of the acts with respect to the stock on hand or ordered before such time, but shall be liable to pay to the right holder a sum equivalent to a reasonable royalty such as would be payable under a freely negotiated license in respect of such a layout-design.
2. The conditions set out in sub-paragraphs (a)–(k) of Article 31 above shall apply *mutatis mutandis* in the event of any nonvoluntary licensing of a layout-design or of its use by or for the government without the authorization of the right holder.

Article 38 · Term of Protection

1. In Members requiring registration as a condition of protection, the term of protection of layout-designs shall not end before the expiration of a period of ten years counted from the date of filing an application for registration or from the first commercial exploitation wherever in the world it occurs.

2. In Members not requiring registration as a condition for protection, layout-designs shall be protected for a term of no less than ten years from the date of the first commercial exploitation wherever in the world it occurs.

3. Notwithstanding paragraphs 1 and 2 above, a Member may provide that protection shall lapse fifteen years after the creation of the layout-design.

Appendix M · Notes

1. For an explanation of the relationship of this section of TRIPs to title 17 of the *United States Code*, see the second paragraph of note 8, chapter 9, *supra*.

2. Article 36 includes footnote 9 that states, "The term 'right holder' in this Section shall be understood as having the same meaning as the term 'holder of the right' in the IPIC Treaty." The IPIC Treaty, which was signed in Washington, D.C., on May 26, 1989, is also known as the Treaty on Intellectual Property in Respect of Integrated Circuits.

3. See note 2, *supra*.

Appendix N

Definition of "Berne Convention Work"

The WIPO Copyright and Performances and Phonograms Treaties Implementation Act of 1998 deleted the definition of "Berne Convention work" from section 101.[1] Pub. L. No. 105-304, 112 Stat. 2861. The definition of Berne Convention work, as deleted, is as follows:

A work is a "Berne Convention work" if—

(1) in the case of an unpublished work, one or more of the authors is a national of a nation adhering to the Berne Convention, or in the case of a published work, one or more of the authors is a national of a nation adhering to the Berne Convention on the date of first publication;

(2) the work was first published in a nation adhering to the Berne Convention, or was simultaneously first published in a nation adhering to the Berne convention and in a foreign nation that does not adhere to the Berne Convention;

(3) in the case of an audiovisual work—

(A) if one or more of the authors is a legal entity, that author has its headquarters in a nation adhering to the Berne Convention; or

(B) if one or more of the authors is an individual, that author is domiciled, or has his or her habitual residence in, a nation adhering to the Berne Convention; or

(4) in the case of a pictorial, graphic, or sculptural work that is incorporated in a building or other structure, the building or structure is located in a nation adhering to the Berne Convention; or

(5) in the case of an architectural work embodied in a building, such building is erected in a country adhering to the Berne Convention.

For purposes of paragraph (1), an author who is domiciled in or has his or her habitual residence in, a nation adhering to the Berne Convention is considered to be a national of that nation. For purposes of paragraph (2), a work is considered to have been simultaneously published in two or more nations if its dates of publication are within 30 days of one another.

Appendix N · Note

1. For the legislative history of the definition of "Berne Convention work," see note 2, chapter 1, *supra*.